A

HANDY BOOK FOR BREWERS

[*ADVERTISEMENT.*]

The Patent Preservative Kalium Meta Sulphite (K.M.S.) referred to in this work is to be had only of the Patentees—

A. BOAKE, ROBERTS, & Co.,

Manufacturing and Consulting Chemists,

STRATFORD, LONDON, E.

Also Caramel, Ant-Acid Finings, and other Specialities.

For further Particulars see Advertisement at End of Book.

A

HANDY BOOK FOR BREWERS

BEING

A Practical Guide to the Art of Brewing and Malting

*EMBRACING THE CONCLUSIONS OF MODERN RESEARCH
WHICH BEAR UPON THE PRACTICE OF BREWING*

BY

HERBERT EDWARDS WRIGHT, M.A.

AUTHOR OF "THE HANDBOOK FOR YOUNG BREWERS"

LONDON

CROSBY LOCKWOOD AND SON

7, STATIONERS' HALL COURT, LUDGATE HILL

1892

"NULLIUS ADDICTUS JURARE IN VERBA MAGISTRI"

PREFACE.

ONE principal aim of this book—which was also that of the previous work on a more limited scale, entitled "A Handbook for Young Brewers," to which the present is a successor—is to give the conclusions of modern research, in so far as they bear upon the practice of Brewing, in such a form that a novice of fair intelligence may understand them.

It will be found, however, that Chapters IV., V., and XIII., as well as a considerable part of the First Chapter, are entirely devoted to practical details, manipulative or structural, whilst every other chapter, except two, has many paragraphs dealing with such questions as they arise.

When referring to arguable points, or to those resting on a single authority, however high, the Author's rule has been to give them as such, and if in any case this rule is departed from it has been done inadvertently; while those points which are generally accepted, or which have been confirmed by the writer's own experience, will usually be found without qualification. If it should sometimes seem that too much weight is given to his personal guarantee, let it be charitably remembered that it is no unusual weakness for authors, when they assume the part of teachers, to think their own conclusions final.

With a book of this kind, a charge of discursiveness is more easily made than avoided. Brewing is an art in which there are so many influences combining to affect the quality of the final product—influences, some of them, of the past, so far as the operator's power of absolutely altering or counteracting them is concerned, yet still potent to seriously modify the results of his later manipulation—that it is hardly possible to treat the successive operations of the working brewer with the orderly precision so easily attained in technical manuals relating to other industries.

As with the *technique* of Brewing, so with the science on which it is based. An art, whose completely successful exponent should not only be an unerring judge of raw material, such as barley, malt, and hops, and have other practical equipments too obvious to catalogue, but should also be a sound chemist and an enthusiastic biologist, may be held to cover so much ground, that it is difficult to say what does not come within its domain. Much, especially in the way of biology, which may at present seem to have but a remote connection with Brewing, will doubtless some day help to elucidate problems which are now obscure.

It may be well to explain the position of the chapter on the Brewery and Plant at the *end* of the book. It was placed there, because it appeared to the Author that the younger students of Brewing, for whom the chapters preceding it are primarily intended, would more conveniently consider general questions from the standpoint of the actual plant amidst which they spend their pupilage, than from the less solid ground of imaginary surroundings; that they would have in the beginning of their studies to deal with arrangements as they are; and that only towards the end of their term would they be in a position to consider with much profit arrangements as they ought to be—or as the Author thinks they ought to be.

Throughout the work, the Author has not scrupled to mention the names of manufacturers or dealers in articles or appliances pertaining to the Brewery, where it appeared helpful to the reader to do so; but having found, after the sheets have been finally passed to the printers, that the Publishers consider it would be a useful feature in the book to insert a few advertisements of matters interesting to Brewers, he wishes it to be clearly understood that he has no personal interest in the matter.

Further, he must make excuse for the absence of the Glossary, to which occasional references have been made in the text, but which it has been found necessary to omit on account of the size to which this book has attained. A glance at the headings of the chapters will show that this increase of size beyond that originally planned is not due to padding or verbiage. The Glossary will probably be published as a separate work.

The Author is glad, in conclusion, to be able to claim for the volume a merit at which few of his readers will cavil—namely, the addition of an Index more copious than is usual in books of this class. He hopes, too, that the Synoptic Table of the various Processes in Brewing and Malting, which will be found in an Appendix, will prove useful to many.

June 1892.

CONTENTS.

CHAPTER I.

INTRODUCTORY.

PAGE

Notes on Chemical Changes—Outline of Processes of Brewing—Malting—Mashing (Infusion, Decoction, and Limited Decoction)—Fermentation (Cleansing, Skimming, Yorkshire Stone Squares, etc.)—Racking—Fining—Storing—Vatting . . 1

CHAPTER II.

BARLEY, MALTING, AND MALT.

Barley the preferable Grain—Six-rowed, Four-rowed, and Two-rowed Barley—"Escourgeon" and Chevalier Barley—Anatomy of the Barley-Corn—Choice of Barley—Over-ripe Grains—Tests for Germinative Power—Situation of Malt-House—Its Construction—Prevention of Mould—Idle Corns—Kilns and Kiln-drying—Last's Patent Ventilators—Construction of Kilns—Furnace and Baffle Plate—Mr. Free on Malting—King's Automatic Regulator—Double Kilns (Stopes')—Chemical Results of Maltster's Operations—Secretion of Diatase and of a Cellulose-dissolving Enzyme—Peptase—Messrs. Brown and Morris's Conclusions—Mr. J. O'Sullivan's Views—Asparagin—Bacterial Theory of Diatase—Data for Judging Good Malt—Pneumatic Malting—Economics of Malting. 53

CHAPTER III.

WATER FOR BREWING.

Pure Water—Varying Ways of Expressing Results of Analysis—Rule for Harmonising—Organic Matter not directly determin-

x   CONTENTS.

PAGE

able—Organic Carbon—Organic Nitrogen—Typical Analyses—
Ratio of Organic Carbon to Organic Nitrogen—Nitrogen as
Ammonia—Nitrates and Nitrites—Ammonia Process—Moist
Combustion Process—Phosphoric Acid and Sulphates in Polluted Water—Heisch (Sugar) Test—Hansen's Method—General
Conditions of Water Supply—Hardness—Sulphates—Bicarbonates—Silica—Chlorides—Effect of various Salts on Type of
Malto-Dextrin—Kainit—Alkaline Sulphates—Carbonates—Iron
—Treatment of Brewing Water—Burtonising—Double Decompositions—Clarke's Process for softening Water—Easy Qualitative Test of Purity of Water—Analyses 93

CHAPTER IV.

HOPS AND SUGARS.

Hops (Goldings, Grapes, Jones, Colegates, etc.)—The Best Districts
—Planting—Poling, etc.—Climatic Conditions—Cost of Production—A Good Sample of Hops—Foreign Hops—Sulphured
Hops—Constituents—Classification of Sugars—Formulæ—Raw
and Refined Sugar—Inverting Sugar in the Brewery—Commercial Glucose 131

CHAPTER V.

THE BREWING ROOM.

Gravity—Brewers' lbs. and Degrees of Specific Gravity—Saccharometers—Converting Degrees Balling into Brewers' lbs.—Baumé
into Specific Gravity—Working out the Brewings—Entry of
Materials—Working out Sparges—Copper Lengths—Parti-gyle
Calculations—Apportioning Hops—Formula for Calculating
"Initial" from "Striking" Heat—Making up Lengths in Fermenting Vessels (Calculations for)—Boiling down to a required
Gravity—Extract per Quarter—Dry or Solid Extract—Extract
per Cent.—Excise Charges—Contents of Squares or Rounds in
Bushels and Gallons—Cost-price Calculation . . . 155

CHAPTER VI.

CHEMISTRY AS APPLIED TO BREWING.

Elements—Compounds—Dalton, Ampère, and Avogadro—Atoms,
Molecules—Formulæ (Empiric and Structural)—Equations

CONTENTS.

(what they mean)—Table of Elements—Their Atomicity—Calculation of Percentage Composition from Formulæ and *vice versâ*—Choosing between Two or more possible Formulæ—Atomicity, Valence or Quantivalence—Saturation; Auto-saturation—Glyptic Formulæ—Compound Radicals—Isomerism—Acids, Bases, Salts—Oxides—Hydroxides (Hydrates)—Basicity Terminations *-ic* and *-ous*; *-ate* and *-ite*—Prefixes *hypo-* and *per-*: Sulphides—Chlorates, Chlorides—Anhydrides—Hydrocarbons — Alcohols — Aldehydes — Carbohydrates—Maltose—Cellulose—Organic Acids—Elements in the Nascent State—Albuminoids in Barley—Amides—Peptones—Asparagin—Analyses (Typical)—Nitrogen—Kjeldhal's Method of Determining it—Iodine Reaction with Starch—Various Qualitative Tests—Iodoform—The Polarimeter 182

CHAPTER VII.

THE LABORATORY.

Essentials of a Laboratory—The Brewer-Analyst's Limitations—Metric System of Weights and Measures—Apparatus and Reagents required—Preparation of Apparatus—Fehling's Solution — Volumetric and Gravimetric Methods — Testing Glucose (Invert), Cane-Sugar, Malt—Normal or Standard Solutions—Equivalence—Albuminoids by Ammonia Process—Soda-Lime Process—Diastatic Activity of Malt—Beer Analysis—Original Gravity by Distillation and Evaporation—Dry Extract, Acidity, etc.—Water Analysis—Combining Results—Soap Test—Free and Albuminoid Ammonia—Oxygen Processes—Hops for Sulphur—Constants—Standard Solutions 218

CHAPTER VIII.

MASHING, SPARGING, AND BOILING.

Objects in Mashing—Restatement of General Principles—Axioms applied to Practice—Noting Acrospire Growth of Malt—Malt of Average Diastatic Capacity—Mode of increasing Dextrin Ratio — Starch — Granulose — Amylo-cellulose — Dextrin — Amylo-, Achroo-, and Erythro-dextrins—Maltose—Equations of Mash-tun Changes—Malto-dextrin Theory—Evidence on which the Theory is based—Isolation of Malto-dextrin—Formula—Modification of Equation Series—Percentage and Type of Malto-dextrins, and their Influence—Limited Decoction—Semi-prepared Raw Material—Hot-grist mashing—Stout and Porter Grists—Brown and Patent Malt—Substitute for—Raw or Return Wort—Dead Mashes—Sparging—Underback—Stewing—Boiling—Adding the Hops—Steam-boiling and Fire-boiling—Open or closed Coppers—Hot Aëration of Wort . . . 276

CHAPTER IX.

FERMENTS IN GENERAL.

Organised and Unorganised Ferments—So-called Inorganic Ferments—Enzymes—Table of Ferments with Functions—Definition of Fermentation—Germ Theory v. Spontaneous Generation—Professor Tyndall's Deduction—Fungi—Why Ferment Organisms must be classed as Vegetable Organisms—Pasteur's Solution—*Aspergillus Niger* as an Example—Raulin's Liquid—Protoplasm — Hypha—Mycelium — Septation — Correlation of Growth—Abortive Mycelia—Modes of Reproduction—Polymorphism and Pleomorphy—Schizomycetes—Hyphomycetes and Saccharomycetes—The Microscope—Hints on Selection and Management of Microscope—Angle of Aperture—Its Parts—Magnifying Combinations—Examination of Yeast . . . 321

CHAPTER X.

FERMENTATION WITH COMMERCIAL YEAST—ITS SCIENCE AND PRACTICE.

Liebig and Pasteur—Conflicting Theories—Professor Huxley's Simile—Traube's Hypothesis—Brefeld's Researches—Adolf Mayer's—Yeast Reacting on its own Tissues—Nägeli's Theory—Dumas—Bourquelot and "Selective Fermentation"—By-products (Glycerine and Succinic Acid)—Inevitable Contamination of Industrial Yeast—Number of Aërial Spores Varies—High and Low Yeast—Three Varieties of the Former—Microscopic Appearance of the Cells—Ordeals which Yeast can Survive—Analysis of High Yeast—Effect of Aëration—Alcohol Percentage and Maximum Density of Wort—Heat Generated—Concurrent Action of Disease Ferments—Attenua-

CONTENTS. xiii

PAGE

tion—Heads—Foxy Smell—Sluggish Fermentations—Fiery Fermentations—Baker's Yeast 357

CHAPTER XI.

CULTURE FROM A SINGLE CELL—WILD YEASTS.

Pasteur's Methods of Purifying Yeast—Survival of the Fittest—Hansen's Theory—Wild Yeasts—Dilution and Gelatine Methods of Isolating a Single Cell for Cultivation—Ascospore Formation; Film or Pellicle Formation—Table of the Preceding, serving for Analysis of Yeasts—Pure Culture on an Industrial Scale—Trials of "Pure Culture" Yeast in North of France—Experience of a Brewer there—"Pure Culture" Yeast in Australia 393

CHAPTER XII.

TREATMENT OF BEER.

Turbidity of Beer—(i) From Defective Yeast—(ii) From Bacteria—(iii) From Albuminoids—(iv) From Hop-resin (and Hop-sickness)—(v) From Amylöins of Abnormally Low Type—(vi) From Mineral Matter in Suspension—Ropiness—Yeast-bite—Antiseptics—Finings—Different Methods of Fining—Storage of Pale and Bitter Ales—Porous Spiles—Sampling—Bottling—Forcing Tray—Simpler Test for Stability in Bottle . . . 410

CHAPTER XIII.

THE BREWERY AND PLANT.

Choice of Site—Purchase or Hire of Existing Brewery—Tower Principle—Semi-gravitation—Structural Essentials—Labour Savers—Stacking Apparatus—Flooring—Wells—Pumps—Transmission of Motion—Shafting—Coupling—Clutch—Keys, etc.—Wheel Work and Belting—Preserving Belts—Screws—The Boiler and its Fittings—Mechanical Stokers—Engine—Sack Hoists—Screens—Liquor Backs—Malt-Mills—"Jacob's Ladders"—Grist Cases—External Mashers—Rakes—Mash-Tuns—Coppers—Under Back and Hop Back—Coolers—Atomising Plant—Climax Aërator—Refrigerators—Ice-Making Machines

CONTENTS.

                                                                PAGE
(Compressed Air: Absorption, Compression: Vacuum)—Fermenting-Tuns and Fittings—Cask-plant—Cask-cleaning—Hints on Cleanliness 440

APPENDIX A.—LIST OF THE HOP-GROWING PARISHES OF KENT 504

INDEX 507

A

HANDY BOOK FOR BREWERS.

CHAPTER I.

INTRODUCTORY.

Notes on Chemical Changes—Outline of Processes of Brewing—Malting—Mashing (Infusion, Decoction, and Limited Decoction)—Fermentation (Cleansing, Skimming, Yorkshire Stone Squares, etc.)—Racking—Fining—Storing—Vatting.

A grain of barley contains, in addition to the husk and germ of the young plant, a considerable quantity of starch and albumen, the latter being variously known as nitrogenous bodies, albuminoids, or proteins. The starch being mostly insoluble at ordinary mashing temperatures, and the albumen of unmalted grain being also, to a great extent, insoluble, and therefore inactive (in the brewer's sense of the word), one principal object of the malting process is to break up and render soluble at those temperatures as much of the valuable starch as possible, and a sufficient amount of the albuminoids.

Among the soluble albuminoids is a body—or group of bodies—called, for convenience' sake, **Diastase**, which, upon the malt being mixed in the mash-tun with water of a suitable temperature, attacks its soluble starch, and converts it into a gummy body called **Dextrin** and **Maltose**, or malt-sugar. And the longer this infusion is allowed to continue at a suitable temperature, the smaller, within certain limits, will the proportion of dextrin be and the larger the proportion of maltose contained in the resulting wort.

The maltose afterwards becomes converted by the action of the yeast—added to start and carry on fermentation—into alcohol and carbonic acid. [Other transformation products, it is true, are formed concurrently, but these may be neglected till a later stage, the object being now merely to indicate the broad general principles upon which the maltster's and, after him, the brewer's art reposes.]

Dextrin, on the other hand, is more or less stubborn as regards conversion into alcohol and carbonic acid, which conversion, indeed, only takes place very slowly and probably after its conversion into maltose.* It is therefore desirable to retain a considerable proportion of unconverted dextrin in the worts where great fulness of palate is required. It is also obvious that the presence of a constituent, undergoing fermentation slowly and slowly evolving carbonic acid gas concurrently with a production of alcohol, is an important factor in the manufacture of a beer which is required to be in continuously good "condition," and one that will carry a firm and permanent "head." In short, as far as present knowledge goes, a wort in which the ratio of maltose to dextrin is high will (as a general rule, which is subject to some qualification) yield a vinous, alcoholic beer, while a wort in which the dextrin present is more than normal will yield a full-flavoured beer, charged with carbonic-acid gas.

Nor is this view, which has until lately been held in the simple form stated, upset, although necessarily modified by, the latest theory as to the formation of quasi-independent bodies called malto-dextrins or amylöins, which theory may be briefly stated here.

Malto-Dextrin (or Amylöin) Theory.—According to

---

* This I believe to be the general tenet, though some investigators, amongst them Payen, have held dextrin to be directly fermentable—*i.e.* withou intermediate conversion into either maltose or dextrose (= glucose or grape-sugar, the product when starch is boiled with certain acids).

this theory malto-dextrins are chemical compounds—
not mere *mixtures*—of maltose and dextrin formed in
malt-wort in proportions varying with the quality of the
malt, of the brewing liquor, or with the system of mashing
adopted, and it is their abundance or comparative absence
which determines the full body (and subsequent " condition ") or the thinness of a beer. According to the
holders of this theory, the *free* dextrin in wort is an almost
uniformly constant quantity; it is only the proportion
combined as malto-dextrin which varies. If it be true
that this fixed proportion of dextrin alone would not
suffice to prevent an excessive " attenuation " of the
beer (*i.e.*, the retention of so small a quantity of unfermented matter that the liquid would not be beer at all
in the actual sense of the word), and that " free " dextrin
is (as the malto-dextrin theorists assert) so stubborn as
regards after-fermentation that the quantity present at
the time of racking would be found practically unchanged
at the end of some months' storage, then the importance
of malto-dextrins cannot be overrated. I shall refer to
them again at the end of this chapter in connection with
the secondary or complementary fermentation in cask,
and hope to deal with the subject more fully at a more
advanced stage.

I must own, however, that though I was at first disposed
to regard the terms " Amylöin " and " Malto-dextrin "
as fresh instances of the regrettable tendency to enlarge
the scientific vocabulary, the existence of such bodies will
certainly help to throw light on certain phenomena of
fermentation otherwise rather obscure.

Peptase.—Another of the soluble ferments (among
which diastase ranks), or unorganised ferments, as they
are sometimes rather unhappily called, in contradistinction
to the organised ferments yeast and its congeners, is
peptase, which, though brought into being during the
malting process, lies mainly, if not entirely, dormant until
suitable conditions, such as those of the mash-tun, stimulate it into activity. To what extent its most favourable

sphere of action differs from that of diastase is a question which must be deferred to a later chapter, the only thing now necessary to be said being that its function is to convert the unaltered protein bodies or albuminoids into peptones, which are apparently—though I do not feel convinced that the action of peptase is so well understood as that of diastase—of the highest importance in nourishing and keeping up the vigour and vitality of the yeast owing to their diffusibility—*i.e.*, their power of passing through the enclosing membrane or cell-wall of the yeast, a power which the unaltered protein bodies, even when soluble, do not possess.

Amides.—Some authorities, however—alleging that the proportion of peptones in malt-wort is always small—are inclined to give primary importance in regard to yeast nourishment to other modifications of the protein-bodies called amides.

Albumen, its constitution; harmful if in excess of diastatic and yeast requirements.—Albumen and the other protein bodies of which it is a type are formed of constituents similar to those of starch (viz., carbon, hydrogen, and oxygen), plus sulphur and nitrogen, whence the name of nitrogenous bodies often given to the albumen-containing bodies or albuminoids. And seeing that, apart from the relatively small quantity required either as diastase or as nutriment for the yeast during fermentation, the presence of these nitrogenous bodies is distinctly hurtful,—being indeed a prime cause of defects which will be treated of hereafter,—it will readily appear that the maltster's object should be to obtain a barley rich in starch and with the minimum of albumenoids.

How small is the quantity of diastase actually required may be imagined from the statement that it is capable of transforming at least two thousand times its own weight of starch into maltose. (Perhaps it would be more correct to say into maltose and dextrin, because in the *brewer's* process the transformation products hardly ever go beyond 80% maltose to 20% dextrin.) Some say it is capable of transforming at least ten thousand times its own weight;[*] and there is even an opinion of authority that the smallest quantity of the said diastase, unchanging itself, is theoretically capable of converting any quantity of starch, if only time be given. I say theoretically, because in practical brewing operations there is always a limit of time which cannot be overpassed; but it may be taken as certain that insufficient conversion of the starch into maltose and dextrin is never caused by insufficiency of diastase, but solely by conditions unfavourable to the activity of that agent—viz., either unsuitable mashing heats—of which more anon; or such a physical arrangement of the starch itself (as in malt made from unkindly barley, badly grown and badly kiln-dried) that the diastase is unable to get at it thoroughly; or, finally, such a high degree of acidity (anything approaching $\frac{1}{2}$ per cent.) of the medium, that diastase would be coagulated, and so rendered inert.

It has seemed in accordance with the scope of this book, which aims at supplementing rather than supplanting practical teaching in the brewery, to set down at the outset the ABC which really lies at the root of the matter, and which may perhaps be called scientific, to distinguish it from that "rule of thumb" that has done such yeoman's service in its time, but which is, at this time of day, hardly up to the level of requirements. The beginner, who has perused the foregoing pages carefully, will now, the writer hopes, be in a position, whilst running through the summary sketch of malting and brewing that occupies the rest of this chapter, to read a little "between the lines," and see to some extent how this ABC comes in as a guide to practice.

Malting.—The first process to be referred to is malting, which is really—albeit many brewers are not maltsters—the earliest and not the least important stage in brewing.

[*] Dubrunfaut said 150,000 times; but he was referring to a portion of the nitrogenous matter which he wished to call "Maltine" (possibly the active part of diastase, but at any rate much less in quantity than diastase would be estimated at).

The barley, which is to be operated on, having been obtained, and the light thin corns removed by screening, or, what is still better, the corns of different sizes having been sorted by *grading* (the object of the latter operation being to get bulks of corn which will germinate similarly under similar conditions), it is then steeped—*i.e.*, covered with water—and allowed to soak in a large fixed vessel called the **Cistern** for fifty hours more or less.

The water then being drained off, the saturated corn is either thrown or allowed to descend (by opening a valve) into the **Couch** or **Couch-frame**. In malthouses of later construction the cisterns are of iron and conical in shape; moreover, they are fixed above the couch-frame, so that, on a valve being opened, the whole of the saturated contents is discharged into the receptacle beneath. This arrangement is much more speedy. A good-sized cistern, which it would take two men working with shovels at least thirty minutes to clear, can be emptied in three minutes, while the work superseded is as heavy as any in the malthouse, and the crushing of a good many corns, that fertile source of mould, is prevented. It may be that in extremely cold weather the free conductivity of the metal would render it an unsatisfactory material for cisterns—it is certain that the steep water should never be extremely cold (never below $50°$); were that the case, such cisterns could be "lagged" with some non-conducting covering.

In the couch the grain rests about a day: twenty-seven hours was the old excise minimum at the time when the grain was gauged in the couch, and the duty calculated on the results of that gauging. Now, however, the use of the couch, not being compulsory, merely depends upon the fact that it is found useful to keep the grain at a considerable thickness at first, in order to encourage a slight rise of temperature, and thereby to favour the beginning of germination.

Malting (continued)—Flooring.—The couch is opened out or "broken," one of its sides, a movable one, being taken out, and the grain partly moved forward, though the couch-frame is still occupied, but so that a much greater area of floor is covered, and the corn lies consequently much less thickly. The thickness will of course vary with the temperature, it being advisable in a general way to spread the grain thinner in warm or muggy weather than when the weather is cold. The object of this is to prevent the temperature of the now growing grain from exceeding the desirable temperature of 60°, and the attendant generation of too much carbonic acid, the escape of which is moreover facilitated by the "turning" or "ploughing" to which "the floors" are subjected, generally twice a day.

Malting (continued)—The Floors.—Upon the day that the couch is opened out the grain becomes a "one-day floor"; upon the following day it is known as a "two-day floor"; on the succeeding days as a "third-day," "fourth-day," "fifth-day floor," and so on. Every day, generally twice a day, "the piece" or "floor" is turned and moved forward away from the cistern and towards the kiln, which is at the opposite end of the malthouse. The turning is effected with broad, flat wooden shovels, and as each shovelful is thrown forward, a dexterous turn of the wrist scatters it thinly and evenly on the floor in front. The usual practice is to skim the surface with one sweep of the shovel, throw that shovelful forwards, and get up the lower layer, so laid bare, in another sweep. In this way a large percentage of the grains, previously lying at the bottom, will now be thrown for a time on the top, and have their chance of absorbing the oxygen needed for healthy growth.

Mode of turning Floors.—The men, as they turn the floors, work from side to side of the malthouse (or from side to middle, and back again to the same side, if the house is a double one), and sometimes they work forward —*i.e.*, following the shovel, sometimes backward—*i.e.*, in front of the shovel. The latter seems the preferable way, fewer corns being crushed—an important point when it is remembered that every crushed corn is not only liable to turn mouldy itself, but that the mycelia of mould run rapidly from the unsound to apparently healthy corns, given favourable conditions for development. When the men follow the shovel (*i.e.*, work forward), the grains which are unavoidably missed cannot escape being crushed between the workmen's feet and the hard floor, if they be trodden on; when, on the other hand, they work backward, they tread upon a yielding layer of unturned grain some inches thick, and comparatively little harm, if any, is done. Felt slippers lessen the risk of crushing, but better still from that point of view is the system of working barefoot practised at Newark. Men, however, who have not been brought up to this system naturally object to begin it.

Germination—Rootlets—Acrospire.—Meantime the rootlets have made their appearance; at first—when the grain begins, as it is said, "to chit"—in a white protrusion at one end of each barley-corn; then they separate, and, if the conditions are favourable to rapidity of growth, this white protrusion soon resolves itself into separate rootlets, three, four, five, six, or even, here and there, seven in number, which grow daily, though they should never grow long and "spindly" (short bushy rootlets are a desideratum), up to the seventh or eighth day from the couch, after which, even though they have been refreshed by judicious sprinkling, the active growth ordinarily slackens, as evidenced by some loss of their pristine brightness of hue.

A less noticeable phenomenon, though some growth is doubtless almost simultaneous with the sprouting of the rootlets, is the development of the **acrospire** or **Plumula.** The acrospire, known to the old malting hand as "the back-spear," starts its growth from the rootlet end on the smooth, not the cleft side of the grain, and grows under the latter's skin to a certain point (about three-quarters the length of the grain), the attainment of which is a sign to the maltster that germination has been carried far enough. This acrospire is what, under the natural conditions of growth in the soil, would develop into the green blade with which we are all familiar, but in the artificial process the growth is stopped far short of that;

indeed it is, as has been said, rarely allowed to traverse more than three-quarters of the length of the grain (never, on any account, being allowed to protrude), this being all-sufficient to call into being the qualities which differentiate malt from barley. What these are, apart from the physical characteristics of greater friability, sweetness, and lower specific gravity (a bushel of good barley weighs about 56 lb., whereas a bushel of malt made from it weighs from 40 to 42 lb.), will be found on pp. 90, 91.

It may be well, however, before referring to the kiln, to add a fairly representative sketch of the progress of a floor of malt supposed to have been steeped in moderately mild weather in spring, and which, though not showing any exceptional vigour in regard to the average number of rootlets produced, exhibits a satisfactory development of acrospire.

Progress of an average floor.—After the usual stay of forty-eight to fifty hours under water in the cistern (the water having been changed at least once), and twenty-four to twenty-seven hours in the couch, its career begins as a one-day floor. Suppose the couch "broken" at 7 A.M., it is probable that an inspection of the grains will reveal the rootlets beginning to protrude here and there, and if the floor be levelled to say three inches, it will be found in the evening, say at 5 P.M., that they are just through in nearly all of them. No turning will be necessary, probably, the first day. On the second morning distinct rootlets will have made their appearance in at least half the grains, and varying from one to three in number.

Turning will be resorted to morning and evening for the next few days—the barley being spread thinner and thinner, and consequently occupying more space until it is a four-day floor, when it may perhaps be advisable slightly to reduce the area over which it is spread. On the morning of the "three-day" floor nearly all the grains will have three well-developed curly rootlets, some of them four. On the evening of the same day all will probably have three rootlets, some four or five, averaging a quarter to a third of an inch in length, and the acrospire will be plainly visible. On the fourth day the rootlets will be well developed, and four or five in number; in the evening the acrospire will be nearly halfway "up." Perhaps on the fifth day the rootlets may show a slight loss of brightness, and it may be advisable to begin **sprinkling,** using about six gallons of water to a quarter of corn as a maximum. The sprinkling is done with a large can, having a straight spout of exaggerated length, which is freely perforated for a considerable part of its length with fine holes, so that a wide and tolerably fine spray is assured. On the evening of the fifth day the acrospire will be fully halfway up, and in some grains possibly two-thirds. On the sixth day, if the rootlets begin to wither, the acrospire should be two-thirds of the way up, and the grain retain its characteristic fresh, cucumber-like smell.

The development of the acrospire is now slower, but on the evening of the seventh day it will be three parts "up" in many cases, and cautious sprinkling may, if necessary, be resorted to. [N.B.—Sprinkling must be restricted by the necessity of sending the floor to kiln not heavily charged with moisture.] On the eighth day "the mellowing" will probably begin, the acrospire being stationary. On the ninth day it may be necessary to leave the floor unturned, and on the tenth, if it be not then ready for the kiln, to let it off with one turning. It will then certainly be fit for the kiln on the eleventh day (as an "eleven-day floor"), but probably before this time mould will have made its appearance, and maybe in such quantity that it will seem advisable to put "the floor" on the kiln a little earlier than its growth otherwise would require. The above details are only given as typical of what occurs in malting a floor of barley when the external temperature is not very low, and where the grain is kept at a moderate temperature, approximating to 60° Fahr., by judicious turning and spreading. In very cold weather the germinating grain may be thirteen or even fourteen days on the floor.

Malting (continued).—It may be mentioned that as

"the floor" nears its next destination, the kiln, on which it will be loaded at an age, generally speaking, varying between nine and twelve days, other younger floors will be following it; and as it is usual to steep about every fourth day, with certain variations to lighten Sunday labour, it is essential that the malthouse floor should be long enough to hold three separate steepings with a small clear interval between, which must be kept scrupulously clear of scattered corns, the edges of each "piece" too being neatly brushed up.

Withering is sometimes spoken of as if it were a separate operation; but though withering-lofts have at times been adopted, it can hardly be so considered. It is, in fact, the getting rid of superfluous moisture by the influence of the air, a riddance which is naturally accompanied by a withering of the rootlets, though the acrospire may still grow slightly; and it is certainly a point of capital importance not to load the green malt on the kiln in a very moist condition. Some maltsters again like to heap up a "piece" of malt for a time before kilning it, whereby a little more heat is generated, the result, as they hold, being greater mellowness. But in any case, the wisdom of endeavouring to get mellowness and friability by withering or heaping must be decided in connection with the freedom from mould which the piece may or may not exhibit. If mould has begun to run it will be advisable to get the "green malt" upon the kiln at once, and not to incur certain damage for a problematical benefit. **Fitness for the Kiln** can be determined by pressing the grain between the thumb-nails, whereupon it should crumble without exuding moisture and without pastiness. The acrospire should be three-quarters "up," as nearly uniformly as possible. The rootlets, which before should have been short and curly (say half an inch in length at the outside), will now be dry and somewhat shrivelled.

The Kiln, of which more anon, consists of a floor either of woven wire or tiles, upon which the green malt has to be loaded, and supported by massive brickwork, within which is the firing-place from twelve to eighteen feet below the floor itself. Rising high above the floor, the upper part of the kiln is generally conical in shape. Stopes says the more closely a kiln resembles a chimney in construction the greater is its effective capacity. Anyhow, large outlet openings, such as are sometimes seen, by leading to over-rapid cooling of the air, prevent that strong upcast draught which is so essential. But on the other hand the openings must be large enough for getting rid of vapour when the green malt is being dried. Cowls are generally better than fixed openings.

Anthracite Coal (Welsh coal), preferable because of its being comparatively smokeless, is burnt. It has on the average 6% or 7% more carbon and about $\frac{1}{2}$% less sulphur than ordinary coal.

The important point is to use *moderate heat at first till the malt is thoroughly dry*. Excessive heat applied to the moist green malt imparts a high colour, besides causing other evils, which will be more fully treated of in Chapter II. The malt stays on the kiln (for drying and curing) from three to four days; and if moderate heat has been used at first, very high temperatures may be employed to finish off without risk.

Double Kilns.—Sometimes an upper kiln is constructed on what is generally known here as the Stopes[*] principle, but one which has long been appreciated in Germany. The green malt is first loaded on the upper floor, for which woven wire is the best material, as holes are generally cut in it—in fact, have to be cut in it—to enable the men to shovel the charge, when properly dried, down on to the lower kiln floor, for which Nuneaton tiles (Stanley Bros.) are as good a material as any. These cut holes are covered with conical wire dissipators or

---

[*] Other patented improvements will, however, be mentioned in the next chapter. In them the aim has very properly been to meet the defect of the Stopes kiln—*i.e.*, the difficulty of *drying* the upper floor at a low heat, and *curing* the bottom floor at a high heat simultaneously.

dispersers, which may also be metal cylinders, with one end absent at the part where they fit over the cut openings. In this case they have an arrangement opening and shutting at the top for letting out the heated air from the bottom kiln without its passing through the layer of malt on the upper kiln.

The double kiln is *theoretically* best, if only the firing can be so arranged that the temperature of the bottom kiln is high enough for imparting flavour and soundness, and the temperature of the upper kiln *at the same time* low enough to dry, without colouring its contents. I say theoretically because, having had very good opportunity of comparing malts made in one house with two double kilns with malts made in another house with two single kilns, I am unable to state a decided preference. If I were forced to state a preference it would probably be for the single kilns as far as we have got. The double kilns involve some alteration in steeping, less is wetted at one time, but the steeping is more frequent—say every other day instead of every fourth day.

The mention of Germany reminds me that the system of drying and curing practised there differs from the usual English method, in that, in that country, heated air alone is allowed to pass through the malt, whilst here the actual products of combustion pass with the heated air. Indeed, an eminent authority, Dr. Graham, thinks this an advantage, holding that the malt, like "a Finnon haddie," keeps all the better for the smoking it receives.

After being thoroughly cured the malt is trodden, either on the kiln or in an adjoining loft, to free it from dried rootlets or "the combes," as they are called. It is then stored, preferably in bins and with "the dust"—*i.e.*, the rootlets—until wanted. Next it is passed over a screen to separate the rootlets, which fall through the mesh of the inclined screen, and is then conveyed to the brewery.

Malt on arriving in the Brewery.—After reaching the brewery the malt is crushed, but not ground, in a malt-mill or malt-mills, whence it is raised, as "grist," while the crushing proceeds, by an elevator or Jacob's ladder, an endless band with cups attached, which as they reach their highest point and begin their descent upside down discharge each its little load of grist into the **Grist-case** or **Hopper**, which commands the mash-tun. This operation takes place, as a rule, on the day before that fixed for the actual brewing.

The **Liquor**, as water is always called in a brewery, is also generally heated each evening for the next day's mash. Some brewers prefer to boil it, and allow it to cool down, adding cold liquor if required. The carbonates, or rather bicarbonates (but not the sulphates), of lime and magnesia are thereby precipitated, and with them any iron present in the same form. The "liquor" may then be treated with one of the standard preparations (generally having a sulphate of lime basis) to assimilate it, as nearly as may be, to some brewing water of repute.

Mashing Systems (Infusion, Decoction, and Limited Decoction).—There are three principal systems of mashing, viz., the Infusion Process, which is the usual English method; the Decoction Process, employed in Germany and elsewhere for the production of Lager beer; and thirdly, a variation of the first with some features of the second, known as Limited Decoction.

In the **Infusion method** the crushed malt and the "liquor" are mixed either in the mash-tun by internal rakes, or they fall into it ready mixed by passage through a mashing-machine, fixed outside the mash-tun, but placed so as to command it. Generally there will be both rakes inside the tun, and one of these external mashers (Steele's, Maitland's, or Riley's, etc.). The mash-tun has a false bottom consisting of perforated or slotted metal plates, which rest on feet so as to be some inches above the real bottom. This interspace and the plates of the false bottom should be covered with the mashing liquor before the grist is started. Where, however, the mixing is done by internal rakes only, it is usual to run all the liquor required into the mash-tun (to the extent of about one-and-three-quarters or two barrels per quarter of malt) before starting the grist, which is then run in *dry* as the rakes revolve and mix it in.

When all the liquor has been run in, before the grist is started, it is advisable to get it a degree or two above the wished-for heat, cooling it down by a revolution or two of the rakes, and if necessary by the addition of cold "liquor." Or a better course still, if time admits of it, is to run nearly the full amount of liquor at a temperature as close to boiling as possible into the mash-tun, so that it may stay there for half an hour or more, and *thoroughly warm the tun*, cooling down by revolutions of the rakes or the addition of cold liquor just before mashing. When the proper heat is attained, any surplus liquor can be run to waste before the malt (grist) is let in. In any case, the mash-tun should be well heated previous to mashing—this is especially necessary when the mash-tun is of iron—so that no cooling of the mash may result. The aim is to get the "**initial heat**" most favourable for inducing certain chemical changes which have already been referred to briefly, and will be further dealt with in the chapter on Mashing and Boiling.

The initial heat (by which must be understood the heat of the mash directly all the malt and all the liquor are together in the mash-tun) may range from 145° to 152° Fahr., or even higher, according to the quality of the malt or the character of the beer that one wishes to produce. To attain this, unless Clinch's system of a preliminary heating of the grist be adopted, a "striking heat," *i.e.*, the heat at which the liquor meets the goods, some 15° Fahr., more or less, above the desired initial, will be requisite. If, on the other hand, the grist be heated, obviously a temperature which approximates to the desired initial will be sufficient.

This "initial" is maintained or slightly raised by the introduction of **"underlet"** or **"Piece Liquor,"** so-called, let under the false bottom; and if there are internal rakes—as there ought to be in all large tuns—it will be the general practice to let them revolve once round the tun, or twice at the most, to mix the underlet and the rest of the mash. Too many revolutions—*i.e.*, too much knocking about of the mash—tend to make the mash "dead," as it is called when the wort drains off badly. Underletting, however, is not the invariable practice, but is often convenient for making up the desired proportion of mashing liquor, which is, as a rule, at about the rate of two barrels for each quarter of malt. Underletting is less needed from the point of view of temperature when the bulk of "the goods" is large, or when the mash-tun, especially if it be of iron, is so thoroughly heated that it acts as a reservoir of caloric for the mash to draw upon.

It should be remembered, however, that the more liquid the mash, other things being equal, the higher will the ratio of maltose be to dextrine in the resulting wort, and consequently the tendency of the latter will be towards greater **attenuation**—*i.e.*, towards a beer containing less unfermented matter but more alcohol. Such a beer, skilfully manipulated, may by the pungency attributable to the increased amount of alcohol and of carbonic acid, with which it should be saturated, delude the taster's palate into an impression of even greater body than one less attenuated may succeed in imparting. On the other hand, there being a tendency, when the fermentation is of a very free and rapid character, to the dissipation and consequent loss of too much of the carbonic acid (representing an equal portion with the alcohol of the solid fermentable matter which the wort once contained), considerable care will be necessary to prevent such a beer drinking thin and poor, or, as the expression goes, "below its gravity."

Rest after Mashing—Wort Circulators.—The mash is next allowed to rest or "stand" for a period that varies from an hour and a half, or even less, to two hours; though in the interval some brewers, who have the requisite appliances, find it to their advantage to "circulate" the wort— *i.e.*, to set taps and convey it to the upper part of the mash-tun, *viâ* some intermediate appliance for raising its temperature. It is then sparged * over the surface of "the goods" (through sparge-arms of larger aperture than those used for the subsequent liquor sparges), at a temperature considerably above that at which it runs from the mash-tun, the double operation—running-off and sparging-on—being carried on simultaneously.

The advantages of circulating are increased and early brightness of tap, and a shortening of the "rest" or "stand," owing both to the first-named advantage and to the fact that the circulation, provided the temperatures be not excessively raised, stimulates the diastasic action which converts the malt-starch into sugar; or, on the other hand, if the command of temperature during the process be without limit, the power which the brewer then has of crippling the diastasic action by a very high heat, and of thereby producing a dextrinous rather than a saccharine wort, or, in other words, one which will yield a full-drinking beer which will improve by storage.

The **two forms of circulator** in use are the one known as **Crockford's** and that patented by **Mr. Bucknall,** of Kidderminster. The former, though no royalty has to be paid, is a somewhat costly arrangement in itself, involving a rotary pump, speeded to at least 1,200 revolutions a minute, considerable lengths of tinned-copper connecting pipe, and a copper vessel with a steam coil in it, which is used for heating the wort as it is pumped up. The opening at the bottom of this vessel (the said opening being connected with its sparge-pipe) is plugged by an overflow pipe, which stands up higher than the coil, so that the latter is always covered while steam is passing

---

* Sparging = sprinkling or distributing liquid (water generally) over the surface of "the goods" (as the malt when in the mash-tun is called) through a sparger. The simplest form of sparger is a copper vessel, with two or three arms, which are perforated with a series of fine holes in the side opposite to the direction in which they revolve; the central vessel being balanced on a pin pointing vertically and fitting into a special socket, and the whole apparatus revolving by the impulse of the water. The central vessel has copper partitions, against which the water impinges.

through it. At the end of the circulating, which may last fifteen minutes, or considerably more if it be found useful, the vessel is emptied by withdrawing the plug-pipe.

Bucknall's apparatus is simpler. A tube connected with the bottom of the mash-tun, or with the small "back" (vessel) into which the taps flow, is so arranged that a jet of free steam admitted into its lower end drives against the wort which has previously been let into the tube, and by the force of its impact (somewhat after the manner of a Giffard's Injector) carries the latter up with it to a height which commands the upper surface of the mash-tun, raising its heat considerably, of course, at the same time. The objections, if valid objections they be, lie in the use of free or naked steam, connoting the possibility of impurities being introduced, and the fact that its condensation adds to the fluidity of the mash. This increase of fluidity need not, however, be excessive, seeing that the principle of latent heat of steam comes into play. The heating capacity of free steam, accordingly, will be four or five times as great as that of steam conducted through coils, a fact which should theoretically render it easy even to boil the wort, as carried up, with a relatively moderate amount of condensation. And if the said steam inlet be well above the level of the boilers, as it would be in most modern plants, the risk of oily matters and other impurities being introduced, especially if certain chemical boiler-compositions be eschewed, is reduced to a minimum.

The remaining steps between mashing and fermentation are roughly and briefly "setting-taps" after the rest in the mash-tun. Shortly after taps are set "tap-heats" are taken; they show a temperature about $2°$ below that which would be registered by a thermometer plunged into "the goods" themselves. The total quantity of "liquor" (=water) required to make up "copper lengths" may either be sparged on—and this sparging goes on simultaneously with the spending of the taps, while the "liquor" supplied through the arms of the

SECOND MASH. COPPER.

sparger should be so regulated that "the goods" are neither drawn nor beaten down; that is to say, the supply should be copious, and yet the holes in the sparge-arms should be fine enough to prevent the liquor from falling heavily, for a light and sponge-like condition of the goods means good drainage, and good drainage generally means good extract.

Or, by another plan, the necessary quantity of liquor may be partly applied by means of a **second mash**, the balance being sparged on. In the latter case "the goods" are drawn somewhat down, say after the first copper is "made up"; taps are then shut, sufficient liquor under and over-let to make the goods fluid enough. The mashing machinery inside the tun is then set in motion, and, after a certain number of revolutions of its rakes, stopped, and "a stand," sufficient to ensure brightness of taps, takes place. A circulator, as above described, will abbreviate this. My own experience leads me to prefer sparging the entire quantity. The extract, if the mash was well made, seems equally good, and the delay caused by the necessary "stand" is avoided—supposing, of course, that there is a second copper ready to be filled.

The copper or coppers being "made up"—*i.e.*, filled to the required depth, generally ascertained by taking the dry dip or number of inches from the top which the surface of the wort is to come up to,*—**hops are added**. Some brewers add them while the copper is being made up, before the length is got; some again add the quantities worked out for each copper all together to that copper; others, with more judgment, add portions, generally different growths, at intervals, boiling the choicest hops the shortest time, with the object of retaining as much of the fine aroma as possible in the wort. When the copper "length" is made up and first boils with the hops it is said to be "through." The coppers may be

* The number of barrels to which these dry inches correspond is ascertained by reference to a Table. Thus suppose 20 dry inches (which is pretty full even for a steam-boiled copper) = 90 barrels, and each inch represents a barrel, then 21 in. = 89 barrels, 22 = 88 barrels, and so on.

boiled either by direct fire action or by steam, the relative advantages of which may be referred to later.

The boiling having lasted from one and a half to two hours (longer than this can hardly ever be needed), the copper is "turned out" or "struck," the boiling wort, hops and all, rushing out through an opened valve or tap into the **hop-back,** a vessel sometimes rectangular, sometimes circular in shape. A circular hop-back of copper admits of the introduction of a sparger, similar to that connected with the mash-tun, for extracting any wort remaining in the hops after the last copper has been pumped out of it. After a rest of about thirty minutes in the hop-back the wort will be pumped, or proceed by gravitation to the **coolers**—open, shallow vessels of wood, iron, or copper—and thence over the **refrigerator** or **refrigerators**, which are, broadly speaking, an arrangement of parallel copper tubes, placed either vertically (of which Lawrence's Vertical Refrigerator is a type) or horizontally (Morton's, etc.), *through* which cold water flows, while the wort flows *over* them in a contrary direction. [To avoid misapprehension on the part of those who have never seen a refrigerator, let me add that the term "vertical" is somewhat of a misnomer; upright would be better. The tubes are in every case—except with certain circular or spiral refrigerators—*at right angles* to the course of the wort.] The object of this passage is to cool the wort from the temperature approaching boiling, say 180°, at which it stands upon the coolers, to a temperature of 60°, or even lower, which is advisable for the commencement of fermentation.

It will be observed that the wort, which is brilliantly clear at the higher temperature, becomes more or less dull when cooled down, from the fact that certain bodies, of albuminous character, soluble in the hot fluid, are thrown out of solution at the lower temperature. It is the business of the yeast, in addition to its vital functions, which result in the phenomena of fermentation (*i.e.*, the production of alcohol and carbonic acid gas from the saccharine matter of the wort), to purge the wort of these factors of turbidity, a purging which is probably effected mechanically, when they are not too plentiful, by the continuous rising of multitudinous yeast-cells to the surface.

Before proceeding further to our description of fermentation, it will be well to refer to certain differences in the method of mashing, as far as they are marked enough to have received special names.

Infusion, Decoction, and "Limited Decoction" Systems of Mashing.—The **Infusion system** is the one described in the foregoing pages, and is the system adopted, with slight modifications, throughout Great Britain. On the other hand, in the great Continental brewing centres the **Decoction system,** so called because portions of the mash are actually boiled or cooked, is preferred. There are, of course, variations, but the usual Viennese system is as follows.

The grist is first mashed with cold water until a homogeneous mixture is obtained, and Thausing says it is considered a sign of good quality in the malt when the mash froths well and has an agreeable smell, and when the water quickly gets a milky appearance. Meantime the water in the copper has been boiled, and enough is now introduced into the mash-tun to raise the heat to a point somewhere between 86° and 100° Fahr.

Next, about one-third of the mash ("goods" and all) is conveyed into a special vessel known as the *maischkessel* (mash-copper) to be boiled, its temperature, however, being brought only by degrees up to 167°. Its appearance is noted from time to time, and, from being milky at first, it gets gradually transparent as the starch is first liquefied and then converted into dextrin and sugar. Two objects have to be kept in view during this procedure—first, the conversion of the starch during the gradual elveation of the temperature up to 167°, and the more completely this takes place the better; and secondly, to elevate the temperature of the remaining two-thirds of the mash by the return to it of the boiled portion. The boiling of the latter, however, is not begun until the milkiness has all disappeared, the time during which it is boiled varying between a quarter and three-quarters of an hour; and until the ebullition is active, the mass has to be kept in constant movement (by revolving arms, with loops of chain depending, which sweep the bottom of the vessel) to prevent burning.

This portion, the first *dickmaische*, as it is called, having been boiled its due time, enough of it is reintroduced into the mash-tun to raise the temperature of the whole to a point between 110° and 126° Fahr., the mashing apparatus being, of course, still revolving. A few minutes having elapsed, a third part of the mash is again taken (second *dickmaische*), and submitted to treatment similar to that undergone by the first, save that the boiling is generally somewhat prolonged. On this being reintroduced into the mash-tun, the temperature of the whole mash should reach a point which varies between 134° and 149°.

This second *dickmaische* having been thoroughly incorporated with the residue of the mash, the mashing is stopped so as to allow some of the solid constituents to subside previous to the abstraction of a third portion, which in this instance is more or less clear wort, and is accordingly called the *lautermaische*. This is generally boiled longer than the previous *dickmaischen*, and, at any rate, the boiling is continued until inspection in a glass shows the coagulated albumenoids being precipitated in large flakes. This having happened, all the *lautermaische* is restored to the mash-tun, the contents of which are thoroughly well mashed once more, so that the final temperature may reach a point between 160° and 167°, this point being, as in the previous operations, higher in the winter than in summer. The "rest" that now ensues is as limited as possible, being, in fact, only continued until the grains are deposited. The mash is, of necessity, much thinner than an infusion mash would be, and the continuous treatment militates against that spongy condition of the goods which is a *sine quâ non* in the latter. The wort should then look dark above the grains—a reddish hue is considered a bad sign—and this will happen ordinarily in half an hour, or but little over.

As regards relative stability, most German brewers would pronounce in favour of decoction beers, but then they are thinking of infusion beers fermented on decoction lines, whereas either system has its own special method of fermentation (to be referred to later) exactly adapted to the tastes of its consumers. So that, considering infusion and decoction beers *as they are*, our conclusions will be widely different, and may be summed up as follows: infusion beers are far more alcoholic, while decoction beers contain a much larger percentage, relative to their original gravity, of unfermented, and therefore nutritive, malt extract. The latter, moreover, owing to the extremely low temperature at which they are fermented, are saturated with carbonic acid gas to a degree unusual in the infusion product. On the other hand, the infusion beer may claim much greater stability, being capable, if well brewed, of standing "on ullage" (*i.e.*, on draught) for many weeks, of keeping and improving in bottle for a considerable time, and even of supporting a voyage to India, without precautions other than those implied in attaining as complete an attenuation in cask as is possible.

Decoction beer, on the other hand, is so incapable of supporting "draught," that the smallest cask of it would become undrinkable before an ordinary family could consume it; and if it be bottled, unless the consumption is to be speedy, "Pasteurisation" (maintaining at a temperature of 140° Fahr. or thereabouts for a time) is an absolute necessity for its preservation. Yet again, no one can deny the refreshing quality possessed by well-iced lager beer (with a temperature so different from that of the lukewarm fluid so often dispensed in summer over English bars), just as no one can deny the superior value, as a digestive stimulant, of light and well-attenuated infusion ale. Decoction beer, therefore, is pre-eminently what Dr. Graham has called it, a "conversation beer." One point of superiority which the bottled decoction beers often exhibit may be noticed—viz., that the deposit, which necessitates considerable care in the pouring out of most English bottled ales, is practically non-existent in good decoction samples, or exists in such a cohesive form (somewhat resembling "the beeswing" in port, but of tougher quality), that there is little difficulty in pouring out the whole contents of the bottle, and that at intervals too, in a drinkable condition.

Limited Decoction is the name applied to a process which begins on infusion lines, the mash, however, after a short rest, and after a certain quantity of strong wort has been drawn off, being boiled in the mash-tun itself by means of free steam, let in under the false bottom, the plates of which it is advisable to bolt down to prevent them from shifting. This boiling, especially where "steely" or hard malt is used, dissolves a quantity of starch, unaffected by the previous mashing temperatures. The mash is then cooled down with cold liquor to a temperature at which diastase is able to act (say 160° to 165° Fahr.), and this diastase is got—the potency of that in the mash-tun having been destroyed by the boiling—by the reintroduction into the mash-tun of that portion of strong wort which was run off soon after the completion of the mash, and which will have been maintained at a temperature, in the meantime, not exceeding 160° F. Upon its thorough intermixture with "the goods," the freshly dissolved starch is rapidly converted into dextrin and maltose (malt-sugar).

Those who adopt the method which is described above will perhaps notice a viscid formation of coagulated albumen, approximating to the *Oberteig*, the grey smeary substance which German brewers find on the surface of their "goods." It represents diastasic factors which have done their work, or, at any rate, in the extremely soluble condition of the starch are no longer required; accordingly its retention by the mash will be no disadvantage, rather the contrary, as its tendency in the ordinary infusion system is, after being coagulated at a temperature of 180° or thereabouts, to redissolve or break up upon prolonged boiling, and thus to become, if not eliminated during fermentation, a possible source of trouble to the brewer.* The brilliancy of limited-decoction worts is remarkable; but further working details must be reserved until the chapter on mashing.

Cleansing and Skimming Systems of Fermentation.—Into one of these two divisions all the various methods adopted in this country fall. Even the "stone-square system" of Yorkshire, so famous in that county, is but a specialised kind of "cleansing," and the employment of subsidiary "dropping squares," frequently used in Scotland and elsewhere, will range as a modified and improved form of skimming.

Skimming System.—The simplest and most usual form of this system is that in which the fermentation is begun and ended in the same vessel (known generally as the fermenting vessel or "gyle-tun," or, according to its shape, as a "round" or "square"). The wort is "pitched," *i.e.*, yeast is added and "roused" in, when but a small quantity of the wort, at a temperature of 60° Fahr. or somewhat higher, is in the round or square. The yeast is added at a rate varying generally between one pound and three pounds per barrel of the intended total quantity, the variation depending on the quality of the beer (heavily hopped or strong ales will usually require more yeast than lightly hopped or low-gravity ales), and the proved strength of the ferment (yeast) in relation to the type of wort. The **pitching-yeast** should be thoroughly drained of beer, and be knocked up into a homogeneous mass. This facilitates oxygena-

* A process has been patented by Mr. B. W. Valentin, with whom, I believe, Mr. Frank Faulkner is now associated, for removing these coagulated albumenoids. It turns upon filtration of the wort, cooled down after coagulation point is reached, through a cellulose filter,

tion, apparently a great initial stimulus to fermentation. Whitish-coloured yeast is preferred to that of darker hue, as indicative of the greater vigour of the multitudinous component cells in the aggregate. Some brewers, with doubtful policy, use yeast which has been "pressed"; some, again, pin their faith upon a preliminary mixture of the yeast with wort at a higher temperature than the usual pitching heat of 60° more or less, rousing them up together in a separate vessel—a hogshead with the head out will do for small quantities—in which the wort stands at 75° to 80°, the top being subsequently closely covered up for some twenty minutes. At the end of that time the yeast will have greatly expanded, and the contents of the vessel are added to the wort running into the round or square, and the whole roused together.

When all the worts are "gathered," *i.e.*, when the two, three, or four "coppers," as the case may be, have all been run over the refrigerators into the fermenting vessel or vessels, **the Exciseman** comes upon the scene, and by taking "dips" and gravities (previously taken and declared by the brewer) arrives at the number of gallons chargeable for duty.

If two or three distinct varieties of beer are produced at the one operation the brewing is called a "**Parti-gyle**."

When several fermenting vessels have to be filled with the *same* sort of beer, it is sometimes the practice, for convenience in assessing the duty, to have one large **gathering-square,** the contents of which are subdivided amongst the said fermenting vessels about twelve or fifteen hours later. Nor does the benefit of such a gathering-square stop at mere convenience; a good deal of coagulated, dirty-looking matter, which has risen to the surface of the otherwise silvery-white head, gets eliminated, and the aëration which the transference involves may also be distinctly advantageous.

A **normal fermentation** is one in which skimming-point (coincident with the beginning of formation of a *yeasty*, as distinguished from a frothy head) is reached in about forty-eight hours from the time of pitching. An earlier time than that would indicate fermentations more or less rapid; a longer period, a somewhat slow type of fermentation. Early stages are the well-known "cauliflower" and "rocky" heads, epithets which, when the heads themselves have once been seen, will require no explanation. The heads rise steadily at first, say until the temperature has risen 5° or 6°, then fall, rising again, as a general rule, if allowed to do so, when the yeast is forming. These early heads are sometimes, though light and frothy in substance, of relatively considerable thickness, especially with medium-strong or strong beers, where the fermentation starts with vigour; thus a head three feet or so in height, the wort beneath it being five feet or so in depth, would be nothing phenomenal. In the case of lightly hopped, light-gravity ales the head will rise much less, but in every case the worts ought to be covered with a coherent head, and must not show any tendency toward what is known as a **Fiery, or Boiling Fermentation.** In the latter case, as the usual yeast-forming point is approached, absolutely no "head" is to be seen, but a rapid evolution of carbonic acid gas, as in a freshly opened bottle of soda-water, perhaps with the formation of great bladdery bubbles filled with the gas, which burst on the surface. This portent, though it may have no ill effect in the isolated brewing, which *may* even be better than the average of brewings, yet points to faulty conditions of mashing or otherwise, which, if persisted in, must end disastrously.

Medium or rather slow fermentations (the latter being quite distinct from **sluggish fermentations,** in which, owing to feeble yeast or unsuitable preparation of wort, attenuation comes almost to a standstill) generally produce a brighter "racking-sample" than quick fermentations are capable of doing.

The temperature of the wort rises as fermentation progresses, and this rise is, of course, a result of the energetic breaking up of some of the wort constituents by the yeast.

The usual rate of rise—unless it be checked by the **attemperator** *—is 1° Fahr. for every brewer's pound of original gravity, which, according to saccharometer indications, disappears, broken up into the ultimate products of fermentation.

Skimming-point, which slightly precedes the formation of a yeasty head, may be about 8 lb. (as shown by the saccharometer) for an 18 lb. or 19 lb. beer—that is to say, when 10 lb. or 11 lb. have apparently disappeared; for a beer of 24 lb. original gravity it will be 10 lb., more or less. The exact point will vary with circumstances and in different breweries, so that experience must decide it. Still more difficult to settle precisely is the question of **temperature.** If the yeast be vigorous, it may be kept low, but, generally speaking, it is advisable to let it run up—*i.e.*, to leave off attemperating a little before the first "skim." Some, however, advocate a reduction of temperature when the yeast is working off, as tending to the latter's readier separation. A relatively low temperature means not only a yeast less liable to liquefy to nothing in summer, but also a beer more saturated with carbonic acid gas, and therefore more brisk on the palate, with more "bite," as some phrase it, and, in addition, with more hop-flavour; but it must not be lost sight of that the greater vinosity often secured, notably in running beers of rather high gravity, by higher fermenting temperatures, often has a similar, and in *their* case a more marked effect in regard to this briskness on the palate.

So that, though some beers of moderate gravity—for example, those of the now usual AK type—will, if the pitching yeast be good, rack perfectly clean and free from "yeast-bite" (a clinging bitter as distinguished from the aromatic fugitive bitter of the hop), even though the

---

* An attemperator is a copper coil, movable or otherwise, placed beneath the surface of the wort in the fermenting-vessel, and through which cold water can be made to run, whereby the brewer is enabled to control the temperature of his fermentations. Attemperators are either movable or fixed, the former for small tuns, the latter for large. A movable attemperator, even for an 80-barrel tun, is rather unwieldy.

temperature at skimming point be not over 66°, it yet seems preferable to give running beers of 25 lb. gravity and upwards a range as high as 70° or 72°, or even, on occasion, higher. Between these two extremes there is of course a happy mean for ordinary running beers of lighter gravity.

But in any case, if low to moderate fermenting temperatures be the rule, the yeast, which, like all other organisms, strives to get into correspondence with its environment (to annex a biological phrase), will soon adapt itself to this procedure; a procedure which is better adapted to produce yeast of uniform type and consequently of uniform activity, than is the constant employment of high heats.

High fermenting temperatures have a tendency to cause irregular development of yeast-cells, some of which under their influence (though of course we are speaking of extremely minute microscopic objects) are of abnormal size—a tendency which is further to be noticed when yeast from strong worts is microscopically examined.

Skimming is generally effected either through **Parachutes** or Griffin & Pearce's **Sluices**. The former consists of a metal vessel (the parachute) shaped like an inverted shallow cone, with the apex removed, where it fits accurately into a tube that passes down through the bottom of the fermenting-tun. This inverted cone, though in the centre of the tun, is capable of being moved up and down from the outside so as to be on a level with the surface of the wort; it also has a valve at the bottom, likewise capable of being opened from the outside, which being done, the yeast immediately flows, with more or less rapidity, down the copper tube aforesaid to a stage below. In the largest tuns this parachute is replaced by a sort of trough-shaped vessel, which extends from the centre of the fermenting tun to its edge, and into which the yeast is pushed by skimming-arms made to revolve at will; the trough, like the parachute, is generally connected with a down-tube through which the yeast passes. Such an arrangement is of course only possible with "rounds." "Squares" may have a similar trough-shaped arrangement at one end, into which a skimming board, depending from a rod stretching right across the square and travelling on wheels, pushes the yeast, or small squares may be hand-skimmed.

Sluices are fixed in an opening cut in the side of the fermenting-vessel, and consist of a movable flat plate of metal (with a projecting lip on the upper edge over which the yeast works), which is raised or lowered by a rack and pinion movement actuated by large wheels on either side. At the lower edge of the frame in which the flat plate works is a strip of hard wood (teak), backed by a slice of india-rubber bedded in the frame; this, if the face of the plate has been planed perfectly true, so that no leakage of wort ensues, will last for years. As the sluices are sent out their cogs are undoubtedly too weak. The yeast, as it comes off, is collected in slate "backs" or squares, resting on girders level with those which support the fermenting tuns themselves; and this, if there be ample space in the fermenting-room for the slate "backs," is a convenient arrangement, enabling the brewer, as it does, to keep his stores of yeast under easy observation.

The first skimming, contaminated by coagulated albumen and hop-resin, which have come out of solution, as the maltose, which retained the latter in that condition, has been gradually decomposed into alcohol and carbon dioxide, etc., should always be rejected from the "pitching" or "store" yeast. So should the last head, consisting largely of aged cells of inferior vigour, **the middle skimmings alone being preserved for subsequent pitching purposes.** Skimming is continued—and both with parachutes and sluices manual or mechanical skimming is necessary—until it is judged that the languishing fermentation has just strength enough to throw up one more thin head, of just sufficient thickness to shield it from the germ-laden atmosphere. The decision is arrived at by removing a few square inches of the head and inspecting the colour

ADVANTAGES OF SKIMMING SYSTEM.

of the fluid beneath. If this appears somewhat black the beer has "finished," and the head will be untouched; if, on the other hand, it looks brownish, the head, or a portion of it, will be skimmed off. When there is any doubt, it is better to leave rather too thick a head than to run the risk of skimming too "closely."

Another advantage of the skimming system is the ease with which the beers can be cooled down by means of the attemperator when the fermentation is slackening. They should undoubtedly be racked at a temperature not exceeding 60° Fahr. in summer, and at one more nearly approaching the normal temperature in winter. For cooling down makes the beer, when racked into casks, much less liable to "fret" or "kick-up"—a defect manifested by the ejection from the bung-holes of a dirty yeasty froth, and a more or less stubborn turbidity of the fluid. It also minimises the risk of "yeast-bite," that very unpleasant after-bitter taste, already referred to, which is often unfairly attributed to the hops, experience seeming to show that the evil is greatly caused by the action of the alcoholic fluid at high temperatures upon the dead or inactive yeast-cells of the protecting head or those still distributed through the beer. Generally speaking, a very good time for beginning this cooling down would be some twenty-four hours after the first skim, precautions being taken in very cold weather. It is more difficult to approve of the practice which some brewers adopt of keeping attemperators running right up to and during the first twenty-four hours of skimming. In beers so treated there seems a tendency, slight though it may be, to yeastiness of flavour.

Dropping Squares or Rounds.—When these (which consist of a second series of fermenting vessels, similar in shape to those in which the fermentation is started but placed on a lower floor than they are) are adopted, the point of attenuation at which the wort is discharged from the upper into the lower series is that, or perchance a trifle higher than that, at which skimming would ordinarily begin; and if there are more tuns than one of the same class of beer to be emptied into a similar number of subsidiary or "dropping" vessels, the wort may be so run down as to blend in its passage. The contaminated first head will be left behind in the upper series of tuns; and though in cold weather there is a liability to a check of temperature, this will be amply compensated by the stimulus which the yeast receives from aëration and rousing.

Cleansing System.—This is the system largely adopted at Burton-on-Trent and elsewhere; and the essence of it is that the fermentation, though beginning in open fermenting vessels as in the skimming system, is finished either in (i) carriage casks, (ii) Burton unions, or (iii) "loose pieces," with or without movable "swan-neck" pipes. Of these, the last two systems are now most in favour. Cleansing in the "carriage casks" (*i.e.*, the casks which "go out into the trade"), though most economical from the avoidance of the waste inseparable from every fresh racking, involves much more labour in "topping up," and there is besides to be reckoned with the almost inevitable necessity of getting the bottom or sedimentary yeast out of each cask by means of a syphon or otherwise.

Apart from these drawbacks and the absolute impossibility of cooling down by attemperating liquor before sending out, the system of cleansing in carriage casks is not without its merits, especially for running beers, in which roundness and palate-fulness are *desiderata*. The *modus operandi* is as follows. The casks, placed in long rows upon stillions (which are long and deep wooden troughs with a slight fall towards one end, where a draw-off plug is fixed in the side and close to the bottom), and with their bungholes slightly inclined to one side, are filled with the fermenting wort by means of a hose. When all the casks are filled as nearly as they can be in this way, the two or three barrels (more margin must be allowed if the quantity altogether is large) remaining in the fermenting vessel will be run into the stillion, and the casks "topped up" by hand with a can, filled at the draw-off plug. This tedious method of filling will have to be improved upon if the size of the gyle (brewing) is considerable: for instance, a long, light, but deep trough, or pipe with nozzles corresponding to the bungholes of the casks, and on which short lengths of smaller hose can be fitted, will greatly facilitate the filling of these casks. In any case, neither trough nor pipe, if pipe it is, must be a fixture. Either should be taken away directly the filling is done, and the pipe should have a plentiful supply of steam driven through it and all the nozzles. Plenty of water, cold first and afterwards boiling, is the best cleanser for the trough.

Yeast will soon begin to work out at the bungholes; and it is a noticeable fact that beer, the head of which has been light or its fermentation even "fiery" (which has been already explained to be a more than usually rapid evolution of carbonic acid gas, filled with which large bubbles form and break at the surface without formation of any yeast), will begin to throw out a comparatively solid yeast soon after cleansing, doubtless owing to the aëration it has received, the rousing, and the increased pressure under which it is working.

It will be necessary to keep the casks topped up regularly—every two hours is none too often during the first twenty-four hours after cleansing—using at first for this purpose the "stillion beer," *i.e.*, any surplus let into the stillion from the fermenting vessel after the casks were filled, augmented by the beer which separates from the yeast soon after it has worked out from the inclined bungholes of the casks. After this, it is preferable to begin topping up with bright clean beer from a previous brewing; and accordingly the surplus from the fermenting vessel must be so regulated that there is practically none left when the topping up with clean beer begins.

Indeed, it is well from the beginning to take more precautions than are always adopted for securing a reasonably clean feed. The yeasty fluid, just as it works off, is obviously unfit to be reintroduced at once into the casks, and may with advantage be drawn off into an additional cask, or into a feeding tank to get the yeast deposited before use. The sooner absolutely clean beer is used the sooner will the fermentation finish, and the more satisfactory will its finish be. As the fermentation languishes the "toppings up" will be less frequent, and when the main crop of yeast has been ejected it is usual to roll the casks into other stores both to make room for other brewings and to assist them to finish, the sedimentary yeast being finally syphoned out. This, of course, necessitates large long stores for rolling, and it is a good plan to have parallel lines of rails for the casks to travel on. In lieu of syphoning, good results are sometimes got by **working out with finings;** finings are added, the casks bunged and then sedulously rolled, after which the bungs are removed, and the yeasty matter, stimulated by the rolling, works out with the finings.

Cleansing in "Loose Pieces," or movable casks, holding generally a little short of three barrels apiece, is conducted on much the same lines as that in carriage casks, except that they are not moved until the beer is racked out of them. And being always, when emptied, rolled out into the yard, they are capable of being thoroughly cleaned without the introduction of steam into the neighbourhood of fermenting beers, where it is objectionable. In this respect they have the advantage over Burton unions, and when fitted with swan-neck delivery pipes with feed-pipe combined, which do away with topping up by hand (often neglected at night), they are quite equal to them in other respects; indeed, I think, superior in this, that the swan-necks and feed-trough can be removed and cleaned directly the active ejection of yeast is over, the rest of the topping up, a very trivial matter, being done by hand. Those who are aware how contaminated soft wood (of which material the feed troughs are made) becomes when in contact with putrescible and yeasty fluids, especially in the summer time, will see how important it is to avoid the risk of passing the later feeds through such a trough which has been in use all the time. Moreover, by moving them at a comparatively early stage, the same trough and swan-necks can be used twice or thrice as often as they could be otherwise.

These loose-piece swan-necks are often so arranged that the same trough serves both as yeast receiver and feed trough; but it is much better to have them quite distinct, the only necessary precaution being to have the bottom of the feed-trough some inches above the bungholes, so that the beer level may be well up the swan-neck pipe. The feed-trough (or tank) may be on the same side as, but at a lower level than, the yeast-receiving trough, or upon opposite sides, as in the sketch. The swan-neck pipe, A, has a tapering flange, F, which fits closely into the bunghole of the "Piece." The swan-neck is not fitted centrally in the 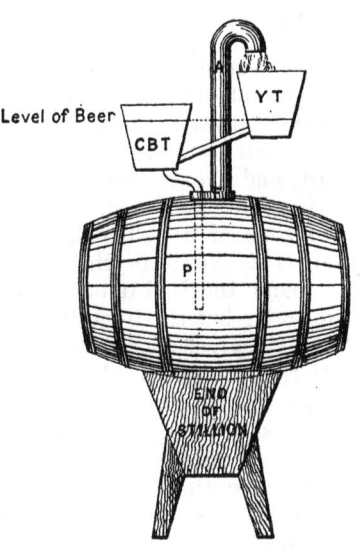 flange, which it just penetrates, and through the wider part a small tube, P, passes, extending a foot or more below the flange and an inch or two above it—just enough, indeed, for a flexible rubber tube to be slipped over the projection and to connect it with the feed-trough or tank, C B T. There may or may not be a cock between C B T and P, but there should certainly be one between the feed tank C B T and the yeast trough Y T.

The trough Y T, of necessity, and C B T, if a trough (but

if a tank a long pipe from it), will run the whole length of the row of pieces, though for the sake of clearness only an end view, and that of one piece alone, is shown. Parts, however, which would be visible if the sketch were a sectional one are represented by dotted lines.

When the gyle (= the whole brewing) is cleansed, the racking hose is put into the Y T, whence it flows into C B T, which, as has been said, is connected with *all* the "pieces." The outlet cock from the fermenting vessel on the floor above is then turned on, and the wort flows simultaneously into all the "pieces." Yeast will soon begin to pour out of the swan-necks into the yeast-trough, and beer (wort) will separate from it. The "drawings" (separated beer) can be run straight into the feed tank, or, what is even better, into a small settling tank, to precipitate the floating yeast, and thence into the feed tank. The latter, if the settling tank command it, can be kept at a constant level by means of a ball-cock arrangement. If the settling tank (not shown in the sketch) cannot be arranged to command the feed-tank, then it would mean additional can-work; but the importance of even a relatively bright "feed" is great enough to be worth this.

If the plan, referred to above, of removing the yeast-trough, feed-trough, and swan-necks when the fermentation has slackened (say two days after cleansing) be adopted, the pieces must stand upon a shallow stillion, or one of ordinary depth, which will receive any yeast which is afterwards thrown out. A strong wind beginning to blow will often cause the pieces, even at a later stage, and when they have virtually finished working, to throw out more yeast.

When swan-necks are not used, or have been removed as suggested, a small protecting cap of yeasty matter will be left covering each bunghole.

Burton Unions.—With Burton unions the principle is the same, but there is a difference in detail. The swan-necks screw into metal bushes fixed in the bungholes, or what correspond to the bungholes; the casks are larger, as a rule, generally holding four barrels, and are enclosed in a wooden frame and supported by trunnions (see Glossary), which rest on bearings fixed on the said frame. The front trunnion has a square head, upon which a handle fits for the purpose of making the casks revolve when they are washed, which is always done *in situ*. The feed-pipes (of 2-inch bore) of Burton unions, instead of passing through the bungholes, as is the case with the " loose-piece " swan-necks, are connected by screw unions, which are permanently fitted in the heads of the casks slightly above the centre.

Burton unions are sometimes fitted with attemperators, which, if fixed, obviously increase the difficulty, already large, of washing them satisfactorily. Of course such attemperators are extremely useful for cooling down the beer when the fermentation has begun to subside, just as they are in the skimming system, but otherwise they are hardly ever necessary. If the temperature be moderate in the larger fermenting vessel at the time of cleansing, the temperature in the unions can hardly ever rise unduly, taking into consideration the fact that the subdivision of the gyle into the smaller vessels, which are probably cooler than itself, generally induces a reduction of temperature.

Cleansed beers, especially Burton-union beers, are often not racked direct from the cleansing casks or unions, but are run into " settling backs " or " racking backs," which are now usually made of large slabs of slate. The uniformity of quality and of attenuation gained thereby are certainly beneficial, but the flattening and risk of contamination by exposure to a germ-laden atmosphere should, in my opinion, be minimised by using the tanks as " racking backs " only, the beer being got out as quickly as possible. But if the tank be used as a " settling-back—*i.e.*, as a vessel in which the beer is left for several hours in order that a certain amount of sedimentary matter may be deposited—a floating cover will intercept many of the contaminating organisms; yet, unless its cleanliness be very thoroughly assured, may cause as much harm as it prevents.

Skimmed beers are often racked on the sixth day from the date of mashing, even when the fermentation is of so slow a type that they have only " come upon the skim " on the third day, but will certainly rack the brighter for a somewhat longer stay in the round; and all bitter ales and strong ales, especially in cold weather, should have at least another day.

Antiseptics (bisulphite of lime, salicylic acid, etc.), if they are used, *may* be added in the racking-back and thoroughly well roused with its contents—though it is far better to add them, albeit more troublesome, in the casks just before they are ready for shiving up. The use of such preservatives should be unnecessary for well-brewed running beers, but they are unquestionably useful, and largely used for those of a stock character.

Yorkshire Stone-square System.—This system, however interesting in itself, need not detain us long. It is one which is hardly likely to be adopted save in response to local demands, and then only after investigations on the spot. The necessary number and costliness of the vessels are against it. Besides the number of the squares other facts tell against that thorough cleanliness so essential for all brewery vessels—viz., the liability of the stone slabs, of which the squares are constructed, to crack under the influence of boiling water (owing to uneven conductivity), and the readiness with which limestone, of which the slabs consist, is attacked by the sulphurous acid of bisulphite of lime; so that practically strong solutions of the caustic alkalies are the only purifiers available.

These are freely spread by mopping with *cotton* mops and left on for a considerable time—say two hours—so that a double inspection is really necessary before the brewer can feel sure of a thorough cleansing having been carried out. If this be consistently neglected a scale will form, behind which putrefying organisms will swarm and contaminate the wort. For such a dangerous scale chloride

STONE-SQUARE SYSTEM.

of lime solution, kept in contact for several days, is recommended as the best solvent; but it is an unsatisfactory material to use where it cannot, from the nature of things, be followed by bisulphite.

The arrangement and method are as follows. The principal squares (which are never large, and are surrounded by another vessel containing water at moderately low temperature) are surmounted by much shallower squares, also of stone, and of the same diameter as that of the lower squares. The large slab which forms the bottom of each upper square also closes in the lower square, and has two apertures, one a "manhole," about eighteen inches in diameter in its centre, the other much smaller, midway between this manhole and the side, and fitted with a pipe which runs downward towards the bottom of the lower square. There is also a valve, which is closed at intervals, so that the feed (the upper square fulfils the part of the feed tank of the Burton-unions) can be made intermittent.

The worts are "pitched" in these vessels (though nowadays one large gathering square for a whole brewing would save an infinity of trouble in the matter of excise declarations), the yeast being usually mixed with wort in the upper square, and then allowed to run into the lower, which has been filled or nearly filled. Periodical rousing, by means of a pump, the number of strokes given increasing with each repetition, is the corner-stone of the system. It begins between twenty and thirty hours after pitching with the pump-rousing of the contents of the upper square, which has had some inches of wort left in it, now, however, allowed, by opening the valve, to flow into the lower square.

Subsequent pumpings are from the lower square into the upper, whence the wort flows back into the lower again through the open valve; these pumpings being continued at intervals till the degree of attenuation is reached at which yeast begins to form. The yeast works out of the manhole into the upper square, and the beer or wort which separates from it flows back into the lower square through the valve. The latter is left open till the fermentation has nearly reached its term, when it is closed for good, any excessive formation of yeast being afterwards skimmed from the manhole. Owing to the enormous degree of aëration and the mechanical rousing which the fermenting worts undergo, the range of temperature can be very much restricted; it rarely exceeds 6° as compared with the normal 9°, 10°, or even 12° of ordinary systems. This limitation of temperature has its advantage in the way of securing solid yeast without a tendency to liquefy in summer time; the separation of yeast from the beer being, moreover, as a rule, facilitated by aëration.

Cleansing in Pontos.—This development of the primitive cleansing idea need not be referred to at length. It is dropping into disuse in London itself, and even for stout and porter, for which it is best suited, so that it is hardly likely to be taken up as a new departure. Wooden vessels (squares or rounds) of small size, with a manhole in the top, out of which yeast flows into the yeast-trough, which has a plug-hole allowing the separating beer to flow, when required, into a settling-trough below, form one feature of the system. Then follows the pumping of this separated beer, when it has deposited its yeast, up to a feed tank or feed tun well above the whole set of pontos, and commanding a small feed cistern (the flow of beer into the latter from the large feed tun being regulated by a ball-cock). The feed-cistern is placed at just the right level to keep the pontos full. There is usually a yeast-trough to every pair of pontos. Such, in brief, are the main features of this arrangement.

Under, or Bottom Fermentation, and Sedimentary, or Low Yeast.—The system of under fermentation (*i.e.*, in which the yeast sinks to the bottom of the gyle-tun instead of rising to the surface) at very low temperatures is the sequel to the decoction system of mashing referred to on an earlier page, and is, perhaps, chiefly of importance to English readers from the fact that the voluminous researches of Continental inquirers, which are so frequently translated for our benefit, have been made mainly, if not entirely, with reference to this method and the type of yeast belonging to it. There is also the further consideration for large exporters that decoction beers, fermented on this plan, are, according to consular reports, gaining ground in many tropical markets, for which their low alcoholic percentage and light character unquestionably fit them, although, as has been pointed out, special "Pasteurisation"—or maintenance for a period at a temperature of 140° Fahr., which for some reason or other has not answered with bottled "infusion-beers"—is required to make the article stable enough for long storage, even in ordinary climates.

The fermentation is carried on in fermenting vessels of small size and in underground cellars, where a very low temperature (say of 38° or 39° Fahr.) is maintained; in fact, the fermentation is started as low as 41° Fahr., and rarely, in the case of lager (or stock beer), reaches 50° Fahr.; 46° or 47° Fahr. would be the more usual finishing temperature. The heat is kept down, not only by the low temperature of the cellar itself, but by vessels of fluted metal (shaped something like a bushel measure, but with a large sloping rim and two handles rising above it), which are filled with ice, and float on the surface of the liquid.

It is a matter of general remark in brewing Lager beer, that the slower the fermentation the better is its flavour and quality. Eleven or twelve days from the time of pitching, the beer is run into store-casks (small vats) in the store-cellar, where it remains a considerable time, often six months. When ripe for use it is drawn off into carriage-casks, the interior of each of the latter receiving a preliminary coating with melted resin, the so-called *Pech* which tends to give lager beer the characteristic flavour which many find somewhat objectionable at first. The superfluity of resin is flared off over a flame, so that the insides of the casks are black.

Racking, Fining, Storing.—Returning to infusion-beers, the temperature at which the beers are let down for racking into casks should not in summer exceed 60°, and in winter should bear a closer relation to the mean temperature of the season. The contents of casks, when the racking temperature has been high, contract under the influence of cold, so that some flattening ensues; moreover, the tendency to "kick-up" is (as has been said) greater in beers that have not been cooled, owing to the presence of certain albumenoid bodies, which the higher temperature keeps in solution, and which consequently go out of solution in the cask itself, instead of being left behind in the fermenting or racking vessels, combined with the action of floating yeast, which remains suspended in greater quantity in the warmer fluid, and is stimulated by the inevitable aëration at racking.

Casks filled with running beer for trade near home are bunged; but it is advisable to "shive" those that have to go by rail, and all stock or delicate ales. The bungholes should be in the bouge (bulge) of the cask only. Some publicans prefer, as taking less room in their cellars, to have the casks up-ended. The bunghole is then in the head, but the beer working out, as it will, upon the addition of finings in summer time, is retained on the top of the cask, flowing back into it through the open bunghole when the first drawing occurs, by which time, covered as it often will be by a free growth of mildew, it can hardly be a desirable addition to the sound contents.

Finings are added either before the beer is dispatched, or by the drayman, or by the customer himself in his own cellar. The latter is, generally speaking, the better course for the beer, if intelligently done; the former the more profitable for the brewer, saving on every cask the quantity of beer displaced by the finings. A common fault is to add too large a quantity. A quart, irrespective of strength, I fear, is the usual amount, and should be the maximum.

"Finings," as used by brewers, depend upon the mechanical action which dissolved isinglass exerts upon

FININGS. ISINGLASS.

the suspended particles, more or less affecting the brightness of the racking sample.

Isinglass, of which the best qualities are simply the swimming-bladder of the sturgeon properly cleaned, is imported from Brazil, Russia, and elsewhere. **Penang** is a good variety. "Leaf 'glass"—as it is called for shortness—is a thin transparent variety, while "Pipe 'glass" has about the shape of a rather small sole, but is two or three times as thick. A fair amount of transparency should be looked for even here.

The isinglass is always dissolved by acids—tartaric, sulphurous, or, more rarely, acetic, as such. In former years, when time was of no special importance, *sour* beer was invariably used, and even now forms an effective, perhaps the most effective, finings for running ales. A good deal of outcry has been made as to the risk of introducing disease ferments (lactic and butyric acid bacteria, etc.), of which a copious supply is assumed to exist in the sour beer; but when it is remembered that the sour beer employed is, or ought to be, brilliant,—and this is coupled with the fact that disease ferments are found in the deposit from such beers, but rarely in the bright beer itself (*cf.* M. Pasteur's experience related in *Études sur la Bière,* French edit., pp. 24, 25),—this outcry will, I think, appear exaggerated.

The first-mentioned acids—tartaric and sulphurous— have each of them their defects as "cutting" agents. The former, though yielding an effective finings, encourages the development of mildew; the latter, though protective against mildew, produces a much less efficient finings. Isinglass "cut" with tartaric acid, to which a proportion of sulphurous acid is afterwards added, yields finings the power of which is not much lessened, while its resistance to mildew is sufficient for all practical purposes. Roche alum is sometimes added in the place of sulphurous acid.

Whatever the agent used, and particularly when it is sour beer, a series of tubs—hogsheads with their heads out—will be wanted. Sieves of varying mesh will also be required to rub the swollen isinglass through, the coarsest naturally being used in the passage from the first tub, or hogshead, to the second, and the finer ones in succession. The rubbing through sieves aërates the finings, and may perhaps be a factor in their action. The process should not be hurried, extending from a month or thereabouts with mineral acids, to six weeks or more when sour beer is the "cutting" agent. In any case, the finings should be distinctly acid; neutral finings, advertised as containing no acids, are not to be recommended. The following are recipes:—

Sulphuric and Tartaric-Acid Finings.—To 7 lb. good isinglass, covered with water, add 1 lb. tartaric acid, dissolved in warm water, and 1 gallon to $1\frac{1}{2}$ gallon of sulphurous acid. Add fresh water as the isinglass swells. Rub through coarse and fine sieves, with intervals between each rubbing. Make up to 72 gallons.

Acetic-Acid Finings.—To 1 gallon acetic acid add 8 gallons of water; mix well, and add 8 lb. isinglass. Fresh water to be added every morning, and the whole to be well "rummaged" until of the consistency of cream. N.B.—1 lb. isinglass makes 10 gallons of finings.

Both of these finings will mix better if diluted with beer; and if two or three parts of the latter be added to one part of either of the above preparations, a quart of the diluted finings ought to suffice for a barrel of any beer. Mr. J. Long, of 43, Eastcheap, manufactures a simple "viscometer" for checking the density of finings.

Stock Beers—Storage.—Pale and other bitter and stock ales are generally "hopped down" or "dry-hopped" with 1 lb., more or less, per barrel, of hops, which ought to be of really choice quality. It is sufficient just to break them apart; in fact, the less they are rubbed the better, both because of the risk thereon depending of producing "fliers,"—*i.e.*, small fragments of hop which draw up with the ale,—and of the danger of introducing more than the normal supply of disease ferments.

The casks of pale ale and other store beers generally

have, from exigencies of space, to be "ridden"—*i.e.*, piled some three tiers high. The plan has this disadvantage, that the porous spiles usually inserted cannot readily be removed and replaced by tight spiles—as should be done—directly their function is duly discharged; this function simply being to let off any great excess of carbonic acid gas, which may sometimes be generated in quantities powerful enough to bulge or even to force out the heads of casks. But anything resembling flattening of the beers should be avoided, the presence of the gas, even to the extent of excessive briskness, being preferable to the reverse.

The Burton brewers, as is well known, stack their ales in the open yard; but this plan is only adopted from exigencies of space, an equable temperature of 55° or 56° Fahr. giving probably the most satisfactory results with store beers. It goes without saying that their temperature at the time of racking should not exceed and may well be lower than the mean storage temperature; and there are good grounds for supposing that the maintenance of the latter at a fairly uniform point, such as the one indicated, is one of the requisite conditions for confirming the satisfactory flavour of the beer.

Our knowledge of the "**secondary**" or, as it seems preferable to call it, the "**complementary**" fermentation, which takes place after the beers are racked into cask, is as yet inexact; but we are free to suppose that a rise of temperature in the store stimulates the less desirable types of **secondary yeast** into activity, to the prejudice of the preferable types. That there is plenty of range between unsuitable and desirable types may be imagined from the fact that no less than *sixty varieties* of yeast alone have been identified in certain top-fermentation commercial yeasts; and this takes no account of other organisms, the bacteria producing lactic and butyric acids (Pasteur's *ferments de maladie*), which certainly have their influence, so detrimental to the stability of beers, enhanced by an elevated temperature.

And here I may perhaps anticipate what I shall have to say under the head of Fermentation, so far as to remark that whereas there used to be an excessive tendency, when M. Pasteur's epoch-making researches first came before the public, to attribute to the malign influence of bacteria all the ills that beer, and especially bad beer, is heir to, so there is now eagerness to attribute them almost entirely to the so-called **wild-yeasts** first differentiated by the distinguished Danish *savant* **Hansen**. This differentiation was effected by continued observation of the ways in which various types, carefully isolated, strive to provide for the continuance of their species, when existing in a condition utterly unsuitable for their development in the ordinary way—*e.g.*, by budding as yeast does. This "second string to their bow," as it were, which yeasts, and some bacteria, have as a protection against extermination, consists in the power to sporulate, *i.e.*, form spores, which may be looked upon as analogous to seeds, and which are capable of re-developing into ordinary cells when suitable nutritive conditions recur. In the case of yeast these spores are associated together in a cell, known as an *ascus*, within the yeast-cell itself, and are therefore known as **ascospores**. The production of ascospores, implying, as it does, an absence of nutrition, is accordingly a starvation phenomenon.

By observing the number of days in which ascospores were produced by yeast-colonies **grown from single cells,** and cultivated under artificial conditions (viz., on blocks of sterilised plaster-of-Paris, standing in shallow saucers of water and covered with a bell-glass), and at varying temperatures practically ranging between 37° and 95° Fahr., and, moreover, by noting the periods at which **films,** or **pellicles,** are formed by such colonies on the surface of fermentable fluids within the same range of temperature, Housen has been able to separate yeast into a number of varieties, one of which (**Saccharomyces Cerevisiæ I.**) is the alcoholic yeast pure and simple, while the influence of some of the other varieties is markedly unfavourable, either in the direction of producing a bitter flavour (yeast-bite) or turbidity. Hence the idea of cultivating a "store" of pitching yeast from a single cell (of course of S. Cerevisiæ I.), which has been practically carried out by Hansen at the **Carlsberg Brewery in Copenhagen,** and adopted in many "under-fermentation" breweries.

For the English top-fermentation system it is alleged to be unsuitable, on account of the difficulty of inducing the essential complementary cask fermentation; but it is noteworthy, as stated by Hansen, that the same objection was raised in the first instance by M. Jacobsen, the public-spirited owner of Carlsberg, and again, that this system of fermenting with yeast cultivated from a single cell is now in full swing in the top-fermentation breweries of the north of France, respecting which I shall have more to say later on. But the grounds on which its unsuitability is maintained may be briefly stated as follows.

Substances known as **Malto-Dextrins** or **Amylöins,** and alleged to be the final mash-tun products of the hydrolysis of the higher dextrins (*i.e.,* of the changes during which they absorb the elements of water), have been isolated from malt-wort. Further, the said malto-dextrins are apparently unfermentable by absolutely pure yeast (**Saccharomyces Cerevisiæ I.**), but are fermentable by other types, notably by one (**Saccharomyces Pastorianus II.**), and possibly by **Saccharomyces Ellipsoideus I.**, or at least the presence of one of these forms seems necessary to degrade the malto-dextrins into maltose, with which alone the pure primary yeast, S. Cerevisiæ, is able to deal.

The elongated cells of S. Pastorianus may be observed in the deposit of really sound bottled ale, but two of its sub-varieties are credited with distinctly noxious influences (yeast-bite and turbidity respectively), and, similarly, a sub-variety of S. Ellipsoideus seems also to be a factor in persistent turbidity. Therefore, however desirable, nay necessary, the fermentation of the malto-dextrins in cask may be, the haphazard employment of all sorts of yeasts, some of which have a beneficial influence, but others distinctly the opposite, seems but a clumsy way to attain it. Surely it will not be beyond the resources of scientific practice to start the primary fermentation with that type of pure yeast which is most capable of splitting up the maltose into alcohol and carbolic acid, and to introduce at the time of racking, or previously, a sufficient proportion of an equally pure culture of those secondary yeasts upon which the needful cask, or complementary fermentation, seems to depend.

Complementary fermentation is stimulated by rolling about the casks into which the ale has been racked, once a day at least, for several days; and this rolling is of great utility when the beer is required to "come round" quickly for bottling purposes. Indeed, a beer that has not acquired cask condition, is not really fit for bottling, the true criterion of fitness (ripeness) being spontaneous clarification, the ale falling, as is said, "star-bright." However brilliant artificially fined beers may be, that condition is only temporary; a fact which is extremely evident in the case of beer fined in the cask into which it was racked, and, for some special purpose, re-racked bright.

The brilliancy noticed at the moment of re-racking speedily gives place to a perceptible haze, doubtless due to the fact that certain previously dissolved albuminoid constituents are thrown out of solution by the oxidation which has taken place, and which the beer, deprived by the racking, fining, and re-racking of a portion of the carbonic acid gas, its natural protector, was unable to resist. A similar result will supervene in bottle when the brightening has been unduly hurried. Either a copious precipitate will be formed, or the ale, freely oxygenated, will leave much to be desired in respect of brilliancy.

Priming, etc.—It is the custom of many brewers to prime their running ales and black beers, especially the latter—that is, to add a solution of some sort of sugar to the finished beers with the object of imparting body or briskness, or both. Excise regulations will only permit a solution having a specific gravity not exceeding 1·150 (water = 1·000), which can be made by diluting a portion of standard syrup, weighing 14 lb. per gallon, with *twice its volume* of water. It is desirable, however, not to get the specific gravity below 1·150°—or, as it is called for brevity, 150°, dropping the 1·000°—which is in itself too low already for the most effective results to be attained. The sugar used may be glucose, if briskness rather than added sweetness is desired; but if it be wished to make the beer more luscious on the palate, then "Invert-sugar" is the material to employ (the levulose, which forms some 50% of it, being less susceptible than its remaining glucose to speedy fermentative changes).

Treating with Malt Extract is sometimes advocated as a panacea. The filtered extract got by steeping half a pound of ground malt for several hours in a quart of cold water is observed to have a distinct influence when daded to 100 barrels of beer in the direction of breaking down the malto-dextrins into maltose; for though malto-dextrins have been stated to be the ultimate *mash-tun* product of the higher dextrins, they, as well as dextrin itself, are capable of further degradation by malt extract made and acting in the cold. However, seeing that the brewer aims at retaining a more or less considerable amount of extract (body) and slowly fermenting matter in his product, it is only when, either through faulty manipulation or the employment of very inferior malt, the dextrin ratio in his wort prior to the primary fermentation was too high—or, as perhaps we ought, in the light of recent discoveries, to say when the proportion of malto-dextrins (and those, too, of what are known as the higher conversions) was in excess, that the addition of cold-water extract of malt can be of any service.

Vatted Beers.—Though vatting, as a practice, is on the decrease in many districts and unknown in some, there is still so much demand for old vatted beers in the West of England that I cannot altogether pass them over.

But there are vatted beers *and* vatted beers. The desire for a more rapid turnover of capital, and the concentration of business in the hands of large firms, has tended to modify the character of vatted beers, which instead of being, as of yore, of very high gravity and supplied to customers unblended, " one way " as it is locally called, are now valued chiefly for the character of age which they impart to the running beers with which they are blended. And as they are blended in proportions often not exceeding 25% of old to 75% of new, it is obvious that the old ethereal vatted character is a secondary consideration; the first requisite being that the vats should come into rapid blending condition, which implies a high degree of acidity, short of sourness however, coupled with absolute brilliancy,—results which are generally secured by fermenting beers of no remarkably high gravity at high temperatures, and supplementing this with rousing and aëration.

But real vatted beers, on the other hand,—*i.e.*, beers brewed to keep in vat—should never show an excess of acidity beyond what the gravity can easily carry. If of high gravity—and high gravity is a *sine quâ non*—they become mellow and vinous, and far more exhilarating with age, in spite of the fact that their alcoholic percentage may actually diminish, or, at any rate, not increase after the stage of vat maturity is reached. This stimulating quality has been attributed to the formation of certain aromatic ethers, amongst which that of ethyl acetate,—formed by the action of acetic acid upon ethyl alcohol (the ordinary alcohol of fermented beverages) and of ethyl butyrate (which in its pure state is used to flavour " pineapple " rum)—may be mentioned as theoretically possible. Acetic acid, the product of the oxidation of alcohol, is always an increasing quantity in old vatted beers, so that the above-stated view respecting the formation of compound ethers is not necessarily shaken by recent scientific evidence respecting whisky, in the case of which similar changes were apparently incorrectly thought to take place.* Nor should the possibility of the action of this acid, or of its aldehyde, upon any unfermented residue of maltose, resulting in the formation of ethereal compounds, be altogether overlooked. However this may be, it is certain that by age strong, well-brewed vatted ales and stouts acquire a flavour attainable in no other way; and accordingly a chance may occur for cultivating a trade in this description of ale, or, what is more likely, that it may be wished to keep vats of strong old stout for blending with running black beers.

Stout Vatting—Keeping up Vats.—If the ordinary English system be followed, vatting is perhaps the only way of getting that amalgamation of flavours which characterises a perfect stout, that slight sub-acidity combined with palate fulness and that close and creamy head, or, in the case of English stouts, rather that close *brown* head so admired by connoisseurs. Accordingly a blend of a vatted stout, having a gravity of 30 lb. or higher (the higher the better), with a sweet running porter of say 18 or 19 lb. gravity, will certainly give far better results than a single stout brewed at 24 to 25 lb. gravity, and sent out unblended. A few words, then, as to the best method of keeping up the uniform standard of the vatted product.

The best plan for that purpose seems to be that two, three, or more vats, according to the trade, of similar quality should be on hand; that when one of the vats is fit for use, a portion of its contents, not exceeding one-fifth, should be drawn off and used, after which the ullage should be made up as rapidly as is convenient with new beer of the same quality; then the second vat should be drawn upon to the same extent, and filled up likewise;

* Dr. Bell, examined before a Parliamentary Committee, stated, in answer to Sir H. Roscoe, that compound ethers and higher alcohols were not increased in whisky by age; that a slight change took place in the acids, but that the increase in value which takes place in "pot-still" (and to a much less extent in patent-still whisky) is due to the disappearance of empyreumatic oils, perhaps as a result of oxidation; though as to the method he could give no opinion.

after which comes on the turn of the third vat, or if the trade be small, of the first vat again, and so on. Ultimately, of course, the vats ought to be drawn off completely and thoroughly cleaned; but if "ullages" be carefully avoided, they can be many times refilled.

I have now, I think, gone through—cursorily, of course, in most instances—all the usual operations in the malthouse and the brewery; and though I may have possibly turned aside occasionally to give explanations or illustrations a little apart from actual practice, albeit intimately connected therewith, the section in the main deals with manipulative details, and thus clears the way for the consideration of more advanced problems or more exhaustive treatment in later chapters.

CHAPTER II.

BARLEY, MALTING, AND MALT.[*]

BARLEY THE PREFERABLE GRAIN—SIX-ROWED, FOUR-ROWED, AND
TWO-ROWED BARLEY—" ESCOURGEON " AND CHEVALIER BARLEY
—ANATOMY OF THE BARLEY-CORN—CHOICE OF BARLEY—OVER-
RIPE GRAINS—TESTS FOR GERMINATIVE POWER—SITUATION OF
MALT-HOUSE—ITS CONSTRUCTION—PREVENTION OF MOULD—
IDLE CORNS—KILNS AND KILN-DRYING—LAST'S PATENT VENTI-
LATORS—CONSTRUCTION OF KILNS—FURNACE AND BAFFLE-
PLATE—MR. FREE ON MALTING—KING'S AUTOMATIC REGULATOR
—DOUBLE KILNS (STOPES')—CHEMICAL RESULTS OF MALTSTER'S
OPERATIONS—SECRETION OF DIASTASE AND OF A CELLULOSE-
DISSOLVING ENZYME—PEPTASE—MESSRS. BROWN AND MORRIS'S
CONCLUSIONS — MR. J. O'SULLIVAN'S VIEWS — ASPARAGIN —
BACTERIAL THEORY OF DIASTASE—DATA FOR JUDGING GOOD
MALT—PNEUMATIC MALTING—ECONOMICS OF MALTING.

BARLEY, owing to the quantity of starch it contains, the activity of the diastase (the agent which converts starch into maltose) in the malted grain, with the facts that its germ is protected when growing by a stout husk, and that the same husk in the mash-tun facilitates the drainage of the worts, is by far the most important grain for the purposes of the maltster and the brewer. It belongs botanically to the family or natural order of the *Gramineæ*. The generic name is *Hordeum*.

In some varieties groups of three flower-bearing spike-lets are found alternately on either side of the central spikelet, each of which are fertile. When this is the case the **six-rowed barley** (*Hordeum hexasticum*) is

[*] I am indebted to the courtesy of Messrs. A. Boake, Roberts, & Co., for permission to reproduce here any portion of my article on " Malting," written in 1889 for their well-known " Diary of the Brewing Room."

produced. When the florets of the central spikelets—*i.e.*, the central row of each series of three—are abortive or infertile **four-rowed barley** is produced; but it is alleged that this is not a very stable type, easily returning to the six-row development when conditions are favourable. However, that it does not too readily revert is evidenced by the preference French brewers show for the four-rowed kind known to them as *Escourgeon* (*H. vulgare hybernum*), which a late writer has wrongly classed with *H. hexastichum*, confusing it with the bigg of northern regions. This preference seems, to a great extent, to be based on the fact that it is sown in winter, and ripens earlier than other kinds.

When, again, only the row attached to the central spikelet on either side is fertilised, the result is a **two-rowed Barley** (*Hordeum distichum*), of which an improved variety, called **the Chevalier,** is the one preferred in England. It is obvious that the barrenness of the lateral rows allow the central row of grains a great chance of development.

As *Escourgeon*, under the name of "winter French," occasionally comes upon our markets, it will not be out of place to mention that it may be distinguished from two-rowed barley not only by less regularity of form, but what will be more perceptible, by the fact that whereas the cleft on the ventral side of the latter is straight and divides the grain into two equal parts, the cleft of *Escourgeon* is crooked, and of the two divisions which it forms one is larger than the other.

Early-sown barley is generally superior *in quality* to late sown; and though this applies to early sowings as compared with later sowings of the same seed, the variety abovenamed (*Escourgeon*) might be worthy of more attention than it gets from brewers here. The writer has seen healthy growing floors of it in July at the brewery called the *Caves du Roy* near Sèvres, though, it must be added, underground, and where artificial cooling was the rule.

Anatomy of the Barley-Corn.

Anatomy of the Barley-Corn.—For a minute description I shall refer my readers elsewhere,* but for a due understanding of the chemical and other changes which are the result of malting, it will be necessary to deal briefly with this part of the subject.

The first thing to notice is the husk, consisting of the **paleæ**—outer and inner palea; the latter being on the cleft or **ventral** side, the former on the side where the acrospire grows, or **dorsal** side, overlaps the inner palea. Beneath the paleæ are two skins, the very delicate **pericarp,** and beneath this the third skin, the **testa.** Both under the microscope exhibit cellular structure, the elongated cells of the former lying in the direction of the length of the grain, while those of the testa are more or less at right angles to it. The larger portion of the grain beneath these skins consists of the **endosperm,** the white and floury portion containing the bulk of the starch granules, interspersed with nitrogenous matter, packed within compartments, so to speak, of cellulose.

At one end of the grain is the **germ,** consisting of the **acrospire** or **plumula,** with the embryo rootlets. This is separated from the endosperm by the **scutellum,** the membranous lining of which, called the **epithelium,** supports a layer of cells emptied of starch.

It only remains to mention the **aleurone** layer, fairly conterminous with endosperm and germ on the dorsal side, a layer of small irregularly angled cells, having dark-coloured granular contents within thickened cell-walls. The contents seem to consist mainly of nitrogenous and fatty or oily matters, but appear to be insensitive to Millon's reagent, the recognised test for proteins. The purpose served by this aleurone layer was long doubtful, but the recent researches of Mr. Horace Brown and Dr. G. H. Morris tend to show that it contains a reserve store of nutriment for the *late* use of the young plant.

* Probably no better general guides can be got than Messrs. Matthews and Lott in their book, "The Microscope in the Brewery and Malthouse."

Accordingly, it is not until the endosperm has been nearly exhausted of its starch (at a stage of growth far beyond that allowed in the malthouse, when in fact the young plant has attained a growth of nearly four inches), that the aleurone cells show marked signs of dissolution.

The operations of malting should not be regarded as isolated; they comprise merely the first, though by no means the least important, steps in the wider process of brewing, and the criterion of success is to be found rather in the superiority of the final product, beer, than in the closeness with which the article malt approaches any given standard.

Thus in certain years a large degree of growth may be most desirable; in others, when the malt in the mash-tun undergoes hydration with greater, and in some cases, with almost too great facility, a less degree of growth would suit the circumstances better. This readiness of hydration, or, in other words, this capacity for yielding a wort rich in maltose, and therefore of a highly fermentable character, is doubtless dependent on conditions other than the growth of the acrospire alone, and indeed rests upon vital conditions of the plant itself, which we have, in general, but limited means of gauging. But we may safely conclude that, under certain circumstances, *e.g.*, a favourable seed time, a sunny, genial summer, a sufficiency of rain to keep the plant in vigorous growth, and a dry harvest, the amount of starch stored up in the cells of the grain will exist in a much higher ratio to the nitrogenous constituents than in dull, cold, and rainy seasons.

We know that starch is formed in plants from carbon, derived from the carbonic acid which plants separate from the air; that the chlorophyll of their leaves, under the impulse of sunlight, in some mysterious way forwards this carbon to be combined with fresh oxygen and hydrogen (elements of the water which the plants imbibe) to form starch, which is then stored away in the plant, as the cells which make up its tissues are formed, and it is therefore not hard to see why in dull and wet seasons—moisture in itself being an all-important factor in dissolving matter and thereby making it assimilable by plants—the nitrogenous constituents of the soil should be much more largely represented in the grain than is the case in seasons of ampler sunshine.

These nitrogenous bodies, as they exist in malted barley, are, it need hardly be said again, not only the source of the so-called diastase, without which brewing, as at present carried on, would be at a standstill, and when modified, of the highly useful peptones and amides, which yield nutriment to the yeast, but also include those inert bodies which cause the brewer such an amount of difficulty, and whose presence it is therefore desirable to restrict by any means that the maltster may have it in his power to adopt. Nor are the above considerations irrelevant, for, if duly kept in view, they will tend more to an understanding of the conditions under which good barley is produced than any amount of dogmatising upon the growth of this region or of that, which might indeed hold good for one particular period, but be utterly faulty at another.

Choosing Barley for Malting.—The grains of barley chosen for malting should be large and even in size, plump, bright in colour, and sweet in smell. The consideration of **size** is even now no unimportant one, although the shifting of the duty which was formerly levied upon malt to the finished product, beer, may have lessened its importance in some eyes, and has probably had its share in inducing maltster-brewers to steep thin barleys, which they would not have looked at fifteen or twenty years ago. For it goes without saying that the large, plump, and full grain is, bulk for bulk, heavier than thinner varieties; moreover, the larger the individual grains, the lower will be the ratio of the somewhat dangerous nitrogenous bodies (dangerous if in excess beyond a very narrow margin), and the higher, conversely, the ratio of the very desirable starch to the total weight. **Uniformity of size** is also of importance, indicating, as it does, grains of the same growth and character; for it is essential that the growth upon the floor should be fairly uniform, and this is hardly likely to be the case with a mixed or uneven grain.

With reference to **the soil** upon which the most suitable barley is grown—and some knowledge on this point often determines a purchase when buyers are well acquainted with their district—I may perhaps quote from myself what I wrote thereon in the article referred to in a footnote.

"Barley grown on sandy loams or land with a calcareous subsoil generally answers best in ordinary years. The soil should be moderately cohesive, well drained, though not excessively dry. In hot, dry seasons, however, very heavy barley of good quality may be secured even upon cold and heavy soils." As no cereal perhaps shows more readily than barley the effect of manure in determining a plentiful yield irrespective of quality, so the heaviest crops of barley are got when it is sown after turnips, fed off upon the land. Where, however, the lease allows it, and the land is good enough, it is of far finer quality when a crop of wheat is interposed. The wheat, coming after the turnips, makes good use of the plentiful fertilising matter in the soil, and as it roots deeply, while barley roots comparatively shallow, they derive many of their inorganic constituents from different *strata*. The barley grown after wheat, then, is the brightest in colour; but to raise it successfully requires a good cultivation of the land, as well as liberty to deviate from the ordinary four-course rotation.

The succession of barley to wheat makes it a matter of some difficulty to eradicate weeds. Factors, not unimportant in the production of a good sample of barley, are the **quality and quantity of the seed-corn** employed. Many farmers are still so unenlightened as to think that the "off-corn" (tail barley) or any rubbish available is good enough for the purpose, while excess in quantity*

---

* Three bushels of seed-corn per acre is sometimes used, but there are good grounds for supposing that half that quantity or less gives better results.

militates against that free "tillering" which so helps the development of the plant. "On the whole, light lands yield a barley richer in starch, or, what is equally important, whose starch-cells are not so crowded together by the pressure of a thick husk or cell-walls as to be obdurate to the successive influences of the malting and mashing processes.

Heavy lands, or those heavily manured with nitrogenous *excreta*, will produce such unkindly, steely barleys, over-rich in protein bodies. It has been proved, over and over again, that the nitrogen in the grain increases with the quantity of the nitrogenous constituents of the soil; in excess—and this applies still more forcibly to chemical manures, such as nitrate of soda or ammonia salts—nitrogenous manures stimulate an excessive development os straw, whereby the barley easily gets "laid" before its ears have stored up their full supply of starch.

The principal characteristics, then, of good barley are even size, a pale yellow colour extending from end to end, and a sweet smell. It should be of fair weight, and, other things being equal, the heaviest barley—at any rate, up to 56 lb. a bushel*—is the best. Besides the fact that the percentage of protein bodies is lower in full plump grain than in poor samples, the husk of the former is relatively thinner. A uniform sample generally weighs better than one in which small and large grains are intermixed. Irregularly developed grains, even of the same growth, will germinate irregularly; and it would certainly be preferable to mix growths uniform in size and general character, than to steep barley, just as received, without removing "the tail," by grading or screening.

Over-ripe grains, moreover, will lose germinative power to the extent of 50% in extreme cases, but unfortunately over-ripeness is a defect not very easy to detect. On the other hand, **barley cut before it is ripe** always grows

* In some parts of the west of England the weight of the sack of four bushels is taken as a basis, and the barley is said to weigh "eleven score," "eleven score, four," etc., as the case may be. The former = 55 lb. per bushel, the latter 56 lb.

badly, frequently turns mouldy on the floors, and has a strong tendency to heat in store. Such barley, however, may be detected by its shrivelled husk, want of plumpness, and, most of all, by its greenish colour. Sometimes a sample of barley gives evidence of two distinct growths having occurred in the same field, caused probably by uneven sowing. The **skin** should be thin and slightly wrinkled; rough, harsh skins indicate barleys which will be sluggish to work, and will give dissatisfaction in the brewery; a barley with a good skin and in good condition flows easily through the fingers when handled.

Note should be taken of any **admixture of other grain,** such as wheat or oats, also of the presence of the seeds of vetches or weeds, which lower the value of the sample, and which there should be machines in every malthouse to remove. Cracked or broken grains, if numerous, ought to influence the rejection of a sample, being great encouragers of mildew. Grains, broken in halves, are most frequent after very hot, dry summers. **Skinned grains** (the husk having been skinned off by setting the threshing machine too close) are worse than broken grains, because no machine yet invented can remove them. **Blackened tips** show that the grain has heated in stack, and become what is termed "mow-burnt."

Reddish[*] or bluish spots indicate germination on the stalk before harvesting, or, at all events, unfavourable

---

[*] Red mould on barley is actually due to *Fusarium hordei*, of which Messrs. Matthews and Lott, in their valuable work, "The Microscope in the Brewery and Malthouse," say : "It is occasionally seen among inferior samples of barley, appearing as a crimson or pink-tinted patch on defective corns, usually at the germinal end; fortunately it does not spread to healthy corns, but it may be communicated to crushed ones." Its appearance, however, is quite familiar enough on growing floors at times. Jörgensen, referring to Matthews' researches on this mildew, says that probably its spores are of greater weight and adhere more closely to the original mould growth than the spores of other organisms—*e.g.* penicillium, mucor, and aspergillus, which are very readily disseminated. The student is advised to study it under the microscope, using the one-eighth or one-tenth objective. Its crescent-shaped spores form a capital object, and are not to be mistaken for those of any other mould.

conditions at maturing. Such a growth is likely to occur when a harvest-time of prolonged wet follows weeks of heat, as was the case in 1881 ; but heating in stack is a result of the grain being carried too soon, to which there is indeed great temptation in wet harvest weather, though that is the very time when less hurry and a larger amount of field-room is required to thoroughly kill the increased undergrowth of clover.

Apart from the added difficulty of drying up the undergrowth, a shower of rain does barley no actual harm. Some indeed hold that the grain which has been subjected to a moderate shower is mellowed thereby, and rendered more "kindly" to work on the malting-floors; others think that the same effect attends the night-dews, which settle so heavily after a warm summer's day, and which, of themselves, deepen the hue even of first-rate barleys towards the end of harvest.

Apart from the indications referred to above it will be necessary after a wet harvest to keep a sharp lookout for **grains which have already germinated.** In extreme cases rootlets may still be perceptible adhering to the grain, or they may have been rubbed off by chance or of malice aforethought. In that case a broken appearance of the germ end, where the rootlets have protruded, and a faint swelling of the acrospire will be the only indications. It is, however, far better to make purchases only of respectable vendors (nor will these cautions even then be thrown away), for rogues will generally endeavour, even when the sample has been satisfactory, to send in the bulk of inferior quality, and the transaction thus occasions positive loss or annoyance, and inconvenience if the bulk be rejected.

The contents of a grain of barley bitten or cut across should be white, floury, and mellow, neither glassy (vitreous) nor of a bluish tinge; in other words, the barley should be kindly. Glassiness of the interior is an indication of the grain having been grown upon a soil too rich in nitrogen ; or it might be suggestive of excessive artificial drying (sweating), possibly sufficient to injure the germinative power.

Tests for Germinative Power.—The vitality of the germ may be decided, Stopes points out, by removing with a knife the skin over the germ end and then observing it with a weak lens. If alive, the germ has a juicy, fairly firm, yellow appearance, like freshly churned butter, or greenish-yellow, like wax. If it be reddish-brown, dark or black, dried or shrivelled, it is *dead*; if grey, of *low vitality*.

A recent communication to the *Brewer's Journal* recommends that to facilitate inspection of the germ, a handful of the grain should be put into a glass of boiling water, in which some washing soda has been dissolved. The outer husk will soon split, it is said, and can be removed by careful washing.

The same writer (Mr. Stopes) also gives what he calls a "fire test," directing it to be carried out as follows. Take from a clear fire a large red cinder, which should be kept by an artificial blast at a uniform heat. Drop the kernels on, one or two at a time. If the corns dance about they may be taken as alive, those that cremate passively are dead. The above manipulation seems a little crude; an iron pan, heated to redness over a Bunsen burner, would surely answer better.

Of other tests for germinative power, the only one perhaps which does not take too long for the purpose of forming an immediate opinion is that devised by **Haberlandt.** First of all, however, it should be repeated that the embryo (visible to the naked eye if the grain be cut in two endwise) is situated at that end of the grain from which the rootlets protrude. It is the plant in miniature, with dormant stalk and rootlets, ready to start into life under suitable conditions. According to Haberlandt, an inspection of the embryo with the microscope, or even with a hand magnifying-glass, will decide the germinating power of the grain with tolerable accuracy.

When a section is taken, he goes on to say, of any healthy embryo, the rootlets look greenish or pale yellow (sometimes distinctly yellow), the plumula being a fair yellow. If treated with sulphuric acid, the yellow colour becomes very distinct in grains of healthy germinative power after two to five minutes, while if the process be continued five to ten minutes, the embryo assumes a rosy-red hue. In grains, on the other hand, which have had their germinative power weakened or destroyed, the rootlets are of a dull yellow or grey, bluish-grey, or brownish, while the plumula is either of a dirty grey, whitish, or brownish hue. The more completely the germinating power has been destroyed, the darker is the colour, as a rule.

This test, whatever it may be worth, is easily applied. The writer's experience with it, however, is that the change of colour to something approaching rosy-red occurs much more speedily than in five minutes. One obvious drawback is that it is quite impossible to assure oneself by collateral experiment that the grains which come well out of the test really possess (though it is most probable that they do) the germinative capacity claimed for them.

Coldewe's Patent.—A useful apparatus giving as speedy results as possible where the question has to be answered by actual germination, consists of a porcelain tray, having a hundred indentations, into which as many grains of barley are placed, germ-end downwards. A glass vessel, into which the tray fits resting on a ledge moulded to receive it, is nearly filled with water. A little sand it placed round the barley, a piece of felt put over to prevent too much evaporation, and the whole apparatus is then placed in a moderately warm situation.

The actual routine of malting, with a few simple, practical hints thereon, occupied part of the first chapter; sundry points, however, require further development.

Situation of the Malthouse in relation to that of the Brewery.—It is nowadays customary and highly convenient to construct a malthouse or malthouses in line with the brewery itself. This not only gives uniformity of façade, but saves labour in more ways than one. A line of rails running into the brewery yard can be used to bring in coal and barley; power for hoisting barley can be got from the brewery engine (though a better plan is to have an independent gas-engine, of *ample power* if only a sufficient pressure of gas can *at all times* be relied on); and the malt, measured up for each day's " grist," can be conveyed by means of an elevator or screw directly into the " hopper," which feeds the malt-mills.

With regard to the **space required for cistern, couch** (which, though not obligatory, as of old, is still often used), **and working floors,** Mr. Scamell gives for the cistern about $12\frac{1}{4}$ cubic feet per quarter of barley, for the couch $13\frac{1}{4}$ cubic feet, and for the working floors from 180 to 200 square feet for every quarter. A later authority says that a 15-quarters house should never have less superficial area of combined couch and floor room than 2,600 feet, if in the south of England, or 2,400 in the north of England or Scotland. This is only 173 to 160 feet per quarter, couch space included. In another place, however, he says that 180 feet is probably the safest average; and that in the construction of the cistern it is not wise to allow less than fourteen cubic feet per quarter.

He would allow a large malthouse a width up to 50 feet, beyond which structural inconveniences occur, as well as the difficulty of keeping the growing floors at a uniform heat, which difficulty is found, the first authority cited holds, in widths of over 40 feet. But this must depend a good deal on the freedom of the ventilation. [The proportions of kiln-floors will be treated later, p. 71.]

Tiles are freely used for working-floors, but, unless most accurately laid, have this drawback, that the jagged edges formed will catch the turning shovel at almost every forward movement, and thereby cause the crushing of many grains, besides harbouring putrescent matter. **Stuart's granolithic flooring,** a sort of hard concrete laid in large slabs, is excellent. **Cement** is held by some to promote a rise of temperature. Nor is iron, as a material for cisterns, theoretically right, it being of great importance to keep the temperatures of the steep liquor from approaching freezing point. Brick, lined with concrete for economy, or with glazed white tiles for efficiency and cleanliness, is a preferable arrangement. This is as regards rectangular cisterns, but the cone-shaped cisterns referred to in Chapter I. have so much in their favour, that one would think twice before constructing a cistern on the older pattern.

Sweating, Steeping (Bohemian Method), Sprinkling.—Sweating of barley on the kiln, if necessary, should be carried on at a temperature not much exceeding 100° Fahr., the barley under treatment remaining a few hours on the kiln; and it is doubtful whether grain, which has already begun to grow, would be benefited by a sweat; certainly, in that case, for safety's sake, the heat employed should be extremely moderate. **The temperature of the steep-liquor** is also, as has been said, a point worth attention. In winter it is often far too low, seeing that a temperature approaching freezing point seriously imperils the vitality of weakly grains, and must delay the germination even of the stronger. A temperature ranging from 50° to 55° Fahr. is a good mean, and the thermometer may be advantageously used at intervals. The **duration of the steep** is, luckily, an open question now. In spite of the authority of so practical a writer as Ford, who would give kindly barley a steep of from sixty-five to seventy-two hours, I hold that our average steep of forty-eight or fifty hours is possibly—except in the case of certain foreign barleys—even too long, and that herein the intelligent foreigner sometimes goes farther astray; except that in **Bohemia** a method, involving double steeping, prevails, which I should gladly see at least tried here.

In carrying out the system thus referred to the grain is first steeped for twenty-four hours, then the cistern is emptied, and its contents put in conical heaps about five feet high. These are sprinkled every hour with cold water, and so turned that the moisture may penetrate every part. During this time the cistern is cleansed, and fresh barley steeped, which is also, after twenty-four hours, placed in similar heaps. Then the first charge is thrown back into the cistern and steeped again for six or eight hours, after which it will have swelled enough and absorbed sufficient moisture. There are really no practical difficulties in the way of trying this method, and it appears to me that the combined aëration and moistening which take place have everything to recommend them. Certainly excessive steeping is detrimental, extracting valuable substances, lowering the vitality of the grain as a whole, causing a degree of moisture which it is difficult to get rid of on the floors, besides favouring the development of mould, and of its complement, acidity.

On the other hand sprinkling, as adapted to the English system of steeping, cannot fully compensate for too short a stay in cistern, it being hardly possible to manage it with regularity enough to promote an even germination under those circumstances. When sprinkling is required it is better to do it in the morning, and have the floors turned afterwards, which gives a better chance of the liquid being regularly absorbed by the grain than sprinkling without a closely following turning—albeit a favourite plan—will do.

And as regards the **prevention of mould**—though it may be greatly limited by thoroughly cleaning and washing the barley before steeping it, preventing by means of curtains or otherwise the access of the dust separated by the screening-machines, and by attention to the temperature of the steep liquor as well as by duly changing the same, and, last but not least, by working at temperatures as low as are consistent with free germination—nothing can be more valuable than **bisulphite of lime.** A 10% solution is most useful for washing cisterns whenever emptied, and most destructive of lactic ferments and spores of mould which swarm there. With doubtful barley, a gallon in the steep liquor to every 20 or 40 quarters, according to circumstances, and, even for sprinkling, liquor containing 1% to 2% may be used without danger. It is useful, too, for bins, but there I must own to a liking for fresh-slaked lime applied hot with a whitewasher's brush.

It is said that **chalk** or **lime** is sometimes used in the steep liquor to reduce acidity and lessen the extractiveness of the liquor. But in view of the fact that the continuous production of lactic acid in the same medium gets more and more restricted by the opposing agency of the lactic acid already produced, and that such production can be renewed by the withdrawal of the latter, which is best effected by causing it to combine with a base to form **lactate of lime,** its benefit in the former case would be more than questionable.

In the latter respect some advantage might accrue if the chalk were freely soluble in water, seeing that, in spite of some opinions to the contrary of leading authorities, of whom Mulder was one, the advantages of hard water for steeping purposes are pretty generally recognised, on the ground that soft water extracts more of the soluble constituents of the barley (over 1% more), of which the loss of the phosphate of potash is the most serious. When hard water is used the phosphoric acid appears to form lime compounds, which remain insoluble until acted upon by the lactic acid, always present, if in minute quantity, in the mash-tun. In any case, potassic phosphate is of extreme importance in the nourishment of the yeast. Moreover, the extraction of soluble phosphates and their presence in the steep water favour the development of mildew, and that soft water more speedily than hard should give evidence of incipient putrefaction is a necessary consequence, implying more frequent changes of liquor. Such changes, from the point of view of the increased drain upon the soluble constituents of the barley, are so far undesirable.

It is further supposed that the lime and magnesia salts in hard water form insoluble compounds with some of the otherwise soluble albuminoid bodies in the steeped barley, and that the effects of this combination may be traced in the greater readiness with which the worts "break" when boiled in the copper. This, I must confess, seems difficult of proof, nor does there seem any reason why such compounds, if they exist, should be more insensible to the influence of the mash-tun lactic acid than the lime phosphates are.

"**Idle corns**" or "**liebacks**" are the grains which do not grow, and include not only those which are really dead, but those of such weak vitality, that anything short of the most favourable conditions prevents their germination.

The capacity for growth of "idlers" of this second class is greatly increased by a moderate kiln-drying of the barley (sweating) before steeping it. Amongst the risks attendant upon an excessive proportion of liebacks are, first, the possible introduction of insoluble starch into the worts, starch which would be rendered soluble by the subsequent boiling in the copper, or even by high sparge-heats when the diastase has become so crippled as to be unable to effect conversion; although it is true that liebacks which have passed through the malting process without germinating have their insoluble constituents modified into a somewhat more soluble condition. A second risk is their liability to mildew.

It is asserted that "liebacks" of the second class may have their germinating power so much increased by the kiln-drying to which malt is subjected, as to be capable of growing if afterwards planted in the earth. Imperfectly cured malt, which has grown, but not produced, for some reason or other, the normal number of rootlets— seven—is, I have good reason to believe, predisposed to do the same, only producing in the soil, however, the rootlets it failed to produce on the floors. In the case of extreme unsoundness and very faulty undercuring, moisture and warmth may even induce the acrospire to sprout in the air.

The presence of a considerable proportion of idlers may be detected by placing a sample from the floor upon the open palm, held at an angle of 30° to 45°; the hand being then slightly shaken with an up-and-down jerking movement, the growing grains will drop off first, leaving most of the ungerminated corns behind.

Kilns and Kiln-drying.—Kiln-drying is often very carelessly performed, the malt being loaded on far too thickly. Moisture is a very potent factor in the chemical decomposition of bodies; so that a high temperature, if dry, is found to be much less energetic in breaking up the various nitrogenous and non-nitrogenous bodies of the malt than a much lower moist one. By placing the malt thickly on the kiln, especially in a very wet state, the conditions most favourable for this decomposition are maintained; and in the case of the albumenoids, this breaking-up is attended by a fermentative or putrefactive action, tending to the development of an excess of acid.

The extreme limit of depth should hardly exceed six inches, under ordinary conditions; beyond this, unless with some special suction arrangements, it is very difficult to dry the malt thoroughly; and if the floor be turned again and again * with the idea of aiding this result the evil is only intensified, such a plan being, as it would seem, one arranged, of set purpose, to keep the moist vapour circulating continuously from the damp stratum below to the dry one above.

On this point Thausing says: "It is known that malt is less coloured by the kiln-drying, the drier it is when the high temperature begins, and *vice versâ*. If the temperature is allowed to rise slowly, and the greatest part of the moisture be got rid of at moderate temperature

* Green malt, therefore, should not be turned, though it may want lightening to allow the vapour to escape. Moreover, on kilns of ordinary construction the bottom layer is often spoilt, and turning will only intensify the damage. It should, therefore, be freely "forked," but never turned till dry to the touch.

(77° to 110° Fahr.), it is possible, later on, to go as high as 167°, and even higher, without producing any coloration of consequence. If, on the other hand, the temperature gets high at first, and while the malt is still charged with moisture, and if the vapour that is formed does not escape quickly, as often happens on badly constructed kilns, then the malt gets much coloured, and empyreumatic produces are formed, which may even be sufficient to overpower the pleasant flavour of the cured malt."

It is undoubtedly possible, and even desirable, to go to a considerably higher heat the last day—when the malt is thoroughly dry—than Thausing recommends. **The finishing temperature** should certainly *not be less* than 180° to 190°. And experiment tends to show that a final temperature of 200° Fahr. (not a fluctuating temperature, reaching that point at intervals, but the maintenance of that temperature for several hours) gives the best results, taking quantity of extract as well as quality into consideration. A lower finishing heat than 200° Fahr. seems to favour increase of extract, though the extract is of a less stable character than that yielded by the higher-dried malt. A higher temperature than 200° tends to impair the amount of extract too seriously for such an elevation to be recommended. [See p. 301 sub. **Maltodextrin,** for a possible clue to this.]

Besides the increase of colour due to caramelisation the application of high temperatures when the grain is moist may cause a loss of diastasic energy, the albuminoids which constitute that force being prone to coagulate under the influence of heat when in a semi-dissolved condition. Steeliness is also an effect of such a premature application of heat. But at the same time we know that the hotter the air is the more moisture it will carry away; and it is possible, to some extent, to utilise this property, counterbalancing the higher temperature by freely admitting larger volumes of air. Hence, it is evident that much more air is required during the drying than during the curing stage.

Last's Patent Ventilators.—This useful innovation, though primarily intended for general ventilation, yet, having considerable influence in bringing the green malt, just before loading on, into a suitably dry condition, and being, moreover, dependent on the draught created by the rush of air through the kiln-fires, may be conveniently referred to here. Without in any way limiting or interfering with the usual lateral ventilation through windows, Last's arrangement consists of a series of openings made in the short wall at the kiln-end of each floor (a dozen or more to each floor), which openings have falling doors to close or partly close them—these doors being either actuated singly, which is the best plan, or all together by a rod.

At the opposite end of each floor (the cistern end) are other similar openings, but less numerous, for admitting the air from outside, and obtaining a longitudinal air-current. The former apertures open out into a space surrounding the kiln, the dunge, in fact, but a dunge carried up to a greater elevation than is usual, so that when the kiln fire is well alight the air rushes down to it through these openings with great velocity.

Construction of Kilns.—Kilns should have a drying surface of at least twenty-five square feet per quarter. (Mr. Stopes thinks the area should never exceed one-fourth or be less than one-sixth of that of the growing-floors, and in another place says that no pale-malt kiln should have a less area than thirty-three square feet per quarter of barley steeped.) The writer named also holds that the combined air-inlets should not bear a higher ratio to the air-outlets than as 4 : 5.

The construction of the roof of kilns requires consideration. A *thin* roof condenses the moisture rising from the green malt. Slates, beneath which are felt and boards with air-spaces between, the inside being soundly plastered, form a roof which gives the best results, though it is important to have the plaster made with lime of good holding power.

Existing kilns have been doubled in capacity on the

principle advocated by Mr. Stopes (though I believe Mr. Corcoran was the pioneer of double-kiln construction in England), which however differs little from the arrangement which has long obtained in many Continental maltings, except that the products of combustion are allowed to pass through the malt, instead of heated air alone being the drying agent employed. And if the kiln-space was not cramped before, it is obvious that the addition of an upper floor will enable steepings to be made twice as often as before, for an interval of two days, instead of four, between each steeping is enough to enable the upper kiln to be ready for a fresh floor of green malt. The chief objection to such an arrangement is one which has been referred to in Chap. I., the difficulty of keeping the temperatures at the desired point on *both* floors simultaneously—say 190° on the lower, and 100° on the upper.*

This difficulty seems to be faced with considerable chance of success in M. Hedicke & Co.'s Twin Kiln. The drying floor is in this arrangement also placed above what the patentees call "the roasting floor"; but as the latter is roofed in (below the drying floor), and has a large tube fitted in the apex of the said roof, which tube passes upward, through the drying floor, direct to the cowl, none of the very hot air passes from this roasting floor into the green malt above to the latter's detriment; and though in a measure this very heated air may be said to pass away to waste, it yet, in its passage out, helps to create a strong upcast draught, and so increases the volume of more or less warm air sucked through the green malt. The heated air admitted to the green malt passes by comparatively narrow air-channels not through, but beside the roasting floor; and side by side with these hot-air channels are channels for introducing such supplies of cold air as may seem advisable. Of course the volume of either can be nicely adjusted.

Furnace and Baffle-plate.—The simplest form of furnace

* See p. 78 for Mr. Stopes' instructions for the management of them.

consists of a grate formed of heavy bars carried on bearers, and set in firebricks. The whole structure, from about the level of the top of the arched opening through which the fire is fed, arching outwards towards the outer walls of the kiln, and forming the **Dunge,** partly used for the storage of coal, is placed as nearly centrally as possible with regard to the kiln floor. There should be inlets for air besides what passes in through the grate, and a damper at the back of the stove helps regularity of combustion.

Baffle-plates, though condemned by Mr. Stopes, have their advantages. They are large flat surfaces of iron, tiles, etc., suspended a short distance above the fire, and from their function are sometimes known as dispersers. Iron baffle-plates have this disadvantage; if they get overheated and much kiln-dust falls on them, the latter burns, with a most disagreeable odour, which passes through the malt above. The best baffle-plates are made of tiles supported on thin strips of iron, supported in their turn by transverse iron rods.

It is of importance, as has been indicated when speaking of the necessity of good supplies of air in the early stage upon the kiln, to get rid of the moisture from the green malt rapidly, though at a low heat. For this purpose **cowls** are far better adapted than the open ventilators often seen, but the most effective arrangement of all seems to be the form of suction introduced by Mr. Free. In the recently arranged large maltings belonging to his firm the kilns are, or can be made, absolutely air-tight chambers, and are each fitted with a Blackman air-propeller placed at the apex of the roof.

These making at first as many as 600 revolutions a minute rapidly draw off the moisture; and it is further claimed that, in the subsequent curing process and when the revolutions of the propeller (fan) have been reduced to 360 a minute, the malt may lie at more than twice its usual depth, and yet that the temperature will be practically uniform (with a variation of, at the outside not more than 10°, a result which, as Mr. Free says, can be attained in no other way) *; that the temperature may be raised even to 230° without unduly colouring the malt; and finally, that the whole process can be effected in half the time taken by the ordinary method. These are, some of them at any rate, great advantages. Even the power of going some 30° or 40° higher than usual in finishing off the malt might be valuable from the point of view of dextrin formation, and need not, with a malt from which the moisture had been so thoroughly extracted, involve a dangerous loss of diastasic power.

When to them and to the alleged greater stability of the extract is added the undoubted increased "tenderness" which results from this method of drawing large volumes of dry, hot air (25,000 cubic feet per minute) through the malt, the added cost of fourpence to sixpence per quarter, at which Mr. Free estimates it, will seem inconsiderable to all who desire real quality of material rather than cheapness. With such advantages, the time may not be far distant when no kiln will be considered complete without some such vacuum arrangement, although the alteration would naturally connote drying by hot air instead of by heat mingled with the products of combustion, as is usual in England.

Mr. Free's own words on the fan system, as compared with the ordinary method of curing, are valuable and very suggestive. "When malt has been worked with great success from the cistern to the kiln, it is by no means uncommon, where the draught is defective, that more injury occurs on the kiln itself than has taken place during the ten or more days that the malt has remained on the floors. The temperatures used in the early stages of drying are of necessity so low, in order to prevent hardness and colour in the malt, that this point forms the

---

* That is to say, if three accurate naked-bulb thermometers be placed in the malt on the kiln, one right down on the tiles, the second 4½ inches higher, the third very near the top, say 9 inches above the first, the temperatures will not vary more than 200°, 195° and 190°.

most favourable opportunity for the formation of mould and acidity; and many brewers who malt for their own requirements will be familiar with the white fungus which spreads itself in large or small patches on the top of a kiln, in which a considerable degree of moisture is still present, together with the mould, which increases with terrible rapidity on the broken and damaged grains until the malt is comparatively dry. This may now be entirely avoided, as under the rapid draught produced by the fan this formation can never take place; and we can rest assured that from the time the malt is loaded until it is fit for curing no deterioration will take place, even though low temperatures be used throughout. Owing to the rapid draught, the steam arising from the malt is barely perceptible, and the top of the grain, instead of being saturated with moisture, owing to the condensation of the steam, is dry and sweet, although the temperature is lower than dare be used on an ordinary kiln. **When one considers how malt is, for the most part, dried**, it does not seem hard to account for the difficulty of producing good results. An article which has, or which ought to have, received the greatest care and attention, is placed upon a kiln for the purpose of effecting the final stage of drying, which it is important should be carried out with the utmost care, and should be both continuous and progressive. Yet what happens? The malt is loaded in the morning, and for the rest of the day is kept at a low temperature. In the evening the fires are banked up, and for the next eight or nine hours not only is the heat not raised, but becomes actually lower. The following morning the fires are made up, and during the rest of the day the malt receives more or less attention; but in the evening the same process of banking-up is repeated, and for the two following days and nights the same operations are continued. Is it to be wondered at that malt deteriorates more quickly on kiln than it ever did on the floor, when a manufacture is carried out on such principles?

A brewer would be much surprised if he were told that

if he partly boiled his wort overnight, then lowered the temperature by many degrees, and finished it the next morning, everything would be satisfactory. Yet this is precisely what is being done in hundreds of maltings in the kingdom. I have never heard of any arguments worthy of consideration used against the principle of drying malt by suction, such as would be produced by aid of a Blackman or similar fan, but I have often heard it suggested whether the fact of drying malt in thirty-six to forty hours would not tend to make it steely. Now the persons who make these remarks must certainly forget the immense amount of time which is absolutely wasted by drying in the manner before described; and so far as the hardness is concerned, I can give the following explanation to the contrary.

"Before using the fan on a large scale, two kilns of exactly the same size and in the same malting were selected, into one of which a Blackman fan was fitted, whilst the other was left in the same condition as had heretofore existed. In the former case the malt was dried and cured in thirty-six hours, but in the latter seventy-two hours were required to do the same work, whilst in size and flavour the fan kiln had a decided advantage; and upon grinding the malt a still greater difference was apparent. Samples were submitted with distinguishing marks upon them to an expert, but not conveying any information as to which was dried by fan, and which by the ordinary kiln; yet in every case the former was identified by greater tenderness, and the colour of its malt-meal was much paler than that of the latter — a point not to be overlooked by those brewers who require a very pale, yet well-cured malt. These facts, however, though very useful to the maltster, might not have been in themselves equally satisfactory to the brewer had other requisites been wanting, more particularly that of stability of the wort. To test this, numerous samples were sent to a well-known analyst, under various numbers or letters; but again, in every case, the fan-dried malt was found to possess less lactic acid and decidedly greater stability than the other samples which had been dried upon one of the best ordinary kilns which have been constructed."

Mr. H. J. King's Automatic Regulator.—The gloomy picture which Mr. Free has so faithfully painted may be falsified in regard to any particular malting by the use of King's (of Newmarket, near Stroud, Gloucestershire) Automatic Regulator. A large iron swing ventilator, accurately balanced on pivots in an iron frame, is placed in a large opening specially cut for it in the brickwork just over the furnace door, and so that it opens or closes at a very slight impulse. Two long brass rods, parallel to each other, are fixed just under the tile floor of the kiln, so that they expand or contract with every rise or fall of the temperature caused by the fire, and so that the expansion of the one rod is *passed on*, through or by the other rod, and added to its expansion to actuate a weighted lever with which the end of the second rod is connected. The lever accordingly, which is in a straight line above the frame of the ventilator, rises or falls as the brass rods expand or contract again, and thus, by means of a slotted rod, opens or closes the easily swinging ventilator. There is an adjusting slide by which the ventilator can be set to open at any temperature, so that the risk of overfiring (*experto crede*) is reduced to a minimum, even when the fires are left for a considerable time. Not only is cold air admitted to the malt directly the temperature reaches the not-to-be-exceeded point, but the draught through the fire from underneath is also checked.

There is another form of regulator also patented by Mr. King, and consisting of a wheel some four feet in diameter, and constructed, as to its outer rim, of a steel tube. The rim of this wheel is about half filled with mercury and a little alcohol. A rise of temperature causes the expansion of the mercury, and so shifts the centre of gravity; the wheel accordingly begins to rotate, and by means of a wire cord passing from a smaller wheel at the end of the shaft on which the large hollow wheel is fixed, opens the ventilator. There are two scale-pans suspended over the smaller wheel, and it is by the amount of weight hung in these that the temperature is determined at which the ventilator is to open.

Instructions for managing Double Kilns (Stopes' pattern).—Though I have made no secret of the opinion that these kilns are ordinarily not adequate to requirements, the patentee thinks otherwise, and gives the following directions (condensed) for managing them.

Green malt to be loaded on the top-floor when fit for kiln.

1st day. Temperature not below 80° or above 100°.

2nd ,, Temperature not below 90° or above 110°. At end of second day lower top floor to bottom.

3rd day. Temperature from 120° to 130° or 140°.

4th ,, Temperature from 140° to 185° or 195° or higher.

The top floor can be ploughed or forked over lightly, if needed, and heats can then be raised or lowered, according to the character to be given to the malt. The bottom floor need not be turned or ploughed.

The regulation of heat and air to be effected by due attention to fires, or adjustment of air inlets and dispersers.

When floors are young and green dispersers can be closed and inlets open. Air is required at this stage.

When the bottom floor is to be finished off at a high heat air can be supplied moderately and dispersers* opened. By these means the bottom floor can be 190° and the top floor 100°.

Sweating of barley to be upon the most convenient floor (preferably the bottom one), and the heat of sweating is not to exceed 115° when the top floor is loaded.

---

* The dispersers referred to are the iron arrangements, shaped like a chimney-pot, only larger, which cover the holes down which the malt is shovelled from the upper to the lower kiln. They have a number of triangular-shaped openings at the top, which can be opened or closed by turning a knob. *Dissipators* are cones of woven wire similarly used for covering those apertures.

Heaping-up the Malt after Curing.—To do this for several hours after the kiln drying and curing is completed is certainly an advantage from the point of view of flavour; moreover, if the malt, in an extremely hot condition, be spread out comparatively thin, there is a tendency to absorb an excess of moisture.

What are the Maltster's Objects in the Preparation of Malt, or rather what are the Results, chemically speaking, which follow his Operations?—He has a grain containing a vast number of cells, each containing granules of starch or protein bodies, or of starch and protein intermingled. In this grain the starch granules are enclosed in an envelope of cellulose, which renders their contents (the **granulose**) practically insoluble in any water much below a boiling temperature. One of his objects, then, is to make these starch granules soluble in water of a lower temperature, and this is effected by alterations in the character of the grain, which have their physical expression in expansion and consequent lightening of texture and the growth of plumula and rootlets, this growth being accompanied by the formation of a slight trace of acid, and maybe of some other solvent, which attacks and breaks down the cellular structure.

Two recent investigators refer this cellulose-dissolving activity to a special **cellulose-dissolving enzyme** (a cytohydrolyst), which, like diastase, is secreted in the "absorptive epithelium." They look upon its secretion, as well as upon that of diastase, as being, to some extent, starvation phenomena, inasmuch as in the presence of relatively-plentiful assimilable carbo-hydrates, *e.g.*, cane-sugar and maltose (but apparently not starch), the secretion seems to be stayed. This rupture of the starch-granule envelope might indeed be effected by other means—*e.g.*, by exposure to sudden and intense heat, as may be noted in a microscopic examination of torrefied grain, where the starch-granules will appear considerably more expanded and ruptured than those even of ordinary malt.

Another object, in one sense even more important,

because it does not seem attainable by any other method, is the transformation of a portion of the insoluble protein bodies into a more soluble form, the result of which is the formation of the bodies known as **amides**, which, together with the **peptones** (another modification), form a store of nitrogenous food for yeast, and the springing into activity, under suitable subsequent conditions, of the two potent factors **diastase** and **peptase**. The diastase, as is well known, is the unorganised ferment which converts starch into dextrin and maltose ; so potent is it as to be capable of converting at least ten thousand times its weight of starch. Indeed, one authority " of light and leading " holds—and certainly there is much to bear him out—that the diastase continues unaltered in the mash-tun, and that a small amount of it can do the work of the largest quantity, if only time be given it.

Nor is the diastasic sphere of action confined to the mash-tun (albeit that of peptase, according to one of its closest investigators, Professor Ullik, seems to be so limited). Diastase, however,—meaning thereby the agency which transforms starch into dextrin and sugar (maltose),—must set to work directly germination begins, or rather, as Mulder puts it, is not the *result* but the *cause* of germination ; that is to say, the conversion of non-diffusible starch into substances capable of diffusion through membranes, which it effects, seems to be necessary before a single fresh cell of the plant can be formed. The student of elementary botany will be aware that every shoot, every rootlet, every part of a plant, is simply an aggregation of cells, which are continually forming at the growing points, and that therefore the necessity of nutritive matter which can pass through or along the cellular tissue, which bounds them, is absolute. This close connection between diastasic action and germination would lead us to expect to find diastase solely in the neighbourhood of the germ, and accordingly Messrs. Brown & Morris claim to have established its secretion in the " absorptive epithelium " (the cellular membrane of the scutellum).

Abstract of Messrs. Brown and Morris's Conclusions.
—I may here condense—though as a complete statement the abstract will be utterly inadequate—the important conclusions of these investigators. Experiment tends to prove the secretion both of the amylo-hydrolyst (diastase) and of the cyto-hydrolyst (cellulose-dissolving enzyme) to be *starvation phenomena* to some extent, because when there is a good supply of assimilable carbo-hydrates —*e.g.*, cane-sugar or maltose—the secretion is checked or even stopped; in other words, the secretive power of the epithelium is only exerted when the supply of tissue-forming carbon compounds begins to fail.

They have further shown that the **relation of the embryo to the endosperm is that of parasite to host,** having cultivated "excised" embryos (embryos detached from the endosperm) in various nutrient media. Cane-sugar, invert sugar, dextrose, levulose, and maltose are all nutritious, but cane-sugar most of all. Lactose, however, does not contribute to the nutriment of the young plant. Even maltose, which is the natural food when the embryo is attached to its own endosperm, seems to be inferior to cane-sugar; and this is explained by the ascertained fact that maltose, when absorbed by the growing embryo, is transformed into cane-sugar, so that there is *a saving of energy* effected by supplying cane-sugar already formed. And from this it follows that the seat of production of the cane-sugar, which the germinated grain contains, is to be sought within the tissues of the embryo itself.

Further experiments made with "excised" embryos from which the absorptive epithelium had been carefully removed by scraping (from the surface of the scutellum), showed that though such a maimed embryo would grow if placed in a readily assimilable carbo-hydrate (cane-sugar, dextrose, etc.), yet that it had utterly lost its power of eroding starch and of dissolving it. On the contrary, embryos retaining their epithelium will liquefy stiff starch paste, embedding themselves in it to an appreciable depth. Rather singularly, the epithelium, removed from its embryo, seems to retain, to some extent, its power of secreting a starch-dissolving enzyme.

Opposing View of Mr. James O'Sullivan.—But, on the other hand, Mr. J. O'Sullivan does not consider that the diastase is secreted in the epithelium alone. Careful experiments made day by day with germinating barley have convinced him that it also exists in the endosperm. From a number of grains he cut off one-third of each, the remaining two-thirds, containing the germ, being rejected. From this he scraped the starch (carefully avoiding that near the husk), which after being mixed with cold water was gradually heated to 149° — 154° Fahr. Even on the first day (apparently corresponding to a "one-day" floor) some soluble starch was found in the filtrate when cooled; more so on the second day—fresh grains corresponding to those of a two-day floor being taken; whilst on the third day, with only three hours' digestion, there was no starch reaction, but only that of a-dextrin. On the fourth day, although the acrospire had hardly started, there was neither soluble starch nor a-dextrin in the filtrate after twenty minutes' digestion, showing that the conversion was complete.

"An interesting observation," he adds, "in connection with the above facts, is, that in no case were there any pitted or corroded starch-granules in the portion of the endosperm employed, and even on the eighth day of germination a like portion af the endosperm showed none. It is evident here that Nature makes no mistake; for although the power to dissolve starch is in a position far removed from the place of the consumption of its solution-products, yet *solution only takes place where the product of the solution is consumed*, and that is the vicinity of the growing embryo."

At the date of the above remarks he held the opinion that the diastase of the endosperm end was probably incapable of dissolving the starch granules, but this he subsequently corrected, having found that an aqueous extract of the endosperm end on the fifth day of germination does possess the power of pitting pure barley starch-granules.

"If we consider the above experiments," he continues, "and believe that the diastase is produced by the embryo, and that it passes out through the scutellum, we must believe two things—that diffusion takes place in opposite directions, not only through the scutellum but also through the endosperm, and that diastase is an easily diffusible body. We know diffusibility is not a property of diastase. The production and presence of naked diastase in the endosperm, no doubt stimulated by the growing embryo, is, to my mind, the most reasonable explanation, and it will carry all the facts, which occur to me, relative to the germination of barley. I say naked diastase, because I believe it is not enclosed in cells, otherwise we could not extract it as easily as we do."

I fail to see that we are reduced to choose between the above assumptions. Messrs. Brown & Morris, in their investigations above mentioned, claim to have established that diastase (as well as the cellulose-dissolving enzyme) is secreted in the "absorptive epithelium," in which case it is of course in practical contact with the endosperm; and even though not in itself diffusible (which we know it is not, otherwise it could act upon the starch granules of unmalted grain in the cold), yet it is conceivable that it may undergo changes sufficient to enable it gradually to permeate the entire endosperm at a rate corresponding with the results of Mr. O'Sullivan's experiments. Fourteen or fifteen years ago Pfeffer (*Landwirthschafftliches Jahrbuch* 1876) showed that this change in the direction of diffusibility (enabling them to pass through membranes) was exercised upon *all* the albuminoids by **asparagin**, a nitrogenous organic compound, having the formula $C_4H_8N_2O_3$.

Then, having performed this function, the **asparagin** seems gradually to disappear as such, being reconverted into a protein body serving as nutriment for the young plant. If this be correct, we must probably look elsewhere for the genesis of **peptase,** to which the peptonisation of albuminoids in the mash-tun is attributed. As to peptase, there seems to be a fair *consensus* of opinion that it exists in germinated, but not in ungerminated barley; that its most favourable medium is a distinctly acid one (*e.g.*, wort containing as much as 2% of lactic acid), in this resembling the pepsin of the gastric juice, whence its name was suggested; and that high temperatures are fatal to it (although solutions of albumen heated to a high temperature under pressure are peptonised, not however by the agency of peptase). Its range is, in fact, as limited as that of diastase. Thausing affirms that the peptase of kiln-dried malt is much more energetic than that of air-dried malt, but gives no evidence to confirm this statement, the correctness of which, in any case, must depend upon the conditions under which the kilning process was carried out.

The "pitting" referred to is the action which is found to occur in the neighbourhood of the acrospire upon the cell-walls (amylo-cellulose) of the starch-cells, whereby the valuable contents, the far more soluble granulose, is set free. Examined under the microscope with one-quarter to one-tenth objective, this pitting is observed to take the form of cracks in the cell-wall, often roughly radiating from a common centre.

In fact, constantly recurring change and reconstruction, in the opposite direction of diffusibility and non-diffusibility, appears to be the dominant note of germination. Starch, albumen, and fatty matters, as such, are not diffusible; yet they are required for the development of the new cells of the embryo and of the rootlets *in which* even starch is found. It is therefore extremely probable that the granulose of the starch, as soon as the confining cell-wall has been eroded by the solvent (cytohydrolyst), gets acted upon by the diastase, and becomes converted into dextrin and sugar, penetrating in the latter form through the scutellum to the embryo, where it forms the material for the formation of new cells—

perhaps being converted into cellulose, too, to some extent —but reverting, as to its unconsumed portion, to the form of starch again in the newly formed cells.

Carbohydrates, both soluble and insoluble, other than starch, are found both in germinated and ungerminated barley. Amongst the former—as the reader who has noted the stimulative effect of various assimilable carbohydrates upon excised embryos will be prepared for—is cane-sugar, the proportion of which is considerably increased during germination, though (and here Mr. O'Sullivan's conclusions appear at variance with those of Messrs. Brown & Morris, who found cane-sugar, as such, more stimulative than either dextrose or levulose) it is, according to Mr. O'Sullivan, rapidly converted, for the nourishment of the young plant, into its assimilable inversion products, dextrose and levulose. That investigator however, states that in germinated barley the former is always in excess of the latter, which points to one of two alternatives (seeing that cane-sugar is by inversion split up into *equal* parts of dextrose and levulose), either that the levulose is more rapidly assimilated by the young plant, or, which is more probable, that dextrose is formed from some of the other carbohydrates.

On these (a and β amylan), on casein, an insoluble albuminoid, and on the mineral matters contained in the germinated or ungerminated barley, there is not space to dwell further than to remark that the latter are, to some extent, withdrawn from the grain, during germination, into the rootlets. The rootlets show upon incineration a much higher percentage of ash (due to inorganic or mineral constituents)—viz., 6% to 10%, whereas barley has about $2\frac{1}{2}$%.

However skilfully the maltster may work his material, a loss of useful substances during germination is inevitable. Valuable starch is turned into worthless cellulose and into acid, which though probably useful in moderation, will represent a distinct waste, as well as be an indication of positive danger if allowed by careless manipulation (too high a temperature on floors, too much heat applied to green malt when loaded on kiln) to become excessive. In any case a loss of weight occurs proportional to the quantity of carbonic acid gas, and even to that of the moisture in excess of the quantity actually applied, which are given off.

Here I must make some reference to what may be styled **the Bacterial Theory of Diastase,** stating the case by drawing upon two works, one of which, " The Parasitical Bacteria of Cereals," by Dr. H. Bernheim, I have only seen extracts of; the other, however, a pamphlet called " Enstehung und Fermentwirkung der Bakterien," lies before me. Dr. Bernheim believes himself to have proved that bacteria capable of promoting germination are to be found in the interior of uninjured corn. He has, he states, produced pure growths of these bacteria, and declares that though their increase is enormously rapid during germination, it proceeds *pari passu* with diastasic capacity. Any experiments made to find out whether barley, to a certainty free from bacteria, can secrete the diastatic enzyme, is foredoomed to failure, because conditions which are fatal to bacteria would destroy the germinating capacity of the grain itself. But one statement, if correct, which he advances, seems a very strong argument—viz., that a pure growth of these bacteria of cereals, cultivated in glutine, possesses the property of so transforming the latter, that its filtrate, if warmed with starch, will, after a few minutes' digestion, convert the latter into dextrin and sugar.

The view that bacteria do possess the power of secreting a diastasic, or at least diastase-like enzyme, is not so much in dispute; indeed, Herr Wortmann's observations seem to prove it, with this limitation, that in a mixture of starch and proteids, bacteria, as long as they are plentifully supplied with proteids, refuse to excrete the diastase-like enzyme, which they produce in abundance if only carbohydrates are available—a statement which forms an interesting corollary to the discovery of Messrs. Brown &

Morris, that the secretion of the same enzyme is inhibited in growing plants by the presence of abundance of assimilable carbo-hydrates.

Herr Albert Wigand, Professor of Botany at Marburg, the author of the pamphlet, seems to have made very careful observations, some of which have been confirmed by, or even have perhaps anticipated those of our latest investigators, notably in regard to the relation of the embryo to its endosperm being that of a parasitic plant to its host-plant, though maybe he does not state it quite so strongly. He says: "The ferment is not necessarily produced, as is generally assumed, by the activity of the germinating plant, but in reality by bacteria, or by a special condition of the protoplasm of certain cells referable to the formation of bacteria.

I derive this conclusion from the following facts:—

1. In the maceration of farinaceous seeds, whether they germinate or not, and equally so in the maceration of flour with water, the starch-granules undergo the said corrosions (*i.e.*, pitting), and in every case bacteria are copiously developed.

2. When bacteria are added to powdered wheat starch, whether the former are got from decaying peas, from beer-yeast, or from decaying flesh, a diastasic action follows.

3. Even when powdered wheat starch is submerged in distilled water and the vessel closed with wadding, numerous bacteria are at once found therein; and some days later isolated corrosions appear, and after a still longer time a part of the starch-granules is completely dissolved in the form of sugar. The same happens in the case of potato-starch, but to a less extent.

From this it may be concluded that in many cases at least the diastasic action is not bound up with the process of germination, but with the activity of bacteria, in this wise, that a fluid ferment, converting starch into sugar, viz., diastase, is excreted by bacteria. . . . Besides this transformation of the starch, a dissolution of the cellulose, resulting in a conversion into sugar, also occurs in the various sorts of corn, which, without doubt, is equally due to bacterial activity. This takes the form of a disorganisation of the cell-walls, which soon melt into shapeless slimy strings, and later on become completely liquefied. In conformity therewith the farinaceous body first appears, as it were, a thick viscous broth, and finally like a milky emulsion. And this dissolution of the cell-walls indeed precedes the conversion of the starch, so that the starch-granules floating freely in the liquid come into contact with the diastase distributed in the latter." [Then after a highly controversial statement about the origin of these bacteria, our author goes on.] "Still what has been said about the origin of diastase requires some important modifications, and indeed limitations. When wheat grains are cut asunder, so that the bottom half alone is provided with a germ, and if the two halves are placed separately in a moist medium, then there at once follows in the germ-containing half an abundant diastasic action, but in the germless half, on the other hand, either (as mostly happens) no diastasic action at all, or at most a very much feebler one. . . . This agrees with the fact that in germination the corrosions of the starch granules begin in the closest proximity to the scutellum.

Yet that it is not the process of germination, but the substance of the germ, which is in itself the source of the formation of diastase, appears beyond doubt from the fact that the latter appears to be developed continuously, even when the germ is kept in check by isolation or cutting asunder. The outer part of the scutellum lying on the farinaceous body of gramineous plants is enveloped in an epithelium of palisade-shaped cells, which, on the one side, have the function of sucking out from the farinaceous body the stores of food liquefied by the germination, and, on the other, of carrying them to the growing plant. It is just in these cells, however, that the source of diastase-formation lies."

Our author adds that although the diastasic influence of the scutellum is essentially heightened as a general rule by germination, yet it is not absolute, for the starch-granules in grains of maize always undergo a conversion into sugar just the same, whether the germ be removed or not, if bacteria are formed in them under the influence of moisture. " On the other hand, though degermed seeds usually undergo no conversion of their starch during maceration, yet isolated *plumulæ* mixed with bean or wheat starch cause abundant corrosions."

I have translated as literally as I can the quotation from Dr. Wigand, though diffuse sentences might bear condensation. It has been my wish, however, to give the evidence for the bacterial origin of diastase as fully as space will allow. Undoubtedly the establishment of this view would tell strongly for the now almost exploded theory of spontaneous generation, save that the conditions obtainable are obviously not such as to ensure that complete prior sterilisation which is necessary to prove or disprove that theory.

What the professor's own contention is may be gathered from his statements that the origin of these bacteria lies in " a transformation of the protoplasm as I" (Dr. Wigand) " have directly observed in the peripheral albuminous cells of a grain of corn," and again that " the protoplasm which fills them (the palisade-shaped cells of the epithelium) undergoes during germination, just as much as during simple maceration, an alteration of character, so that the mass, at first finely granulated in an irregular way, is transformed into a number of larger regular granules of equal size, which exhibit an active swarming movement of vital character, and between which, here and there, small rods are also found. If a section made through the scutellum, so that the contents of the wounded cells find their way into the surrounding water, be kept under a covering-glass, then within a day those little dancing bodies, which have become free, *are transformed into the usual rod-like bacteria.*"

Good Malt, Data for judging.—The section will be incomplete without a brief catalogue of the physical aspects of the malt best calculated to carry out the chemical programme which the brewer wishes to arrange. Good malt, then, will be free from crushed and mouldy grains and adherent rootlets. It should be of a uniform bright colour, free from dark-tipped grains, and with a thin smooth skin. The skin on either side of the acrospire should never have the "cridled" look of barley which, Ford says, "proves one of two errors—either that it has been forced too much in the young stage of malting, hence the conversion was not perfect, or that the heat upon the kiln was too high before the steam was well off." A rough wrinkled skin may also indicate insufficient ripening of the barley from which the malt was made.

When bitten, malt should be tender, yet crisp, full of flour from end to end, and with no ricy tips. Hard or vitrified particles in the flour indicate either excess of nitrogenous matter, or too sudden an application of heat on the kiln; the extract from malt containing them is seldom satisfactory. Partial over-curing—some of the grains having their contents semi-caramelised like those of brown malt—must be guarded against. Such grains are easily detected with a little practice. Their presence indicates very faulty drying conditions, and they may give far too deep a tint to the worts. When the acrospires taken from a few of the grains spring asunder under the knife upon being cut, it is a guarantee against excessive slackness and, to some extent, of proper curing, though the expert empiric determines this by the amount of flavour. Whether the acrospires should be two-thirds or three-quarters up is a matter of taste. I should prefer three-quarters as a general rule (especially when the barley is not kindly, if they can then be got to grow so far), but uniformity is the main thing. Undergrown stuff, which is virtually almost barley, should never be bought.

In sampling it is no bad plan to count out 100 grains and divide them according to their degree of growth, thus getting the percentage of grains which are three-quarters " up " or more, two-thirds " up," one-half " up," less than half, idlers, etc. Lastly, in buying malt, a lookout should be kept for holes, generally near the acrospire, the work of weevil. These, by the way, should be looked for most carefully when purchases of foreign barley are made. Similar holes have lately come under my notice in a sample of Morocco barley; but in this case the punctures were the work of grubs or caterpillars which had eaten out the greater part of the interior, and assumed the chrysalis form, the slough of which was generally to be found within the husk; though sometimes the developed, though defunct, moth was in evidence.

Pneumatic Malting.—Though I have not space to say much about Pneumatic Malting, which has not hitherto found great favour amongst English maltsters, it cannot be ignored, especially as the modern development of the drum system (Henning's patent) bids fair to obviate previous drawbacks. In the original system of M. Galland the germinating barley was placed in closed vessels provided with a suction-fan, which exhausted the air heated by the vital processes and contaminated by carbonic acid gas, and sucked in air kept cool and moist by being drawn through a bed of coke, on which cold water was continuously sprayed. In spite of the obvious drawback that the grain, incapable of being shifted, grew into a tangled mass, and that the malt had the character of being less tender than that produced in the ordinary way, very good beer was produced by using it.

Certainly some of M. Galland's own beer, brewed at Maxéville near Nancy, was far and away the best French beer I have ever tasted, and not inferior to Viennese brands of repute. The former inconvenience is obviated by the introduction of revolving drums, arranged so as to take a wetting apiece, and capable of being supplied with cooled, moist, and pure air; and it is claimed, moreover, that the erection of a malting on this system results in great economy in prime cost, space, and working expenses.

The Economics of Malting.—Though one man can work a 15-quarter house wetting 45 quarters a fortnight, it takes from ten to twelve men and a foreman in large houses to work an average of 480 or 490 quarters in the same time. Of course, unless the single hand is an exceptional man, the work in the larger houses is better done. This is equally true, assuming the foreman to be efficient, if the men are individually less skilful than the "single-handed" worker. Coal brought in at 20*s.* a ton, or even under, may (though I don't advocate cheap materials myself) be made to dry from 30 to 35 quarters; and thus the nett expenses (excluding interest on capital, remuneration for personal attention, expenses in attending markets, and similar items which the maltster for sale must reckon in) should not exceed 1*s.* 6*d.* per quarter, and may be kept below it if malt-dust and kiln-dust sales cover 25% of this gross expense, as they may very well do.

This, too, without allowance for increase, which varies from 3% or 3½% in well-managed brewers' malthouses, to anything you please in maltsters'. Of course, too, the season makes a difference. With good dry barley a 5% increase is not unusual, and where foreign barley is malted more may be looked for; at least, where the malt is used in the brewery *by measure,* while the barley itself comes in *by weight,* the increase seems to become something phenomenal. Of course any increase, beyond some 5%, is only apparent.

Nowadays the natural desire of maltsters, who are not brewers, for increase, conflicts with their equally natural desire to get weighty malt by undergrowing it.

CHAPTER III.

WATER FOR BREWING.

PURE WATER—VARYING WAYS OF EXPRESSING RESULTS OF ANALYSIS—RULE FOR HARMONISING—ORGANIC MATTER NOT DIRECTLY DETERMINABLE — ORGANIC CARBON — ORGANIC NITROGEN — TYPICAL ANALYSES—RATIO OF ORGANIC CARBON TO ORGANIC NITROGEN—NITROGEN AS AMMONIA—NITRATES AND NITRITES—AMMONIA PROCESS—MOIST COMBUSTION PROCESS—PHOSPHORIC ACID AND SULPHATES IN POLLUTED WATER—HEISCH (SUGAR) TEST—HANSEN'S METHOD—GENERAL CONDITIONS OF WATER SUPPLY — HARDNESS — SULPHATES — BICARBONATES — SILICA—CHLORIDES—EFFECT OF VARIOUS SALTS ON TYPE OF MALTO-DEXTRIN—KAINIT—ALKALINE SULPHATES—CARBONATES—IRON—TREATMENT OF BREWING WATER—BURTONISING—DOUBLE DECOMPOSITIONS—CLARKE'S PROCESS FOR SOFTENING WATER—EASY QUALITATIVE TEST OF PURITY OF WATER—ANALYSIS.

PURE water may mean one of two things—viz., either the pure water of the analytical chemist, corresponding as closely as possible to the formula H_2O, or, on the other hand, it may mean, and generally does mean, water which, though charged with gases such as carbonic acid and nitrogen, the origin of which (beyond the quantity derived from the air*) may be referred to the oxidation of organic matter, and with a reasonable quantity of dissolved solid or saline constituents, yet shows no evidence of recent contamination to anything like a dangerous extent. Contamination, even in a past not necessarily very remote (of which a high amount of total inorganic

---

* Which in the case of carbonic acid, the principal gaseous product of oxidation, seems to be small. Thus lake water contains at most 1 part in 400, whereas *good* well water may have quite 8 gallons CO_2 in 100 gallons of water.

nitrogen—*i.e.*, nitrogen existing as ammonia and nitrates —is held to be an index), must be taken into consideration; for though the condition of things which produced it may have ceased for a time, there is a possibility that the stoppage may be only intermittent—*i.e.*, that the aëration, soil-filtration, etc., which have broken up the original organic matter may fail, and the pollution be renewed.

The former type of purity is probably never found uncombined in nature, and even laboratory experiments have failed to eliminate the trace of nitrogen, which prevents the ideal formation of H_2O from being attained. In fact, it has been suggested that it is this inseparable trace of nitrogen which alone renders the boiling of water, in the ordinary sense of the word, a possibility, that, without it, heat would reduce the fluid into its elements. However this may be, the distilled water of the chemist is far from being absolute H_2O, though sufficiently near it for all the purposes of his operations.

Of dissolved saline constituents the brewer tolerates, and indeed desires, a larger quantity than would always be wished for in a drinking water, where the presence— though allegations as to their injuriousness to health have yet to be proved—of salts of lime and magnesia in the form that precipitates on boiling (the bicarbonates, or so-called carbonates) is clearly undesirable in view of the deposit produced by them—the too-well-known "fur"—in kettles and domestic boilers.

But for actual brewing operations it seems to be clear, in spite of some revision of views formerly held, that relatively large quantities of sulphate of lime, or gypsum, more moderate quantities of the carbonate, though this is perhaps more questionable, and magnesic salts, or, on the other hand, the chlorides (calcic, magnesic, or sodic) which characterise a different type of water, are all in different ways distinctly useful.

But in any case, freedom from pollution is the question of capital importance, and the proportion of saline constituents is in the second line. I shall therefore deal with the more important point first, and as it appears to me that considerable mental confusion occurs in consequence of the varying methods of stating the results of analyses, I shall touch upon these several methods at some length, and trust to be able to throw a little light upon what they signify, for the benefit of those who have had little or no experience of operative water analysis.

Results are expressed sometimes in parts per 100,000 (German analyses in parts per 10,000); sometimes in "grains per gallon," which is equivalent to parts per 70,000 (a gallon = 10 lb. of 7,000 grains each), while "free and albuminoid ammonia" is estimated in parts per million—*i.e.*, milligrammes in the litre.

The following rules for converting results into uniform shape may be found useful:—

1. To convert parts per 100,000 into grains per gallon, multiply by ·7.

2. To convert grains per gallon into parts per 100,000 divide by ·7.

3. To convert grammes per litre into grains per gallon (*i.e.*, parts per 1,000, into parts per 70,000) multiply by 70.

(Consequently to convert milligrammes per litre into grains per gallon multiply by 70 and divide by 1,000, or multiply by ·07.)

Organic Matter not directly Determinable.—The actual amount of organic contamination (animal or vegetable) cannot be determined directly by any known method of analysis, but it is supposed that sufficient *data* for forming an opinion can be got by the three methods, which are ordinarily employed, or a combination of them. These are—

1. The combustion process, with which the name of Dr. Frankland is identified.

2. The ammonia process. (Free and albuminoid, otherwise saline and organic ammonia.) Prof. Wanklyn's process.

3. The moist combustion, or permanganate and potash, process.

Some details of the working of the latter two methods, the last in its simplest form, will be given in the chapter on laboratory work. Their practical bearings only will be considered here. The combustion process being too lengthy and difficult for amateur analysts, no attempt to describe the manipulation will be made here, or elsewhere, except in general terms; but an effort will be made to explain the results stated to be obtained by it, premising, however, that in carrying out the process, a small measured volume of water, amounting to a litre if the impurity is likely to be small, is evaporated to dryness, the carbonates having been got rid of previously by treatment with sulphurous acid solution. With the residue (every precaution having been taken to avoid loss or gain) an admixture of pure dry copper oxide is made, and the mixture is then heated in a furnace in a combustion tube of hard glass. The oxygen thereupon set free from the oxide attacks the organic matter and decomposes it, the resulting carbonic acid and nitrogen being then determined, and the amounts expressed in terms of **"organic carbon"** and **"organic nitrogen."**

Against this method Professor Wanklyn, championing his own ammonia process, has argued that the ignition of a water residue involves loss of the nitric acid, which exists in considerable quantity in most waters, and its replacement by an equivalent of carbonic acid [$HNO_3 = 1 + 14 + 48 = 63$ replaced by $CO_2 = 12 + 32 = 44$], this loss of weight being far larger than the organic matter. He also claims to have shown that where solutions of substances containing a known quantity of nitrogen have been tested, the experimental error has been so great as to annihilate the claims of the combustion process to any sort of accuracy.

Again, "previous sewage contamination," which is another feature of Dr. Frankland's method and the Registrar-General's reports, is also objected to by Sutton (Volumetric Analysis) *as introducing a theory*, and as placing a water without a trace of previous sewage contamination upon the same level as one with ·032 part of total inorganic nitrogen per 100,000, owing to the deduction of 320 made as a correction for the average inorganic nitrogen in rain-water. He prefers simply to state the total inorganic nitrogen—*i.e.*, the once organic nitrogen now represented by inorganic compounds, ammonia, nitrates, and nitrites, into which it has been transformed by oxidation. Professor Wanklyn goes further, and disputes the correctness of measuring defilement of water by the presence of nitrates and nitrites, which often come, he thinks, from the geological strata traversed by the water and apart from any possible contamination by organic matter.

Appended below are four fairly typical analyses borrowed from Sutton's "Volumetric Analysis,"* which will serve as a text for a few remarks on the meaning of organic carbon and nitrogen, their ratio to one another, etc. Except the hardness (and even hardness *may* be some indication, seeing that impure waters are generally very hard, owing to the fact that animal *excreta* contain large quantities of lime) and the "total solids," nothing is determined that has not to do with the purity of the water; for chlorine, though generally taken to be combined with sodium in the form of common salt (chloride of sodium), may in conjunction with other *data* have an important bearing on the question of contamination or freedom therefrom.

It may be useful to append to this set of analyses another set made by Messrs. Crookes, Odling, and Tidy of the London Water Supply, for the month of October 1881. It is expressed somewhat differently, and the numerical results are given in grains per gallon, whereas the first set are in parts per 100,000. As will be seen, the chlorine is calculated as common salt (in the analytical process chlorine is first determined by nitrate of silver solution, the result being multiplied by the factor 1·647), and the total solids are not given.

* A book published by Messrs. J. and A. Churchill, to be recommended to those who wish for a systematic handbook of the subject.

TABLE I.

Expressed in parts per 100,000.	Total Solids.	Organic Carbon.	Organic Nitrogen.	Ratio of Organic Carbon to Org. Nitro.	Nitrogen as Ammonia.	Nitrogen as Nitrates and Nitrites.	Total Inorganic Nitrogen.	Total Combined Nitrogen.	Chlorine.	Hardness. Temp.	Hardness. Perm.	Hardness. Total.
GLASGOW WATER (from Loch Katrine)	Clear, very pale brown	2·40	·124	·014	8·9 : 1	·001	·003	·004	·018	·76	…	…	·2
CATERHAM WATER WORKS (Deep Well) 1873	Clear	27·68	·028	·009	3·1 : 1	0	·021	·021	·030	1·55	15·2	6·0	21·2
Average Composition of Unpolluted Water.													
Deep Well Water— 157 samples	…	43·78	·061	·018	3·4 : 1	·010	·495	·505	·523	5·11	15·8	9·2	25·0
Spring Water— 198 samples	…	28·20	·056	·013	4·3 : 1	·001	·383	·384	·397	2·49	11·0	7·5	18·5

TABLE II.

Expressed in grains per gallon.	Appearance.	Matters in Suspension.	Ammonia.	Chlorine.	(Equal to Common Salt.)	Nitrogen.	(Equal to Nitric Acid.)	Initial Hardness.	O. required to Oxidise Organic Matter.	Organic Carbon.	Organic Nitrogen.	Free O. in Cubic Inches.
NEW RIVER COMPANY	Clear	None	None	1·12	1·82	0·203	0·914	15·7	·021	·055	·009	2·10
EAST LONDON COMPANY	Clear	None	·001	1·29	2·12	0·190	0·856	15·6	·040	·107	·014	2·02
LAMBETH COMPANY	Clear	None	·002	1·17	1·92	0·182	0·819	14·8	·064	·134	·020	2·07
GRAND JUNCTION COMPANY	Clear	None	·001	1·15	1·88	0·151	0·680	14·6	·053	·109	·014	2·09
SOUTHWARK AND VAUXHALL COMPANY	Clear	None	·001	1·15	1·88	0·168	0·756	14·6	·060	·121	·020	2·09

Before passing to the other heads of the analyses, a word or two more as to the suspicion attachable to the presence of chlorine in somewhat large quantity will not be out of place, in view of the rather large amount that the deep-well samples in the first set of analyses contain. Sutton holds that a water containing more than three or four parts of chlorine per 100,000 should be suspected (seeing that human urine contains about 500 parts per 100,000), but Wanklyn, more cautiously, says that five or ten grains of chlorine per gallon are not an absolute bar, even for drinking purposes, but only a reason for suspicion under certain circumstances.

In the particular case in question, if the water containing 5·11 parts of chlorine per 100,000 (=3·57 grains per gallon) showed a high proportion of organic nitrogen, say much above ·02, it would stand condemned of being unfit for use where a high standard of purity is desirable. A water, however, corresponding exactly to the average of these 157 samples would pass muster. Of course all the conditions would have to be passed in review; and the fact of the water coming from a deep well would tell distinctly in favour of the chlorine *not* being due to recent contamination, and therefore innocuous, if not positively beneficial, which, if combined with calcium or magnesium, it might very well be.

Hardness (temporary and permanent), as well as "total solids," will be referred to later.

Organic Carbon and Organic Nitrogen.—From these the existing condition of the water in respect of organic contamination is to be inferred. In a good water, fit for domestic purposes, the proportions should not under ordinary circumstances exceed ·2 part of organic carbon and ·02 part of organic nitrogen per 100,000. As Sutton, however, points out, the brown, peaty upland waters may contain much more organic carbon, derived from vegetable sources, than this without being condemned, although under usual oxidation influences the proportion, and consequently its ratio to the organic nitrogen, ought to be rapidly reduced. In deep wells, on the other hand, organic carbon, as might be expected, generally falls below the average.

In surface waters from cultivated soil or shallow wells the usual proportions range higher, organic carbon ·25 to ·30, organic nitrogen ·04 to ·05.

Ratio of Organic Carbon to Organic Nitrogen.—The ratio may vary from as much as 10 (or even in extreme cases 20) of carbon : 1 of nitrogen in upland waters and rivers near their source, to equality—viz., 1 of organic carbon : 1 of organic nitrogen—in polluted wells, and accordingly will furnish a useful indication of the origin of the organic matter—for example, thus :—

When the ratio of organic carbon to nitrogen is very high the organic matter is of *vegetable* origin; when the ratio is very low the organic matter is of *animal* origin. The significance, however, of these ratios seems, according to Sutton, to be obscured by the results of oxidation, which in the first case causes a more rapid loss of carbon, so that an originally high ratio of carbon to nitrogen gets considerably reduced; in the second case, on the other hand, the nitrogen disappears more rapidly, so that the ratio, originally low, increases.

Nitrogen as Ammonia (NH_3)—Ammonia in ordinary natural waters seems generally to be due to animal contamination. In upland surface waters, Sutton says, it seldom exceeds ·008 part; in water from cultivated land the average is about ·005. Wanklyn, speaking of "free ammonia," says when it exceeds ·08 part per million (= ·008 per 100,000) it almost invariably proceeds from fermentation of urea into carbonate of ammonia, and is a sign that the water consists of diluted urine in very recent condition. This water, he adds, will also be found "loaded with chlorides."

Ammonia being very readily oxidised to nitrates and nitrites, its presence in quantity generally indicates absence of oxidation, and usually coincides with the presence of organic matter. This general statement is more specifically borne out by Dr. Frankland, who states that he has succeeded in isolating certain microbes, which he calls **nitrifying organisms,** and which make ammonia (itself the product of decomposition) combine with the oxygen of the air, whereby it is converted into nitrous and nitric acids. These microbes are remarkable for the simplicity of their food requirements. They will produce nitric acid from ammonia in liquid practically destitute of organic matter. Indeed, it is only in such starvation media that they establish their supremacy; in more nutritious media other organisms crowd them out. In sewage, the professor adds, we find *no nitrification but much ammonia.* In such a liquid the nitrifying organisms bide their time till the other organisms have consumed all available nourishment and are perishing from want, then they step in.

Nitrogen as nitrates and nitrites, *i.e.*, combinations of nitric and nitrous acids (derived from oxidation of nitrogenous organic matter, probably as above) respectively with the bases (lime, etc.) existing in the water. The average, though variations are considerable, in deep wells is ·5 part per 100,000, in springs somewhat lower, but in water from some shallow wells, as might be expected, higher.

They are generally considered to be referable to the oxidation of *animal* matter, and, as such, pointing to a defilement (past as far as they themselves are concerned) of the water. Professor Wanklyn, as we have seen, objects even to this, holding them to be often derived from the geological strata which the water passes through. But he points out that vegetation processes in lakes and rivers are calculated to withdraw nitrates from the water.

However innocuous in themselves for potable purposes they may be, some interesting experiments by M. Émile Laurent seem to show that nitrites, at all events, are undesirable in a brewing water. Harmless as they would probably be in a neutral liquid, the nitrous acid set free from them in a faintly acid medium, such as fermenting wort, apparently exerts a very destructive influence on the growth and fermentative power of yeast.

Total Inorganic Nitrogen.—The sum of the nitrogen existing as ammonia + that present as nitrates and nitrites, being an indication of *past* contamination (as the organic nitrogen is of *present* contamination), it is therefore, apart from the possible evil influence of nitrites referred to above, mainly of importance as showing only *potential* mischief, which will not become actual as long as the necessary oxidising conditions of aëration and filtration continue. Obviously though, a high proportion of inorganic nitrogen renders the recurrence of actual contamination more probable.

The average quantity yielded by deep wells is ·5 part, by springs about ·4 part per 100,000; but though the conditions remain very constant for each well or spring, the range is very wide. As has been said before, "total inorganic nitrogen" corresponds nearly (certain rather arbitrary corrections being made) with Dr. Frankland's "previous sewage contamination."

The Ammonia Process depends upon the more or less brown coloration which water containing ammonia gives on the addition of a definite quantity of "Nessler's solution," and after the free, or as it is sometimes called, the saline ammonia has been determined in this way, the practice is to get at the albuminoid organic ammonia by adding a quantity of potash and permanganate solution, which, with the aid of heat, converts the existing nitrogenous matter into ammonia, and this is then determined by "Nesslerising" as before. In practice it is usual to take 500 cc. to distil over 200 cc., part of which is "Nesslerised" for the free ammonia, then to add the permanganate-potash to the 300 cc. left. More precise directions will be given in the chapter on laboratory work.

Objection made to Ammonia Process and its Answer.—Fault has been found with this process because there are nitrogenous organic substances which yield no albuminoid ammonia. But this inconsistency, as far as water is concerned, makes the process all the more valuable, seeing that the only one which is likely to occur, viz., urea, is just the one which is provided for. Chance nitro-compounds might, if detected, vitiate the conclusions to be drawn from the analysis.

The General Conclusions to which Professor Wanklyn comes are—Deep spring water is often so pure as not to yield ·01 part of albuminoid ammonia per million, and unless mixed with surface water does not yield as much as ·05 part. Free ammonia exceeding ·08 part per million almost invariably proceeds from fermentation of urea into carbonate of ammonia, and is a sign that the water consists of *diluted urine in very recent condition*. This water will also be found "loaded with chlorides." Much albuminoid ammonia, which generally "comes over" slowly, little free ammonia, and almost entire absence of chlorides, indicate *vegetable contamination*. Any water containing ·02 to ·05 part of albuminoid ammonia per million may be classed as very pure (of course when free ammonia is well under ·08), but there is good ground for suspecting a water containing a considerable quantity of *free* ammonia along with more than ·05 part per million of albuminoid ammonia. In the absence, or nearly so, of free ammonia a water need not be condemned on the score of its albuminoid ammonia unless the latter amounts to something like ·10 part per million.

The Permanganate or Moist-combustion Process, so called because it depends upon a combustion (in a chemical sense) of organic matter by oxygen set free from the permanganate, is, as Professor Wanklyn points out, very useful as an auxiliary to the ammonia process in helping to decide between ammoniacal deep spring water and sewage water. Such a quantity of potassium-permanganate ($KMnO_4$) is taken that 1 cc. of the standard solution = 1 milligramme of oxygen (or $\frac{1}{10}$ milligramme in the simpler process described in the laboratory chapter), and accordingly the number of cubic centimètres of the solution required just to retain a faint trace of the pink tint characteristic of the permanganate, exactly corresponds with the number of milligrammes (or tenths of milligrammes) of oxygen consumed by the organic matter in the quantity (usually one litre) of water dealt with. The results of the process are expressed in reports as "oxygen required to oxidise organic matter."

Professor Wanklyn states that the general conclusions to which his investigations point are that water distinctly of first-class purity does not consume more than ·5 *milligramme* of oxygen per litre (= ·035 grain per gallon), while average drinking water consumes from four to six times as much. Dr. Tidy considers water absorbing not more than ·05 grain of oxygen per gallon to be very pure, and those consuming between ·05 and ·15 grain of medium purity.

Objection made to the Permanganate Test.—Dr. Hassall has stated that though the permanganate readily gives up its oxygen to organic matter and nitrous acid (HNO_2) it fails to do so to nitric acid (HNO_3), the latter being an acid in the highest degree of oxidation of which it is susceptible; and this is the case even when the said acid is present in very large quantity, and therefore certainly indicating pollution, which, though not actively going on, may easily recur. On the other hand, its ready loss of colour in the presence of nitrous acid may lead, as in example No. 1 lower down, to the conclusion that a large quantity of albuminoid organic matter exists; in other words, that the water is undergoing extensive pollution at the time of analysis, whereas there is only evidence of past contamination—a much less serious state of things.

Dr. Hassall also points out that the permanganate is very sensitive to protoxide of iron—as might be expected, seeing that the iron compound always takes up oxygen very readily and passes to a higher oxide. This sensitiveness to the protoxide of iron, however, is apt to be misleading; for however undesirable from a brewer's point of view the presence of an iron salt may be, the reasons are different from those which make fair organic purity an essential. Instructive instances of employment of permanganate, where its indications were misleading, are given below.

	Total Solids.	N. as Nitrates and Nitrites.	Equal to Nitric Acid.	Organic Nitrogen from Albuminoid Ammonia.	Equal to Albuminoid Organic Matter.	O. required by the Organic Matter, Nitrites, etc.
No. 1.	120·8	2·30	8·87	·011	·14	·52
No. 2.	58·10	3·18	11·55	·006	·07	None.

	Total Solids.	N. as Nitrates and Nitrites.	Organic Nitrogen from Albuminoid Ammonia.	Equal to Albuminoid Ammonia.	Protoxide of Iron.	O. required by Organic Matter, and Protoxide of Iron.
No. 3.	23·0	None.	·01	·12	·39	·095

Remarks on the above.—In No. 1 a large quantity of the permanganate was decolourised by *nitrous* acid, and therefore the albuminoid organic matter (existing contamination), though really of very small amount, would, if this test alone had been relied on (the oxygen being multiplied by eight as the rule is), have come out 4·16 grains per gallon instead of only 0·14 grain. In No. 2 the absence of any action on the permanganate would lead to the conclusion that this was a very pure water; it had, however, been exposed to such extensive contamination in the past, that it would be hazardous to rely on the conversion of organic nitrogen into the innocuous nitric acid being always so completely and punctually performed. No. 3 shows how the decolourisation of the permanganate by the protoxide of iron may help to condemn a water otherwise extremely pure and suitable for drinking, if not for brewing purposes.

To summarise, as far as we have them, the analytical data which determine the purity of a water.

(i) Organic carbon should not much exceed ·2 part nor organic nitrogen ·02 part per 100,000.

(ii) Free ammonia should not exceed ·05 part, with the same of albuminoid ammonia per *million*.

(iii) Water consuming ·05 grain or less of oxygen per gallon is very pure; between ·05 and ·15 of medium purity.

Slovenly or Incomplete Statements.—It is perhaps impossible, except by such a comparison as the above, to bring the different systems "into line"; though there is reason to think that some unscrupulous analysts use the easier ammonia process, but state the results in terms of organic nitrogen (N = $\frac{14}{17}$ of the ammonia), a practice which Professor Wanklyn justly reprobates.

And though it is anticipating somewhat, this seems a suitable place for referring to his strictures on one mode of stating the results of analysis in regard to mineral solids—namely, that of stating the quantity of each metal and each acid radical in a given quantity of water. Of course, in analysing water, the sulphuric acid, the chlorine, the lime, the magnesia, etc., are determined as such, but it is usual to combine them on certain definite principles—*e.g.*, to combine the sulphuric acid with lime rather than with magnesia, the chlorine with sodium, and to get as much of the latter compound (sodium chloride = common salt) and carbonate of lime as the data will admit of.

On the other hand, it is claimed that a statement of results uncombined does not lend itself "to cookery," but only states ascertained facts. However, it does not readily show whether the water is acid, basic, or neutral; and to ascertain this the puzzled recipient "must divide every quantity of metal or acid radical by its equivalent, then add up the two sets of numbers, and note whether base or acid radical predominate."

Phosphoric Acid, Sulphates, and Hardness (?) as Evidence of Pollution.—Dr. Hassall says, that as phosphoric acid in a combined state as phosphates is a very common constituent of our food, its presence even in minute quantity is an evidence of pollution by sewage, but Wanklyn maintains that except as infinitesimal traces phosphates cannot co-exist with carbonate of lime in a clear water, supporting his contention on the ground that, upon dropping a few drops of a clear solution of phosphate of soda into a beaker of bright, clear water containing carbonate of lime, there will presently occur, upon stirring, a precipitate of phosphate of lime. [But refer next paragraphs on " Sugar (or Heisch) Test " as to phosphorus in an organic form of combination.] Dr. Hassall also suggests that sulphate of lime may, because of the presence of combined sulphuric acid in food, be indicative of sewage contamination; at any rate, as has been pointed out, owing to the large quantity of lime which animal *excreta* contain, polluted water is usually very hard.

Sugar (or Heisch) Test.—The value of this, the so-called Heisch test, has been questioned. The method is as follows. To a large test-tube containing a small quantity of the water to be examined, a little well-boiled (sterilised) sugar-solution is added, the tube then being closed with a sterilised plug of cotton-wool. It is kept for two or three days at forcing tray temperature (say 80° Fahr.), and if no fungoid filmy growth develops, the water is pronounced pure. But Dr. Frankland's experiments in 1871 tend to show that water known to be contaminated produces no film in the *absence of phosphates*, but does produce it directly phosphates are added, in which case its indications would be delusive.

But Messrs. Matthews and Lott ("Microscope in the Brewery and Malthouse," p. 151) have a higher opinion of the test. "It is performed by taking about 250 cc. of the water to be tested and adding to it 1 to 1·5 grain (? gramme) of pure recrystallised cane-sugar. The bottle containing these is put on the forcing-tank, and the appearance noted at different intervals during several days. Some waters remain quite clear, others become opalescent or milky, while those of the worst class go turbid, and smell strongly of butyric acid. The microscope will show the nature of the bacteria present. The test, according to Professor E. Frankland, indicates phosphorus in the water, and this contention has been sustained by one of us in a series of experiments on a great many samples of water; and as a rider to it the fact has been established *that butyric fermentations occur in the waters containing most phosphates,* other marked signs of contamination being at the same time afforded by chemical analysis" [The italics are the present writer's.]

Further, the former writer, referring to the fact that waters which develop organisms when tried by this test fail to do so after boiling, filtering, and retesting, says (*Brewer's Guardian,* 509), "It is not that the organisms originally present have been killed, but that the main feeding material has departed with the phosphoric acid"—precipitated on expulsion of the carbonic acid gas—"for the addition of mere traces of phosphoric acid to boiled water will suffice to give a fresh growth of organisms."

He adds that he has convinced himself by experiment that phosphorus in the organic form of combination, *e.g.*, in egg albumen, is a richer food for bacteria than inorganic phosphates + sugar, and that waters containing phosphorus in this form may be boiled and filtered and yet give bacterial growths, the phosphorus when in this form not being eliminated by boiling. As a consequence, waters which contain carbonates of lime and magnesia, and which develop organisms with the Heisch test after being boiled and filtered, probably contain organic matter of an albuminous character.

Hansen's Method.—The latest development of research in connection with the fitness of a water supply for brewing, tends towards simplicity, and promises results at least as satisfactory as, and far more intelligible than those of the more elaborate processes. In A. Jörgensen's words, "The principle of the method is that it is only necessary to know, for brewing purposes, whether the water contains such organisms as are capable of developing in wort and beer. To this end small quantities of the water in its original or diluted state are added to a series of flasks containing sterilised wort and sterilised beer. An examination of the flasks after incubation in a thermostat at 25° C. (= 77° Fahr.) for fourteen days will then afford information regarding the nature and number of the organisms present in the water in question."

Conditions of Water-supply, Spring and Well-water. —As the careful analyst, having to pronounce upon the qualities of a water, likes to learn as much about its source as he can, so the brewer may very well make himself acquainted with the conditions which determine a plentiful supply or the reverse, conditions, moreover, which stand in some relation to the quality. We may divide such supplies into spring and well water, the former not necessarily meaning a spring gushing from a rock or hill, but often merely a supply of water which rushes suddenly into a well, which is being sunk, when a porous stratum connected with a more or less distant gathering ground of rain is struck.

Thus clay is impervious to rain, and much money has been spent, where it has run deep, in fruitless efforts to get a sufficient supply of water therefrom; but if in such an attempt a porous stratum (of limestone, chalk, gravel, sand, etc.) were to be struck which ran without a " fault " * to some far-away and extensive gathering ground (*i.e.*, a large extent of porous soil) at a higher level, then a copious supply of water—spring water—would be obtained. And if the level of this distant gathering ground were very high compared with the depth to which the well was sunk, the water would rise up in, or even overflow the top

* A fault, geologically, is a break in the continuity of a stratum or strata, owing to the forces, which have been at some time or other at work, having first severed and then raised the strata on one side of the cleavage above or away from those on the other. The " throw " of the fault, as the amount of vertical displacement is called, may vary between an inch and several thousand feet.

of, the well, and would thus form what is known as an **Artesian well**.

On the other hand, if a well is sunk in a porous water-gathering soil, or even into and through a very shallow basin of clay, overlying such porous strata, which crop out all around the clay and extend for some distance, the water obtained will not be, in the same sense of the word, spring water, but well water. Such a supply of water is not obtained at once even in water-gathering strata; it is only when the water-level—a level varying at different seasons with past rainfall—and which is known as "the plane of saturation," is reached, that any considerable quantity of water can be obtained.

This "plane of saturation" is not uniformly level in the sense that the surface of a lake is level, but, the liquid being sucked up into the pores of the stratified rocks (much as a sponge absorbs water) by capillary attraction, it will vary with the porosity of those rocks, and the narrower the pores the higher the water will mount in them. Obviously, if one of the higher points of "the plane of saturation" be struck, the rate of percolation must be extremely slow.

In any case, the comparative slowness with which a sufficient supply of water percolates from such a saturation area into a well, will show the mistake that is sometimes made in sinking deep wells into the chalk. Of course, if a copious stream be struck, well and good; but this is always a chance, and it may be missed merely by a few feet. Consequently the safest and cheapest plan appears to be directly good water (taking the lowest dry-season "plane of saturation") is reached, to leave off sinking downwards, and to drive "headings," at right angles to the shaft, both on the chance of striking a spring and, still more, to form reservoirs in which the water can steadily accumulate. It is quite possible to sink and bore a well 500 or 600 feet deep into chalk without striking a proper spring, and the owner of such a well, sunk without "headings," can never rely, if he should want several hundred barrels of water for refrigerating, etc., on being independent of outside water supplies.

Natural Purification of Water.—The purification of water—that is, the conversion of organic matter, whether animal or vegetable in origin, into harmless constituents—is effected by means of the oxygen dissolved in the water. This process is as much a burning, and as much and no more an oxidation, as when coals are consumed in a grate. The oxygen of the air being much more soluble in water than its nitrogen, the ratio of oxygen to nitrogen is much greater in water than in air, so that the former is obviously in a very active state.

Accordingly, whether it be dissolved by the water directly out of the air, or be found by the latter imprisoned with air in the pores of the soil it traverses, it oxidises the carbon to carbonic acid (CO_2); that is to say, it turns noxious matter into a harmless and even desirable ingredient, which increases as the water gets more and more pure; though of course it is, in itself, no index of purity, as fresh contamination may be going on concurrently, and so the proportion of carbonic acid gas be ever increasing. As has been stated, good spring water may very well contain 8% by measure of carbonic acid. Again, oxygen oxidises the nitrogen of animal origin into nitric acid (HNO_3), which combines with the bases present (lime, etc.) to form nitrates. Nitrites, the salts of nitrous acid (HNO_2), point to partial, and perhaps incomplete, oxidation.

Hardness.—The so-called hardness of water is usually determined by the soap-test—*i.e.*, by shaking up a measured quantity of water with a measured quantity of a standard solution of soap, and observing the point at which the lather formed becomes permanent. The absence of lather at the first addition depends upon the fact that, where lime and magnesia are present in water, the soap forms insoluble compounds with them (oleates and stearates of lime and magnesia), and that only when they are entirely abstracted does the lather begin to form.

The readiness with which soap lathers when used with rain or other soft water is a matter of common observation. More details for manipulation will be given in the laboratory chapter.

In England the hardness is calculated on the (most probable) assumption of its being due to carbonate of lime, each grain per gallon shown to be present being called "one degree of hardness." On the Continent the estimation is generally expressed as caustic lime and in parts per 100,000. Obviously any such statement in terms of one salt is only conventional, and may cover a considerable error—*e.g.*, if much magnesia be present : 40 parts of magnesia in its simplest form of combination are theoretically able to precipitate as much soap as 56 parts of lime; and indeed Wanklyn says that one equivalent of magnesia consumes as much soap as one and a half equivalent of lime—hence, he says, 75 degrees of hardness count for 42 grains of carbonate of magnesia.

The hardness considerably decreases, as a rule, after boiling ; that is to say, a permanent lather is formed at an earlier stage with boiled water ; and it is accordingly useful to determine and state the degrees of hardness before and after boiling. Another name for the degrees of hardness which disappear is **"temporary hardness,"** that which remains after boiling being **"permanent hardness."** The temporary hardness is due to what are really bicarbonates (though often spoken of as carbonates) of lime or magnesia, though it hardly corresponds exactly, as even after prolonged boiling some two grains of carbonate per gallon remain in solution. Moreover, in some cases, some degrees of hardness are masked by the concurrent presence of carbonate of soda. But the general effect of boiling, or of a temperature near boiling, is to drive off the carbonic acid, which alone keeps the lime, etc., in solution, and thereby the bicarbonates are converted into carbonates, which precipitate. The permanent hardness is referable to the sulphates of lime and magnesia or to chloride of calcium.

The popular view (once universally held), that a good proportion of the sulphates mentioned, and particularly of that of lime, somewhat limits the solution of nitrogenous matter and of the colouring matters and bitter principles of the hop, is contested as to the former point by later investigators, who assert that the amount of nitrogenous matter extracted by a mash made with distilled water is practically identical with that extracted in a mash made, under precisely similar conditions, with a water treated with sulphate of lime (say twenty grains per gallon of anhydrous salt); indeed that, if anything, the distilled water showed the best results, the proportion of the desirable peptones and amides being higher in its case, though the total nitrogen (and *a fortiori* the proportion of the undesirable nitrogenous bodies) was somewhat lower.

The late Mr. Southby, experimenting with a hard water (containing as much as 55·7 grains per gallon of sulphate of lime and 13·8 grains of sulphate of magnesia) against distilled water, was, I believe, the first to prove that the benefit of water containing sulphates of lime and magnesia did not—as far as the malt was concerned—depend upon a diminished solution of nitrogenous matter, which he found to be practically identical with hard or with soft water (varying only by a decimal point), but on the fact that the sulphates appeared to exert some subtle influence which caused the nitrogenous matter, when rendered insoluble by boiling in the copper, to separate in a distinctly flocculent form; the wort, when filtered and diluted, showing very bright, whereas the distilled-water wort was cloudy throughout, even after filtration.

Obviously then, this suspended matter, which in the latter case is not unlikely to be the cause of a somewhat persistent turbidity, will in the former case be readily separated by drainage through hops in the hop-back, by precipitation on the coolers or by the mechanical action of the yeast. Thausing, recording experiments on decoction lines with waters dosed with sulphate of lime (gypsum) to a considerably larger extent than in Mr. Southby's experiments—viz., with as much as 140 grains per gallon and upwards—notes a similar effect. The wort ran from the mash-tun (the *Läuterbottich*) unusually light and brilliant, and after 1½ hour's boiling "broke" exceptionally well.

Further, Mr. Southby points out that these sulphates of lime and magnesia existing in the mashing liquor exert a slight, but distinct antiseptic influence—in other words, render the wort more capable of resisting the attacks of injurious organisms; and when it is considered what a relatively long time worts lie in a comparatively unprotected state, even in the best-arranged breweries, this benefit will not appear unimportant.

Second Benefit conferred by Presence of Sulphates. —Another recognised benefit of sulphate of lime in the brewing water is a limitation in the extraction of the rougher bitter flavour of the hop: thus the Burton brewers, using water containing very large quantities of that salt, are able to add probably half as many hops again as users of a water of which the hardness mainly depends on carbonates.* This is, of course, where high quality and a considerable amount of hop flavour are desired, a matter of great moment, and to it, I have very little doubt, the creamy softness which characterises the best Burton samples, with all their "cleanness" and "finish," is due.

There is an opinion, too, that another point in which water containing sulphate of lime has an advantage over water not containing it, is that **less colouring matter is extracted** by the former from the malt and hops, or, if extracted, that it is precipitated during boiling.

The most desirable proportion of these "permanent-hardness" sulphates (lime and magnesia) seems for general

---

* An analysis, for example, will be found at the end of this chapter, of a water (B) with which, even when moderately treated with sulphate of lime, it is found impossible to use more than ten to twelve pounds of hops per quarter, even for pale ales; much lower quantities being obligatory for bitter ales of less gravity.

purposes to vary between thirty to fifty grains per gallon, and even the latter amount might give unsatisfactory results in breweries, where it is the custom to derive a substantial portion of the extract from sugar in any shape. For black-beer brewing the presence of lime and magnesia sulphates are not beneficial.

Bicarbonates.—As has been already mentioned, the lime and magnesia held in solution, when combined with carbonic acid gas in the form of bicarbonates, are precipitated as carbonates when the carbonic acid is driven off by heat. Accordingly, if the brewing water were always submitted to a somewhat prolonged boiling and separation of the precipitate, the action of these salts would be *nil* as regards the mashing and boiling operations; but, as the heating of mashing and sparging liquor is usually conducted, doubtless appreciable quantities find their way, in the shape either of bicarbonates or carbonates, into the mash, where they form, in combination with the lactic acid present in the malt, lactates of lime or magnesia.

I believe that the presence of this normal lactic acid of sound malt (as distinct from the abnormal acidity of unsound malt) is an advantage, and that its abstraction is not only undesirable from the point of view of flavour, to the piquancy of which it almost undoubtedly contributes, of soundness which it helps, being, as far as it goes, a specific poison to the injurious organism known as *Bacterium lactis*, but that just as *in moderate quantity* it aids the action of the diastase, so in ampler measure it assists the action of the peptase (which requires an acid medium) in its important function of peptonising the albuminoid constituents of the wort, or, in other words, rendering them available as yeast nutriment.

Nor should I be surprised if subsequent experiment were to show it to be not without influence upon the extraction of a desirable hop flavour. For each of these reasons, fairly certain or purely conjectural, the retention of the lactic acid may be assumed as a thing to be aimed at, and accordingly the presence of bicarbonates or carbonates *may* explain certain negative, or worse than negative results which sometimes attend the so-called "Burtonising" of brewing water—*i.e.*, adding preparations containing sulphate of lime and other salts, or allowing the water to flow through a gypsum-tank on its way to the hot liquor-back.

Not wishing, however, to be accused of overstating the case, I may say that the quantity of carbonate of lime required to neutralise lactic acid would be as $10:9$. Now taking the normal proportion of free acid (calculated as lactic) = ·2 to ·3 per cent., the former of these being one part in $500 = 140$ grains per gallon. But the total carbonates in a water containing 20 grains of them per gallon would, taking the above ratio $(10:9)$ and assuming 1·25 gallon to be required to produce 1 gallon of wort, only neutralise (and that, if all the carbonates took part in the reaction) 22·5 grains of lactic acid or barely one-sixth part. However, it may be added that careful experiments by Dr. G. H. Morris have shown the acidity percentage in sound wort from the mash-tun to be not higher than ·073.

Although boiling and filtration (or even decantation) will eliminate carbonates in a laboratory, the same thing is not so easily done in a brewery. Boiling, however, is certainly an advantage, even if the removal of the carbonates be not specially desired, being destructive of any full-grown organisms which may be in the water as well as a stimulant to their spores or germs, invulnerable, as such, even to boiling temperatures, to assume the form of developed organisms, as which they are capable of being destroyed by boiling or even lower temperatures.

On the other hand, the presence of moderate quantities of carbonate of lime and magnesia is circumstantial evidence of the good quality of the water containing those salts. There are occasionally large fissures in the chalk formation, through which polluted water may find its way wholesale; but as a general rule, owing to the filtration and aëration which the fluid undergoes while passing the pores of masses of chalk, it is usually extremely pure provided it is drawn from fairly deep wells.

Silica is only of importance to the brewer inasmuch as in conjunction with carbonate of lime it forms that rock-like precipitate known as "scale" in boilers, etc., or "fur" in kettles, and which tends to choke the supply-pipes leading from the hot liquor-backs to the mash tun. This risk of gradual stoppage of the pipes is another reason for a preliminary boiling of the mash-liquor, in a distinct vessel if possible, where the precipitate can be more easily dealt with.

It is impossible to remove this scale by tapping the pipe or expanding it by the sudden application of heat outside because of the envelope of non-conducting composition with which the latter is usually covered; nor are the copper pipes capable of standing much rough scraping, so that the only alternatives are either to sacrifice the pipes when they get nearly choked, or to treat the separate lengths with strong muriatic (commercial hydrochloric) acid, which, though a dirty and unpleasant job, can be so managed that the scale gets broken and loosened sufficiently for a moderate scraping with a long-handled scraper to remove considerable pieces of the scale, especially after a short soakage with alkaline water and steaming.

The writer has carried this plan out more than once, and when the scale has been of a very obdurate nature; but he has found that contact with the acid must be for a prolonged time, say for twenty-four hours, and that the pipe, with a dummy-flange, cut out of sheet iron and bolted on to each end, must be shifted from time to time (the dummy flanges are better than bungs, which are apt to be blown out owing to the rapid evolution of gas), and that only small quantities of the acid can be put in at a time.

Silica is present in most waters, a thing not to be wondered at when we remember how omnipresent it is in nature. It has been pointed out by J. O'Sullivan that the cellulose fibres of barley husks and of the chaff of wheat are shaped, so to speak, on a skeleton of silica; and in fresh water streams and the depth of ocean are innumerable multitudes of tiny Diatoms reabsorbing and forming their myriads of minute shells from the silica continuously eroded by rain, and carried down to their sphere of operations by streamlets into rivers, and rivers into seas, and reforming anew with their allies the Foraminifera (which construct their shells of carbonate of lime), the sedimentary rocks, just as those which underlie this earth of ours were formed and reformed in countless bygone ages.

Chlorides.—As some brewing centres have gained fame in consequence of the water available there containing sulphates, so others depend for their value mainly on chlorides. Chlorides of calcium and magnesium appear to determine, especially in conjunction with those of sodium and potassium, a full and rich flavour, which those who have tasted certain Scotch ales and compared them with their English rivals will be aware of.

A proportion of chlorides which might be expected to give marked results would be about seven or eight grains of calcic chloride per gallon, six or seven grains of magnesic chloride, ten grains of potassic chloride, and eight of that of sodium per gallon. It may be found advisable to increase the calcic at the expense of the magnesic salt and the sodic at the expense of the potassic, but it will not be overlooked that many waters already contain chloride of sodium (common salt) in some quantity.

The improvement effected by adding this alone is easily put to the proof, and a good deal more than the quantity given can sometimes be used with advantage, especially in the brewing of black beers. The other salts of course will be cautiously added, it being always advisable for the brewer, in this as in other changes, to feel his way before materially altering the character of his beer.

I may perhaps state that I have known common salt to

SALTS AFFECTING TYPE OF MALTO-DEXTRIN.

be added at the rate of one pound per quarter of malt to the liquor in the mash-tun (there were internal rakes only, so that all the liquor was got in before mashing began) without any restrictive effect upon the subsequent fermentation. This, at the rate of two barrels of mashing liquor per quarter, would actually amount to ninety-seven grains per gallon. This amount would, however, be diluted to at least the half by sparges by the time that the wort was gathered in the copper; but even then the quantity was high, and might easily reach the excess on which prosecutions have from time to time been based.

Effect of various Salts on the Type of Malto-Dextrins.
—Dr. Moritz, in a valuable paper on Malto-dextrins (the *compounds* of maltose and dextrin which are stated to impart palate-fulness and condition), gives some interesting parallel mashes of malt (1) **With Distilled Water**; (2) **With Gypsum** equal to 50 grains SO_3 per gallon = 85 grains of the anhydrous salt; (3) **With Calcic Chloride**, 37·5 grains per gallon.

The experiments were made, apparently, not so much to determine the actual amount of malto-dextrin, as whether it was of the higher or lower type (see p. 295)—*i.e.*, one in which dextrin preponderated, or one in which maltose preponderated. As will be seen, the water treated with calcic chloride gave a wort containing a lower type of malto-dextrin,—*i.e.*, one which would ensure rapid condition, and therefore, according to present views, would answer best for short-storage beers.

The gypsum liquor, showing higher malto-dextrins, appeared to be suited for long-storage beers. The distilled liquor gave less malto-dextrin altogether, a lower quantity, in fact, than is deemed desirable.

It will not be overlooked, however, that these are laboratory experiments which sometimes show different results—and not least of all when dealing with the types of malto-dextrins—from actual brewery operations. The results were as follows:—

(1) $\begin{cases} \text{Maltose} & . \quad 6\cdot29 \\ \text{Dextrin} & . \quad 6\cdot88 \end{cases}$
$\qquad\qquad$ ——$13\cdot17$

(2) $\begin{cases} \text{Maltose} & . \quad 6\cdot80 \\ \text{Dextrin} & . \quad 9\cdot12 \end{cases}$
$\qquad\qquad$ ——$15\cdot92$ $\Big\}$ As Malto-dextrin.

(3) $\begin{cases} \text{Maltose} & . \quad 9\cdot01 \\ \text{Dextrin} & . \quad 6\cdot35 \end{cases}$
$\qquad\qquad$ ——$15\cdot36$

Kainit.—In some cases Kainit, which is a natural mixture of salts, may be added with advantage in its purified state. As far as my own experience goes, I used it rather freely with one water, which was practically river-water filtered, adding 2 oz. per barrel of mashing liquor (which works out 24 to 25 grains per gallon), but without chloride of sodium; on the other hand, with the water, B, given at the end of this chapter, no benefit could be traced. According to Langer ("Lehrbuch der Chemie," u.s.w.) it contains 20% of potassium sulphate, its formula being $K_2SO_4 + MgSO_4 + MgCl_2 + 6\ H_2O$, or potassium sulphate, magnesic sulphate, and magnesic chloride + 6 molecules water of crystallisation.

Sulphates of Potash and Soda.—Different opinions exist as to the sulphates of potash and soda. Mr. Southby, however, says there is "no doubt that the sulphates of the alkalies have a tendency to cause thinness of palate and a peculiarly poor and, at the same time, harsh flavour in ales. It has been also said that they prevent the ales fining, but I have never been able to find any proof of this assertion."

As a rider to this statement I cannot resist appending, towards the end of this chapter, two analyses (A and *a*) of the same water, the supply of a brewery turning out export beers of considerable stability and, as I am credibly informed, ales, in which a much larger proportion of hops is used than by the brewers employing water B and b, yet without the "harsh flavour" spoken of being apparent.

Carbonate of Soda or Potash.—Whatever the truth about the sulphates, there is universal agreement as to the carbonates of soda and potash. They are distinctly bad, and even for black-beer brewing, for which they have sometimes been thought desirable, the same may be affirmed to a moderate extent. The extractive nature of the water containing them determines the solution of colouring matter from the materials employed, as well as the extraction of a rank bitter from the hops; it also probably facilitates the extraction of an intractable type of nitrogenous matter, and, perhaps more demonstrably, by masking the acidity of the wort, leads to a precipitation of useful peptones.

For getting rid of these obnoxious ingredients treatment with sulphurous acid or with calcic chloride has been suggested. The addition of the former, which of course must be used in the proportion indicated by the sums of the respective atomic weights ($Na_2CO_3 = 106$: $H_2SO_3 = 82$)—*i.e.*, 41 parts *by weight* of the acid to 53 parts by weight of the sodic carbonate, would result in the formation of sulphite of soda. This, which I believe was the basis of a certain so-called "Material" used with a view to producing a factitious paleness of wort, might have a similar result, sulphurous acid—a well-known *bleaching* agent—being again set free (as in the case of the "material") from the sulphite by the agency of the lactic acid of the mash. [It has been remarked, by-the-bye, in the use of the material, and even attributed to it as a merit, that casual contamination of the brewing water, which might otherwise be unsuspected, becomes revealed by an exceedingly pronounced sulphuretted-hydrogen smell, which the beer brewed with the said polluted water develops, it being alleged—with what correctness let those who use it say—that no such smell occurs with it when the brewing water is pure.]

Moderate alkalinity might be neutralised by utilising

the free sulphurous acid in bisulphite of lime. Thus, supposing the bisulphite to contain 580 grains of free anhydrous sulphurous acid per gallon, the use of 1 pint per quarter of the mash, which is usually considered safe enough, would neutralise about $1\frac{1}{2}$ to $1\frac{3}{4}$ grain per gallon of sodium carbonate.

The use of calcic chloride is recommended on the assumption that one of the so-called "double decompositions" will take place, resulting in the formation of chloride of sodium and carbonate of lime.

Iron in Water, of which traces are very general, exists usually in the form of bicarbonate of iron ($FeH_2C_2O_6$), which is precipitated on the expulsion of the CO_2 by boiling. It is also found as ferric sulphate or as protoxide of iron. A good deal of mysterious damage is attributed to iron—but certainly iron in solution forms with tannic acid (which, it will be remembered, is an important constituent of hops), tannates of inky hue, thus acting prejudicially in two ways—viz., imparting a bad tint to the product, and diverting part of the tannin from its proper function of precipitating a portion of the albuminoids (as tannates of albumen).

The development of "fuzzy heads" in fermentation has been supposed to be an outward visible sign of the presence of iron in some form, an opinion I merely state without intending to endorse it. If the water contains carbonate of lime, the latter, being precipitated on boiling, or to some extent as that temperature is approached, will carry down the iron with it; but in the event of there being iron but no carbonate of lime in the water, treatment of the water with carbonate of soda (5 or 6 grains per gallon) has been suggested, the carbonate of soda being afterwards rendered harmless by the addition of calcium chloride in excess, as recommended above. Of course time must be allowed for the precipitate to settle after boiling if such treatment is necessary; and it would be almost imperative to have a distinct hot liquor-back for boiling, whence the purified water could be slowly run into the vessel from which the mashing "liquor" is drawn.

Treatment of Brewing Water—Burtonising—Double Decompositions.—The treatment of brewing water for special defects has been referred to more than once in the last few pages, but there has, further than this, been so much anxiety to make brewing waters tally with Burton analyses that one cannot ignore it. Still it does not follow, as a matter of course, that the mere addition of sundry salts, and especially of sulphate of lime (gypsum), is going to produce the identical thing. Nor would it be well always to do so.

Brewers, who from the conditions of their trade or the arrangement of their plant find it advisable to use large percentages of sugar (invert or glucose), will certainly not find it to their advantage to use waters highly charged with gypsum. Whatever the cause—and I do not feel called upon to pronounce decidedly, though it may be conjectured, in the light of M. Hansen's discoveries, that the conditions are such as to give the predominance to some undesirable form of secondary (wild) yeast—the conjunction of a water containing much calcic sulphate with the employment of a considerable proportion of sugar, certainly seems to influence the production of beers having what, for want of a better name, may be called a "wiry" character.

If, however, it be desired to pass the water through gypsum, a good form of tank for the purpose is one with a central division going from the top to within about a couple of inches of the bottom. Both partitions (see illustration, next page) are then filled with pieces of gypsum (purchasable at Newark-on-Trent), and the water, being turned in, on one side, at B, speedily flows underneath the central division, $a\,a\,a$, and rises on the other side, flowing through the outlet, C, away to the heating tanks. The water is thus always flowing steadily, without any rush, as long as the inlet tap, by which its rate of flow should be regulated, is open. The tank need not be more than 4 feet 6 inches long by 4 feet 6 inches deep, by 3 feet wide. G G is the gypsum bed.

In such a tank the water, of which an analysis is given at the end of this chapter under heading B, acquired the character of *b*. The tank was only used for two hours, during which time not more than 16 barrels passed, including the quantity standing in the tank before the operation began; but this quantity was made up to 70 or 80 barrels with the ordinary liquor. Consequently, it

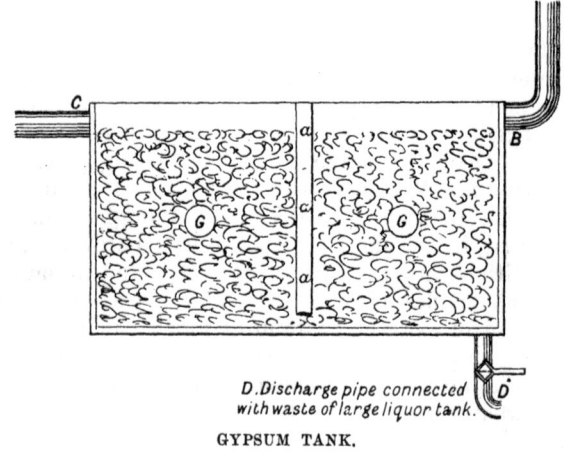

D. Discharge pipe connected with waste of large liquor tank.

GYPSUM TANK.

appears that the liquor which actually passed through the tank would have been impregnated (assuming the analysis to be correct) to the extent of 80 or 100 grains per gallon at least.

To carry off any slimy matter which may accumulate in the tank, a pipe with a stop-cock of wide aperture fitted to some point in the bottom of the tank, and with its other end connected with the waste-pipe from the large liquor-back, is probably the most effective arrangement. If, directly the stop-cock is opened, a downward rush of water from the larger reservoir be also started,

DOUBLE DECOMPOSITIONS. CLARKE'S PROCESS.

considerable suction will be caused, and the slimy matter thoroughly drawn away.

Double decompositions are those reactions in which two compounds take part, with the result of a formation of two fresh compounds. Thus in the one mentioned above, where calcium chloride added to water containing carbonate of soda forms calcium carbonate and sodium chloride, the formula $CaCl_2 + Na_2CO_3 = CaCO_3 + 2\ NaCl$ not only emphasises the fact but tells us, because

$$
\begin{array}{llll}
Ca = 40 & Na_2 = 46 & Ca = 40 & ^*Na = 23 \\
Cl_2 = 71 & C = 12 & C = 12 & Cl = 35\cdot5 \\
\hline
CaCl_2 = 111 & O_3 = 48 & O_3 = 48 & \\
& \hline & \hline & 58\cdot5 \\
& Na_2CO_3 = 106 & CaCO_3 = 100 & \times\ 2 \\
& & & \hline \\
& & & 2\ NaCl = 117
\end{array}
$$

that 111 parts by weight of calcic chloride added to 106 parts of sodium carbonate produce 100 parts of calcic carbonate and 117 of common salt.

A number of years ago Dr. Graham pointed out the probability of a similar double reaction upon the addition of sulphate of lime and chloride of sodium to water, resulting in the formation of sodium sulphate and calcium chloride.

Clarke's Process for Softening Water.—As this process is adopted in at least one very large brewery to my knowledge with useful results, it may be serviceable to set down the *modus operandi* here, as the patent rights have now expired. For each 1,000 gallons of water about 1 oz. of quicklime is required for each degree of hardness (*i.e.*, each grain of hardening matter per gallon reckoned as carbonates of lime). The quicklime being thoroughly slaked in a pailful of water the milk of lime thus obtained is poured into the cistern containing say 100 gallons of the water, which has to be softened, or any multiple thereof according to the quantity dealt with. The remaining 900 gallons (or a corresponding multiple) is then run in and roused to mix.

* Na (= Natrium) is the symbol for Sodium.

The whole body of the water will now appear very milky owing to the formation of chalk, the carbonic acid which kept it in solution being abstracted by the caustic lime, this latter combination also resulting in the formation of more chalk, which gradually precipitates, and at the end of about twelve hours leaves the water clear enough for drinking purposes. If greater precision be aimed at, a drop or two of silver-nitrate solution may be added at intervals to a sample withdrawn in a white cup from the cistern. As long as there is lime in excess it will give a yellow or brownish coloration; but as soon as this gets very faint the inflow of hard water should be stopped.

Professor Wanklyn indicates a way for **accelerating the softening process.** He points out that, on performing the process in a large glass vessel, it will be seen that a layer of quite clear water makes its appearance on the top, and gradually extends downwards. "If we ask how this water has become clear, the only answer that can be made is, that the precipitate has moved down to the layer of water beneath it, and thereby rendered that layer thick; for had the precipitate not descended into it, it would, like the top layer, have become clear. In the same way, this second layer, by its depositing, renders that beneath it turbid. If such a vessel of water took six hours to clear, we should expect that by dividing it into six layers by means of five diaphragms, equidistant from each other and from the top and bottom of the water, that the water would clear in one-sixth the time, or one hour. On making the experiment, this is found to be the case.

To test this matter more fully, what may be called a "subsidence filter" was constructed. It consisted of a wooden box 12 inches square and 20 inches deep, containing 24 plates of sheet zinc $\frac{3}{4}$ inch apart. Each plate had 6 holes punched in it, 1 inch in diameter. The holes were near to the side, and had their edges turned up a little. The plates were so arranged that the holes were not opposite each other. A small tap came from just below the lowest plate. Another box like this, but without plates, was also constructed. Both boxes were charged with freshly softened water, containing chalk suspended in it. The water took about eight hours to clear in the box without the plates, and was quite clear in the one with the plates at the end of twenty-five minutes." The lesson learnt from this operation on a small scale might easily be applied on a larger basis, or might be extended to mechanical filtration generally.

Easy Qualitative Test.—If sudden doubt be felt as to the purity of the water supply, certain methods are available, which, though too "rough and ready" to be placed among tests proper, may yet be depended on as far as they go. One of these consists in the addition of a few drops of Condy's Ozonised Fluid to the suspected water, sufficient to give it a faint pinkish tinge. If organic matter be present the pink disappears in a greater or less time, and a brown precipitate (oxide of manganese) is formed, the organic matter being oxidised or burnt up; but if the water be pure, the pink colour remains. This action of the "Condy" may be manifested by putting into some water coloured with it a strip of clear white blotting paper, which consisting, as it does, of cellulose and other organic matter, will have the same effect upon the tinctured water.

Colour and Smell.—If two white glass cylinders (Nessler cylinders) be filled, one with the suspected and one with distilled water, and placed side by side on a porcelain tile, a yellow or brown tint (observed by looking down through the depth) in the former indicates organic matter, but not *necessarily* (unless in water previously pure) of a very objectionable type; for instance, water from a peaty source is often highly coloured.

Again, some of the water may be shaken up in a large wide-mouthed bottle, and the nose applied at once. Any objectionable smell will be more readily detected if the water be slightly warmed.

Organic Matter detected by Ignition of dry solid Residue.—Evaporate some of the water to dryness in a platinum dish, then hold over the flame of a Bunsen burner and observe if it blackens; this will indicate an appreciable amount of organic matter. A slight charring indicates a small amount of organic matter. As upon further heating the brown colour produced by the charring goes off, the maximum charring must be watched for.

Seeing that a sudden and temporary pollution of a water supply is within the range of possibilities, and might occur at a time when the immediate stoppage of the brewings would be impossible, it is well to be prepared with a remedy. If chloride of lime be boiled with the water at the rate of ten grains of the former to each barrel of the latter, the organic matter will be oxidised, and any chloride of lime remaining can be neutralised by the addition of a similar quantity of bisulphite of lime. But this, at best, can be only a temporary measure, and no delay should occur in getting a supply of pure water.

I now conclude this lengthy chapter—on a most important subject, however—with the analyses previously referred to as A and a and B and b.

Analysis A.

	Parts per 70,000.
Solid Residue at 212° Fahr.	29·42
Ammonia (= ·366 parts per million)	·0256
Albuminoid (= ·05)	·0035
Chlorine	3·99
Equal to Sodium Chloride (Common Salt)	6·57
Hardness before boiling (total)	2·91
,, after ,, (permanent)	1·63
,, lost in ,, (temporary)	1·28
Nitrogen as Nitrates	*Nil.*
Equal to Nitrate of Lime	,,
Organic Carbon	·123
,, Nitrogen	·0348
Ratio of Carbon to Nitrogen as	3·6 : 1
Total combined Nitrogen	·055
Fermentative action on pure Cane-sugar	Practically *Nil.*
,, ,, ,, (after boiling)	*Nil.*
Nitrites	,,
Appearance	Clear.

ANALYSIS a.

(*Same water, but a year or two later.*)

Ammonia	0·025
Carbonate of Lime and Magnesia	7·36
Sulphate of Lime and Magnesia	1·01
Alkaline Sulphates	12·42
Carbonate of Soda	3·10
Chloride of Sodium	6·67
Silica, etc.	·66
Alkaline and earthy nitrates	*Nil.*
Organic matter	·23
Total solid matter in grains per gallon	31·45
Hardness before boiling—degrees	5·25
,, after ,, ,,	·8

The report sent with A said: " In appearance it was clear, and it did not exert any appreciable fermentative action on a solution of pure cane-sugar. The analysis of the organic constituents, made by the combustion process of Drs. Frankland and Armstrong, shows the water to be one of average purity. The ammonia is doubtless of natural origin, and should not be confounded with the ammonia resulting from sewage decomposition. The albuminoid ammonia is not very large. The organic matter is more than usually exists in naturally pure water, but is of comparatively harmless character, and not resulting from sewage origin. Nitrates are absent, and the amount of salt, though high, is not of sewage origin, and therefore is not a sign of contamination. The hardness is by no means large, the principal part of the mineral matter no doubt consisting of alkaline salts. It is a water of average purity, and should produce good black beers, but is too soft to produce the best mild and pale ales."

It is interesting to compare the above independent analyses, which, though showing discrepancies—notably in the matter of hardness*—are fairly concordant in a general sense.

The other analyses, more than once referred to, are

* Various salts produce hardness, *e.g.*, the following numbers, repre-

below. B is the natural water, b the water after partial treatment in the gypsum tank.

The results are stated in grains per imperial gallon of 70,000 grains.

	B	b
Nitrogen as Nitrates and Nitrites	·1648	
,, = Nitric Acid	·74	
Oxygen required to oxidise organic matter	·074	
The mineral constituents are probably combined as follows:—		
Sulphate of Lime	3·71	33·10
Sulphate of Magnesia	...	...
Carbonate of Lime	16·37	16·37
Carbonate of Magnesia	6·61	6·61
Sulphate of Soda	...	...
Sulphate of Potash	...	...
Carbonate of Soda	...	...
Chloride of Magnesia	...	·71
Chloride of Sodium	3·80	3·80
Nitrate of Potash	1·19	1·19
Oxide of Iron	·21	·21
Silica	·84	·84
Organic matter	·59	·59
Total Solids	33·32	63·42

The report sent with the above was: " I find this water to be fairly pure; it shows no evidence of recent sewage contamination. The small amount of nitrogen, as nitrates and nitrites, which is present, is in all probability of mineral origin; no alkaline carbonates are present. In passing over the gypsum it has taken up 29·39 grains of sulphate of lime, and ·71 grains of chloride of magnesia per imperial gallon."

senting grains dissolved in each gallon of water, will give the respective quantities required to produce one degree of hardness:—

Calcic Chloride . ·7889	Magnesic Chloride . ·6229	Sodic Cholride ·8305
,, Carbonate ·7128	,, Carbonate ·6091	,, Sulphate 1·0104
,, Sulphate ·9689	,, Sulphate . ·8651	

CHAPTER IV.

HOPS AND SUGARS.

Hops (Goldings, Grapes, Jones, Colegates, etc.)—The Best Districts—Planting—Poling, etc.—Climatic Conditions—Cost of Production--A Good Sample of Hops—Foreign Hops—Sulphured Hops—Constituents.

Classification of Sugars—Formulæ—Raw and Refined Sugar—Inverting Sugar in the Brewery—Commercial Glucose.

Hops.

Hops, as known to brewers, are the strobiles, or greenish-yellow cones, of the female plant, consisting of broad and partly overlapping scales. The male plant used at one time to be cultivated—that is to say, a very small percentage of them among the female plants, say 1 in 200 or 300, with the view of securing fecundation—but such a course is now regarded both on the Continent and in England as unnecessary. Botanically the hop (*Humulus lupulus*) belongs to the *Urticæ* or nettles.

As is well known, Kent is the hop-growing county *par excellence*. There is something in the soil of its lower greensand belt, and again in the loams and the kindly loamy clays of the so-called Thanet, Woolwich, and Reading beds, which is particularly favourable to the production of a good quality crop; while, on the other hand, the heavier clays of the district, known as the Weald, are more remarkable for quantity, the crop there often in good years approaching, or even exceeding, a ton per acre. In East and Mid Kent and Farnham the average yield is about $6\frac{1}{2}$ to 7 cwt. per acre. A list of the principal Kentish hop-growing parishes distinguished as East, Bastard East, Mid, North (or the Hill), Weald, and West Kent, will be found as an appendix.

A very capable authority,* himself a Mid Kent grower, says: "It is very remarkable that, given the very finest land in Mid Kent, and the most scientific methods of cultivation, with the very same climate, hops cannot be grown equal in quality to those produced in the contiguous East Kent districts barely ten miles distant; and again, the hops grown in the adjacent Weald of Kent cannot 'hold a candle,' in the matter of quality, to the produce of genuine Mid Kent land. The distinction in the colour, shape, style, and general appearance of the flower-cones is most marked, and discoverable by the veriest tyro (!). The most inexperienced brewer can detect the difference of brewing value in the copper, and the most juvenile merchant can 'spot' the Weald of Kent hops by the coarse and large leaves, the thick strigs, and the comparative want of refinement in the flavour."

Mr. Whitehead also says (which is perhaps going rather far) that good judges can tell at a glance the difference between genuine East Kent hops and those from Bastard East Kent, and that there is at least 10% difference in their value.

The different kind of hops grown in England comprise the Golding and its varieties (Bramling, White's Early, Buss', and Fuggles'), the Grape, with its improved sorts (White Bine, Williams' White Bine, Cooper's White, and the Mathon), the Jones, the Colegate, and the inferior early sorts known as Meophams and Prolifics.

Of these, **Goldings**—and the original stock has not been improved upon—are by far the best. Their strobiles are about the size of a Kentish cob-nut, roundish in shape, and not growing in clusters like those of Grapes. Bram-

---

* Charles Whitehead, Esq., of Barming House, near Maidstone, whose excellent little book, "Hops from the Set to the Skylights" (published by Effingham Wilson, Royal Exchange, at 2s.), I have found of great use.

lings come to pick about ten days earlier than ordinary Goldings, but have not their fine quality; while Buss' and Fuggles' are picked later, although the last-named come early into flower.

Grape Hops rank next to Goldings. In the improved varieties more compactness has been attained (the old-fashioned sort labour under the imputation of being too coarse and large, and of having a thick strig, which shows plainly "in the sample"), but all of them have larger cones than those of the Goldings, and all their cones grow in clusters. Of the improved varieties, **Cooper's White,** an early sort, and **Mathons,** which come next to pick, and which are a very good sort of hop, with many of the qualities of Goldings, are freely grown in the Worcester and Hereford "hop-yards."

Jones' Hop.—A rather coarse hop with large strobiles, grown largely in the Weald of Kent and Sussex, also to some extent in other counties, but not in East Kent. They require to be picked when just ripe, otherwise the petals readily become detached, forming "fliers."

Colegates.—A coarse, strong hop, yielding wonderful crops in the Weald of Kent and Sussex. The chief argument in favour of growing them is that, coming, as they do, late to pick, they often, under the influence of a late spell of favourable weather, grow away from the vermin which has ruined earlier and choicer sorts. Their strobiles are smaller than those of Goldings.

As regards the value of the hops they produce, the authority before quoted ranks the different districts in the following order: East Kent, Bastard East Kent, North Kent, Mid Kent, West Kent, Weald.

North Kents (or the Hill) and **West Kents** are by the trade included in Mid Kent, but my own experience of Mid Kent brewing is that North Kents are very highly esteemed by brewers there, for a delicacy of flavour rather than potency; although, as Mr. Whitehead says, Mid Kent growers do not like to confess any inferiority of their own produce. The finest hop land in England, he says, is that from Chatham to Faversham, and from Faversham nearly to Canterbury for some miles, chiefly below the line of railway, upon various clays, loamy clays, and loams of the Thanet, Woolwich, or Reading beds and the Oldhaven beds overlying the chalk. As the chalk appears again, the loam surface decreasing in thickness, the hopground becomes less valuable; but below Canterbury, in the district from Chilham to Barham Downs east, hops of first-class quality are grown on somewhat sandy loams upon chalk, although the crops are smaller and the poles required are shorter.

Thus far I have only spoken of Kent, but in many breweries, **Farnhams**—*i.e.*, real Farnhams, Farnham Town district hops—are preferred even to East Kents. At one time, when the writer was in the habit of using choice Farnhams frequently, he generally found that when any gyle of pale ale was of especial merit, this appeared, upon reference, to be concurrent with the fact that a larger percentage of Farnhams than usual had been employed in its production.

On the other hand, in some districts, or it may be in some plants, where copper hopping has to be light, and where the pale ales go very speedily into consumption, Farnhams may give less satisfactory results than the milder and delicate hops of Worcester and Hereford. There seems indeed to be a certain astringency, combined with the great aroma of Farnhams, which makes their position in relation to other hops comparable with that of the highly flavoured, astringent, Indian teas, in relation to the milder produce of China.

The hop-districts of Surrey and Hampshire "march together" more or less, the most favourable soil being that referred to by Gilbert White as "the malm, a sort of rotten or rubble stone, which when turned up to the frost and rain moulders to pieces, and becomes manure to itself," a soil found in the neighbourhood of his parish of Selborne, in Hants, and Farnham, in Surrey. These combined districts, where "Farnhams" and "Country

Farnhams" grow (marked with the bell, as Kentish hops are with the horse), are confined within comparatively narrow limits, about five or six miles wide by twenty or thereabouts in length. Worcester and Hereford hops grow upon certain formations either of the new or old red sandstone, or the alluvium of certain rivers, " Teme-side " hops perhaps have the preference; but the most favourable hop-growing soil in both Worcester and Hereford is a red loamy soil on the old red sandstone.

Planting, Poling, etc.—Two or three sets, as the root-cuttings, from which the young plants grow, are called—two usually giving better results than three—form " a hill," and " the hills " are disposed in a series of parallel straight lines about 6 feet apart, so that each hill is 6 feet from its neighbours in front and behind, as well as to left and right. The length of the poles required varies with the different sorts, Goldings taking the longest—viz., 14 to 18 feet; Colegates come next with poles from 12 to 16 feet; Grapes grow on poles from 10 to 12 feet long; and Jones on shorter poles of 8 or 10 feet.

The climatic conditions required for a thoroughly good growth of hops, are, briefly, weather such that the ground can be kept clear of weeds, and " a good crumb " attained—viz., a thorough disintegration of the soil for the root fibres to run in; further, the absence of prolonged spring frosts, which check the growth of the young plants, a check which, it is supposed, make their juices more grateful to the winged and wingless *aphides* (" the fly," or " lice "); freedom, too, from spring drought, which encourages the attacks of " the flea "; and from very hot and dry summers, which bring " the red spider." After a sudden check caused by cold weather, mildew, the work of a parasitic fungus (*Spærotheca Castagnei*) may manifest itself by white spots upon the leaves, and is perhaps more to be dreaded than the other enemies of the hop plant.

If it (the *Spærotheca Castagnei*) attacks the hops when in burr (*i.e.*, the incipient cone), it prevents the development of the latter, arresting its growth at once; if it attacks the cone it soon takes possession of the delicate internal tissues, a few hops so attacked utterly spoiling the sample.

There is another fungus, too, familiarly known as "**the rust**," which attacks the leaves of the cones, rapidly turning them from a delicate golden hue to a dull creamy colour. The best remedy for either kind of mildew—though owing to the forward state of the hops when rust appears it is not easy to use it then—is sulphur freely applied by a machine with a revolving fan. For aphis blight soft soap and water, with an infusion of tobacco, squirted over the plants, is the favourite remedy. Against the flea soot and lime are used, but are not considered very effective. A thunderstorm, accompanied by rain, is the only thorough remedy for the attacks of red spider. Ladybirds, on the other hand, are welcome visitors, being destroyers of *aphides*.

The above forms a very cursory sketch of the ills that the hop is heir to, but will be enough to show the difficulty of prognosticating the crop and the truth of the old saw, which looks upon the prospect of the yield as being full of peril up to July 25th at least—

> "Until St. James is come and gone
> There may be hops or there may be none."

And, even then, high winds may prevail just before and during picking, and do incalculable damage to the hops, lessening their condition, and bruising and browning the tender scales of the cones.

Cost of Production.—This amounts on well-managed land to about £40 an acre, of which 20% goes for manure and its application; over 30% for picking, drying, and selling; and 7% for interest on capital. There are other outlays for digging, dressing, poling, tying, earthing, tying top-shoots or "ladder-tying," "nidgetting," etc., which, though individually moderate, make up a considerable aggregate. The annual cost of poles is estimated at £5 5s. per acre, though this amount will be reduced where mixed kinds of hops are grown, seeing that the old Golding poles can be used for those hops which take shorter poles. But it is false economy to use poles large enough for fully established hop-plants to pole plants, especially Goldings, in the first or second year of growth.

The cost in Worcestershire and Herefordshire appears to be about the same, though one grower, living near Malvern, in his examination before the select committee of the House of Commons, put it as low as £30 per acre, and another explained how they were produced more cheaply on the Shropshire border than in Kent and Surrey. The same witness considered £5 per hundredweight, if maintained, a fairly remunerative price for Worcester and Hereford hops.

A good sample of hops should be of a bright greenish-yellow, inclining more to yellow than green, leaving, when rubbed in the hand, yellow traces, with a fragrant and powerful aroma, and a smooth and oily feel. There should be plenty of the yellow powder or lupulin, and that sample which shows stout, thick hops where it has been cut will be *cæteris paribus* the fullest of "condition." The stems should be darker than the corresponding strobiles, which will show that the hops have not been bleached with sulphur.

I may supplement the above, taken from the early edition of this book, by Mr. Whitehead's valuable summary. In a perfect sample the cones as seen on "the face" should be whole, with the strigs completely free from moisture, and the lupulin or gold-dust adhering to the bracts. But very few leaves should be seen, and the cones should be single and not in bunches, and of a brilliant pale gold colour. A pungent aromatic odour should proceed from the sample, without the slightest *soupçon* of the peculiar sweet "gingerbready" smell, as of heated clover hay, indicative of too much heat having been employed in the drying process.

Upon rubbing down some of the sample in the hand

there should be no residue of fibrous substance, but the whole should chaff finely, leaving a yellowish resinous deposit upon the fingers, necessitating the use of much soap to remove it. Good judges can determine at a glance, by looking at the sides of a sample, as to the "thickness" or "condition" of the hops and the state of maturity at which they were picked, by the colour, quantity, and general appearance of the seeds, whole, or cut through by the knives. If hops have been scientifically dried and well managed the sample will be most elastic, and may be compressed easily into a small compass, and upon the pressure being removed will spring back to its former size. This is a most valuable index of thorough and judicious desiccation.

The seeds should be firm and dark in appearance, and should "cut hard" before gathering. When hops are, in merchants' parlance, "mashy"—*i.e.*, showing a considerable proportion of small fragments on the face of the sample— they are not fit for "dry-hopping" (hopping down in cask) with, because the small pieces give trouble as "fliers" when the ale is drawn, and because "mashiness" indicates some loss of the most valuable properties, either through over-ripeness or careless curing.

The **"tare,"** or deduction allowed for hop-pocketing, is 6 lb. per pocket.

Of **foreign hops** the best growths are those of **Saaz** (in Bohemia) and of **Spalt** (in Bavaria). These, as with us, are divided into a town district (Stadt Saaz and Stadt Spalt), which stands highest in value, and a "country" district (Spalter Nebengut, Saazer Bezirkshopfen, and Kreishopfen). The Bavarian mark best known in England is that of **Hollertau,** which however ranks after those already named; in fact, the high prices which Austrian and German brewers are willing to pay for them prevent the exportation of the highest qualities. The two main varieties of hop grown are red and green hops (*Rothhopfen* and *Grünhopfen*), of which Professor Thausing (in his " Theorie ŭ. Praxis der Malzbereitung und Bierfabrikation ") says: "The red hop has bine, which is reddish-coloured on the sunny side, and cones, which remain relatively small and, upon drying, assume a hue between yellowish and reddish. The cone-leaves (bracts) of this kind of hop are tender, the strigs thin, the hop-powder possesses a pleasant aromatic smell, and the seeds are very small.

This variety is the higher in quality, and demands for successful development better soil and better climatic conditions than the green hop, the bine of which is quite green in colour, and whose cones, upon drying, retain a pale green hue. The cones of the green hop are mostly larger, have coarser bracts and strigs, and the seeds are generally larger than those of the red hops. Nor has the green hop the pleasant flavour of the red, but more or less suggests that of garlic. Its yield, however, is, as a rule, greater than that of the red hop."

The pick of Würtemburg and Baden hops ranks nearly, if not quite, with Hollertau, and before the best growths of Alsace.

American Hops.—America is *the* factor which our native hop-growers have to reckon with, particularly as the hops sent thence—in spite of their flavour somewhat suggesting that of black-currant leaves—are very useful, and far preferable to inferior Continental sorts, for ales in which some amount of "finish" is expected. Indeed, it was admitted by a Herefordshire grower, before the Select Committee on the Hop Industry, that "the chief competitors of Worcester and Hereford hops were those from California and the Pacific States, which are of good quality, well packed, and are increasing in estimation in the market."

Good colour is characteristic of most samples, especially of those baled as Californians; most of all, perhaps, those from Washington Territory have a uniform pale *yellow* or golden hue, which our most "coloury" hops could hardly rival. Good specimens, too, will retain this colour with little appreciable loss as "yearlings," a fact which I take to be due partly to the regular solar conditions under which they have ripened, but mostly to the fact that no over-stimulating manures have been used to force a crop. A corollary of this is that they make good yearlings, and are often better used at that age than when new.

Belgian Hops.—These, imported under the marks of Alost and Poperinghe, are only used in beers where no particular "style" is expected. The chief hop-growing districts of Belgium, besides those named, are around Mons, Namur, Hal, Asschè, Hensies, and Opwyck.

French Hops.—The French hop-growing area has been greatly restricted by the loss of Alsace and Lorraine, but the north of France—the chief beer-producing centre of that country—yields a considerable quantity of hops, which are, I understand, absorbed by the local trade. Burgundy produces hops, which are met with under that brand in England, and indeed the product of its famous *Cote-d'or* may rival fine Bavarians. The writer has seen fine-flavoured specimens from sources so far apart as the Dordogne, the borders of Savoy, and the neighbourhood of Bordeaux, though not upon the English market.

Sulphured Hops.—With regard to the sometimes necessary use of sulphur, a good deal of prejudice, which some deem groundless, exists. Sulphur is employed in two ways. (1) It is sprinkled, as has been said, on the plant, to check blight and mildew. (2) It is burnt under the hops while on the oast, and thus reaches them not in the form of sulphur, but as sulphurous acid.

Now as regards the first method, even if some particles of sulphur have lodged in the hops, it is in its unoxidised state insoluble; and even in experiments which have been made with it, mixed in equal proportions with yeast, it has been found no hindrance to the fermentative action of the latter, the only effect being the production—in itself far from desirable—of a small percentage of sulphuretted hydrogen. It is therefore, say those who do not object to that flavouring ingredient, chiefly objectionable as indicating unhealthy conditions of growth.

As regards the second method of application, a Bavarian Commission, with Liebig at its head, came to the conclusion, after two years of exhaustive inquiry, that the process was not prejudicial to the fermentation, and was beneficial to the hop itself.

However this may be, English brewers are not, as a rule, disposed to regard sulphured hops with favouring eyes. The sulphuretted-hydrogen smell which the conjunction of sulphur with yeast has been shown to determine, may be, and indeed seems to be, transitory; but there is no record that the researches of the Commission went far enough to decide what effect, if any, it has in conjunction with yeast of the secondary type (after, or complementary fermentation in cask); and until this is determined we must look upon the presence of sulphur as undesirable.

The most important Constituents of the Hop are—
1. Essential, flavouring oils.
2. Resins.
3. Bitter principles, intimately associated with the resins.
4. Tannin.

Chemists disagree widely about the quantity of essential oil present in the hop, and whether it be homogeneous or of two kinds, one of which is volatile at 212°, and the other at a higher temperature. R. Wagner found in dried hop-cones about .8% of hop-oil. "It has," says Thausing, "when obtained from fresh hops, a clear yellow colour, a spicy taste, and agreeable smell. It is very slightly soluble in water (1 part in 600 parts of water), but readily in alcohol and ether. The hop-oil not only volatilises on boiling, but also at ordinary temperatures in the air passes into fugitive acids, especially into valerianic ($C_5H_{10}O_2$). In old hops the oil has been oxidised to this acid, whence their characteristic smell."

For this reason the preparation and maintenance of hop-oil—which otherwise would be very desirable, as a means of getting a maximum of flavour and of preservative qualities too—has been attended with difficulty.*

* This was written before the Brewers' Show, at which Messrs. Boake & Co. exhibited a first-rate sample.

The oils, resins, and bitter principles appear to be very closely connected with each other. This combination being broken up by boiling, the resins and the associated bitter principles are set free, the oils being partly volatilised (which occasions the agreeable fragrance of a boiling wort copper) and partly distributed through the wort. Long boiling is, of course, a disadvantage as regards retention of the essential oils, but is required to break up their combination with the resins and bitter principles, which would otherwise be, to a great extent, lost with some of the aromatic oil itself.

I rather hold the opinion that the resins, when dissolved, check the volatilisation of the essential oil; which theory, if it be correct, points to the advisability of more minutely subdividing hops, when added to the copper, than is usually done. It is apparently to the resins that the discoloration of the heads during fermentation and just before the yeasty stage is largely due. The resin, held in solution by a strongly saccharine medium, goes out of solution, as the maltose gets withdrawn or broken up by fermentation, and conglomerates on the top of the wort. It may be safely said, I think, that invert sugar has a similar solvent effect; it will be observed, when extract consists, to a greater extent than usual, of invert, that the "dirty-head" period is often prolonged—*i.e.*, lasts to a lower point of attenuation than the average one. This may be owing to the fact of *more* resin having been dissolved, as well as to that of more sugar remaining undegraded at a comparatively late stage.

The fourth important constituent is **tannin or tannic acid**,* which, combining with certain of the soluble albumin-

* Certain of the tannins belong to the glucosides, bodies which break up, under the influence of dilute acids or of ferments, into sugars or cognate bodies. Tannin is precipitated by gelatine from a clear solution, and use is made of this fact in the determination of the amount present in a sample of hops. The difference between the amount of permanganate solution decolorised by the two solutions (before and after the gelatine treatment) gives the oxygen required to oxidise the tannin. The *exact* point when all the tannin has been oxidised is got by addition of indigo, which is decolorised by oxygen but less readily than tannin.

ous matters of the wort, forms an insoluble precipitate (tannate of albumen) with them, thus freeing the wort from constituents which would affect the brightness and stability of the beer produced from it. Further consideration of boiling will be deferred to a later chapter.

The hops used for "dry hopping" or "hopping down" must be ripe and full of aroma. They, in particular, ought to be free from sulphur directly applied, as this undoubtedly shows that all the conditions of disease have been present, a matter which, in the absence of boiling to destroy or weaken the spores, is likely to be specially dangerous. Comparatively easy means of determining the presence of sulphur in any given sample are within the reach of the non-professional analyst, and may be found in the laboratory chapter.

Storing Hops.—Hops should be kept in a dry, darkish (even light-proof) store, free from draughts, as air and light both favour the slow oxidation whereby the hop-oil is converted into valerianic acid, which has a disagreeable and somewhat rancid cheesy odour. It is therefore unwise to buy so heavily as to be overstocked with "yearlings," though some proportion of these should be used when the new crop first comes in.

There seems, however, ground for supposing that the bitter principle, too, becomes seriously modified in old hops, so as to yield a clinging or fixed bitter, which does not readily leave the palate; whereas, on the other hand, the fugitive bitter of the new hops leaves the palate clean. It is not impossible that the fresh-hop bitter may be akin to the glucosides, which have been referred to in a footnote under tannin, and that its almost instantaneous disappearance from the palate may be due to a conversion affected by the saliva.*

That this is not a question of merely academic interest

* Mr. M. A. Adams, in a most interesting paper read before the Society of Public Analysts, instanced salicin, a well-known glucoside and very bitter substance, of which, if a few drops of its saturated solution be placed upon the tongue, the bitterness soon disappears.

may appear more clearly at some later time, if ever the Legislature insists upon classifying beers into those which are bittered solely with hops, and those into which some bittering ingredient other than hops has entered. Now a cursory analysis will not easily distinguish the bitter of old hops from that of quassia and other kindred bitters, which though wholesome enough in themselves, are undoubtedly regarded by the public with prejudice, although Mr. Adams feels certain that by carrying the analysis further it is quite possible to do so.

In estimating the coming yield (with regard to the question of purchasing or not), it may be well to remember that it is generally over-estimated when the summer has been backward, and the crop is accordingly what is called a "top-crop," and that, where high winds prevail during picking, the quality and condition of the hops are much decreased; but on the other hand, very little faith should be placed in the predictions of a total blight, the favourite theme of those who have hops to sell. Yearlings—the hops of the previous season—never have the market or brewing value of good new hops. Those of two seasons back are "olds," hops more ancient still are "old-olds." Obviously, such hops can have little or no brewing value, and, unless well preserved, are even likely to damage the flavour of the product.

Sugars.

The sugars form two out of the three groups into which the important bodies known as carbohydrates (so called because, in addition to carbon, they contain hydrogen and oxygen in the proportion in which these two elements combine to form water, 2 : 1) are separated.

The types of sugar most important to brewers are—

(1) **Glucose, Grape-sugar, or Dextrose,** which is commercially prepared from either separated starch, or from a starch-containing grain, by boiling either material with sulphuric acid under pressure, the acidity being afterwards neutralised.

INVERSION OF SUGAR.

(2) **Saccharose, Sucrose, or Cane-sugar** (including beet-root sugar), some being "raw," others "refined," but neither fermentable without inversion, which, however, readily takes place under ordinary fermentation conditions by the agency of invertase (invertin) * which healthy yeast secretes.

(3) **Invert Sugar,** separable into equal parts of dextrose and levulose (fruit-sugar). It is obtained, commercially, by boiling a solution of cane-sugar to which a small percentage of sulphuric acid has been added. This operation is, as with glucose, effected under pressure to save time, and in both cases the sulphuric acid, which itself undergoes no change (its action being catalytic), has to be subsequently neutralised with whiting. Sulphate of lime is then formed, and precipitates on standing, or it may be removed by filtration.

A second commercial process, one to utilise the activity of invertase, the soluble enzyme mentioned above, has been patented by Mr. Tompson, of Burton-on-Trent; the process, as I am credibly informed, being a satisfactory one. The only objection which might be urged against this method is based upon the probability of raw sugar, teeming with bacteria and their spores, being sometimes used. Now it is easy to see that the double boiling, which the sugar receives in the sulphuric acid process, would probably be sufficient to destroy those spores as well as the adult bacteria; but in the yeast process such a

* Recent researches (by C. O'Sullivan and F. W. Tompson) show that the dry solid matter of yeast contains 2% to 6% invertase; that caustic alkalinity of the medium is instantly fatal, while on the contrary slight acidity is favourable ; and that a sample of invertase which had induced hydrolysis of 100,000 times its own weight of sugar was still active. According to Thausing, E. Donath found that a small quantity could invert a solution of cane sugar in 10 to 15 minutes at ordinary temperatures. Donath says this interesting substance is not to be regarded as an albuminous body, though the investigators named above found that the substance isolated by them gave (with most of the other members of the invertase group to which it belongs) a red reaction with Millon's Reagent, the test for proteins or albuminoids.

temperature, during inversion, is impossible, the maximum favourable temperature for invertase being about 140° Fahr.

Several brands of invert sugar, prepared by the sulphuric acid process, are before the public. It is also possible, and many brewers find it profitable, to invert cane-sugar in the brewery itself, but without pressure, so that the boiling has to be prolonged. The method of doing this will be given later in the chapter.

(4) **Maltose** plays a prominent *rôle*, but not being commercially produced it belongs more to the chapter on Mashing, where it will be referred to.

Their accepted formulæ are—

Glucose Group—$C_6H_{12}O_6$—consisting of—

(a) Dextrose, glucose, or grape-sugar (reduces "Fehling ").*

(β) Levulose or fruit-sugar [invert sugar is a mixture of a and β].

(γ) Galactose, a sugar unfermentable by yeast, which is formed + dextrose, if sugar-of-milk or gum-arabic is boiled with dilute sulphuric acid.

Cane-sugar Group—$C_{12}H_{22}O_{11}$—consisting of—

(a) Saccharose, sucrose, or cane-sugar (does not reduce Fehling).

(β) Lactose, or sugar-of-milk ($C_{12}H_{22}O_{11} + H_2O$), occurs in every sort of milk, and can be separated by evaporation from milk, the casein of which has been coagulated by means of rennet. It reduces Fehling.

(γ) Maltose, the sugar formed by the action of the diastase of malt upon its, or other, starch. Maltose reduces Fehling's solution, but to a less extent than glucose or invert sugar is capable of. Its

---

* The Fehling's solution, which will be more fully treated in the chapter on Laboratory Work, is an alkaline solution of copper sulphate (to which it owes its blue colour). Certain sugars, *e.g.*, glucose, invert, and maltose, have the property, when boiled with the Fehling, of discharging the blue colour and precipitating the copper of the sulphate as a red precipitate of cuprous oxide.

HYDROLYSIS. SUGARS.

exact or comparative reducing power is not definitely fixed, varying from 65 : 100 (O'Sullivan) to 62 : 100 (Brown and Heron), and even to 61 : 100. Probably the varying dilution of the Fehling may account for some discrepancy.

If now we compare with the above formulæ that of the third group of carbohydrates—viz., the cellulose group to which starch belongs $(C_6H_{10}O_5)_n$,—we shall see that the difference between it and the formula of glucose consists of two atoms of hydrogen and one of oxygen in each molecule (or more strictly speaking of multiples of those numbers, seeing that the undetermined n of the starch molecule, in any case, represents a large figure), the same difference which we find existing between the first and second of the above formulæ when for the sake of comparison the formula of the glucose group is doubled. We thus see that the conversion of starch into glucose, and the alteration of cane-sugar into invert sugar, and again that of starch into maltose, are equally hydration processes, *i.e.*, the elements of water in some way or other enter into combination, and effect important changes as a result of the action (hydrolysis) which is set up.

The simplest equations,* which express the reactions, are therefore

$$C_6H_{10}O_5 + H_2O = C_6H_{12}O_6.$$
Starch and water — Dextrose,

and

$$C_{12}H_{22}O_{11} + H_2O = C_6H_{12}O_6 + C_6H_{12}O_6.$$
Cane-sugar water — Dextrose and levulose.
Invert sugar.

Commercial Cane-sugar.—Commercial sugar is obtained either from the sugar-cane or beet (*Beta vulgaris*), the latter being far inferior to the former for the brewer's

* The latest hypothesis of the starch molecule is much more complex, and supposes it to consist of five so-called amylin groups, each of which is $(C_{12}H_{20}O_{10})_{20}$; but it will be observed that the ratio of each element to the other is maintained, so that though the points of hydration may be much more numerous than once supposed, there is hydration none the less.

purposes, owing to certain objectionable flavours which, except in the best refined samples, are only too prominent. Maple-sugar is also extensively used in America; the Java palm also yields sugar where it flourishes; and certain grasses, *Sorghum vulgare* and *Sorghum saccharatum*, have been cultivated for the same purpose in the United States, and even tried, but without success, owing to our uncertain summers, in the United Kingdom.

Accordingly, when we speak of cane-sugar apart from chemical surroundings, we mean the produce of the sugar-cane as distinguished from beet-root sugar. In spite, however, of objectionable flavours and even a slightly lower degree of sweetness in its finished samples, beet-root sugar is a formidable rival to cane-sugar, not only on account of the bounties paid to foreign exporters by their Governments, but because, owing to the comparatively stable nature of the crop, the factories dealing with the raw material can keep longer at work, and because the beet-root juice contains a smaller proportion of uncrystallisable sugar than that from sugar-cane. It is only, in fact, by adopting the most improved methods (amongst them extraction by the diffusion process instead of by crushing) that the planters of British Guiana have been able to hold their own. As it is, Demerara sugar from that colony is perhaps the best and purest in the world.*

The amount of crystallisable sugar in a juice forms its standard of value,—the "refining value,"—and may vary considerably, even in samples which actually contain the same amount of sucrose. Especially in the case of cane-sugar, the natural acid of the juice in a hot climate tends to invert part of the sucrose, and this inverted sugar is not only non-crystallisable itself, but prevents the crystallisation of an equal quantity of uninverted sugar. Ash is also a factor in non-crystallisation, one unit, roughly speaking, rendering five units of sugar uncrystallisable.

* It may be interesting to note that the best sugar tends to connote the worst rum, and *vice versâ*. Demerara rum and Jamaica sugar bear witness.

But from the invert-sugar maker's point of view this is probably not a question of much moment, although it is supposed that the removal of a portion of the crystals, before inversion, is not an unknown operation.

Cane-sugars are divided into raw and refined. In preparing the former, often only the crudest method is used; for instance, the syrup, whether decomposition has set in or not, is just boiled down to crystallising point over an open fire, and this point being reached, the fluid is run into casks, which are then turned bung downwards for the uncrystallised portion to run out. This, the molasses, is then reboiled in order to get another supply of crystals.

Such being the method employed, it is not surprising that low-class raw sugars, Barbadoes, Jaggery, or Bastards, and indeed ordinary unrefined sugars generally, contain impurities of a revolting character. Among these are fungus spores (probably including that of *Leuconostoc mesenteroides*, supposed to be the cause of the viscous fermentation of sugar refineries, the so-called *Froschlaich*, frog-spawn, or *Gomme de sucrerie* of German or French refiners), bacteria, and bacilli in hosts, not to speak of the *acarus sacchari*, or sugar mite, an insect visible to the naked eye in its adult stage, but existing either in the egg or as a developed organism. This insect is the cause of the complaint known as " grocers' itch " to those who have what is technically known as " the handling,"* but which we may translate by its more sinister synonym, " the manipulation " of sugars. Beside these, fragments of sugar-cane, except as indicating not the most careful manufacture, are unimportant items.

Dr. Hassall, who had had a large experience in the analysis of all sorts of foods, stated that out of 72 samples of brown sugar, purchased at various shops, microscopic

* " Handling " consists largely of mixing various qualities—*e.g.*, coarse dark with light-coloured attractive sugars, with such unholy skill that the fraud (for it is palmed off at the price of the best) shall not be apparent. On account of the difficulty which sugars having a large crystal offer to this sort of " handling," I understand that they are somewhat out of favour with the trade.

fragments of sugar-cane were present in all but one; sporules and filaments of fungus in nearly all; the *acari* were found in 69 of the samples, and often in considerable quantity.

The present writer has detected, amid a horde of disease ferments, what he believes (as firmly as he can without the check of after cultivation) to have been a growing spore of *Leuconostoc mesenteroides*; and the probable connection of this organism with subsequent ropiness should not be lost sight of, especially in view of the facts, that if any beers show a tendency to become ropy, English black beers do so (in bottle if at all), and that these are the very beers in which crude, unrefined sugars are most largely used.

Were it not for these abominations there would be much to be said in favour of dark-coloured raw sugars for the manufacture of porter and of ales, other than pale or bitter ales, owing to the undoubtedly more pronounced flavour imparted by them than by the higher qualities of refined; but, as matters stand, they are only fitted, in their crude state, for a "running trade" in a not very high-class article, the producers of which have made up their minds to face the necessity of frequent changes of "pitching" or "store yeast," with all the drawbacks involved therein.

The case might be somewhat different if a previous inversion of this raw cane-sugar were the rule, because the boiling with the acid, which takes place the day before the inverted product is used, when inversion is carried out in the brewery itself, would certainly destroy existing adult bacteria, and what is even more important, because more difficult, it would facilitate the destruction of the spores of those bacteria, which, *as spores*, can survive even a prolonged continuous boil, but which, when the boiling is intermittent, are stimulated into assuming the adult form by the first boiling, and in that phase of their development are ready to be slain by the second.

But for this, it is not very easy to see the advantage

of inverting (which some *do* dispute, though the majority consider it a self-evident proposition), because we know that yeast secretes a ferment or enzyme called invertase (invertin), quite apart from its well-known *fermentative* action upon certain saccharine bodies, and that this enzyme, which indeed—as we have seen—can be entirely separated from the yeast (not losing, at any rate, if not gaining, vigour by such separation), has the function of inverting cane-sugar into a mixture of dextrose and levulose—*i.e.*, of converting the non-fermentable into a fermentable sugar.

Thus it will be seen that it really is difficult to say why a perfectly pure cane-sugar, uninverted previously, should not, if boiled with the wort in the usual way, get inverted in the fermenting vessel and give satisfactory results; unless it could be shown, which, as far as I know has not been done, that the inverting enzyme *must* be separated, or that yeast engaged in vigorous reproduction and fermentation is incapable of secreting it. This may be so to a certain extent. There is analogous evidence in the case of another enzyme, diastase, the secretion of which by the special organ of the grain seems to be " a starvation phenomenon "—*i.e.*, to be at a standstill when there is a plentiful food supply in a very assimilable form.

In the case of common unrefined sugars the facts, first, that the yeast-crop would be severely handicapped in its struggle for existence by the introduction of a horde of bacteria, probably in a very active condition, and again that such sugars contain nitrogenous bodies of uncertain and presumably unstable character, afford good reasons why the neglect of previous inversion, and that too by boiling with acid to minimise one of these evils at least, is not to be thought of.

This, accordingly, will be the place to introduce a description of the method of inverting cane-sugar in the brewery, premising that, in comparing costs, the brewer will remember that he gets the use of a material giving an extract of 84 brewers' lb., or thereabouts, per 2 cwt. as against 70 or 72 brewers' lb., given by invert [or in other words he puts into his own pocket the profit made by the increase of bulk, and again another profit—for that increase of bulk (19 parts cane, 20 invert) cannot account for the greatly lessened extract—due to fixation of water]. Again, he saves the expense of evaporating his product down to ostensible dryness, or at least down to a concentrated form, which the invert-sugar maker must do to bring his wares into transportable bulk.

So that, evidently, if a good supply of real and unmixed cane-sugar can be depended on, there is a good margin to make the operation of inverting one's own sugar a profitable one.

Against this may be set the fact that the brewer has not time to remove by filtration through animal charcoal, as the invert-sugar maker does, the colour imparted by the boiling with sulphuric acid, so that there would be a difficulty in using sugar home-inverted on the sulphuric-acid system for pale or delicate-coloured ales. For these, then, if previous inversion is a *sine quâ non* (of which I, for one, am not convinced), Tompson's patented Yeast Inversion Process must be resorted to, as it imparts no colour. Its manipulation is easier, too; but, as has been said, unless sugars of the highest class are employed, one safeguard is lost.

The following is the method suggested by Dr. Graham, who did so much to emancipate practical brewing from rule-of-thumb tradition :—

To Invert Cane-sugar.—Fill a kilderkin nearly to the brim with water, then add 10 pints of sulphuric acid (spec. gr. 1840, water = 1000). Then, disregarding the decimal, because exact measurement with the dilution is not necessary, 10 pints of the undiluted acid weigh $22\frac{1}{2}$ lb. (1 gallon being taken = 18 lb.) = 360 oz. But the 18 gallons dilute acid = 144 pints—*i.e.*, each pint of it corresponds to $2\frac{1}{2}$ oz. of the original acid. After these preliminaries the next steps are as follows :—

INVERTING CANE-SUGAR.

(1) Run into the dissolving tun 22 to 23 gallons of boiling water for each cwt. of sugar to be inverted.

(2) When ready to add the sugar, put in the dilute sulphuric acid in the proportion of 2 pints per cwt. of sugar.

(3) Add the sugar, distributing it carefully; turn steam on full, and as soon as the sugar is in put on the lid.

(4) When the contents begin to boil the steam may be reduced. Actual hard boiling is unnecessary, though a temperature of 212° must be maintained.

(5) Boil for two hours. When steam is off and lid removed, add whiting, gradually and with great care, otherwise the contents of the vessel will effervesce so much as to boil over.

(6) The whiting being added (say 10 oz. for every 2 pints of the dilute acid), the steam is to be turned on again for half an hour so as to mix the whiting.

(7) The solution should settle before draining off; also it would be well to run it through a (strong) calico filter.

The designer of this method was content to have this inversion take place on the same day that the sugar was to be used. In another modification of this system, which differs in mere points of detail (*e.g.*, in using 1 lb. of acid and 2 lb. of whiting per cwt. of sugar, and in making up the bulk of the boiling liquid to exactly one barrel inclusive of the sugar), it is recommended to invert the sugar a half-day before using it, say in the afternoon of the day before the one on which the sugar is to be used. It is advisable to test the solution with litmus paper, in order to be sure that the acid is neutralised.

Commercial Glucose is manufactured upon similar lines, that is, by the action of dilute acid, at a temperature of boiling, upon starch. In this country rice, maize, and for one brand sago, are employed, but any source of starch will do. A good deal of the Continental glucose is made from potato starch. The process is as follows: the rice, maize, or other amylaceous substance is mashed in water containing 1 to 3% of sulphuric acid; after mashing it is run into a receiver, where heat is applied by means of jets of steam ; or extracted starch may be either boiled with the dilute acid in an open tank, or heated in a strong cylinder of copper at a high pressure, which greatly expedites conversion.

The conversion may be stopped just when the liquid (cooled down) ceases to give a blue reaction with iodine, in which case the percentage of dextrin in the product will be high.* If the process be pushed further, and especially if it be carried on under pressure, dextrose (with a little maltose) will be the chief product. The acid is neutralised with whiting or limestone, which results in the formation of a precipitate of sulphate of lime. Neubeuer, having made numerous analyses of commercial glucose (probably all of German make), found its average composition to be, fermentable sugar 61·08 ; dextrin and kindred bodies (non-fermentable) 20·54 ; ash (chiefly gypsum) ·34 ; water 18·04. And the largest quantity of the latter came out as high as 23·66%!

A good deal of prejudice against the use of sugar exists amongst the public, but its employment can in no sense be stigmatised as adulteration : indeed it would be difficult, if not impossible, to brew the beers which the public taste demands without that valuable adjunct. Glucose tends to determine "dryness," "invert" a more luscious character.

---

* Modern research speaks of amylöins. But whatever the view about these alleged chemical compounds of maltose and dextrin, there is certainly room for controversy as to the identity of the dextrin-products of the acid process with those of malt-wort. Practice tends to brand the former with less stability.

CHAPTER V.

THE BREWING-ROOM.

Gravity—Brewers' lbs. and Degrees of Specific Gravity—Saccharometers — Converting Degrees Balling into Brewers' lbs.—Baumé into Specific Gravity—Working out the Brewings—Entry of Materials—Working out Sparges—Copper Lengths—Parti-gyle Calculations—Apportioning Hops—Formula for Calculating "Initial" from "Striking" Heat—Making up Lengths in Fermenting Vessels (Calculations for)—Boiling down to a required Gravity—Extract per Quarter—Dry or Solid Extract—Extract per Cent.—Excise Charges—Contents of Squares or Rounds in Bushels and Gallons—Cost-price Calculation.

Gravity.—Probably the first thing the beginner hears of, as soon as he has got some idea of the geography of the brewery, is "Gravity," which may be either expressed for every-day purposes in the so-called **brewers' lbs.**, or in **degrees of specific gravity** (the latter being the scale upon which Excise charges are based), both of them being standards adopted for stating the strength of a particular wort before fermentation, and indeed as a means of classifying it later on, according to its value when a finished product. Thus it is usual to speak of an 18 lb. beer, a 20 or 25 lb. beer, etc.,—even though the specific gravity scale is now commonly and interchangeably used,—and we are wont to say that such and such a beer "drinks" or "does not drink its gravity," the latter verdict being obviously one which the careful brewer endeavours to avoid.

"Lbs. gravity" or "brewers' lbs." then may be defined as those lbs. only by which the weight of a barrel of any wort exceeds the weight of a barrel of water—for instance, a gallon of water weighs 10 lb., therefore a barrel weighs 360 lb.; and a barrel of wort weighing, say 380 lb., would be said to be of the gravity of 20 lb. (strictly brewers' lbs.); and the resulting beer, after fermentation, would be known as a 20-lb. beer, irrespective of the loss of weight, which may show a good deal of variation, but is certain to be considerable, consequent upon the splitting up of the solid constituents of the original wort into carbonic acid, some of which disappears, and alcohol, which is lighter even than water.

This extreme lightness of alcohol accordingly makes the quantity of solid matter removed or split up by fermentation appear to be even greater than it really is; in other words, the alcohol, being so much lighter than water, yet the ordinary saccharometer, which the brewer uses, being incapable of estimating it otherwise than as water, masks a certain portion of really unfermented matter. So that what brewers call the **Final Attenuation,** that is to say, the weight which a barrel of the beer at the close of the primary fermentation would show over the weight of a barrel of water (and which is one-quarter, one-fifth, or sometimes less, of the original gravity), is a purely conventional statement, involving more than one departure from strict accuracy.

Saccharometers.—But it being manifestly inconvenient to be compelled to weigh a barrel, or even a measured part of a barrel, whenever the gravity of a wort has to be ascertained, various saccharometers have been devised, which by a nice adjustment of added weights, increasing with the density of the wort, enable the brewer, as he reads off the numbered mark on the stem to which the instrument sinks in the liquid, to find out the gravity with great ease.

The saccharometers generally used in England are either the old pattern known as "Dring and Fage's," or "Long's," or the specific gravity one known as Bate's in Germany Balling's saccharometer (graduated to show

how many parts by weight of dry, pure, cane-sugar, or parts equal thereto, are present in the solution taken at 14° Réaumur = 63½° Fahr.). In France and elsewhere an instrument on the same principle, known as Baumé's hydrometer or *pèse-sirop*, is used; but, unfortunately, this class does not appear to be constructed on a uniform plan. A formula is given below for converting Baumé into degrees of specific gravity, it being understood that the formula is for an instrument graduated so that a liquid of 1,480° of specific gravity marks 48° on its own scale. Also a similar formula for converting degrees Balling into brewers' lb., with a comparative table, too, of the same equivalents, side by side with one showing the degrees of specific gravity, with their equivalents in brewers' lb.

Balling (Degrees).	Brewers' Lb.	Degrees, S.G.	Brewers' Lb.	Degrees, S.G.	Brewers' Lb.	Degrees, S.G.	Brewers' Lb.	Degrees, S.G.	Brewers' Lb.	Degrees, S.G.	Brewers' Lb.
1	1·5	1001=0·36	1021= 7·56	1041=14·76	1061=21·96	1081=29·16
2	2·9	1002=0·72	1022= 7·92	1042=15·12	1062=22·32	1082=29·52
3	4·4	1003=1·08	1023= 8·28	1043=15·48	1063=22·68	1083=29·88
4	5·8	1004=1·44	1024= 8·64	1044=15·84	1064=23·04	1084=30·24
5	7·2	1005=1·80	1025= 9·00	1045=16·20	1065=23·40	1085=30·60
6	8·7	1006=2·16	1026= 9·36	1046=16·56	1066=23·76	1086=30·96
7	10·1	1007=2·52	1027= 9·72	1047=16·92	1067=24·12	1087=31·32
8	11·6	1008=2·88	1028=10·08	1048=17·28	1068=24·48	1088=31·68
9	13·1	1009=3·24	1029=10·44	1049=17·64	1069=24·84	1089=32·04
10	14·6	1010=3·60	1030=10·80	1050=18·00	1070=25·20	1090=32·40
11	16·0	1011=3·96	1031=11·16	1051=18·36	1071=25·56	1091=32·76
12	17·6	1012=4·32	1032=11·52	1052=18·72	1072=25·92	1092=33·12
13	19·1	1013=4·68	1033=11·88	1053=19·08	1073=26·28	1093=33·48
14	20·6	1014=5·04	1034=12·24	1054=19·44	1074=26·64	1094=33·84
15	22·1	1015=5·40	1035=12·60	1055=19·80	1075=27·00	1095=34·20
16	23·6	1016=5·76	1036=12·96	1056=20·16	1076=27·36	1096=34·56
17	25·2	1017=6·12	1037=13·32	1057=20·52	1077=27·72	1097=34·92
18	26·8	1018=6·48	1038=13·68	1058=20·88	1078=28·08	1098=35·28
19	28·4	1019=6·84	1039=14·04	1059=21·24	1079=28·44	1099=35·64
20	30·0	1020=7·20	1040=14·40	1060=21·60	1080=28·80	1100=36·00

The equivalent brewers' or saccharometer lbs. in the first of the above tables are, if anything, a shade high; **the annexed formula gives closer results.**

Let B = deg. Balling, and s = brewers' (or saccharometer) lbs., then—

$$B = \frac{260\ s}{360 + s}, \text{ and } s = \frac{360\ B}{260 - B}.$$

Thus suppose we want the equivalent of 14° Balling—

$$s = \frac{360 \times 14}{260 - 14} = \frac{5040}{246} = 20\cdot 5.$$

Formula for converting Baumé into specific gravity—

Sp. grav. $= \dfrac{148{,}000}{148 - \text{deg. Baumé}}.$ Accordingly, e.g., 9° Baumé $= \dfrac{148{,}000}{139} = 1065°$ sp. grav.

But there is a good deal of variation, owing to indefinite standards of adjustment in respect to the latter saccharometer.

It may be added that it matters not what quantity of the wort is taken if only the saccharometer can float in it freely. In practice the quantity generally taken is that contained in a tall narrow sampling can, wherein the saccharometer can sink down to the topmost mark on its stem without touching bottom.

Degrees of Specific Gravity—Definition.—Each degree of specific gravity is equal to one-thousandth part of the gravity of distilled water at 60° Fahr., water being, as it were, the unit; but instead of unity its value is taken as 1,000 in order to avoid awkward fractions. It will be seen that "a degree of specific gravity," then, means no definite and uniform weight, but is merely the expression of the relation between the gravity of any wort and that of water. A gallon of wort taken from a barrel of 1,050 or 1060 sp. gr. will be equally of 1050 or 1060 sp. gr. (bearing the same relation to a gallon of water that the larger quantity does to a barrel), but, according to the definition, each of its degrees will only equal $\frac{10}{1000}$ lb. = ·01 lb., whereas each of those in a barrel would equal $\frac{360}{1000} = \cdot 36$ lb.

But, inasmuch as specific gravity, equally with brewers' lbs., states the excess of the weight of wort over water (because the 1000 is in general practice dropped and only the degrees in excess quoted), it is plain that there will be a constant uniform ratio between the two, which enables a gravity expressed in one standard to be converted into the other. Thus the ratio between 1 degree of sp. gr. and 1 brewers' lb. is

As $1000 : 360 =$ as $25 : 9 =$ as $1 : \cdot 36$.

Rule to convert Degrees of Specific Gravity into Brewers' Lbs. and vice versâ.—Multiply the given degrees by ·36, or multiply by 9 and divide by 25.

Ex.—To find the equivalent of 57 degrees in brewers' lb.

$$57 \times \cdot 36 = 20 \cdot 52 \text{ or, } \frac{57 \times 9}{25} = 20 \cdot 52.$$

Rule to convert Brewers' Lbs. to Degrees of Specific Gravity.—Divide by ·36, or multiply by 25 and divide by 9.

Why 2 cwt. of Sugar only give about 84 Brewers' Lb. Extract.—The fact that any given quantity of cane-sugar, which practically all dissolves, only gives brewers' lbs. to the amount of rather over $\frac{1}{3}$ of its own weight, may for a moment puzzle the beginner, but it is to be explained as follows.

A gallon of sugar weighs say 16 lb., or in other words, the specific gravity of sugar $= 1 \cdot 6$; if then 1 gallon of sugar were to be put into a barrel and 35 gallons of water added, there would then be 36 gallons, weighing altogether $16 + 350 = 366$ lb.; or, as has been explained before, a mixture having the gravity of 6 brewers' lb. would be produced. Therefore it takes 16 lb. of sugar to yield 6 brewers' lb., in other words, 1 brewers' lb. corresponds to $\frac{16}{6} = 2 \cdot 6$ lb. of sugar dissolved; or again 2 cwt. will yield 84 brewers' lb. extract $\left(\frac{224 \times 6}{16} = 84 \right)$.

And even this applies only to cane-sugar. Invert sugar

and glucose give much lower extracts, a fact which the necessary presence of water of hydration is insufficient to explain. By totalling up the atomic weights of invert sugar, for example ($C_{12}H_{24}O_{12}$ = 144 + 24 + 192 = 360), and subtracting from it the total atomic weights of cane-sugar ($C_{12}H_{22}O_{11}$ = 144 + 22 + 176 = 342), it will be seen that the water of hydration is only as 18 : 360, or 5%. The explanation must therefore lie in the presence of water of crystallisation, which invert sugar and many apparently dry samples of glucose contain.

Working out the Brewings.—This is a very simple operation. As a general rule, the number of barrels required, of different qualities and gravities, will be set down first—say on Saturday for the whole of the coming week—with the rounds (fermenting vessels) allotted to each. (The last is obviously a most necessary precaution, especially where the rounds are numerous, as they are in an extensive trade conducted on the skimming system, and of varying size, since otherwise a mash might be made without suitable rounds being available to run the worts into.) From the quantities that one intends to brew × their gravities the quantities of malt and sugar are calculated for each brewing respectively.

For example, we set out to brew on one day 132 barrels of bitter ale at $17\frac{1}{2}$ brewers' bs., and 75 barrels of XX at $18\frac{1}{2}$ brewers' lbs. Then $132 \times 17\frac{1}{2}$ = 2312, and $75 \times 18\frac{1}{2}$ = 1387, or 3699 = the total number of brewers' lbs. required. Then suppose we wish to get at least 25% of the extract from invert sugar, consigned say in 3 cwt. casks (which may be estimated as giving 105 brewers' lb. per cask), we see at a glance that 9 casks (= 945 brewers' lb.) is close enough for our purpose.

Then 3699 − 945 = 2754, and 2754 ÷ 85 (the assumed extract per quarter for fair malt) = $32\frac{1}{2}$ quarters nearly. So that our brewing consists of $32\frac{1}{2}$ quarters of malt, assumed to give an extract of 85 lb. and 27 cwt. of sugar. Of course malt may give a larger extract than the one indicated; it may also, if made from poor barley, give a much lower one. The excise standard = 79·2 lb., and if this is not attained, owing to either material, plant, or system, or two or all of them being faulty, "the charge," instead of being levied on the defective produce, is levied upon the material used.

For calculating the proportion of hops required, 2 cwt. of sugar are generally taken = 1 quarter malt (as the Excise formerly reckoned), though, as a matter of fact, the extract of that quantity of invert sugar or of glucose is considerably less than that yielded by a quarter of malt, so that, strictly speaking, the total lb. of such sugar used should be divided by 256 (lb.) instead of 224 to arrive at its equivalent in malt; 2 cwt. of good cane-sugar, however, give approximately the same extract as a quarter of malt.

Obviously, too, the hops should be so distributed among the various coppers as to bear a fairly close relation, not only to the number of barrels in each, but to their gravity as well. This point, however, will be more conveniently dealt with when we come to speak of parti-gyles.

Entry of the Malt and Sugar.—The exact quantities of malt or sugar which one intends to use have to be entered in the Brewing Book supplied by the officer of Inland Revenue, and this must be done at least two hours before use [the intention to brew having been notified in the same way at least twenty-four hours before]. When the malt weighs less than the standard weight (42 lb. per bushel) it is reduced into the said standard weight for entry. For example, suppose our $32\frac{1}{2}$ quarters of malt, being freely made, weigh only 40 lb. a bushel, *i.e.*, 2 lb. short of the standard, then the working is as follows:—

$32\frac{1}{2} \times 8 = 260$ bushels; $260 \times 2 = 520$ lb. short, this $\div 42 = 12\frac{8}{21}$, *i.e.*, 12 bushels off $32\frac{1}{2}$ quarters = 31 quarters for entry.

The quantity of sugar is reduced to lbs. for entry.

Sparging for Copper Lengths.—As the conditions vary a good deal it will be impossible to lay down a rule precise enough to meet all cases; it will therefore perhaps elucidate the matter better if we now proceed to mash our $32\frac{1}{2}$ quarters (on the morning after entry of materials has been made) in imagination.

The mash being made with two barrels to the quarter, including underlet, the total quantity on "the goods" = 65 barrels. Deducting from this $24\frac{1}{2}$ barrels (because "the goods" imbibe and retain a considerable quantity of the liquor, which may be roughly estimated at 27 gallons per quarter), we get $40\frac{1}{2}$ barrels from the mashtun, without reckoning sparge. Accordingly, the difference between this and the sum total of the copper lengths will represent the quantity of liquor required as sparge (less any liquor run into coppers direct without being sparged).

This being a parti-gyle, consisting of two distinct kinds of beer, we shall desire not to mix the coppers in the fermenting vessels; accordingly the first and second coppers will go for the BA and the third copper for the XX. But this would be impossible if we made up the first copper entirely with wort; we accordingly run in a considerable portion of plain liquor into both first and second coppers, and moreover keep back a portion of the strong "first runs" in the underback for mixing with and bringing up the gravity of the third copper to XX standard.

A moment's reflection will show that if we get a copper of given length, say of 100 barrels, we are not likely to get 100 barrels from it into the fermenting round; and for this there are several causes.

(i) The copper dip is taken on boiling wort, whereas in the F. V. it stands at 60° or thereabouts (= a shrinkage of 4%).

(ii) Waste during boiling (amount varies with conditions, atmospheric pressure, and amount of wind, the depth of the copper in relation to surface, etc.).

(iii) Retention of wort by hops (60 lb. hold back about 1 barrel).

(iv) A relatively small amount retained in the intermediate vessels, hop-back and coolers.

We take all these causes in the aggregate, and find that the loss will generally average a known amount, within a barrel or thereabouts, at all events, and on that we base our calculations. Suppose we arrange our three copper lengths at 88, 65, and 80 barrels respectively; experience, say, tells us that we may expect to get in the rounds 76, 56, and 72, the former two totalling up 132 barrels, or exactly the amount required for the BA, the latter being purposely run short, so as to allow of the desired length of 75 barrels being made up by a sparge over the spent hops.

But this is not all. As before said, a considerable quantity of plain liquor must be run into both first and second coppers to get their blend down as low as $17\frac{1}{2}$ brewers' lbs. This plan—seeing that the amount of liquor run into coppers has to be deducted from sparge—will have the incidental advantage of preventing an excessive sparging of goods, which is certainly to be avoided. Let us see **how the quantity of liquor which we have to run in is to be calculated.**

The first "runs" from the mash-tun will probably be found to weigh 35 brewers' lb. or thereabouts; but as we intend to keep back 22 barrels in the underback for the third copper, we shall not be far off the mark if we take the average gravity of the wort which reaches the first copper a little lower—viz., at 32 or 33 lb. As we wish to get the first copper to turn out (*i.e.*, to weigh after boiling) a little, but not much, in excess of the gravity required for the BA, let us fix the gravity at 17 lb., which, after boiling, will give a wort in the fermenting vessels of 18·5, more or less, according to the duration and vigour of the boil (our own estimate is based upon what may be considered a rather short boil of $1\frac{1}{2}$ hour for the first copper).

Then $88 \times 17 = 1496$ total brewers' lb. required. If we use 12 cwt. of invert, giving an extract calculated in brewers' lbs. as 420, there remain $(1496 - 420) = 1076$ lb to get from the wort. Then $\frac{1076}{33} = 32 \cdot 6$, or, for first copper, $32\frac{1}{2}$ barrels of wort $+ 55\frac{1}{2}$ barrels of liquor $+ 12$ cwt. of invert sugar.

Then, as we calculate to get from the first copper 76 barrels at $18\frac{1}{2}$ lb., or 1 lb. over the desired gravity, the running-down gravity of the second copper must be $\frac{76}{56} = 1 \cdot 3$ under the desired gravity, viz., 16·2. Perhaps 14·7 might be a sufficient "in-copper" gravity; but if, on the other hand, there is a fairly full copper, such as can be safely boiled by steam, perhaps the loss by boiling, and consequently the increase of the copper's running-down gravity, would be less than if a harder boil was attained by fire. We will accordingly assume 15 lb. to be the required "in-copper" gravity for the second copper.

We will now take the average gravity of the wort making up second copper = 23 lb. (but this must obviously be a question of experience; it will be found sufficiently close under the conditions predicated).

$65 \times 15 = 975$ total brewers' lb. required.

$975 - 105$ (from 3 cwt. sugar) $= 870$.

$870 \div 23 = 38$.

Or 38 barrels of wort to 27 barrels plain liquor and 3 cwt. invert sugar.

It may be mentioned that as it is practically impossible to ensure that *absolute* uniformity of "in-copper" gravities which would be necessary to secure an unvarying gravity of the produce if the entirety of two coppers are blended, it is advisable rather to underdo than to overdo the gravities, as they can be brought up to the required mark by the addition of a little more sugar in the coppers, whilst lowering them, when in excess, is not so easy.

It will be found almost essential in this sort of partigyle brewing, or if much sugar is used, to have some kind of **apparatus for dissolving cask-sugar,** such as a copper trough, long enough to hold two casks and fitted in a

SUGAR-DISSOLVING APPARATUS.

stout wooden frame. The trough will have two plug-holes commanding each copper if the latter are side by side, or the contents can be carried some distance by shoots. There are steam nozzles just above where the casks lie, and steam pipes being fitted on them, are forced through holes bored into the sides of the casks exactly opposite the bungholes. The bungholes are of course downward, and the sugar, as it is melted, flows out of them.

To return to the sparges. The total "in-copper" length required being $88 + 65 + 80 = 233$ barrels, out of which $40\frac{1}{2}$ barrels are yielded by the mash and $55\frac{1}{2} + 27 = 82\frac{1}{2}$ barrels are plain liquor, not sparged, or altogether 123 barrels. Then $233 - 123 = 110$ barrels to be sparged.

This quantity (110 barrels) should be quite sufficient sparge for $32\frac{1}{2}$ quarters, and if a sample of the last runnings be caught just when the third copper length is made up, it will probably not be found to weigh more than 1·5 brewers' lb., and very possibly less. Personally, I do not care to get worts much below 2, although one needs to be assured then that the sparging apparatus is in good order, and that the sparge-liquor is evenly and lightly distributed; because it may happen that, owing to imperfect sparging, the liquor falling much more copiously in one place than the other may "channel," and then, in very flagrant instances, it would be possible for the "last runs" to be of very low gravity, and yet the major part of "the goods" be unexhausted.

I have purposely taken a rather simple parti-gyle as an illustration. I might, however, fill my pages with an infinite variety, in some of which two mash-tuns might be used, without exactly suiting the requirements of any of my readers. I will, however, to illustrate what has been said about apportioning the hops to the various coppers, not only according to their length but also with some regard to their gravity, take a very straightforward brew—viz., 200 barrels of XX at 18·5.

The total brewers' lbs. required being $18.5 \times 200 = 3700$, if we wish to get 20% of the extract from invert sugar we shall find that 21 cwt. at 35 lb. ($= 735$ lb.) is the quantity required.

Then $\dfrac{3700 - 735}{85 \text{ (extract per qr.)}} = 35$ quarters of malt (strictly speaking 34·88).

The materials, therefore, are 35 quarters of malt and 21 cwt. of invert sugar.

Though in the brewing of light gravity ales, where sugar is used to any extent, I should always advocate a quantity of unsparged liquor (proportioned to the quantity of sugar) being run into the copper in lieu of sparging the entire length; yet in this instance we will suppose the whole quantity, except what drains from the mash, to be sparged.

Seventy barrels being used for the mash and underlet, the goods will keep back 26 barrels, so that only 44 barrels can be reckoned on from the mash-tun.

Our copper lengths will be (say) $85 + 60 + 82 = 227$ barrels in all three coppers. Then we shall want $227 - 44 = 183$ barrels of sparge.

Of course, if a second mash is adopted—but this is generally unnecessary if the first mash was properly made—the quantity of liquor so used must come off the sparge-length of 183 barrels. No set rule need be given for dividing the sparge liquor, but as it is advisable to "keep the goods up" at first, the quantity of liquor sparged on by the time that the first copper is made up should not be very far short of that copper-length + such a quantity of strong wort as is run into, or kept back for, the second and third coppers to bring their gravity up.

And I must say that I think the plan of equalising gravities by keeping back strong wort for second and third coppers is one to be greatly recommended. It greatly simplifies calculations (even a chance mistake in mixing copper lengths in the rounds need not produce very dire consequences), it renders the hopping an easier

PROPORTIONS OF HOPS TO COPPERS.

matter; moreover, worts of low gravity are known to have a tendency to extract a rank bitter from the hops. And though such a manipulative detail belongs more to another chapter, it may be said here that starting the sparging some 10 or 15 minutes before the taps are set is often a help in "keeping up the goods."

Though in brewing only one description of ale, we cannot, if the division by the assumed extract and other preliminary simple calculations have been correctly done, go wrong, let us act, nevertheless, upon the commendable plan of equalising gravities to a certain extent—*e.g.*, if we get the "in-copper" gravity of our coppers respectively 19 lb., $16\frac{1}{2}$ lb., and 14 lb., and supposing we boil the first copper only $1\frac{3}{4}$ hour against 2 hours' boil of the other two, they will run down into the fermenting vessels of the value say (the boil not having been a very rapid one) of 20·8, 18·6, and 16·0 at least.

Apportioning the Hops (assuming the above gravities).—Suppose we use for XX hops to the amount of 5 lb. per quarter. Reckoning 2 cwt. sugar = 1 quarter malt, then $35 + 10\frac{1}{2}$ (21 cwt.) = $45\frac{1}{2}$, which × 5 = 227 lb. of hops divisible amongst the three coppers.

```
Then taking Copper I.,   85 Barrels @ 19 lb.   = 1615
    ,,      ,,    II.,   60    ,,     16½ ,,   =  990
    ,,      ,,   III.,   82    ,,     14  ,,   = 1148
                                                ────
                                                3753
```

Then the proportions are represented by the following rule-of-three sums based on the fractions: for Copper I., $\frac{1615}{3753}$, or (in round numbers) = $\frac{16}{37}$; for Copper II., $\frac{990}{3753} = \frac{10}{37}$; for Copper III., $\frac{1148}{3753} = \frac{11}{37}$.

```
  I.  37 : 16 :: 227 =  98
 II.  37 : 10 :: 227 =  62
III.  37 : 11 :: 227 =  67
                       ───
                       227
```

Working out Hops at lbs. per Barrel.—In parti-gyle brewing, and especially where beers are being brewed which have to be differently hopped, it is by far the most convenient plan to work by the ascertained proportion per barrel in preference to proportion per quarter. And this is really the best system in every case, because the extract per quarter may easily vary 5 brewers' lb., or more, with varying qualities of malt; so that if the proportion be calculated per quarter, the smaller quantity of beer yielded by the inferior malt will get the same quantity of hops as the larger quantity of beer yielded by an equal quantity of the better malt.

Thus, for argument's sake, we want to brew a running pale ale of 22 lb. gravity, hopped with 12 lb. of hops per quarter (giving 85 lb. extract) and an AK of 18 lb. gravity hopped with 8 lb. per quarter. Then the proportions per barrel are for the PA $(85 : 22 :: 12) = 3\cdot1$, and for the AK $(85 : 18 :: 8) = 1\cdot7$.

Assuming that we want to get 50 barrels of the former and 75 of the latter, and that we shall get them from the first two coppers (which are of the lengths just given, viz., 85 and 60 barrels respectively), then the total hops required for both descriptions of ale $= (50 \times 3\cdot1) + (75 \times 1\cdot7) = 283$. But if the first copper be got of such a strength as to turn out—or rather run down into the F.V.'s—at 22 lb., seeing that it will run about 75 barrels, we shall want $75 \times 3\cdot1 = 232$ for the first copper, leaving 51 for the second. In practice, if the worts were to be more blended than in the case under consideration, we should probably rather underdo the worked-out proportion for the first copper, and accordingly rather exceed it for the second, seeing that the stability of the extract in the first copper is presumably greater than that of the second. This being so, one would like to support the second copper by adding hops somewhat in excess, where possible, of what its gravity really warrants. Or, if the flavour generally obtained permits of returning hops, we might keep to the precise

INITIAL HEAT AND STRIKING HEAT. 169

proportions, but, as counselled in Chap. VIII., only very lightly boil a portion of the best hops assigned to the first copper, and return as many as possible to the second copper.

Formula for calculating Initial Heat from "Striking Heat."—Though not likely to be much used in practice, it may be useful to have such a formula. Of course it is applicable to a mixture of any two bodies whose specific heat * is known, but, as in our own case, it will be used solely for mixtures of malt and water. The lettering used may be arranged with special reference thereto. So when

W. M. = weight of malt (*i.e.*, total weight used),
S. H. M. = specific heat of malt (= ·42),
A. T. M. = actual temperature of malt,
W. W. = weight of water,
S. H. W. = specific heat of water (but as this is taken = 1, it really may be left out of calculation),
A. T. W. = actual temperature of water,

then the general formula will be—

$$\frac{\text{W.M.} \times \text{S.H.M.} \times \text{A.T.M.} + \text{W.W.} \times \text{S.H.W.} \times \text{A.T.W.}}{\text{W.M.} \times \text{S.H.M.} + \text{W.W.} \times \text{S.H.W.}} =$$

I. H. (initial heat).

Supposing, then, we mash each imperial quarter of 336 lb. malt with 2 barrels of water (= 720 lb.) at 165°, and we find, by plunging a mash-tun thermometer into the grist-case, that the A. T. M. = 62°, then our calculation comes out as follows: [We take a single quarter of malt for the calculation and 2 barrels of water to keep the numbers down.]

$$\frac{336 \times \cdot 42 \times 62 + 720 \times 1 \times 165}{336 \times \cdot 42 + 720 \times 1} = \frac{127549 \cdot 44}{861 \cdot 12} = 148 \cdot 1.$$

This approximates pretty closely to the actual *mixing* heat; but it must not be forgotten that a chemical action,

* For information on Specific Heat, see Glossary.

more or less energetic, immediately begins, during which heat is set free. Moreover, the mash ought to fall into a mash-tun so well heated as actually to gain rather than lose heat. Consequently, when the diastasic action is vigorous, and the heating of the mash-tun, especially if an iron one, has been efficiently performed, the mash-tun too being of such a size and so placed that the radiation of heat is inconsiderable, we should expect the temperatures of the mash taken at the finish—*i.e.*, when all the mash is in the mash-tun (and which, though inaccurately, is called the "initial heat") to show 3° or 4° higher.

Making up Lengths.—Although I hold with equalising copper gravities so far that very little calculation will be requisite, it will be desirable to give certain forms to meet cases in which such equalisation is not possible.

I. To find in what proportion worts of two different gravities must be mixed to obtain a certain bulk at an intermediate gravity.

(a) To find the bulk of stronger wort. **Rule.**—Multiply the given bulk by the degrees (or pounds) of gravity under the gravity required of the weaker of the two worts, and divide by their difference of gravity.

Ex.—How much wort at 85° must be combined with wort at 14° to produce 1000 gallons at 57?

Degrees under $(57 - 14) = 43°$
Difference $\quad (85 - 14) = 71°$

$$\frac{1000 \times 43}{71} = 605\frac{45}{71} \text{ gallons at } 85°.$$

[The correctness of which may be proved as follows—

$$605\frac{45}{71} \times 85 = 51478\frac{62}{71}$$
$$394\frac{26}{71} \times 14 = 5521\frac{9}{71}$$
$$\overline{1000 \times 57 = 57000}]$$

MIXING WORTS.

Ex.—How much wort at 30·6 gravity must be mixed with wort of 5 lb. gravity to obtain 80 barrels at 21 lb. gravity per barrel?

Lb. under $(21 - 5) = 16$
Difference $(30·6 - 5) = 25·6$
$\dfrac{80 \times 16}{25·6} = 50$ Barrels at 30·6

Proof.
$50 \times 30·6 = 1530$
$30 \times 5 = 150$
$\overline{80 \times 21 = 1680}$

(β) To find the bulk of weaker wort. **Rule.**—Multiply the given bulk by the degrees (or pounds) of gravity of the stronger of the two worts over the gravity required, and divide by their difference of gravity.

Ex.—How much wort at 14° must be combined with wort at 85° to produce 1000 gallons at 57°?

Degrees over $(85 - 57) = 28$
Difference . $(85 - 14) = 71$

$\dfrac{1000 \times 28}{71} = 394\dfrac{26}{71}$ gallons at 14°.

Ex.—How much wort at 5 lb. gravity must be mixed with wort at 30·6 to produce 80 barrels at 21 lb. gravity?

Lbs. over $(30·6 - 21) = 9·6$
Difference $(30·6 - 5) = 25·6$
$\dfrac{80 \times 9·6}{25·6} = 30$

Proof.
$30 \times 5 = 150$
$50 \times 30·6 = 1530$
$\overline{80 \times 21 = 1680}$

II. To ascertain the proportions in which two worts of different gravities must be mixed to get an intermediate gravity.

Rule.—Find the difference of gravity of the two given worts above and below the required gravity. State these differences (inversely) in the form of a fraction, and reduce the fraction to its lowest terms. [The example given is in brewers' lbs., but of course the rule holds equally good for degrees.]

Ex.—In what proportion must worts at 29 lb. and at 8 lb. gravity per barrel be combined to produce a gravity of 20 lb.?

$$20 \text{ lb.} \begin{cases} 29 \\ 8 \end{cases} \asymp \frac{12}{9} = \frac{4}{3},$$

i.e., 4 barrels at 29 lb. to each 3 barrels at 8 lb.

III. To ascertain the proportions in which worts of four different gravities may be mixed to produce an intermediate gravity.

Rule (*a*)—State the differences of gravity of all four worts above and below the required gravity, but inversely. This column will give proportions at the gravities in the same line.

Ex.—What proportions of worts at 20°, 37°, 63°, and 80° respectively will give a combined gravity of 57°?

```
           Difference reversed
       ⎛ 20  ...  23 (Barrels at 20) × 20 =  460
  57°  ⎜ 37  ...   6 (    ,,        37) × 37 =  222
       ⎨ 63  ...  20 (    ,,        63) × 63 = 1260
       ⎝ 80  ...  37 (    ,,        80) × 80 = 2960
         ──                                    ────
         86                              57 = 4902
```

Obviously, though, other combinations of these gravities might be made which would give the same combined gravity, and in the event of the brewer having to blend four different worts (not a plan to be recommended), he would find it simpler to arrange his coppers so that *equal* quantities of the three weaker worts would be run in, and so that only the proportion of them *taken as a whole*, and the proportion of the strongest wort required to bring the gravity up, must be calculated. And of course the stronger wort, which is naturally the first copper, might easily be the only one whose precise gravity he knows at the beginning of his calculation. If he has worked out the assumed total extract correctly he may, having got his first copper ready to run down at a gravity of 80°, know that his remaining three coppers will average a gravity of 40° $\left(\dfrac{20 + 37 + 63^*}{3}\right)$, but he cannot be sure that they will be precisely 63°, 37° and 20°. So that we have

Rule β.—Get the average gravity of the second, third, and fourth coppers, and using that as one term and the gravity of the strong wort as the other, proceed as in Rule II. Assuming the average gravity to be 40°

$$57 \begin{cases} 80 \\ 40 \end{cases} \!\!\!\!>\!\!\!\!< \dfrac{17}{23} \qquad \textbf{Proof.} \begin{cases} 17 \times 80 = 1360 \\ 23 \times 40 = 920 \\ \overline{40} \times 57 = \overline{2280} \end{cases}$$

i.e., 17 barrels of first wort and $7\tfrac{2}{3}$ of each of the others in each 40 barrels.

Boiling down Copper to get a required Gravity.

Ex.—A brewer wants in his gyle-tun wort of a gravity of 70°, but finds in his copper 85 barrels at 62°. How much must he boil away?

Rule.—Multiply the given bulk by its gravity, and divide by the required gravity. Or multiply by the difference between the two gravities and divide by the required gravity. [The first calculation will give the bulk to which the copper is to be boiled down, the second the amount to be boiled away. And one proves the other.

$$\textbf{Ex.} — (a) \quad \dfrac{85 \times 62}{70} = 75\tfrac{3}{7}.$$

$$\textbf{Ex.} — (\beta) \quad \dfrac{85 \times 8}{70} = \dfrac{9\tfrac{5}{7}}{85}$$

N.B.—This, of course, means the amount actually to

---

* They can of course only be these gravities with an average of 40°, if they are equal lengths; but if they are at those gravities, though unequal lengths, they will average 40° for any F.V. into which equal lengths are run, though more or less, as the case may be, on the whole.

be boiled away + evaporation on coolers. The usual difference between copper-length and the quantity got in the gyle-tun depends on shrinkage, and retention by hops as well as on these factors.]

Working out Extract per Quarter.—In the paragraph on working out the brewings mention was made of the extract given by a quarter of malt. The so-called extract (which of course differs from the "solid" or "dry extract" to be mentioned shortly) is the apparent extract perceptible by the saccharometer, and generally ranges between 80 and 90 brewers' lb. per quarter of 336 lb. Forming, as it does, a ready means of classifying malts, from one point of view, the extracts should be worked out on the morning following the brew at latest.

> **Rule.**—Multiply the barrels got by the gravity (or each lot of barrels by their respective gravities, if there are various gravities), deduct the number of brewers' lb. given by sugar, and divide the remainder by the number of quarters brewed.
>
> > **Ex.**—Suppose we brewed 200 barrels at 18·5 lb. from 34 quarters of malt and 21 cwt. of invert sugar. Then $200 \times 18·5 = 3700$ lb.; $3700 - 735$ (lbs. from sugar) $= 2965$; $2965 \div 34 = 87·2$ extract per quarter.

Dry or Solid Extract may be defined as "the amount of solid matter which a wort contains, whether derived from malt or other material."

It is generally arrived at by multiplying the extract per quarter, as ordinarily calculated, by 2·597 (2·6 approximately), though a factor as low as 2·538 has been advocated as being more correct.

Let us suppose we have an extract, as ordinarily taken, of 88·7 per quarter, this $\times 2·597 = 230·353$ dry extract.

Extract per Cent.—We can now make use of the ascertained amount of dry or solid extract to calculate the percentage of extractive matter which the malt yields. This we do by taking the solid extract and dividing it by

3·36 (in other words, multiplying by 100 and dividing by 336, the weight of a standard quarter of malt), and we accordingly find $230·353 \div 3·36 = 68·55\%$.

The necessity of working out the solid extract may be dispensed with by multiplying the ordinary extract by the factor ·7729 (which is $2·597 \div 3·36$). Thus $88·7 \times ·7729 = 68·55\%$.

[If, however, the lower factor 2·538 be taken for estimating solid extract, the factor for getting percentage out of ordinary extract will be ·755. The variation is due to a difference of opinion as to the amount of gravity added by any given quantity (say 1 gramme in 100 cc.) of starch transformation products. The higher factors depend on the assumption that 1 gramme of malt extract in 100 cc. raises the density of the infusion by 3·85° (water being 1000). This is admitted to be true for sugar solutions at 1050 (though rather too low for those of lower gravity and too high for those of higher), but is alleged not to be high enough for accuracy when starch-transformation products are being dealt with. Mr. O'Sullivan, in fact, considers that 1 gramme of such products in 100 cc. at 60° Fahr. raises the density 3·95—in other words, that such a solution will have a specific gravity of 1003·95.]*

Excise Charges.—The Excise charges are levied either upon the material used, or upon produce. 84 lb. of malt or other grain, or 64 lb. of invert sugar or glucose, are expected to yield 1 barrel of wort of the specific gravity

---

* Another way of working out the percentage extract, which will show how the higher solution value affects the extract in an opposite sense, is based on the fact that as 3·85 (or 3·95, as the case may be) shows the density value of 1 gramme of solid extract in 100 cc., so it shows the value of 1 lb. in 100 lb.—*i.e.*, 10 gallons of water. Accordingly the specific gravity, over $1000 \times 3·6$ (to bring the 10 gallons up to a barrel) $\div 3·85$, give the amount of solid extract *per barrel*. Hence the percentage extract can be got. Suppose we have 190 barrels at 52° from 40 quarters malt. Then—

$$\frac{52 \times 3·6}{3·85} = 48·62 \quad \text{and} \quad \frac{48·62 \times 190}{40 \times 3·36} = 68·7\%.$$
(Solid extract per barrel.)

of 55° at least, less 4%, and in the event of any lower yield the charge is upon material. Passable material and fair skill ought to ensure in every case a sufficient extract to avoid a "material charge." We will accordingly deal with the charge upon produce first.

The amount levied is 6s. 3d. per barrel, formerly of 57°, but now of 55°, from which an allowance of 6% is made for waste and loss during fermentation. This deduction, however, is not made daily, but is taken off at the month's end from the total number of gallons chargeable. To enable the charge to be levied, the quantity produced has to be brought into gallons, and these calculated into gallons of the standard gravity of 55°, whereupon their number is entered by the Excise officer in the "specimen book," and the brewer, to avoid chance of mistake, should check the calculation.

Suppose in one F.V. he has 130 barrels at 1048, and in another 70 barrels at 1053, or concisely 48 and 53, then

130 × 36 × 48 = 224640
70 × 36 × 53 = 133560

358200 which ÷ 55 = 6513 gallons chargeable.

These totals should be entered daily in a small book kept for the purpose, and added up at the end of the month, just as the officer does to get at the amount payable as duty. Any odd gallons, less than 36, are carried forward to the following month.

Let us suppose we have 135021 gross gallons at 55° with 27 "odds" from the preceding month. Then the calculation will be

$$
\begin{array}{r}
135021 \text{ (gross gallons at 55)}. \\
8101 \text{ (6\% deducted)}. \\
\hline
126920 \\
27 \text{ ("odds" from last month)}. \\
\hline
\end{array}
$$

36)126947.

6/3 { | 5 | $\frac{1}{4}$ | 3526 and 11 gallons over ("odds" for next month).
     | 1/3 | $\frac{1}{4}$ | 881 10 0
     | | | 220 7 6

£1101 17 6 payable.

It has been mentioned that, if the amount and gravity of wort produced do not come up to a certain standard, the charge, instead of being levied upon produce, is levied upon material—*i.e.*, the charge is made, not upon the quantity which the brewer actually gets, but on what he ought to have got. Consequently, he pays a higher duty on what he actually gets than the 6s. 3d. which the more competent brewer pays. Although "material charges" ought only to have a theoretical interest to those who devote any study to brewing, it may be well to enlarge the catalogue of materials with the quantities which are expected to produce one barrel of beer at 1055. These are malt 84 lb.; raw cane-sugar 56 lb.; invert or glucose 64 lb.; No. 1 syrup (weighing 14 lb. per gallon) 68 lb.; and No. 2 syrup (weighing 13 lb. 2 oz. per gallon) 82 lb.

A calculation made on the above basis gives a number of gallons which, less 4%, constitutes the "minimum yield," and on this, if the actual yield fall below it, the charge is made. Both charges are subject to the 6% deduction when the monthly accounts are made up.

It is sometimes necessary for the brewer to work out the contents of a round or square vessel, which is either in position or is intended to be put up; and to do this he may avail himself of the following divisors or factors.

Contents of Square or Round Vessels in Bushels or Gallons.—Having got the number of cubic inches in his vessel (in the case of rounds, diam. × diam. × depth, all in inches), he has the choice of either dividing by a divisor or multiplying by a factor.

Gives result in	Divisors for		Factors for	
	Squares.	Circles.	Squares.	Circles.
Gallons	277·274	353·036	·0036065	·0028326
Bushels	2218·192	2824·29	·00045082	·00035407

Ex.—Suppose we have a rectangular vessel 14 ft. × 15 ft. × 5 ft. = 168 × 180 × 60 inches = 1814400 cubic inches.

Then $\frac{1,814,400}{277\cdot274}$ = 6543 gallons = 182 barrels (nearly).

A speedier way of reckoning the Above.—This, which is correct enough for practical purposes, consists in dividing the *cubic feet* by 6 and adding 4% as correction. This gives the answer in *barrels*, thus—

14 × 15 × 5 = 1050 cubic feet

$\frac{1050}{6}$ = 175, and 175 + 7 (4% of 175) = 182 barrels.

Cost Price of Beer.—Where a competitive trade is done, it is necessary, and it is never superfluous, to know the cost of each barrel of beer at the moment of production, or rather of delivery. The difficulty is to know precisely what expenses beyond those of actual malt, hops, and sugar used, and of duty chargeable, to divide and apportion strictly to each individual barrel, and which to lump together in a more general manner. On the whole, we should feel inclined to place in the first class those expenses which *do* bear a more or less close relation to the number of barrels produced—viz., those under the headings of coal, wages and salaries, rail (carriage inwards of materials and outwards of finished produce), horses, finings, etc., while those which either would not vary at all, or would vary very little with the number of barrels produced, are such items as interest on capital at 5%, losses on rentals, wear and tear of plant, repairs of plant, etc. The two last are obviously correlated, and where, as large firms generally do, brewers have their own mechanics, repairs are largely included under the head of wages. Accordingly, it seems fairer to divide the sum total of these less elastic items by the average number of brewing days, assigning an amount equivalent to the quotient so obtained to each day; the result of which, of course, will be that the larger the number of barrels brewed on any particular day the lower will be the debit of each individual barrel in respect to those items. And this is what really occurs. A sudden influx of trade, resulting in an appreciable increase of the output, would not practically increase those items, whereas it would at once increase the other expenses under the heads of coal, railway charges, etc., and, if permanent, would increase those under the head of wages and salaries also, though perhaps not to the same extent. On the other hand, this method of dealing with the elastic (or progressive) expenses and the non-elastic (or unprogressive) expenses has this disadvantage, that, if it is the practice, from some motive of convenience, to brew only a relatively very small gyle on any one day of the week, then the barrels brewed will be unduly overweighted with the latter set of expenses; but, save for this, it seems far the best working plan.*

We may take the following amounts as fairly average ones per barrel for the different items of progressive expenses. Coal, $3\frac{1}{4}d.$ per barrel; wages and salaries together, $2s.$; rail and horses, $2s.$ $11d.$ per barrel. Of course, where beer is sent long distances by rail, the latter item may be much increased for the particular consignment. The calculation given refers to distances within a wide, but still reasonable, trade radius. The amount of what have been called the unprogressive expenses—by which again are meant those which do not increase in strict unison with the increase of trade—must of course vary considerably with circumstances; but we will, for the purposes of our calculation, assume them to be £3,550 per annum, and the number of brewing days in the year to be 251 (we are speaking of a concern producing 50,000 barrels or more yearly), then, in accordance with the scheme sketched above, each of these days will be debited with a sum of £14 $2s.$ $11d.$, in addition to the other items more directly concerned in production. It may be mentioned that loss

* Bad debts should be taken into account, but as they do not necessarily increase in direct ratio with the trade, are here included in the "non-progressive" expenses.

on public-house rentals, whether the houses be leasehold, and relet at a lower rental than they are held at, or freehold, and let at an annual sum which does not represent 5% on the investment, being wholly incurred to secure "tied trade," should be charged solely on the beers brewed for such tied trade. But upon family-trade ales, or public-house ales going into the free trade, no such charges are incident. Accordingly they have been left out of the calculation of cost price given below.

Cost Price Calculation.

Produced 210 Barrels AK @ 17·6 = 3696 lb. ⎫
    ,,   66 ,,   XX @ 18·7 = 1234 ,, ⎬ 3 : 1
Bunged down 198 Brls. AK and 63 Brls. XX = 261 Brls.

Materials (as below)—Extract 85·2.

	£	s.	d.	£	s.	d.
Malt, etc., 5 Qrs. No. 1, Flaked @ 42/- =	10	10	0			
,, 10 ,, Foreign Malt @ 35/- =	17	10	0			
,, 33 ,, Pale English @ 42/- =	69	6	0			
				97	6	0
Saccharum, 15 cwt., No. 2, Invert @ 17/- =	12	15	0			
,, 9 ,, ,, 3, ,, @ 16/- =	7	4	0			
				19	19	0
				117	5	0
Deduct for grains sold @ 2/8 per qr.				6	8	0
Cost of gravity-giving material				£110	17	0

[Divide between AK and XX in proportion 3 : 1, *i.e.*, £83 2*s*. 9*d*. and £27 14*s*. 3*d*.]

AK.

	£	s.	d.	£	s.	d.
Proportion of ext. yielding material				83	2	9
Hops—112 lb. Worcester	7	0	0			
,, 224 ,, Mid Kent	15	0	0			
Dry Hopping—99 lb. East Kent	10	12	0			
				32	12	0
Duty				54	0	0
				£169	14	9

XX.

	£	s.	d.	£	s.	d.
Proportion of ext. yielding material				27	14	3
Hops—28 lb. Belgian	1	3	0			
" 44 " Weald Kent	2	9	6			
				3	12	6
Duty				18	3	9
				£49	10	6

The larger amount ÷ 198 = 17s. 1¾d., and the smaller ÷ 63 = 15s. 8⅔d.

Then we have—

	AK.		XX.	
	s.	d.	s.	d.
Cost for Materials and Duty	17	1¾	15	8⅔
Wages and Salaries	2	0	2	0
Coal	0	3¼	0	3¼
Railway, Horses, etc.	2	11	2	11
Finings, Shives, and Bungs	0	1	0	1 1/12
Fixed (unprogressive) charge	1	1	1	1
Cost per Barrel	£1	3	6	£1	2	1

Or, making a kind of Balance Sheet, we have—

Dr.   *Cr.*

	£	s.	d.		£	s.	d.
To Malt	97	6	0	To 198 Brls. AK @ 23/6	232	13	0
" Saccharum	19	19	0	" 63 " XX @ 22/1	69	11	3
" Hops	36	4	6	" Grains	6	8	0
" Duty	72	3	9				
" Coal	3	10	8				
" Wages and Salaries	26	2	0				
" Railway and Horses	38	1	3				
" Finings, Shives, etc.	1	2	2				
" Fixed charges	14	2	11				
	£308	12	3		£308	12	3

CHAPTER VI.

CHEMISTRY AS APPLIED TO BREWING.

ELEMENTS—COMPOUNDS—DALTON, AMPÈRE, AND AVOGADRO—ATOMS, MOLECULES—FORMULÆ (EMPIRIC AND STRUCTURAL)—EQUATIONS (WHAT THEY MEAN)—TABLE OF ELEMENTS—THEIR ATOMICITY—CALCULATION OF PERCENTAGE COMPOSITION FROM FORMULÆ AND *VICE VERSÂ*—CHOOSING BETWEEN TWO OR MORE POSSIBLE FORMULÆ—ATOMICITY, VALENCE OR QUANTIVALENCE—SATURATION; AUTO-SATURATION—GLYPTIC FORMULA—COMPOUND RADICALS—ISOMERISM—ACIDS, BASES, SALTS—OXIDES—HYDROXIDES (HYDRATES)—BASICITY—TERMINATIONS *-IC* AND *-OUS*; *-ATE* AND *-ITE*—PREFIXES *HYPO-* AND *PER-*: SULPHIDES—CHLORATES, CHLORIDES—ANHYDRIDES—HYDROCARBONS—ALCOHOLS—ALDEHYDES—CARBOHYDRATES—MALTOSE—CELLULOSE—ORGANIC ACIDS—ELEMENTS IN THE NASCENT STATE—ALBUMINOIDS IN BARLEY—AMIDES—PEPTONES—ASPARAGIN—ANALYSES (TYPICAL)—NITROGEN—KJELDHAL'S METHOD OF DETERMINING IT—IODINE REACTION WITH STARCH—VARIOUS QUALITATIVE TESTS—IODOFORM—THE POLARIMETER.

CHEMISTRY, as a science, has for a number of years been separated into two divisions, originating in an apparently fundamental difference now recognised as no longer absolutely existing. This supposed difference, which referred the origin of all the various groups in the second and, from the brewer's point of view, most important division to life-processes or the functions of organisms, was the cause of these divisions receiving respectively the names of inorganic and organic chemistry.

But it having been discovered within the last fifty or sixty years that several of the compounds included in the latter, or so-called organic division, can be produced in the laboratory without the intervention of any animal or

CHEMISTRY OF THE HYDROCARBONS.

vegetable life-functions whatever, it has become evident that the term organic is somewhat of a misnomer, and it is only its convenient conciseness which maintains it against the preferable title of the **Chemistry of the Carbon Compounds**, or (seeing that the carbonates fall within the realm of inorganic chemistry) the still more preferable one of the **Chemistry of the Hydrocarbons and their Derivatives.**

It is beyond the scope of this book, however, to attempt to treat these divisions separately; the most that can be done here is to enunciate a few general principles as introductory to the hints on laboratory work in the next chapter for those who are ignorant of chemistry, and to enable them to approach the consideration of those important carbon-compounds (compounds in which carbon always enters into more or less intricate combination), starch, dextrin, cane-sugar, maltose, the alcohols, etc., with a mind capable of appreciating the significance of chemical *formulæ*.

In our study of matter we are confronted with certain substances known as **elements**—over seventy in number, though but few of them comparatively occur in any quantity, many being extremely rare. These elements are so called because they are incapable of being split up into simpler constituents by any known process; they constitute the simplest form of matter known to science.

Although it has been suggested that the large list of elements now identified may be a tribute rather to the imperfection than the perfection of analytical methods, and that they are modifications of some single substance, possibly hydrogen, it would be travelling too far into the region of the hypothetical to do more than glance at this theory; and indeed the regularity with which the substances, which we now regard as elements, combine to form definite and more or less stable products, renders it probable that the final limit of subdivision has been reached.

A Compound may be formed of two elements (*e.g.*, NaCl,

sodium chloride or common salt, or H_2O water). Complex substances may, however, consist of four, five, or more elements (*e.g.*, albumen, consisting of carbon, hydrogen, oxygen, nitrogen, sulphur, and possibly phosphorus). The brilliant hypotheses of Dalton, Ampère, and Avogadro* (though difficult of direct proof) having systematised all known facts, we are justified in taking it for granted that the elements combine in certain definite proportions, and always in the same proportion or in simple multiples of them, unless in the rare cases of an element having a double atomicity, of which more anon. They are assumed to consist of atoms ($ἄτομος$ = indivisible), which may be defined accordingly as "the smallest quantities of elementary matter which can take part in a chemical reaction." Two or more atoms, whether of the same or of different elements, combine together to form a molecule (it is supposed, indeed, that the ultimate particles of most elements, at least in the gaseous state, consist of two or more similar atoms), and a molecule may therefore be defined as "the smallest quantity of elementary matter, which can exist in a free state." This definition, however, hardly covers the full employment of the term, for it is usual to speak, for instance, of the molecule of water, H_2O, which, as shown, by its formula, consists of atoms of hydrogen and oxygen in the proportion of 2 : 1.

And here it may be said that the formulæ usually given —the **empiric formulæ,** as they are called (in contradistinction to **structural formulæ,** which impart information as to the reactions which have taken place)—give merely the relative number of atoms of each substance in a solid body (however exact they may be for one in a gaseous state); for example, the formula given above for common salt, NaCl, which merely expresses the fact that sodium (Na. for natrium) enters into combination with chlorine (Cl) in the proportion of 1 : 1, possibly ought to be

* Avogadro's hypothesis, summarised, is that "Equal volumes of all gases contain the same number of molecules under the same conditions of pressure and temperature."

written Na_nCl_n, n standing for an unknown and probably very large number.

This question of the complexity of the molecule comes still more to the front when we find, what is so puzzling at first sight, that varying substances like starch, dextrin, and cellulose, on the one hand, have the same empirical formula ($C_6H_{10}O_5$), and consequently, the same percentage composition, and cane-sugar and maltose ($C_{12}H_{22}O_{11}$) on the other. They are, consequently, more correctly expressed as $(C_6H_{10}O_5)_n$ and $(C_{12}H_{22}O_{11})_n$, *i.e.*, taken n times. And it may be added, with regard to starch, that in order to form an equation explanatory of the successive changes that take place during the mashing process, it is necessary to assume for n a value of at least 20, or of 10 if the formula be doubled to bring it into line with that of maltose; and later researches warrant a rearrangement and amplification even of this formula 10 ($C_{12}H_{20}O_{10}$).

Structural formulæ are, as it were, the condensed expression of the conclusions drawn from the reactions; for example, the empiric formula of acetic acid = $C_2H_4O_2$, but its **structural or constitutional formula** C_2H_3O, OH, whilst showing its percentage composition, also shows that one atom of oxygen and one atom of hydrogen are so linked together as to be capable of undergoing substitution by some other atom (thus comporting themselves like a single atom), and again of recombining under suitable conditions. This is what actually happens; *e.g.*, when acetic acid is treated with phosphorous trichloride PCl_3 it is converted into acetyl chloride, according to the equation $3\ C_2H_4O_2 + PCl_3 = 3C_2H_3OCl + PO_3H_3$ = (three molecules of acetic acid and one of phosphorous trichloride become three of acetyl chloride and one of phosphorous acid). Further, if the acetyl chloride so formed be brought into contact with water, a reaction *in a contrary sense* ensues, acetic acid being regenerated in consequence of the hydrogen and oxygen from the water taking the place of the chlorine in accordance with the equation $C_2H_3OCl + H_2O = C_2H_4O_2 + HCl$.

An equation, which expresses in concise form the reaction to which it relates, is so called because the weights indicated by the combined symbols, if any, and formulæ, on the one side of the sign = exactly correspond with the weights indicated by the combined symbols and formulæ on the other; and it may not be superfluous to say that as every element has its symbol, so that symbol represents a definite and constant relative weight of that element. Thus, to take a very simple form $H_2 + O = H_2O$ signifies not only that two atoms (or molecules) of hydrogen combine with one of oxygen to form water, but that exactly 2 lb. of hydrogen combine with 16 lb. of oxygen to form 18 lb of water; and the statement obviously stands, if for lb. we read grains or tons or anything between the two, so long as the same value is kept throughout.

The most important Elements, from our technical point of view, are those in the following list. The meaning of the fourth column will be explained in the next paragraph.

Those marked (M) are metals. The others are non-metals or metalloids. Those marked (H) are halogens.

Name.	Symbol.	Atomic Weight.	Atomicity, Valence, or Quantivalence.
Hydrogen	H	1	Monad, Monatomic, or Univalent.
Chlorine (H) ...	Cl	35·5	,,
Iodine (H) ...	I	127	,,
Potassium (M)	K	39	,,
Sodium (M) ...	Na	23	,,
Silver (M)	Ag.	108	,,
Oxygen	O	16	Diad, Diatomic, or Bivalent.
Sulphur	S	32	,,
Barium (M) ...	Ba	137	,,
Calcium (M)...	Ca	40	,,
Magnesium (M)	Mg	24	,,
Copper (M) ...	Cu	63·5	,,
Nitrogen	N	14	Triad (sometimes Pentad).
Phosphorus ...	P	31	,, ,,
Carbon	C	12	Tetrad, Tetratomic, or Tetravalent.
Silicon	Si	28	,,
Iron (M).........	Fe	56	Diad and Tetrad.

Atomicity, Valence, or Quantivalence, are synonyms expressing the varying capacity which an atom of each element has for fixing atoms of other elements. Thus the atom of certain elements such as hydrogen, potassium, sodium, chlorine, silver, etc., have only the capacity of fixing *one* atom of another element, and accordingly those elements are called **monatomic,** or **univalent,** or **monads.** An atom of the diatomic, bivalent, or diad elements, *e.g.*, oxygen, calcium, sulphur, etc., has the capacity of fixing *two* monad atoms or *one* diad. Similarly, each atom of a triatomic (trivalent or triad) element is able to fix three monad atoms or one diad and one monad. One atom of the tetrad carbon can fix four monad atoms or two diads; a pentad atom can fix five monad atoms or two diad atoms and one monad atom, and so on. To denote atomicity the marks ' (for monad), '' (for diad), ''' (for triad) are sometimes used; thus Mg'' reminds us that magnesium is diad.

(Later paragraphs on saturation and auto-saturation continue this subject.)

Calculating percentage Composition from Formulæ.—Having now the atomic weights of several of the elements before us, it may be useful to give a rule for calculating the percentage composition of a substance (*i.e.*, the weight of each element in one hundred parts by weight of the compound, all expressed in the same terms) from its formula.

> **Rule.**—The atomic weights of the elements forming the compound are to be added up and a series of rule-of-three sums (corresponding in number to the number of elements composing the compound), of which the first term is the sum of all the atoms; the second term is always 100; the third term being the atomic weight of each element in turn.

Thus, taking acetic acid $C_2H_4O_2$, $C_2 = (12 \times 2) = 24$; $H_4 = (1 \times 4) = 4$; $O_2 = (16 \times 2) = 32$, which together $= 60$,

Then,

(1) 60 : 100 :: 24 = 40
(2) 60 : 100 :: 4 = 6·66
(3) 60 : 100 :: 32 = 53·34

That is to say, the percentage composition is carbon 40, hydrogen 6·66, oxygen 53·34, which added together = 100.

Conversely, **to get the Formula from the percentage Composition** (ascertained, let us suppose, by analysis). We find out, for example, that a compound (and we will take acetic acid again) has the percentage composition of carbon 40; hydrogen 6·66; oxygen 53·34, and we get at the formula in two steps. First, the amount of each element ascertained must be divided by its atomic weight—thus

$$C = \frac{40}{12} = 3\cdot33$$

$$H = \frac{6\cdot66}{1} = 6\cdot66$$

$$O = \frac{53\cdot34}{16} = 3\cdot33$$

Next, these amounts are to be divided by the lowest amongst them (in this case 3·33); we accordingly get CH_2O, whereas the accepted formula of acetic acid = $C_2H_4O_2$, which is equally in accordance with the percentage proportions of the elements; it might equally be $C_3H_6O_3$ and so on.

This brings us face to face with the important fact that percentage composition does not necessarily show the correct formula (though it does so in the majority of cases), which has to be decided generally by determining the molecular weight. The molecular weight equals the sum of the atomic weights, corresponding with twice the vapour density compared with that of hydrogen taken as unity.* Exact experiment has shown the vapour

* To avoid the necessity of referring to hydrogen explicitly and con-

density or specific gravity of the vapour of acetic acid (compared with hydrogen = 1) to be 30·07, consequently the molecular weight = 60·14. But if CH_2O were to be taken as the formula of acetic acid, $C = 12$; $H_2 = 2$; $O = 16$ = 30 only. It is therefore evident that $C_2H_4O_2$ is the correct formula, the discrepancy of ·14 being due to almost inevitable experimental error.

The molecular weight of a substance, of which the percentage composition is known, may be either expressed M.W. = $\dfrac{100}{\text{lowest product of first step}}$, or some simple multiple of it—in the case of acetic acid M.W. = $\dfrac{100 \times 2}{3 \cdot 33}$ 60 (approximately).

The real molecular weight of acetic acid can also be arrived at by considering its only silver salt, **silver acetate,** in which one atom of hydrogen is replaced by one atom of silver. [Silver is *monad, vide* the table of the elements and paragraph succeeding it on Quantivalence]. Experiment shows that 100 parts of silver acetate contain 64·68 parts (nearly) by weight of silver.

tinuously as unity when in fact a litre of it weighs ·0896 gramme, the term "krith" is sometimes used in stating the specific weight of *gases*. [On the other hand, solids and liquids have their specific gravity stated as compared with water, 1 cc. of water = 1 gramme; gold = 19·3; iron 7·8 grammes, etc.] A "krith," then, = ·0896 gramme, the weight of a litre of hydrogen weighed at 0° centigrade and under a pressure of 760 millimetres of mercury (= 29·92178 inches). Accordingly the specific weight of hydrogen is said to be 1 krith; that of chlorine 35·5 kriths; that of oxygen 16 kriths; and so on. And assuming the number of molecules in one litre of any and every gas to be correctly computed at 6,106,000 *trillions,* the weight of each molecule of hydrogen would be ·0896 gramme ÷ that enormous divisor. Similarly the weight of each molecule of chlorine would be 3·1808 (= ·0896 × 35·5) divided by the same huge number.

I mention this to emphasise the hypothesis (Avogadro's) that under uniform conditions of pressure and temperature the number of molecules in every equal measure of every gas in equal. Not as sometimes stated, that the molecules of different gases are *necessarily* equal *in size*, only that each different molecule occupies an exactly equal space. For aught that is known, each molecule may move freely therein, like, for instance, a pea in a bladder.

Then the atomic weight of silver being 108, and one atom of hydrogen being replaced by one atom of silver, either 30 parts acetic acid give 137 parts of silver acetate, or 60 parts acetic acid give 167 parts of the acetate. Let us now multiply the parts by weight (64·68) found in 100 parts of silver acetate by 1·67, and if we find, as we do, that the product corresponds with the atomic weight of silver (108), we conclude that 60 parts of acetic acid, by parting with one atom of hydrogen and taking in its stead one atom of silver, yield 167 parts of silver acetate, or that the correct formula for the acid $= C_2H_4O_2$ and nothing less.

Or it may be put thus:—

$$\frac{35\cdot 32 \text{ (got by subtracting 64·68 from 100)} \times 108}{64\cdot 68} = 58\cdot 98$$

the weight of the carbon, hydrogen, and oxygen combined with one atom of silver. But in the acid, instead of the atom of silver, there is an atom of hydrogen; adding the equivalent of this to 58·98 we get 59·98, which practically $= 60$, the error of ·02 being an experimental one which one can hardly expect to lessen unless by repeated trial.

I have dealt rather at length with this point, not only because questions bearing upon it are sometimes asked in examination papers, but chiefly because of its intrinsic importance, in view of the complexity of formula exhibited by several of the substances in which we are specially interested.

Saturation of Atoms.—Though an atom may form a compound in which its full power of fixing other atoms is not exercised, such a compound is more or less unstable, the tendency of every atom being to fully saturate itself, that is, to combine with *all* the atoms which it has the power of annexing. That this tendency towards complete saturation is not always very pronounced may be seen from the fact that nitrogen fixes only *three* monad atoms to form the, in one sense, stable compound, ammonia (NH_3), though it is pentatomic, *i.e.*, fixes *five* atoms in ammonium chloride (NH_4Cl). It has been suggested that the term *atomicity* should be reserved for the maximum capacity of saturation, while the capacity of inferior saturation (or combination) should be expressed by *Quantivalence*. In this sense nitrogen would be *pentatomic* in the ammonium chloride, and *trivalent* in ammonia.

Auto-saturation or Auto-combination.—It is supposed that certain atoms, and we may especially signalise the tetravalent carbon atom, can combine with other atoms of the same element to form a compound-atom of greater atomicity than the original component atoms. Thus two carbon atoms, each of which is capable of fixing four atoms, combine together, each of them in the combination using up one of their valences, so that the combined carbon atom (or molecule) will now have the capacity of fixing *six* monad atoms. This is generally graphically expressed by a sketch, known as a **Glyptic formula** (which, it is hardly necessary to say, is purely illustrative, and in no other way purports to represent what occurs), in which the tetravalent atom of carbon is represented with four arms, thus (as a), the coming together of two such atoms (as β) with six arms, and the coming together of three atoms (as γ) with eight arms, *i.e.*, forming a combination capable of fixing eight monad atoms. Similarly, four auto-combined carbon atoms will form a compound atom (molecule) capable of fixing ten monad atoms, and so on. The importance of this view lies in the bearing it may have upon the great complexity of many of the carbon compounds.

Compound Radicals.—There are certain atomic groups

(molecules) which appear to play the part of a single atom in regard to combination. They are known as radicals or compound radicals. Like the elements, these radicals have their special atomicity. Thus NO_3, the radical of nitric acid (HNO_3), is monad; SO_4, the radical of sulphuric acid (H_2SO_4), is diad; PO_4, the radical of phosphoric acid (H_3PO_4), is triad. Again, P_2O_7, the radical of a compound of some import in water analysis, pyrophosphate of magnesia ($Mg_2P_2O_7$), is tetrad and fixes two atoms of the diad magnesium.

Accordingly, it is tempting to extend this principle, with Mulder, to compounds of the greatest complexity. His view may, in one particular case, be stated as follows. The formula of albumen, according to him (but see Lieberkühn's on p. 204), is 10 ($C_{40}H_{31}N_5O_{12}$) + S_2P), and if we betake ourselves to totalling up the atoms we shall get the enormously complex molecule $C_{400}H_{310}N_{50}O_{120} + S_2P$. But if we assume the existence of a compound radical "protein," having the formula $C_{40}H_{31}N_5O_{12}$ *and comporting itself as a single atom*, the molecular structure of albumen is greatly simplified. It must, however, be admitted that this notion is now discredited in many quarters. Thausing says, "The non-existence of protein is gradually becoming evident."

Isomerism.—I have referred to the notion of compound radicals and of auto-saturation as possibly throwing some light on isomerism, a term expressing the fact that sundry substances, with distinctly different characteristics, have the same elementary composition. Well-known instances are starch, dextrin, and cellulose, equally expressible, as far as their percentage composition is concerned, by the formula $C_6H_{10}O_5$, and the hexacid alcohols, mannite and dulcite, $C_6H_8(OH)_6$, which, though only distinguishable by the most delicate chemical tests, have this remarkable difference, that the former is able to nourish a certain *bacillus* (identified by Dr. Frankland), which excites ethylalcoholic fermentation in it, whereas in a solution of dulcite the same bacillus becomes inert.

ISOMERISM. OXIDES.

These dissimilarities, combined with similarity of elementary composition, *may* be explicable by the existence of dissimilar compound radicals within each molecule of their structure ; or again, it is evident that though the percentage of an element present in any given substance will not vary whether its atoms are auto-combined or not, yet that their capacity for saturation (*i.e.*, for fixing the utmost number of other atoms) will be different in the two cases as regards that particular element ; and as this implies the possibility of very numerous variations of grouping, it may be at the root of the mystery. Without insisting too strongly on this, it is certain that there are substances, varying considerably from one another, but containing *the same elements in the same proportion by weight*, and these substances are known accordingly as **isomeric** or as **isomers.**

Acids, Bases, Salts, (Oxides *).—Acids may be either

1. Oxy-acids (oxygen acids) formed by the combination of certain non-metallic elements with oxygen, with addition of water (*e.g.*, sulphuric and phosphoric acids).

[But note that all elements, except fluorine, can combine with oxygen to form *oxides.*]*

2. Hydracids = those in formation of which halogens unite with hydrogen, the compound then combining with water (*e.g.*, hydrochloric and hydrofluoric acids, etc.).

Bases are metallic oxides (basic oxides).

Salts are produced by the action of acids upon bases, resulting in a *loss of hydrogen*, which is replaced by an equivalent of a metal ; *e.g.*, nitric acid (HNO_3) neutralised with soda yields sodium nitrate $NaNO_3$.

---

* **Oxides** are acid, alkaline, or neutral. (1) **The acid oxides** = the oxy-acids, are compounds of O and non-metals or metalloids. (2) **The alkaline oxides** = bases ; compounds of O and metals. (3) **Neutral oxides**, which are either exceptions to (1), as water, which when pure is neither acid nor alkaline, or to (2), as oxides of the so-called heavy metals, insoluble in water.

Or in other words, an **acid** is a substance containing hydrogen, which it readily exchanges for a metal when treated either with a metal or with a metallic compound called a base. **A base**, again, is a substance containing a metal, combined with oxygen and hydrogen. It readily exchanges its metal for hydrogen upon being treated with an acid. The products of the action of an acid on a base are, in the first instance, *water*, and next a neutral *salt*.

Familiar bases are caustic potash KOH, caustic soda NaOH, and caustic lime CaO_2H_2, called respectively potassium, sodium, and calcium **hydroxides** or **hydrates**.

Basicity is a term used to express the power that acids possess of parting with their hydrogen and replacing it with a metal. Thus they may be monobasic (hydrochloric, nitric), bibasic (carbonic, sulphuric), or tribasic (phosphoric).

Sometimes, however, a bivalent metal (or base containing such a metal) forms a salt with an acid which contains but *one* atom of hydrogen in the molecule (*e.g.*, nitric acid), and it is then believed that one atom of the metal (copper, for example) acts upon the hydrogen atoms of two molecules of the acid thus:—

$$Cu + \left. \begin{matrix} HNO_3 \\ HNO_3 \end{matrix} \right\} = Cu \left\{ \begin{matrix} NO_3 \\ NO_3 \end{matrix} \right. + H_2 \text{ or } Cu + 2HNO_3 = Cu(NO_3)_2 + H_2.$$

But as a rule, the metals combine to form the salts in obvious relation to their atomicity. (*E.g.*, $BaSO_4$, in which one atom of bivalent barium has displaced two atoms of hydrogen from sulphuric acid to form barium sulphate.)

Mineral and Organic Acids.—Acids are spoken of as **mineral** (sulphuric, nitric, hydrochloric, and generally all those which contain no carbon), or **organic** (acetic, lactic, oxalic, including all those which have such a supremely interesting relation with the brewer's products). Carbonic *acid* with the formula H_2CO_3 is to be regarded as hypothetical (only its anhydride CO_2 being produced), but its salts, the carbonates, are stable compounds, containing the diad radical CO_3 (*e.g.*, sodium carbonate Na_2CO_3 and calcium carbonate $Ca''CO_3$).

Names of Acids.—The usual terminations are *-ic* or *-ous*, which difference signifies that although the elements composing them are identical, yet that the proportion of oxygen is lower in the latter (*e.g.*, sulphuric acid H_2SO_4 and sulphurous acid H_2SO_3). Again the prefixes *hypo-* ($\upsilon\pi\grave{o}$ = under), and *per-* (short for $\upsilon\pi\epsilon\rho$, very or more) are used in the names of certain acids to signify a proportion of oxygen less than that in the *-ous* acid when the former is prefixed, and greater than that of the *-ic* acid when the *per-* is prefixed. Thus hypobromous (HBrO) or hypochlorous (HClO) and perbromic ($HBrO_4$) and perchloric ($HClO_4$) acids are known.*

Sulphates, Sulphites, Nitrates, Nitrites.—Sulphates are the salts of sulphuric acid, sulphites of sulphurous acid. Similarly nitrates are the salts of nitric acid, nitrites of nitrous acid.

Sulphides are compounds of sulphur with a metallic element.

Chlorates are salts of chloric acid, but **chlorides** are compounds of chlorine, either with metals (metallic chlorides), with which it readily combines, with non-metals, *e.g.*, HCl, which with water forms hydrochloric acid, or with a radical, like ammonium, NH_4, with which it forms ammonium chloride. [When ammonia NH_3 in gas or solution is brought into contact with HCl, ammonium chloride having the composition of NH_4Cl is formed, and therefore, to compare it with metallic chlorides, it is assumed that NH_4 is a radical acting like a metal.]

Anhydrides are binary compounds containing oxygen, and are converted into acids on the addition of water,— *e.g.*, sulphurous anhydride $SO_2 + H_2O = H_2SO_3$ sulphurous acid. CO_2 carbonic acid gas, or carbon dioxide, is carbonic

---

* But *per-*, *-ic*, and *-ous* are also used for certain compounds of iron, chromium, and manganese. Thus the proto-salts of these metals are those in which the metal is diad; while in the per-salts two atoms together act as one hexad. The latter are sometimes called *Sesquicompounds*. The proto-salts of iron are also called ferrous salts, the per-salts are ferric-salts; *e.g.*, ferrous sulphate, $FeSO_4$, and ferric sulphate. $Fe_2(SO_4)_3$ are respectively the protosulphate and the persulphate of iron.

anhydride. So the term *anhydrous* (= waterless) is used as an epithet of a salt freed from water.

Hydrocarbons.—The simplest compounds of carbon are those which contain only carbon and hydrogen—the hydrocarbons. All the other more complex carbon compounds (*i.e.*, all the organic acids, the sugars, starch, dextrin, the alcohols, etc.) may be considered as derivatives therefrom. And it may be useful, as an aid to remembering their formulæ, to note two peculiarities.

(1) The number of hydrogen atoms in a molecule is always an *even* number.

(2) The number of hydrogen atoms in a molecule is never greater than twice the number of carbon atoms + 2.

The hydrocarbons which contain this maximum of hydrogen are *complete* or *saturated* hydrocarbons, and may be represented by the general formula C_nH_{2n+2}.

Of these hydrocarbons there is a series increasing regularly by CH_2—viz., methane CH_4, ethane C_2H_6, propane C_3H_8, butane C_4H_{10}, pentane C_5H_{12}, and hexane C_6H_{14}. Space does not permit of any lengthy reference to these and their derivatives, but a linear arrangement of formulæ will show the relation between ethane, its alcohol (ethyl alcohol, which is the alcohol produced in fermentation), its aldehyde, and its acid (acetic), which is characteristic throughout.

C_2H_6. : C_2H_6O. : C_2H_4O. : $C_2H_4O_2$.
Ethane. Ethyl or ordinary alcohol. Acetic aldehyde. Acetic acid.

Alcohols then may be looked upon either as hydrocarbons in which one or more atoms of hydrogen have been replaced by hydroxyl OH (in which case the structural formula will be C_2H_5OH for ethyl alcohol), or as water in which half of the hydrogen has been replaced by a radical, a compound of carbon and hydrogen.

If we compare ordinary alcohol and a more complex alcohol, glycerine, this possible relation with water can be more readily seen.

$$\left.\begin{array}{c} H \\ C_2H_5 \end{array}\right\} \begin{array}{c} OH \\ ,, \end{array} = \begin{array}{c} H_2O \text{ Water.} \\ C_2H_6O \text{ Ethyl alcohol.} \end{array}$$

MANNITE. DULCITE. ALDEHYDE.

$$\left.\begin{array}{l}H_3 \\ C_3H_5\end{array}\right\} \begin{array}{l}O_3H_3 = 3(H_2O). \\ = C_3H_8O_3 \text{ Glycerine.}\end{array}$$

The mention of glycerine as an alcohol will doubtless be news to some students; but it will be remembered that some is formed during the brewer's fermentation process; there are, however, many alcohols of more complex structure containing 4, 5, 6, or more carbon atoms in the molecule. Of those containing 6 atoms of carbon the hexacid or hexyl alcohols, mannite and dulcite, both with the formula $C_6H_8(OH)_6$, may be again mentioned, for more reasons than one. First, because of their close relation to real sugars, as shown by the fact that nascent hydrogen acting upon glucose or upon invert sugar produces mannite, and again, acting upon sugar of milk or galactose, produces dulcite. Secondly, on account of the formation of mannite in the lactic fermentation of sugar, and of its probable importance in connection with mucous fermentation and "ropy" beer. Thirdly, because of the interesting fact (already mentioned) that a certain bacillus is able to distinguish between the two. And lastly, because modern chemistry regards glucose and its isomers, having the formula $C_6H_{12}O_6$, as aldehydes of these hexyl alcohols, having the formula $= C_6H_{14}O_6$, an aldehyde (*alcohol dehydrogenatum*) being an alcohol which has lost hydrogen.

This view is based on the facts that glucose readily takes up oxygen (just as acetic aldehyde does), especially in alkaline media—*e.g.*, reducing copper oxide CuO to cuprous oxide Cu_2O (in the test with Fehling's solution to be after described), and also that nascent hydrogen converts it into mannite.

But although ordinary alcohol is theoretically connected with the hydro-carbon ethane, which is actually found in some of the gases given off by petroleum wells, and which can, moreover, be built up synthetically from methane (marsh-gas), it is to the fermentation of sugar that we look as *the* source of alcohol.

Taking glucose (dextrose) as the type of sugar, the simplest equation that can be given is

$$C_6H_{12}O_6 = 2(C_2H_6O) + 2CO_2.$$
Glucose = Alcohol and carbonic acid.

Or taking other sugars in turn

$$C_{12}H_{22}O_{11} + H_2O = 4(C_2H_6O) + 4CO_2$$
Maltose and water = Alcohol and carbonic acid.

Or,

$$C_{12}H_{22}O_{11} + H_2O = 2(C_6H_{12}O_6).$$
Cane-sugar and water = Invert Sugar.

$$C_6H_{12}O_6 = 2(C_2H_6O) + 2CO_2.$$
Invert Sugar = Alcohol and Carbonic Acid.

But, as a matter of fact, these formulæ are only partially true, insomuch as they do not account for other transformation products, of which the most important are glycerine and succinic acid. More elaborate equations are accordingly necessary to account for these, which will be more properly dealt with under the head of fermentation.

The **aldehydes** are, as has been hinted, to be regarded as alcohol from which hydrogen has been abstracted (*alcohol dehydrogenatum*), although acetic aldehyde—or, as it is sometimes called, ethyl aldehyde—is actually formed in the laboratory, and equally so in the brewer's products by an oxidising agency.

According to the above view the oxidation of alcohol into acetic acid takes place by two reactions, thus:

$$C_2H_6O + O = H_2O + C_2H_4O$$
Alcohol and oxygen = Water and aldehyde
$$C_2H_4O + O = C_2H_4O_2$$
Aldehyde and oxygen = Acetic acid.

Though it may occur perhaps sometimes according to the equation

$$C_2H_6O + O_2 = H_2O + C_2H_4O_2$$
Alcohol and oxygen = Water and acetic acid.

Aldehyde may, however, be reduced into alcohol again by causing it to combine with hydrogen, though its normal course in a beer subjected to oxidising influences would be to combine with more oxygen to form acetic acid.

It is thus a decidedly unstable compound, and much more volatile than alcohol, so that the characteristic flavour it will impart, even to beer, is more or less transitory.*

Carbohydrates (and Albuminoids).—The remaining substances of most importance to the brewer are the carbohydrates and the albuminoids, the former so-called because they contain carbon, hydrogen, and oxygen, the two last elements being in the proportion in which they exist in water.

Of the carbohydrates the most important groups are—

The glucose group $C_6H_{12}O_6$ (including dextrose, or grape-sugar, and levulose, or fruit-sugar).

The cane-sugar group $C_{12}H_{22}O_{11}$ (cane-sugar, maltose).

The cellulose group $(C_6H_{10}O_5)_n$ (starch, cellulose, and dextrin).

This is the usual classification of the text-books. But a later and more exact grouping—albeit no completely satisfactory one has yet been made—is on the following lines (abridgment from C. O'Sullivan, with one alteration explained at the end).

* A case in point occurred within the writer's experience early in 1891. Some hogsheads of light ale had been bottled, but just before the bottling was completed a fairly good, or at all events a practised judge, tasted the ale and pronounced it "pricked," and the corks were ordered to be drawn. The writer thought this verdict incorrect, but was only in time to save a few bottles from being emptied. These were kept, with the result that the ale was perfectly sound, bright, and in fine condition several months later; the deposit, which was small, consisting only of normal cells, chiefly of *Sacch. pastorianus*. It transpired that the hogsheads had been given far too much vent, so that oxidising influences were excessive. Probably the aldehyde so formed, which had procured the over-hasty condemnation, soon passed into acetic acid, which the ale, being sound enough, was able to carry.

Class I.—Saccharans $n(C_6H_{10}O_5)$. Soluble in water, insoluble in alcohol, yielding $n(C_6H_{12}O_6)$ bodies by action of acids, without formation of intermediate bodies.

[a and β **Amylan, Dextran, Levulan, the Galactans,** etc.]

Class II.—Saccharens $n(C_6H_{10}O_5)$. Insoluble in water and in alcohol, yielding $n(C_{12}H_{22}O_{11})$ bodies, *e.g.*, maltose—by action of certain zymases or certain acids, and finally $n(C_6H_{12}O_6)$ bodies by action of acids.

[**Cellulose, Starch, Inulin,** etc.]

Class III.—Saccharins $n(C_6H_{10}O_5)$. Soluble in water, insoluble in alcohol. Converted by certain zymases into $n(C_{12}H_{22}O_{11})$ bodies, and by acids first into those bodies, afterwards into $n(C_6H_{12}O_6)$ bodies.

[**Maltodextrins, Dextrin(s), Glycogen,** etc.]

Class IV.—Saccharons (sugars, with sub-groups).

(a) *Saccharoses*, $n(C_{12}H_{22}O_{11})$. Soluble in water and in alcohol below absolute. Converted by acids, and, as to some, by zymases into $n(C_6H_{12}O_6)$ bodies.

[**Sucrose (cane-sugar), Maltose, Lactose,** etc.]

(β) *Glucoses*, $n(C_6H_{12}O_6)$. Soluble in water and alcohol.

[**Dextrose, Levulose, Galactose,** etc.]

(γ) *Aromatic compounds* of no special interest here.

Class V.—Mucilages, Gums, Glucosides, etc. (See Glossary).

The alteration made has been to use "Saccharons" for the name of Class IV., and "Saccharoses" for sub-group *a*, instead of the contrary. The writer, with all diffidence, suggests that it is a greater aid to memory, as well as more consistent.

[A substance called **Dextran** (isomeric with dextrin), and known as "gum of fermentation," *gährungsgummi*, so named by Scheibler, who proved its formation during the viscous fermentation of sugar-beet juice. The organism producing it seems to be, in that case, *Leuconostoc mesenteroides*. The fact that its appearance is so much dreaded in sugar refineries, with the other alleged fact that some formation of it takes place concurrently with that of mannite in viscous fermentation of wines, etc., point to a connection with the unpleasant phenomenon of "ropiness." Though apparently concurrent, Monoyer showed grounds, as long ago as 1862, for believing that mannite and gum were the results of distinct operations, and that their proportions varied. It is interesting to note, while on the subject of "ropiness," that white wines are more subject to this malady than red, a fact supposed to be due to a deficiency of tannin.]

Maltose, as has been said, is the sugar produced by the action of diastase in the mash-tun upon starch; and the change is often expressed by the following simple equation, though the actual steps are much more complex, as will be seen in the chapter on mashing, etc., the starch-molecule being very much larger:—

$$3 (C_6H_{10}O_5) + H_2O = C_{12}H_{22}O_{11} + C_6H_{10}O_5$$
$$\text{Starch and water} = \text{Maltose and dextrin.}$$

The conversion of maltose into alcohol, and the formulæ connected therewith, will be referred to in one of the chapters on Fermentation (Chap. X.).

Cellulose is the substance of all vegetable tissues. It is found, perhaps at its hardest, in the date-stone, at its softest in the delicate membrane of the yeast-cell, forming the woody fibre of trees or the husk of barley. Its connection with its isomer, starch, may be seen in the interesting fact that purified cellulose dissolved in concentrated sulphuric acid, and afterwards diluted and boiled, is converted into dextrose (grape-sugar) and dextrin. [It will be remembered that starch, boiled with a very dilute solution of sulphuric acid similarly, though, of course, much more readily, becomes hydrated into a similar mixture, or, if the boiling be prolonged, almost entirely into dextrose.]

The Organic Acids may be mentioned as having an interest for brewers, namely, lactic acid, $C_3H_6O_3$, and butyric acid, $C_4H_8O_2$. Their connection with the hydrocarbon series C_3H_6 and C_4H_8 is obvious, but the brewer's main interest in them centres in the fact that their presence in his wort is most undesirable, though, as regards the former, this statement must be taken with the qualification that a limited amount of lactic acid, due to that normally present in the soundest malt, is an essential ingredient of beer, assisting to give piquancy to the finished beverage, and in the mash-tun stimulating the action of the peptase in its work of fitting the albuminoids to become food for yeast, and again, in the copper, preventing the said peptones from being precipitated by heat or the hop-tannin.

Both acids are produced by specific ferments, of which there are apparently more than one type in each case (thus butyric acid is produced by the agency of *Bacterium butyricum*, otherwise *Bacillus amylobacter*, and perhaps by *Bacillus subtilis*; lactic acid by *Bacterium lactis*, *Pediococcus acidi lactici*, and *B. subtilis*), and the course, taking cane-sugar as a starting-point, would be

$$C_{12}H_{22}O_{11} + H_2O = 2\,(C_6H_{12}O_6)$$
Cane-sugar and water = Glucose,

next the glucose is broken up, yielding lactic acid,

$$C_6H_{12}O_6 = 2\,(C_3H_6O_3)$$
Glucose = Lactic acid,

and, lastly, the lactic acid is converted into butyric acid,

$$2\,(C_3H_6O_3) = C_4H_8O_2 + 2CO_2 + 4H.$$

Lactic acid = Butyric acid and carbon-dioxide and hydrogen.

Of course with maltose, having the same formula as cane-sugar, for a starting-point, the initial equation would be different, unless we could show that maltose does undergo, as some suppose, a hydration into dextrose. Otherwise, the first equation might be

$$C_{12}H_{22}O_{11} + H_2O = 4\ (C_3H_6O_3).$$

These equations further explain the formation of lactic acid in germinating barley, cane-sugar being a known constituent of the ungerminated grain. Nor is it necessary in this case to assume the intervention of a special ferment, the water for hydration being so accessible. Moreover, as will be shown later, when speaking of asparagin (under amido compounds), carbon and hydrogen are set free in the formation of this soluble amide from an insoluble nitrogenous body, and this carbon and hydrogen may be oxidised into carbonic acid gas and water, or the elements of the latter may be all the more ready in their nascent state to enter into the fresh combination which the equation indicates.

And speaking of **elements in their nascent state,** *i.e.*, at the moment of their liberation, it is a matter of certain observation that they possess more active properties then than when they are in the free state.

Accordingly, it is by no means improbable that the development of sulphuretted* hydrogen H_2S, producing the so-called "stink" in certain stock beers, may be connected with a butyric fermentation. It will be noticed, on referring to the equations, that in the formation of butyric acid hydrogen is set free. What is then more likely than that in its nascent state it wrests sulphur from one or more of the sulphur compounds present, whether sulphates of the brewing water, bisulphite of lime, sulphurous acid due to the hopping, or the sulphur of the albuminoids?

* However, a specific organism *Beggiatoa* (the *B. alba* and other sub-varieties) busies itself with decomposing sulphur compounds in water (mostly in hot sulphur springs) setting sulphuretted hydrogen free. In whatever way it proceeds, whether by abstracting oxygen and setting hydrogen free to combine as indicated, or otherwise, such water, enclosed in a flask with Beggiatoa, soon develops H_2S.

Butyric acid is classed among the fatty acids, to which acetic acid, too, belongs, and combines the flavour of the latter with that of rancid butter.

Succinic Acid—$C_4H_6O_4$—is formed in the alcoholic fermentation of saccharine wort, and in other ways which have only a chemical interest. It and lactic acid are the two acids normal to beer, which remain in the residue when a measured quantity of the liquid is being distilled for analysis, while acetic acid passes over with the distillate. The former two are accordingly classed as fixed acid, both being calculated as lactic, while the acetic acid is classed as volatile acid.

The Albuminoids, although they play the most important rôle in animal nutrition, are far from being, as a class of compounds, completely understood. But it is certain that they contain nitrogen and sulphur in addition to carbon, hydrogen, and oxygen, and possibly phosphorus. The simplest formula (Lieberkühn's) assigned to them is $C_{72}H_{112}N_{18}O_{22}S$ from the following percentage analysis of albumen.

		Limits of variation.
Carbon	53·3	50·0 — 55·0
Hydrogen	7·1	6·9 — 7·5
Nitrogen	15·7	15·0 — 18·0
Sulphur	1·8	0·3 — 2·0
Oxygen	22·1	20·0 — 24·0

The above proportion of nitrogen is very fairly constant, and 100 divided by it gives the factor 6·36, by which the total nitrogen found in any substance (*e.g.*, by the soda-lime combustion process) is multiplied to arrive at the percentage of albumen. It must not be overlooked, however, that the calculation of all nitrogen into albumen may lead to error. For instance, mucedine, a nitrogenous body in barley or wheat, has, when derived from the former, the following composition assigned to it—Carbon 53·97; Hydrogen 7·03; Nitrogen 16·98; Sulphur 0·68; Oxygen 21·34. Again, the nitrogen may be present in the form of peptones or amides, the former of which weigh more, owing to the hydration which has taken place, than does the albumen from which they are derived, and consequently are relatively poorer in nitrogen, while amido compounds, on the contrary, are relatively richer in nitrogen than the bodies of which they are transformation products.

The albuminoids, so called from their best-known representative, the albumen of eggs, are bodies of an extremely unstable nature, some of which are, at all events when in excess, a great source of difficulty to a brewer. Modified, however, into peptones (either by the action of peptase at relatively low temperatures and in a moderately acid medium, or by boiling under pressure), certain of them become desirable constituents of wort, and being then capable of diffusing through the cell-membrane of the yeast, which is impervious to unmodified albumen, they play an all-important part in the nutrition of that ferment.

Of the albuminous bodies in barley, some are soluble, others insoluble, in water, but the ratio of the former to the latter is increased by the malting process. These soluble bodies are, however, thrown out of solution in various ways, amongst which may be specified as most important:—

(a) By boiling—causing a separation of flocculent matter. This precipitation indeed commences a good deal below the boiling temperature (viz., at $158°-160°$ Fahr.).

(β) By action of the hop-tannin. The tannic acid of the hop combines with albumen, precipitating it as *tannate of albumen*.

The following nitrogenous bodies have been identified in barley (about 12% altogether):—

1. **Casein**—insoluble, or very slightly soluble both in hot and cold water; but soluble in alcohol and dilute alkali, but not in acid.

2. **Fibrin**—insoluble in water, but soluble in strong alcohol in the cold (in a 30—70% solution only when boiled), in dilute acids, and alkalies.
3. **Mucedin**—slightly soluble in cold water, somewhat more so in hot. Boiling, however, appears to alter its character in so far that the cloudiness it induces, instead of subsiding with comparative speed, lasts for weeks. It is soluble in 60%—70% alcohol (Tralles), in dilute acids, and alkalies, but seems to be precipitated from the two latter solutions upon these being made neutral.
4. **Albumen (vegetable)**—soluble in cold water, but precipitated as to part at 158°—168° Fahr. [It can be precipitated even from a cold solution by adding a few drops of nitric acid.]

It is supposed that during the germination-stage of the malting process, possibly during the kiln-drying, a portion of the gluten is transformed into **amides**, which, though perhaps less diffusible than **peptones,** may serve in a less degree as yeast-nutriment, being, like the peptones, uncoagulable by boiling temperatures.* Nor are either of them affected by tannic acid in a slightly acid medium like wort, although the peptones, at any rate, are precipitated by it in a neutral one. Amides, Professor Ullik holds, are in no way the product of peptase, but are formed independently of peptones. Chemically, they may be regarded as substitution products of ammonia NH_3, in which one or more atoms of hydrogen are replaced by acid radicals, according to the formulæ

$$N \begin{cases} C_2H_3O \\ H \\ H \end{cases} \quad N \begin{cases} C_2H_3O \\ C_2H_3O \\ H \end{cases} \quad N \begin{cases} C_2H_3O \\ C_2H_3O \\ C_2H_3O \end{cases}$$

Acetamide.   Diacetamide.   Triacetamide.

---

* But it *is* held, on the other hand, that amides (owing to their crystalline character) are much more diffusible than peptones, and that they, in fact, afford yeast and bacteria most of their nitrogenous food. In this view real peptones exist in small quantity, having passed into

Or again, Acetamide may be looked upon as acetic acid in which the hydroxyl (OH) is replaced by an amido group, as appears in the formulæ,

$$\underset{\text{Acetic acid.}}{CH_3 - \overset{O}{C} - OH} \qquad \underset{\text{Acetamide.}}{CH_3 - \overset{O}{C} - NH_2}$$

Amides are generally neutral, the acid hydroxyl having been replaced.

The amido-compounds are typified in the animal body by urea, uric acid, glycocoll, etc., and in the vegetable world by glutamine and asparagine, the latter having the formula (in which, however, the relation to ammonia is not readily seen) of $C_4H_8N_2O_3$, or structurally of $\left.\begin{array}{l} H_2N \\ HO \end{array}\right\} C_4H_3 (NH_2) O_2$.

The important researches of Pfeffer have shown that certain non-diffusible protein substances are in leguminous seeds (peas, beans, lentils, etc.), and in germinating barley (according to Lermer) converted into **Asparagin**, and, as such, become capable of passing through the new cell-walls of the young plant, the change being attended with the setting free of carbon and hydrogen (legumin, as to which Pfeffer's observations were recorded, being poorer in nitrogen and richer in carbon and hydrogen than its transformation product), which are either oxidised into carbon-dioxide (carbonic acid gas) and water, or are perhaps converted into non-nitrogenous vegetable substances. Apparently the asparagin itself is *re-converted* into protein matter as growth advances, carbon and hydrogen being absorbed with aid of light.

amides—hydrolytic action going further with malt-extract under suitable conditions than in animal digestion (where the action of pepsin stops with the formation of peptone). Taking the nitrogenous matter, its relative proportions as belonging to the albuminous group or the amide group have been estimated for barley and malt. Barley, albumen group = 63% ; amide = 37% ; malt, albumen group = 46% ; amide = 54%.

Mr. A. H. Allen, referring to Schulze and Barbière as recommending that the true *soluble albuminoids* should be distinguished from *peptones*, and these again from the *amido-compounds*, says: "For the qualitative detection of albuminoids the formation of a precipitate on adding acetic acid and potassium ferro-cyanide will suffice. For the precipitation of the *albuminoids* various reagents, such as tannin, ferric acetate, cupric acetate, plumbic hydroxide, etc., should be employed on separate portions of the solution, the precipitate containing least nitrogen being considered that which represents the true albuminoids. The peptones, which in nutritive value are equal, or nearly so, to the albuminoids"—more than equal as far as yeast alone is concerned—"may be precipitated from the filtrate by means of phosphotungstic acid. The *amido compounds* which remain in the solution from which the proteids and peptones have been precipitated are typified by asparagine and glutamine, and may, if desired, be determined by boiling the solution with an acid, and then estimating the ammonia from the amount of gas liberated by sodium hypobromite."

To avoid any change of composition in the nitrogenous bodies during extraction, the same investigator recommends the extraction to be made first with cold and then with hot water, or else with dilute alcohol.

It is hardly to be supposed that these analytical niceties will be within the experimental limits, to which the average brewer must confine himself, but my hope has been by referring thereto to throw a little light on the difficult and complex, but most important bodies dealt with in the few preceding paragraphs.

It will be instructive to append here two careful analyses by O'Sullivan of pale malt, as indicating the final modifications effected by the malting process. It is stated that every constituent was determined directly, and the closeness with which the totals approximate to a hundred speaks for the accuracy of the methods employed.

	No. 1.	No. 2.
Starch	44·15	45·13
Other Carbohydrates (of which 60%—70% consists of fermentable sugar), Inulin(?) and a small quantity of other bodies soluble in cold water	21·23	19·39
Cellular matter	11·57	10·09
Fat	1·65	1·96
Albuminoids.		
(α) Soluble in alcohol sp. gr. ·820, and in cold water ... ·63		
(β) Soluble in cold water and at 68° C. ... 3·23		
(γ) Insoluble in cold water but soluble at 68°—70° C. ... 2·37	13·09	
(δ) Insoluble at 68°—70° C. but soluble in cold water (= albumen proper) ... ·48		
(ϵ) Insoluble in cold water and at 70° C. ... 6·38		
— albuminoid totals (No. 2: ·46, 3·12, 1·36, ·37, 8·49)		13·80
Ash	2·60	1·92
Water	5·83	7·47
	100·12	99·76

Nitrogen, the characteristic constituent of all these so-called protein or albuminoid bodies, is a remarkable element. Itself a tasteless, colourless, and inodorous gas, and (under certain circumstances) a singularly inert substance—a species of chemical ballast, as it were—supporting neither combustion nor life, and not readily combining with other bodies, it yet forms compounds of exceedingly powerful properties—viz., with hydrogen, the powerful alkaline base ammonia (NH_3); with oxygen and hydrogen, nitric acid; with excess of chlorine, a dangerous explosive, as it will indeed with many other substances.*

Nitrogen in carbon compounds is estimated in various ways. One, known as the **absolute method**, consists in a combustion of the compound, mixed with copper oxide, in a tube, in which there is also a layer of copper foil, which

---

* This malign readiness may be amusingly illustrated by soaking a crystal of iodine in strong ammonia. The iodine, getting pasty, combines with the nitrogen of the NH_3 to form nitrogen iodide, which, as soon as it is dry, will explode with a loud report, almost at the lightest touch.

of course becomes highly heated. All the air must be carefully exhausted before the operation begins, and at the end all the gases (which, if the substance contained nothing beyond carbon, oxygen, hydrogen, and nitrogen, are only three in number, viz., CO_2; vapour of water, H_2O; and free nitrogen) are also exhausted. The water-vapour of course condenses, the CO_2 (carbon dioxide or carbonic acid gas) is absorbed on passing the gases through a solution of potassium hydroxide (caustic potash), and the nitrogen, thus separated, can be collected and measured, and its weight easily calculated.

The **Soda-lime Method** and **Dr. Graham's Adaptation of Professor Wanklyn's Ammonia Process** for the determination of nitrogen are both described in the next chapter, with working details.

Kjeldhal's Method, of which there is more than one modification, is based upon the conversion of the organic nitrogen into ammonia by a treatment, which begins with heating a measured quantity of the powdered substance ($\cdot5$—1 gramme) with a mixture of equal parts of concentrated pure sulphuric acid and Nordhausen (fuming) sulphuric acid, with the addition of one or two grammes of phosphoric anhydride (P_2O_5), which must obviously be free from nitrous or nitric acid. At the end of the whole operation the nitrogen is determined from the ammonia.

The heating (just short of boiling) is kept up for a varying period (*i.e.*, until the mixture loses its dark colour, due to caramelisation of the substance, and turns yellowish or faintly red). Powdered permanganate of potash is then cautiously added in small quantities at a time, because the reaction is very violent—heating being temporarily stopped—till very slightly in excess (shown by a greenish colour of the solution). This completes the oxidation (nitrogen into ammonic sulphate). When cool, concentrated caustic soda (sp. grav. 1·3) is added in excess to decompose the ammonic sulphate, but carefully poured down the side to avoid loss of the ammonia which it liberates. The mixture is now distilled, with special precautions, which include the addition of a few pieces of zinc before the caustic soda, to prevent the violent bumping which would otherwise occur, and the ammonia which comes over is received into standard acid. At the close, when all the ammonia has come over, this mixture, in which the acid is in excess, is " titrated " (as in the soda-lime process), and the ammonia estimated from the difference between the amount of acid before the ammonia was distilled into it, and that which remains after. The ammonia multiplied by $\frac{14}{17}$ gives the amount of nitrogen, which multiplied by 6·3 gives the latter in terms of albuminous matter.

Certain other tests, which are merely qualitative, *i.e.*, which only reveal the presence of such and such an element or compound, but do not give the quantity as a quantitative analysis does, may find a place here, instead of in the next chapter.

Iodine added to a fairly cool solution of starch produces an intense blue colour (iodide of starch, or, more correctly, iodised starch, the formation being apparently not a definite compound), which disappears on heating, it is supposed because the heated water takes up more iodine of which the starch is accordingly deprived, but which reappears on cooling (once). An aqueous solution of iodine is better than a tincture (alcoholic solution), but the iodine is very sparely soluble in water, until a crystal of potassium iodide is added, whereupon immediate solution occurs. With erythro-dextrin iodine gives a reddish-brown colour, which tinges starch-blue more or less violet when both are present. The affinity of iodine being greater for starch than for erythro-dextrin, it is possible by the addition of a very little, and that dilute, iodine solution to cause the starch-blue to develop first and the redder coloration upon a further addition of iodine. It is further possible, by the cautious addition of very dilute ammonia to such a mixture, to cause the red-brown coloration to disappear while the blue remains. Iodine is a very delicate test for starch, giving a bluish tinge even at such extreme dilution as one drop of starch paste in a quart of water, or putting it otherwise, a liquid containing $\frac{1}{500,000}$ its weight of starch-paste strikes a blue colour. With the final, if there be a *final* type of dextrin, known as achroo-dextrin (ἄχροος = uncoloured), no reaction is produced.

But with wort, which is a composite fluid, the first drop or two of iodine solution may be decolourised (it should be added drop by drop if the wort be in a test-tube), therefore the operator must not draw hasty conclusions, but should add sufficient iodine for certainty. If, upon testing the wort some time before the copper lengths are secured, the erythro-dextrin reaction appears, it will be wise to lower the sparging heats, for the reaction may soon be that of soluble starch. And according to Lintner, erythro-dextrins are themselves liable to be thrown out of solution by the alcohol formed in the beer wherein they exist, and consequently a certain degree of haziness may result. Matthews, however, disputes this view of Lintner's, holding that, when dextrins are precipitated by alcohol, they tend to agglomerate without causing any troublesome opalescence.

Nitrites (in Water).—" The best qualitative test for nitrites," says Sutton, " is to acidify the water moderately with pure sulphuric acid, then upon adding potassic iodide and starch liquor, the occurrence of the well-known dark blue colour of starch-iodide reveals the presence of nitrites immediately." [This turns upon the fact that nitrous acid, set free from its compounds, the nitrites, by sulphuric acid, combines with the potassium of the iodide liberating iodine to produce its blue reaction with starch. Note that potassium-iodide, as such, produces no blue colour with starch.]

But a blank experiment with distilled water should be tried, to make sure of the purity of the sulphuric acid.

TESTS FOR NITRATES AND NITRITES. 213

Nitrates and Nitrites in Water—The Indigo Test.—
Colour a little of the water with indigo solution, then add
twice the bulk of pure sulphuric acid (which sets nitric
or nitrous acid free from their salts). Then, if there are
nitrates or nitrites present, the blue colour will be discharged; in the contrary case it will remain. The importance of having pure sulphuric acid, free from nitric
acid, is again evident. This test can be made very fairly
quantitative by having the indigo solution (made by
dissolving pure indigo carmine in distilled water) of such
a strength that 10 cc. are decolourised by 10 cc. of a
standard solution of a nitrate—*e.g.*, 1·011 gramme of
potassic nitrate dissolved in a litre, of which 10 cc. will
contain ·0014 gramme of nitrogen. Then if 10 cc. be run
into a measured quantity of the water, and the colour
remains after the sulphuric acid is added, the quantity
actually decolourised by the nitrates in the water can be
ascertained by " titrating back " with the standard potassic
nitrate.

The Phenol-Sulphuric Acid Test.—Water, evaporated
just to dryness in a platinum or porcelain dish, is treated
with a solution (about one drop per cc. of the water) made in
the following manner. To a small quantity of pure crystalline carbolic acid (phenol) is added four times its weight
of pure and strong sulphuric acid. The mixture is then
heated to boiling for a few minutes, cooled, and diluted
with half its bulk of pure water.

The dish is then placed on the water-bath again, whereupon the mixture will acquire a violet-red colour if nitrates
are present. With ·5 grain per gallon the colour is intense.
[The phenol-sulphuric mixture should be kept in a stoppered
bottle.]

Another Qualitative Test, operated upon the " total
solids " of water, is given in the next chapter.

Millon's Reagent for Proteids is made by dissolving
quicksilver in an equal weight of nitric acid (of density
1·41), then gently warming and diluting the solution with
twice its weight of water. There must be a trace of free

nitric acid. The liquid is to be decanted from the deposit which separates after standing for some hours. It colours protein bodies red.

The Biuret Reaction for Peptone.—If a solution of peptone be made strongly alkaline with caustic potash or soda, and a few drops of an excessively dilute solution of copper sulphate be added, a beautiful rose-red colour is produced. This reaction was at one time considered characteristic of peptone, but it seems to occur (with somewhat violet shade) with albuminoids. [The employment of a dialyser to separate the diffusible peptone from other non-diffusible albuminoids might make this test of value, but the writer has not tried it.]

Iron, Test for.—Boil about 500 cc. of the water and collect the deposit, in which all the iron precipitates as a hydrated oxide—ferric oxide—upon a filter-paper, free from iron. Anything adhering to the boiling flask should be washed off with pure hydrochloric acid, which should also be used for washing the filter residue. If the filtrate now contain an iron-salt, there will be, on treatment with potassium-ferro-cyanide (yellow prussiate of potash), a marked precipitate of Prussian blue.

Or add 2 cc. of nitric acid and 1 cc. of ferrocyanide of potassium to 100 cc. of the water; whereupon in the presence of iron the usual blue colour will be produced. It may be advisable to boil the water with the nitric acid to ensure solution of the iron before adding the ferrocyanide. This test also may be made quantitative by having a standard solution of iron, and comparing the colour given by it at various dilutions on addition of the ferrocyanide of potassium with that given by the water actually under examination. Two Nessler tubes on a white tile should be used.

Organic Matter in Water.—Evaporate a portion to dryness in a platinum dish (70 cc. will do). When dry, hold over the flame of a Bunsen burner. If the residue becomes charred it is a sign of the presence of organic matter, more or less according as the charring is considerable or slight. Watch closely for maximum charring (brown colour), as it goes off on further heating.

Alcohol, Iodoform Test for.—Add to the liquid which is being examined a little iodine solution and a little potash solution; on warming gently, a yellowish turbidity appears, and crystals frequently separate out on standing. This substance is iodoform, which is insoluble in water. The reaction is so extremely delicate that by it 1 part of alcohol in 300,000 of water can be detected. Concentration of the alcohol by fractional distillation has even enabled a millionth part of alcohol to be detected.

Optical Activity—Polariscope—Polarimeter.—As the expressions "optical activity," "angle of rotation," etc., may be occasionally used and are frequently to be met with in papers dealing with brewing from a scientific point of view, a brief account of the polariscope or polarimeter may stand here. Be it premised that though used in some laboratories and capable in expert hands of facilitating analyses of compound fluids into the composition of which either type of sugar enters, the manipulation is not to be taught by book; accordingly, such analyses, when described in the next chapter, are by the volumetric method (Fehling's solution) entirely.

The action of the polarimeter is based upon the fact that certain substances, or solutions of them, have the property of causing certain optical alterations in a ray of polarised light passing through them, the correction of which by means of a mechanical adjustment (a milled head actuating a wedge-shaped piece of quartz which is fitted with a scale that moves with it), and then a comparison of the movable scale with another fixed scale, called the vernier, enables the observer to measure the angle of rotation and classify it either as a right-handed (+) or left-handed (—) rotation.

Without entering too far into detail, it may be said that the polarimeter (of which there are various makes) consists generally of a long telescopic arrangement, capable of being accurately focussed so as to get a sharply defined "field," and placed horizontally with a lighted lamp at the end. In the centre is a movable tube 100 mm. or 200 mm. long (according to the density of the solution) for containing the fluid to be examined. Two Nicol's prisms, known respectively as the polariser and the analyser (made, in a special way, of the crystal known as Iceland spar), are on either side of the movable tube; also there is a plate of double quartz (*i.e.*, made of two qualities of quartz, having the one a right-handed and the other a left-handed rotation) towards the lamp-end of the apparatus, while, towards the eyepiece end, are first (nearest the movable tube) a plate of left-handed quartz, then, nearly adjoining it, a plate of right-handed quartz, divided diagonally, and so disposed that while one of the divisions is fixed, the other can be moved upwards or downwards by the milled head mentioned in the last paragraph, and thus the thickness of right-handed quartz in the line of vision be increased or decreased. Obviously, if it has to be *increased* in order to correct the optical disturbance produced by the contents of the tube, then the latter have a left-handed rotation; if the thickness has to be *decreased* a right-handed one.

The optical alterations are either in (1) colour; disappearance of the uniform tint, "the transition tint," whereupon half the field becomes red, the other violet; (2) striation, *i.e.*, appearance of dark bands which cross the field; or, (3) half-shadowing, *i.e.*, where one half of the field on one side of a vertical line is dark, the other half light, instead of both being uniformly illuminated, as should be the case at starting. [A slight movement of the milled head, equally with the insertion of the tube containing a solution of an organic substance, produces these alterations.]

The half-shadow instruments are preferable in the case of coloured liquids, and for those observers who have a difficulty in appreciating slight variations of colour, and so getting the exact transition tint.

Some of these instruments are constructed for use with

a monochromatic sodium flame, but one of the half-shadow polarimeters (Schmidt & Haensch, of Berlin) is used with *white* light, *i.e.*, gas or an oil lamp.

Symbols are used to denote rotating power, and they vary somewhat with the kind of ray employed. When the ray is what is known as the "mean yellow"—*i.e.*, the middle colour of the spectrum of a ray of white or ordinary light (as used with transition-tint polarimeters), it is $[a]_j$ (j. for *jaune*=yellow), $[a]_D$ implies the monochromatic sodium ray, and $[a]_R$ a red ray—*i.e.*, a monochromatic light got by interposing a piece of red glass between the lamp and the polarimeter.*

Sometimes the further addition of the figures 3·86 at the right side of these symbols occurs, and this means that a solution having the specific gravity of 1003·86 (1 gramme sugar in 100 cc. approximates very closely to this specific gravity) has been used.

Recommending the habitual inspection of worts with the polarimeter, Mr. Heron says that "as a general rule the specific rotatory power of a wort should not fall below 105 $[a]_D$ or rise higher than 122 $[a]_D$, the former indicating an abnormally low percentage of dextrin and large excess of soluble nitrogenous matters, the latter a very high percentage of dextrin, resulting probably in extremely high attenuations and cloudy beers, fining only with difficulty." Albuminoids give a marked left-handed rotation, while dextrin-compounds, as their name implies (*dextra* = the right hand), maltose, etc., give a more or less right-handed rotation.

* To convert $[a]_D$ into $[a]$ × 1·114; to convert $[a]_j$ into $[a]_D$ × 0·898, but the relation 24 : 21·54 is only true for the carbohydrates.

CHAPTER VII.

THE LABORATORY.

Essentials of a Laboratory—The Brewer-Analyst's Limitations—Metric System of Weights and Measures—Apparatus and Reagents Required—Preparation of Apparatus — Fehling's Solution — Volumetric and Gravimetric Methods—Testing Glucose (Invert), Cane-Sugar, Malt —Normal or Standard Solutions—Equivalence—Albuminoids by Ammonia Process—Soda-Lime Process—Diastatic Activity of Malt — Beer Analysis — Original Gravity by Distillation and Evaporation—Dry Extract, Acidity, etc. — Water Analysis — Combining Results — Soap Test — Free and Albuminoid Ammonia — Oxygen Processes — Hops for Sulphur — Constants — Standard Solutions.

A ROOM with gas and water laid on, and with ready means of conveying the latter away when running in a continuous stream for cooling; a plain wooden working bench 2 feet 6 inches wide and 3 feet high, with cupboard underneath to hold the larger apparatus and shelves above for the reagents; an earthenware tank (to resist acids) let in flush with the top of the bench, and which may be procured, of Doulton's make, for 7*s.* or 8*s.*; a separate shelf, *free from vibration*, to stand the balance on, is all that will be absolutely necessary beyond apparatus and reagents for the performance of any of the tests or analyses referred to in this chapter.

The gas should be conveyed along a pipe running just above the working bench or table, and below the shelves; and the pipe should have three or four small straight-nozzled taps, on which india-rubber tubing can be slipped and permanently kept to connect them with the Bunsen burners. There should also be a gas-burner of the

OUTLINE OF ANALYSES.

ordinary type, but with its bracket fixed a good deal lower than is usual—*i.e.*, within easy reach of both hands together, for the purpose of bending glass tubing and rounding rough edges.

It is advisable to have good ventilation and a fire; and where experiments with sulphuretted hydrogen or chlorine are likely to be performed there should be a separate chamber (one 2 feet by $1\frac{1}{2}$ feet will do) with glass doors, and connected by a pipe to the flue of the fire. But these are outside the range of the modest experimenter, who limits his inquiries to points practically connected with brewing.

These points will be—

Analysis of sugar (glucose, invert, etc.).

Analysis of malt (determination of extract, diastatic value, acidity, albuminoids, etc.).

Testing hops for sulphur (here the sulphuretted hydrogen evolved requires no special precautions).

Determination of original gravities of beer (either by distillation or by the evaporation process).

Analysis of water (determination of free and albuminoid ammonia by Professor Wanklyn's process; and possibly the amount of oxygen required to neutralise organic matter); determination of total solids; hardness, before and after boiling; proportions of carbonates and sulphates of lime and magnesia, of chlorine (generally combined as chloride of sodium, or common salt), and, if time allow, of the alkalies.

Further than this the amateur can hardly be expected to go. Indeed, the operative brewer will not easily secure the freedom from interruption which even the comparatively simple water-analysis referred to demands.

The Metric or Decimal System of Weights and Measures offers such obvious advantages in the way of rapidity of calculation and absence of confusion arising from ambiguity of weights of the same denomination,* that it is now generally adopted. Only in expressing the saline constituents of water it is most convenient to express them

---

* *E.g.*, the lb. Avoirdupois is heavier than the lb. Troy; but its ounce is lighter than the Troy ounce.

in grains per gallon; but even here an easy decimal relation enables the metric weights and measures to be used. For instance, Professor Wanklyn recommends 70 cc. (cubic centimetres) of water to be operated on. This quantity (flasks, marked to measure it, can be obtained) contains 70,000 milligrammes, or exactly the number of grains which a gallon of water contains; so that the result obtained with it *in milligrammes* is exactly equivalent to grains per gallon, and may be expressed as such without alteration. And if this quantity should appear too small for any determination, it is a simple matter to take any multiple of it, dividing the result obtained by that multiple.

Note, that the Greek-derived prefixes *deka-*, *hecto-*, *kilo-*, and *myria-*, are used for the multiples of metres, litres, and grammes, while the prefixes of Latin derivation, *deci-*, *centi-*, and *milli-*, are used for decimal parts of them—*e.g.*, a kilogramme = 1000 grammes; a milligramme = ·001 gramme.

A litre (= 1·76 pint), a name given to the cubic decimetre, contains 1000 cc. (cubic centimetres). One cc. of distilled water at its greatest density, 4°C. (about 39° Fahr.) = 1 gramme. In practice 1 cc. at ordinary temperature is taken = 1 gramme; then a litre is reckoned as containing 1000 grammes or 1,000,000 milligrammes, and use is made of this in determining "free and albuminoid ammonia," which is stated in *parts per million*—*i.e.*, the number of milligrammes found when a litre of water is operated on.

The **Apparatus and Reagents required** will be—

(1) APPARATUS.

Thermometer, graduated up to 300° C. (for drying oven).
3 Bunsen burners (one with rose).
Drying-oven.
Desiccator.
Porcelain basins (evaporating).
Platinum dish and foil.
Beakers (assorted).
Glass evaporating basins (4).
Watch glasses (pair).

Funnels, glass (3).
Stoppered flasks (with mark for measuring solutions, 2 of litre size, 2 of 500 cc., 1 of 250 cc., 1 of 100 cc., 1 of 70 cc.).
Burette (100 cc.).
Burette-stand (white wood).
Pipettes (100 cc., 70 cc., 50 cc., 25 cc., 20 cc., 10 cc., and 5 cc.).
Pipette (2 cc.) for Nesslerising

APPARATUS AND REAGENTS FOR ANALYSES.

APPARATUS (*continued*).

may be made out of glass tubing.
Graduated 10 cc. pipette.
Test-tubes (2 doz.) and stand.
Liebig's condenser (glass) and stand.
Filter-papers (coarse grey and Swedish).
3 Boiling-flasks (Bohemian glass).
3 large flasks (for wash-bottles and boiling).
Specific gravity bottle and counterpoise.
Glass-tubing (1 lb. assorted).
Vulcanised tubing (for gas), about 12 feet.
Vulcanised tubing for general use, 3 feet assorted.
Glass rod (for stirring rods).
Cork-borers (set of).
Files (triangular and rat-tailed).

Balance and weights.
Glass cylinders (for Nessler test) with flattened bottoms, and file-marked for 50 cc.
Retort (for Liebig's condenser) and iron retort-stand.
White glazed tile.
Tinned water-baths (2).
Brass crucible tongs.
Blocks of wood (various thickness) for elevating Bunsen burners, etc.
Winchester quarts (3 or 4).
2 Squares of fine wire gauze.
3 Sand-dishes.
Tripod stands (2 or 3).
Glass scale-pans for balance.
1 Pipe-clay triangle.
Combustion tubes.
India-rubber cork.
Assorted corks (4 doz.)
Pestle and mortar.

(2) REAGENTS.

Ferrocyanide of potassium.
Acetic acid.
Animal charcoal.
Basic acetate of lead.
Litmus paper (red and blue).
Litmus (solution of).
Sulphuric acid (pure for analysis).
Hydrochloric acid (pure for analysis).
Nitric acid (pure for analysis).
Ammonia solution (pure).
 ,, decinormal solution of.
Carbonate of soda.
Caustic soda.
 ,, potash.
Calcic chloride (pure).
Cochineal (about 8*d*. oz.).
Alcohol.
Methylated spirit.

Iodine (solution of crystals).
Iodide of potassium.
Indigo solution.
Sulphate of copper.
Rochelle salt (sodium potassio-tart).
Perchloride of mercury.
Ammonium chloride.
Nitrate of silver.
Potassium chromate.
 ,, permanganate, pure crystallised.
Potassium ferrocyanide.
Oxalic acid.
Ammonium oxalate.
 ,, carbonate.
Barium chloride.
Iron proto-sulphate.
Sodium amalgam (or mercury and metal sodium).

[The apparatus and chemicals as arranged by Mr. Wright are supplied by Messrs. Townson & Mercer, of 89, Bishopsgate Street Within, London, packed in case complete, at £12. 10s.]

Preparation of the Apparatus.—Fit the wash-bottles with corks bored with two holes, through which bent glass tubes are to be passed; one short and bent at a wide angle passes just through the cork, the other bent at a sharper angle has the end of its shorter limb contracted nearly to a point, while the longer straight limb passes through the cork and nearly to the bottom of the flask. [Glass tubing is bent by holding it, a hand on either side of the flame, in the upper part of a gas-jet, and turning it round all the while to get it softened uniformly. Then by *gentle* pressure it can be bent at any required angle. A pointed end is got by softening as before described, and moving the two hands wider apart. A nick with a file where the tube is drawn to a very small bore will enable the operator to break it at the desired place, as it will enable him to divide all other glass tubing of moderate size. Rough edges may be filed, and made smooth in the gas-jet.]

If then the flask is filled with distilled water and the cork with its tubes fitted closely, upon blowing through the shorter tube water is driven out of the pointed tube in a fine spray, just adapted for washing filter residues. Arrange the **drying-oven.** The cheaper japanned sort has three movable legs. Fit a perforated cork into the small opening and fix your thermometer (graduated up to 300° C.) firmly in the cork, so that the quicksilver end is in the interior of the oven.

Slip one end of convenient lengths of vulcanised tubing over the straight-nozzled gas taps, and the other over the inlet pipes of the Bunsen burners. (N.B.—If the tubing be a shade small for slipping over readily, wetting the pipe will facilitate matters.) Get the **desiccator** ready. If you have the cheapest form, which, except the cover, is moulded in one piece, place a few bits of pumice-stone in the lower portion, and pour in sulphuric acid enough to nearly cover them. [The sulphuric acid absorbs moisture greedily, and therefore keeps the desiccator *dry.*] Fit on the perforated zinc on which your glass pan or platinum dish is to stand, and smear a little lard round the finely ground edge on which the cover fits. This will keep the cover from slipping, and make the interior perfectly air-tight.

Put **the balance** on its special shelf. If one of Becker's cheap balances (price about 32s., turning to a milligramme*), which are quite good enough for the student-operator, be used, a rectangular glass case, procurable from an operative bird-stuffer for about 5s., will protect it as well as the expensive balances are protected by their specially made cases. The setting-up and adjusting of the balance (by the little screw disc at one arm) must be learnt from some one who knows how to do it, though the task is simple enough.

Before proceeding to actual work, it is necessary to get the weight of, or "to tare," (i) the two or three glass basins which will be used; (ii) the platinum dish, which will be used for igniting residues; (iii) the specific gravity bottle—filled with water at 15.5° C. (=60° Fahr.), under which conditions its contents are supposed to weigh 50 grammes, but are seldom exact. [The counterpoise = weight of *empty* bottle, is put in scale-pan with the weights.]

The glass basins and platinum dish must be previously dried in the drying-oven at 100° C., and put without loss of time into the desiccator to cool, and the weighing quickly done. Let us assume that glass pan No. 1 (scratch the figure on it with a file) weighs 27·922 grammes (*i.e.*, 27 grammes and 922 milligrammes), that glass pan No. 2 weighs 23·203 grammes, the platinum dish 14·216 grammes, and the water-filling specific gravity bottle 49·983 grammes.

We will now suppose the student with all his apparatus and reagents carefully arranged to hand, in strict attention to Sir H. Roscoe's dictum that **"he who works in a mess will frequently have his mind in a muddle."**

The first thing to do will be to make the copper-

* The balance turning to half a milligramme and in a mahogany case can be bought for about £2 10s.

sulphate solution known as **Fehling's Solution** or **Fehling**, which is more satisfactory than buying it ready-made,* though it can be so procured at Messrs. Townson & Mercer's of Bishopsgate Street, and of other dealers in chemical appliances. Decimal weights and measures are used throughout, as more convenient and easy.

Fehling's Solution is the test-reagent for glucose and maltose; its use depends on the fact that, though it can be boiled alone without undergoing change, yet the addition of a trace of grape-sugar is enough, upon warming, to precipitate from the *blue* solution a portion of the copper as protoxide—Cuprous oxide Cu_2O—and the larger the amount of grape-sugar added, up to a certain point, the greater will be the amount of copper precipitated, till a point is reached when all the blue colour derived from the sulphate is gone, and all the copper lies at the bottom of the vessel as a red precipitate.

It is prepared as follows, the ingredients being :—

34·64 grammes sulphate of copper
173 ,, Rochelle salt (sodium potass. tartr.)
60 ,, caustic soda.

Crush rather more of the sulphate than is likely to be required, and dry between blotting-paper. Dissolve the salts separately, and mix *after* they are dissolved, adding the caustic soda *last*. Make the whole up to 1 litre. (N.B.—The ring scratched round the neck of the flask a short distance below the stopper is the mark up to which the flask is to be filled. Use distilled water.) [Or where the test is infrequently used the solutions may, to avoid deterioration, be made up separately, the copper solution in one 500 cc. measure and the Rochelle salt and caustic soda in another, and *carefully mixed in equal quantities* as required. Allen advises, as rendering the solution more

* Note that the solution must be kept away from the air and light, otherwise it is liable to undergo a change which makes it untrustworthy. On this account old Fehling should be tested by diluting a small quantity with its own bulk of water and heating to boiling for a few minutes. It ought to remain perfectly clear.

TESTING THE FEHLING.

permanent, 180 grammes of Rochelle salt and 70 of caustic soda.]

Then 10 cc. of this solution corresponds to ·05 gramme of glucose; that is to say, if such a quantity of any saccharine solution as contains ·05 gramme of glucose be run gradually into a porcelain dish, already containing 10 cc. of Fehling which has been raised to boiling point (over a Bunsen, with or without a sand dish) and be stirred meanwhile with a glass stirring rod, the mixture being still kept boiling, the strong blue colour of the Fehling will disappear, and the liquid become clear as water, or nearly so, but with a red precipitate of cuprous oxide (Cu_2O). A yellowish tinge is a sign that too much of the sugar solution has been run in (the caustic soda gets to work when *all* the copper salt is precipitated), but if the exact point at which the blue disappears be read off (the saccharine liquid is run in from a burette* graduated into cc. and tenths of a cc.), it is manifest that the percentage quantity can be readily calculated. An example or two will make this clear.

First of all, however, it is advisable to test the correctness of the Fehling itself. This is done by taking some of the purest cane-sugar that can be got (that which is sold, or which used to be sold, as Finzel's crystals), of which 2·5 grammes, dried *moderately* in drying oven, is dissolved in about 200 cc. of water and boiled for one hour with 2 cc. of purest hydrochloric or sulphuric acid, which is afterwards nearly neutralised (*i.e.*, so that it will only *very faintly* redden blue litmus paper) with carbonate of soda or with standard potassic hydrate (caustic potash), and finally made up to a litre.

Suppose the burette filled with 100 cc. of the above

---

* A burette is a rather long tube of stout glass, stoppered at the top and with a glass cock at the bottom, capable of letting out the contents drop by drop. It contains 100 cc. of fluid, and is graduated in front, so that the number of cc. run out, or any fraction of one, can be easily read off. It is placed in a vertical position on a simple stand in front of the operator. The cock of glass, well ground in, can be treated with a little lard to make it quite watertight, if necessary.

now inverted sugar-solution, 10 cc. of Fehling (it is sucked up into a 10 cc. pipette, so as just to come up to the mark round the upper stem) is placed in a porcelain dish, which is then heated over a Bunsen burner. A small quantity of the sugar solution (about 2 cc. at a time to begin with) is then run in and boiled, the mixture being stirred all the while. When the blue colour begins to get faint add the sugar solution drop by drop; finally when the colour is gone and the deep-red cuprous precipitate lies at the bottom of the dish, read off from the burette the quantity run in. Suppose this to be 19·1 cc. Then the calculation will be as a Rule of Three sum.

$$19\cdot 1 : 40{,}000 :: \cdot 05 = 104\cdot 712$$
[40,000 = 1000 (cc.) × 40 to bring the 2·5 of sugar up to 100 grammes in order to get percentage.]

Then it will be necessary to subtract 5% (= 5·235) from this, because 100 parts cane-sugar = 105 parts glucose.

104·712 − 5·235 = 99·477 % of cane-sugar in the sample, a high but very probable percentage. Wherefore the Fehling may be taken as correct.

Volumetric and Gravimetric Methods.—The above, or any analysis of glucose, invert-sugar, etc., conducted on similar lines is known as the volumetric method. Another method, as follows, is known as the gravimetric method.

About 30 cc. of Fehling is added in a beaker to 50 cc. well-boiled and boiling water [it is well to have this beaker within another beaker of boiling water]. Then a known volume of the glucose-containing liquid, but not enough to discharge *all* the blue, is added, and the boiling continued for 12 to 15 minutes. Then the precipitated Cu_2O is quickly filtered, washed with well-boiled water, dried and ignited in a porcelain crucible with the filter-paper * for 20 minutes. The ignition should convert

---

* It is needless to say that the ash of the filter-paper should be taken into account (tared). Half a dozen or so of the kind and size used may be ignited and the ash carefully kept together and weighed. The total

the Cu_2O into black cupric oxide CuO, which is then cooled in the desiccator and quickly weighed, as the oxide is very hygroscopic. The CuO found multiplied by ·4535 will give the quantity of glucose in the quantity of the solution which was added.

The factor for *cane-sugar*, after inversion, is ·4308.

But if the ignition is only enough to burn the filter-paper without converting the Cu_2O into CuO the factors employed should be ·5042 for glucose, and ·4790 for sucrose (cane-sugar) after inversion.

Want of space prevents any gravimetric calculations being appended, but the student will be able from the above data to make his own calculations; he will find it instructive to check his results got by volumetry by those that the gravimetric method gives him.

Examination of Commercial Glucose (or Invert-sugar).—Dissolve 2·5 grammes in 500 cc. water (= 100 grammes in 20,000 cc., which will be the middle term of the first Rule of Three sum below).

There will be two separate determinations—(a) to determine the percentage of existing glucose; (β) to determine the dextrin.

(a) Boil 10 cc. of Fehling over a Bunsen as before, and run in solution as previously directed from the burette. Then suppose it takes 15·2 cc. to just precipitate all the copper. The calculation will be—

$$15 \cdot 2 : 20{,}000 :: \cdot 05 : x$$
$$\frac{20{,}000 \times \cdot 05}{15 \cdot 2} = 65 \cdot 78\% \text{ of glucose in sample.}$$

Preparatory to determination β 200 cc. of the above solution is taken, and with addition of 4 cc. sulphuric acid boiled for 3 hours.

It is then cooled and made up to 250 cc. at 15·5° C. (= 60° Fahr.). Consequently, in the second solution the

divided by 6 may be recorded in the note-book on some page easily referred to, with tares of the other things (*e.g.*, platinum dish, specific gravity bottle, glass evaporating basins) frequently used.

glucose will be dissolved in the proportion of 100 grammes in 25,000 cc., which number will accordingly be the middle term.

As before, 10 cc. of Fehling is boiled, and the solution run in from the burette. Suppose it takes 16·7 cc. to neutralise this time. The calculation will be—

$$16·7 : 25,000 :: ·05$$

$$\frac{25,000 \times ·05}{16·7} = 74·85.$$

74·85 − 65·78 (ascertained glucose) = 9·07, but from this 10% has to be deducted, viz., ·907 (because 9 parts dextrin = 10 glucose), which leaves 8·16.

Consequently the brewing value of the commercial article appears to have been

$$\begin{array}{ll} \text{Glucose} & 65·78\% \\ \text{Dextrin} & \underline{8·16\%} \\ & 73·94\% \end{array}$$

Examination of Raw or Refined Cane-sugar.—Two grammes of cane-sugar are dissolved in 100 cc. water, and boiled for 1 hour with 2 cc. strong sulphuric acid to invert it, and made up to 500 cc. (the acid should be neutralised).

Suppose it takes 13·3 to precipitate the Cu_2O (10 cc. of Fehling to be used as before), the calculation will be

$$13·3 : 25,000 : ·05$$

$$\begin{array}{r} ·05 \\ \overline{13·3)1250·00} \\ 93·98 \end{array}$$

Deduct $\frac{1}{20}$ part, because 95 parts cane = 100 invert $\bigg\} = \dfrac{4·69}{89·29\%}$ of cane-sugar in the sample.

[But note that very many samples of raw cane-sugar contain considerable quantities of invert, to determine which a preliminary trial with Fehling, before boiling with acid, would be necessary.]

Difficulty of deciding when the Right Quantity has been run in (testing Filtrate for Copper).—Owing to impurities, albuminous and other, in the solution which is being tested, its heating with the Fehling sometimes produces a muddy or dull greenish appearance, the precipitate refusing to settle. It is then very difficult to decide when the right quantity of the saccharine solution has been added. To determine if any copper remains unprecipitated, a little of the mingled fluids may be filtered (the filter-paper on the filter being previously washed with a little hot water) into a beaker. It is there made slightly acid with a few drops of acetic or hydrochloric acid, after which *one* drop of potassium ferrocyanide solution is added. The presence of any copper in the filtrate will be revealed by a more or less brown coloration, according to the amount of copper present.

Testing Malt for Maltose and Dextrin.—This is done in three operations. (1) Five grammes of the malt are taken after crushing (with a small pestle and mortar or a coffee mill kept for the purpose) and mixed with 100 cc. of distilled water in a beaker. The beaker is then placed on a sand-bath over a steady flame, and during the first half-hour raised to 60° C. (=140° Fahr.), at which heat it is maintained for an hour longer. Then it is boiled, filtered (the residue being well washed), cooled, and made up 500 cc. (The per cent. proportion for the Rule of Three sum will be 100 grammes in 10,000 cc.)

The first test is made as before with 10 cc. of Fehling (the malt-wort being run in from the burette and boiled as before). Then suppose it takes 13·6 cc. to precipitate all the Cu_2O, the sum will be—

$$13·6 : 10,000 :: ·05 : x = 36·76.$$

(2) The next step is to take 100 cc. of the above solution, adding 3 cc. sulphuric acid, and boil for three

hours. After boiling, nearly neutralise, as in previous inversions, and make up to 250 cc.

Then 100 cc. (*i.e.* one gramme) having been taken and made up to 250 cc., 100 grammes would take 25,000 cc., which × ·05, as usual, = 1250.

Then supposing, on trying the above solution with Fehling, that 16·5 is required to precipitate;

$$\frac{1250}{16\cdot 5} = 75\cdot 75,$$

deducting from which the previous "glucose" reading, we get $75\cdot75 - 36\cdot76 = 38\cdot99$ (= apparent dextrin as glucose); from this 10% has to be deducted so as to reduce it to glucose; therefore $38\cdot99 - 3\cdot89 = 35\cdot1$.

This will give us glucose 36·76, dextrin (apparent) 35·1 or 71·86 in all; but yet another correction has to be made. The first determination made, though expressed in terms of glucose, really represents maltose, and of this, according to C. O'Sullivan, 100 parts have only the same reducing action upon Fehling that 66·66 parts of glucose have. Accordingly to bring the glucose indication into maltose, we must add the half, thus $36\cdot76 + 18\cdot38 = 55\cdot14$ of maltose.

Obviously, this large alteration of the percentage got by operation 1 will necessitate a correction for the dextrin got by operation 2. The steps are—

$$55\cdot14 \times \frac{100}{95} \text{ (to increase by } \tfrac{1}{20}\text{)} = 58\cdot04.$$

From 75·75 (got in 2nd operation)
deduct 58·04
─────
17·71
10% off 1·77
─────
15·94 = dextrin.

[N.B.—These apparently complicated corrections are necessitated by the fact that the determination in the first operation shows *maltose*, but in the second operation *glucose*. The maltose percentage obtained has, accordingly, to be translated into its equivalent of glucose

($55 \cdot 14 = 58 \cdot 04$), which equivalent is subtracted from the total : the remainder $17 \cdot 71 =$ dextrin, expressed as glucose, and from this, accordingly, a tenth has to be deducted. The formulæ and their values on which these corrections are based are as follows :—

$$
\begin{array}{ccc}
\text{Glucose.} & \text{Cane-sugar and Maltose.} & \text{Dextrin.} \\
\hline
C_6 = 12 \times 6 = 72 & C_{12} = 12 \times 12 = 144 & C_6 = 12 \times 6 = 72 \\
H_{12} = 1 \times 12 = 12 & H_{22} = 1 \times 22 = 22 & H_{10} = 1 \times 10 = 10 \\
O_6 = 16 \times 6 = 96 & O_{11} = 16 \times 11 = 176 & O_5 = 16 \times 5 = 80 \\
\hline
180 & 2)342 & 162 \\
 & \overline{171} &
\end{array}
$$

Whence it will be seen that the molecule of maltose only weighs $\frac{19}{20}$ of the glucose molecule into which it is converted by boiling with dilute sulphuric acid ; and that the dextrin molecule weighs $\frac{9}{10}$ of the corresponding glucose molecule.]

(3) Meantime 50 cc. of the infusion should have been evaporated over water in glass evaporating basin No. 1, and then dried for $1\frac{1}{2}$ hour in the drying oven at 100 C., after which it is quickly put into the desiccator, cooled, and rapidly weighed. Suppose the gross weight $= 28 \cdot 296$ grammes. Then $28 \cdot 296 - 27 \cdot 922$ (weight of glass basin) $= \cdot 374$.

The 50 cc. taken $= \frac{1}{2}$ gramme, therefore it will be necessary to multiply the nett weight by 200 to get the solids of 100 grammes.

$\cdot 374 \times 200 = 74 \cdot 8$ (dry soluble extract), the difference between which and the maltose and dextrin got will include albuminous matter, acidity, ash, colouring matter, etc.

So that the results got can now be tabulated as far as the maltose and dextrin are concerned.

Maltose . . . . . $= 55 \cdot 14$
Dextrin . . . . . $= 15 \cdot 94$
Lactic Acid, Sol. Albuminoids,
    Ash, etc. . . . . $= 3 \cdot 72$

$74 \cdot 80$ Dry soluble extract.

It will be useful to append here three analyses by Dr. C. Graham, purporting to show the influence of high kiln heats on the character of the infusion products which the malt subsequently yields.

	80° C. (170° F.)	100° C. (212° F.)	120° C. (248° F.)
Maltose	57·01	52·44	51·32
Dextrin	14·92	18·49	19·35
Lactic Acid	0·56	0·49	0·31
Soluble Albuminoids	2·09	1·60	1·50
Colouring Matter, Ash, etc.	1·49	1·38	1·32
Total dry solids	76·07	74·40	73·80

[Qualified by the malto-dextrin, or amylöin theory. The above results must, however, be considered in the light of recent evidence on the existence of malto-dextrins or amylöins, which are supposed to be *definite compounds* of maltose and dextrin, combined, however, according to the type, in very varying proportions. It is supposed that, though the *free* maltose may vary, the *free* dextrin is practically constant in quantity—viz., 20% of all the starch which has undergone hydrolysis.

To quote one of the arch-priests of the new cult: "In the ordinary methods of analysis, the maltose, whether free, or combined as malto-dextrin, will appear entirely as maltose, while the dextrin, whether combined or free, will appear as dextrin. Consequently, in the ordinary analysis, we get our total maltose and our total dextrin, quite irrespective of the amount of each which is free and the amount which is combined. Here are two typical analyses where the percentages of total maltose and total dextrin expressed on 100 parts starch are the same. The figures chosen are integral, so as to make the point as clear as possible.

	A.	B.
Free Maltose	65 ⎫ 75	73 ⎫ 75
Combined Maltose	10 ⎭	2 ⎭
Combined Dextrin	5 ⎫ 25	5 ⎫ 25
Free (stable) Dextrin	20 ⎭	20 ⎭

THE AMYLÖIN THEORY.

In both these cases the total maltose is 75, and the total dextrin 25, so that had these worts been analysed in the ordinary way, and without regard to malto-dextrins, they would appear the same in constitution; and they would naturally be regarded as about to yield the same results as regards attenuation, and as regards general character of finished beer. But the recognition of the malto-dextrins indicates that, although identical in respect of total maltose and dextrin percentages, the worts will yield *entirely* different results. For instance, wort A will not attenuate to nearly so low a point as wort B, and the beers yielded by these worts will be entirely different in palate, rate of conditioning, stability, and brightness."*

Let us examine this contention a little. The examples are owned to be hypothetical, and they are indeed so extremely hypothetical as to be at variance with the analytical results given in another part of the same paper. In those examples it appeared that as the quantity of malto-dextrin increased, the type rose also as a general rule; that is to say, the malto-dextrin compound contained less and less maltose and more and more dextrin. It was only when the quantity of malto-dextrin was low, that its type also was so low as to bear the proportion of maltose 2 : dextrin 1 (as in the hypothetical example A), and this was only in the case of an undercured malt, while those purporting to give the results of mash-tun determinations never showed a lower proportion of maltose to dextrin than maltose 1 : dextrin 1.

Therefore, even if the amylöin theory be proved up to the hilt, it appears that the want of precision lies within much narrower limits than the above hypothetical example would make it, and that if the dextrin found be worked out as a percentage of actual starch or rather of the carbohydrate portion of the soluble extract, any surplus shown above the 20% of stable dextrin will give a fair indication not only of the amount but of the type of

* "Transactions of the Institute of Brewing," iv., No. 6. Paper by Dr. Moritz.

malto-dextrin likely to be formed under the given conditions.*

Of course the indication will not always be very exact, but if the surplus of dextrin is low we may take it that neither quantity nor type is likely to be high; if the surplus of dextrin is high that type, almost certainly, and quantity, most probably, will be high. And it may be added that the dextrin should apparently come out a shade higher than analyses give it, seeing that recent researches have gone far to prove that there is an unfermented residue in beer which is not maltose but which yet has cupric-reducing power; and owing to this amount not requiring correction (for if it were glucose it would ferment away), the correction "maltose into glucose" is somewhat lessened, so that the dextrin amount is fractionally increased.]

Acidity in Malt.—The method of testing for acidity here to be described is based upon chemical equivalence and the use of solutions accurately titrated or standardised.

For example, three distinct kinds of solution will be required; a standard or normal acid solution made with oxalic acid; a corresponding normal alkaline solution of ammonia, or of what is perhaps preferable, sodic hydrate (pure caustic soda); and a solution of litmus, though litmus paper can be made to do. All these can be bought ready prepared, but for the sake of clearness the preparation of the standard acid and alkali solutions will be explained here, the method of making the litmus solution being left to the end of this chapter.

Of the other solutions, not only are standard or normal solutions required, but also one $\frac{1}{10}$ of the strength, and another $\frac{1}{100}$ of the strength, that is to say, 100 cc. and 10 cc. respectively of the normal solution diluted to a litre (1000 cc.). The decinormal, *i.e.*, the $\frac{1}{10}$ solution, is written shortly $\frac{N}{10}$, the centinormal $\frac{N}{100}$.

* The, 20% of stable dextrin is calculated on the *starch* of the malt. This, by referring to Mr. O'Sullivan's analyses in the previous chapter

TESTING ACIDITY IN MALT.

' It has been said that the preparation of the standard solutions is based upon equivalent values, that is to say, the atomic weights are totalled up in each case, and their sum gives the exact quantity which corresponds to, or neutralises, each of the others. Only it must be noted that in the case of oxalic acid, which is a *bivalent* compound, only half the quantity represented by the total weight will be required. It will be worth while to set forth the calculation at length.

Oxalic Acid—$C_2H_2O_4 + 2\ H_2O$.

$H_2 = 2$; $C_2 = 24$; $O_4 = 64$ . . . $= 90$
The two molecules of water of crystallisation $= 36$
$\overline{126}$

Of which half, as stated above, viz., 63 grammes, is dissolved in a litre to make the normal solution; consequently the $\frac{N}{10}$ solution contains 6·3 grammes and the $\frac{N}{100}$ solution ·63 gramme.

Ammonia NH_3.

$N = 14: H_3 = 3 = 17$.

Accordingly 17 grammes in a litre will make the normal solution.* [63 grammes oxalic acid correspond to 17 grammes ammonia, and 6·3 of the first to 1·7 of the latter.]

Sodic Hydrate NaOH.

$Na = 23 : O = 16 : H = 1 = 40$.

---

the reader will see averages about 45%. The stable dextrin will accordingly average about 9% on the malt, so that the amount above this, in our analysis 6·94, may be taken as approximating to combined dextrin.

* Best got by taking about 19·32 cc. of *liquor ammoniæ fortior* having a specific gravity of about ·880 and making up to a litre. But in any case it, as well as the sodic hydrate solution, must be standardised against the normal oxalic acid—*i.e.*, when equal bulks are mixed and tested with litmus paper, there must be neither acid nor alkaline reaction.

Accordingly 40 grammes in a litre will make the normal solution, of which 1 cc. will neutralise the acid of 1 cc. of the normal oxalic acid solution. But oxalic acid is not the acid of malt or beer; these are lactic or acetic. We will, therefore, compare their molecular totals with those already taken, to learn what relation those acids bear to the standard alkaline solutions.

Lactic acid ($C_3H_6O_3$).

$$C_3 = 36 : H_6 = 6 : O_3 = 48 = 90.$$

Consequently 90 grammes lactic acid = 17 grammes ammonia, or 40 of sodium hydrate. That is to say, 9 of lactic acid = 1·7 of ammonia or 4 of sodic hydrate, and so on. Conversely a litre of either alkaline solution (normal) will represent (*i.e.*, neutralise) 90 grammes of lactic acid, a litre of the $\frac{N}{10}$ solution will represent 9 grammes, and a litre of either alkaline $\frac{N}{100}$ solution will represent ·9 gramme (this equivalence will be used in the calculations).

Acetic acid ($C_2H_4O_2$).

$$C_2 = 24 : H_4 = 4 : O_2 = 32 = 60.$$

Therefore 6 and ·6 grammes acetic = 9 and ·9 lactic acid in neutralising the alkaline solutions. Accordingly a litre of either normal alkaline solution = 60 grammes acetic, and a litre of the $\frac{N}{10}$ and $\frac{N}{100}$ solutions 6 and ·6 grammes respectively.

Preparing Infusion for Acidity Test-process, and Calculation.—Ten grammes are mashed as before, and made up to 500 cc.—50 cc. of the above are taken; *i.e.*, 1 *gramme of malt* is dealt with.

The $\frac{N}{100}$ ammonia is used, run in from a burette upon the 50 cc. in a porcelain dish and tested at intervals with litmus paper. Suppose it takes 4·7 cc. of the $\frac{N}{100}$ ammonia before neutrality is produced. We have seen that 1 litre (*i.e.*, 1,000 cc.) of $\frac{N}{100}$ ammonia = ·9 lactic acid. So the calculation will be—

1 gramme (the quantity of malt dealt with) took 4·7 cc. Therefore 100 grammes would take 470 cc.

1000   470 :: ·9

= ·423% lactic acid.

[Mr. Allen, however (in *Commercial Organic Analysis*) says: "The normal proportion of free acid, calculated as lactic acid, is not more than ·2 or at most ·3 per cent.; ·4 per cent. is unusually high, and denotes unsoundness." This is going rather far. It will be observed that two of Dr. Graham's analyses show proportions exceeding this, even one with malt dried at 212°. Of course even this finishing temperature is compatible with unsoundness acquired by previous unskilful handling.]

Albuminous Matters.*—Very concordant results, although its trustworthiness has been disputed, can be got by using Professor Wanklyn's ammonia process, albeit specially devised for determining the amount of pollution in water. For this method three standard solutions will be required, instructions for the preparation of which will be found at the end of this chapter. These solutions are (1) Nessler's solution; (2) standard ammonium-chloride solution; (3) solution of potash and permanganate of potash.

* It must be confessed that the determination of albuminous matters, though generally forming part of an ordinary malt analysis, is not altogether satisfactory. Strictly, the nitrogen found, ought to be stated in terms of amides, peptones, albuminoids, etc., by the complicated process of Professor Ullik. Although in two samples of malt the total nitrogen may come out the same, stated as albuminoids, yet in one these may be low, and the amides high in amount, and the reverse in the other. Obviously, the malt with the most of its nitrogen in the form of highly assimilable amides would give the most satisfactory results.

More detail will be found when the testing of water for "free and albuminoid ammonia" is described, but it may be said here that the test depends on the fact that a small quantity of Nessler (in practice 2 cc. are used in each 50 cc. of water) reveals the presence of even extremely minute traces of ammonia (1 part in 10,000,000) by striking a tint more or less brown, according to the quantity of ammonia present. The tint is compared with that produced by Nesslerising a second 50 cc. of water, to which a known volume of the ammonium-chloride solution has been added, and when an exactly similar tint is produced (which can be matched quite closely by placing the two tubes side by side on a white tile, and looking at them *through their depth*), the amount of ammonium-chloride solution used in the five or six successive Nesslerisings is read off and translated into ammonia.

In water analysis, after the portions containing the free ammonia have been distilled off and tested, the residue is boiled with some of the permanganate-potash solution, in order to convert the organic matter into ammonia, in which form alone it can be estimated by this process. The same method is adopted in estimating the albuminous matters in malt-extract. Care must be taken to use "ammonia-free" distilled water for the cylinder (test-tube) to which the ammonium-chloride solution is added for comparison, and that solution must be run in *before* the Nessler. The 2 cc. pipette used to measure the Nessler, which can be made by the operator out of a piece of glass tubing, will do to stir up the contents of the cylinders.

Let us now proceed to the actual operation. Take a flask of water two-thirds full, to which a little freshly ignited carbonate of soda has been added. Connect the retort by the beak-shaped tube with the condenser (india-rubber stoppers, suitably perforated, make the tightest joints), and bring the naked flame of a Bunsen burner under the retort. [Of course before the contents of the retort begin to boil, cold water must be flowing continuously through the outer tube of the condenser in order to condense the vapour which comes off.] The vapour as it is condensed is to be caught in one of the Nessler cylinders, file-marked, so that 50 cc. can be accurately caught each time.

Test the first distillate with Nessler to ensure that all the free ammonia is got rid of, which would otherwise vitiate the result, and as soon as no coloration is produced, 10 cc. of wort (made by mashing 10 grammes as before, and making filtrate up to 1 litre), representing accordingly ·1 gramme of malt, is added, and the real distillation begins. After the first and second distillates have been tried with Nessler (the second should be nearly colourless), 100 cc. of the permanganate and potash solution, previously boiled with 200 cc. of ammonia-free water, is added. [N.B.—A few pieces of pumice-stone, or broken clay pipe put into the flask, will prevent its "bumping," and possibly breaking. The broken pipe should be heated to redness in a platinum dish or crucible till all the darkish colour which it assumes is gone.]

The first 100 cc. distilled over is taken and made up with "ammonia-free" water to 500 cc. Five separate distillates—or six if the coloration continue marked—are taken, and should be made up to 500 cc. like the first, as long as the coloration is considerable. 50 cc. of each 500 cc. (or of the 100 cc. if undiluted) is Nesslerised, and the parallel results got with ammonium-chloride solution noted, and used as a basis of calculation as follows.

[The first two distillates of 100 cc. each are supposed to be diluted to 500 cc.; the others not to require such dilution, but in each case only 50 cc. is Nesslerised.]

(1) 100 made up to 500.   50 cc. took $2·25 = 22·5$
(2) 100   ,,   ,,   500.   50 cc. ,, $1·25 = 12·5$
(3) 100 (undiluted)   50 cc. ,, $2·25 = 4·5$
(4) 100   ,,   50 cc. ,, $1·5 = 3·0$
(5) 100   ,,   50 cc. ,, $·5 = 1·0$
                                         ─────
                                          $43·5$

i.e., 43·5 cc. of the ammonium-chloride solution are used to produce a series of tints equal to those produced by the ammonia evolved from 1 gramme of malt.

But each cc. of the ammonium-chloride solution = ·00001 gramme of ammonia.

I.e., 0·1 gramme = ·000435 of ammonia, and 100 grammes of the malt = ·435 gramme of ammonia.

Rule.—Now multiply the ammonia got by 5·2* to get the albuminous constituents of the malt.

$$·435 \times 5·2 = 2·262 \text{ albuminous matter.}$$

Accordingly we are now able to fill up the gaps which were left in the analysis of the extract from a sample of malt (p. 231). This will now stand—

Maltose	55·14
Dextrin	15·94
Albuminoids	2·26
Lactic acid	·42
Ash, colouring matter, etc.	1·04
	74·80

Estimation of Nitrogen by Soda-Lime Process. (*a*) **Soluble Albuminoids.**—This method consists in heating the substance dissolved in the smallest possible quantity of water—or malt may be mashed, the wort being just evaporated to dryness, and the dry solids carefully scraped up—with a mixture of caustic soda and caustic lime, called soda-lime,† in a combustion tube, which is either of iron and closed at one end, or of hard glass with one end drawn out to a point, which can be broken off when desired. The nitrogen of the albuminoids is thereupon converted into

---

* This factor 5·2 corresponds with the factor 6·3 used for calculating albuminous bodies from total ascertained nitrogen $6·3 \times \frac{14}{17} = 5·2$ [17 parts ammonia contain 14 nitrogen].

† Can be bought ready for use at Messrs. Townson & Mercer's at 1*s.* 4*d.* per lb.

SODA-LIME PROCESS.

ammonia, which is led into a known quantity of normal hydrochloric, sulphuric, or nitric acid contained in a special bulb apparatus, where it combines with its equivalent quantity of the normal acid. The amount of *acid* remaining unneutralised is then determined by titration, which amount deducted from the known volume in the tube gives the amount neutralised by the ammonia evolved during the combustion. [On the equivalent principle referred to in the paragraph on acidity determination, the normal solutions contain respectively in 1 litre 49 grammes sulphuric acid, $H_2 SO_4$ (half weight of total atoms), 36·5 of hydrochloric acid, HCl; 63 grammes of nitric acid, HNO_3; 40 grammes of sodic hydrate, NaHO, and 17 of ammonia, NH_3.

Accordingly, as stated before, any measure of one of the normal acid solutions neutralises *exactly the same measure* of the ammonia or sodic hydrate, if the solutions be correctly made.]

The **Combustion-tube,** some 20 inches long, must first have the bottom covered to the depth of about 3 inches with coarsely granulated (not powdery) soda-lime. Then the dissolved substance, with the rinsings as sparingly done as possible, is run in, and after a few minutes' rest the tube is about three parts filled with soda-lime; or, if it be malt, the carefully evaporated extract, care being taken to secure every particle by rubbing the dish out with a portion of soda-lime after thoroughly scraping out the contents, is put into the tube. We will assume that the amount operated on represents the dried soluble solids from 5 grammes of malt, mashed with cold distilled water in a beaker, the temperature having been gradually raised to 140°, and maintained thereat for one hour. [If a concentrated solution, however, is operated on, an asbestos plug, lightly put in, will prevent any soda-lime being carried over when heat is applied and steam generated.]

Five cc. of normal acid is now run in the special bulb apparatus (Will & Varrentrapp's), which must afterwards be connected with the combustion tube. The connection must fit quite tightly, and precautions must be taken to prevent the cork or stopper, which fits into the combustion tube, from getting burnt. [N.B.—A piece of cotton waste, wetted and hung upon the end of the combustion tube and on the cork in question, and with its two ends dipping into a basin of water underneath, will keep the end of the tube cool.]

The bulb itself must be put in a vessel of cold water as soon as the combustion tube has been placed in the furnace, with its end (that towards the bulb) projecting some three or four inches.

After the combustion tube has got red-hot and vapour has ceased to come off (if the solution was employed), the bulb apparatus is detached, and its contents and subsequent rinsings emptied into a porcelain dish. Alkali solution is now run in from a burette, and when neutrality is just reached (if a few drops of litmus solution have been previously added, the point is just when its red gets a tinge of violet, or red and blue litmus paper may be alternately tried), the quantity is read off, and the calculation is as follows:—

Suppose the quantity of N. alkali run in is 3·7; then—seeing that 5 cc. of N. acid was run into the bulb—1·3 gramme will have been neutralised by the ammonia given off.

But each cc. corresponds to ·017 gramme of ammonia (because 1000 cc. contain 17 grammes) or to ·014 nitrogen (ammonia contains $\frac{14}{17}$ of nitrogen).

Therefore ·014 × 1·3 = ·0182 gramme of nitrogen from 5 grammes malt, which × 20 (to bring to percentage) = ·364.

·364 × 6·36 (a factor got by dividing 100 by the average percentage of nitrogen which albumen contains) = 2·315 albuminous matter.

Total Albuminoids (by Soda-Lime).—The above will give the soluble albuminoids; if the total albuminoids are required it will be necessary to take the *dry grist*, carefully reweighed after grinding, and to heat the tube to redness, beginning at the end near the bulb. There should be a portion of soda-lime at the lower end of the *glass* tube, and a portion, likewise unmixed with malt, at the upper end, the grist mixed with the bulk of the soda-lime occupying the space between. The object of having a glass tube and of its being drawn to a point at the bottom is that when the combustion is thoroughly over and the ammonia practically all evolved, the point may be broken off and a gentle current of air blown through, which carries into the bulb any of the ammonia which has been left behind. The calculation will be similar to that already given.

Accuracy of the Soda-Lime Method.—Opinions differ as to this; but it seems that, except in the case of certain compounds, which either do not yield their combined nitrogen as ammonia or not the whole of it, the method may be trusted. With substances very rich in nitrogen the addition of sugar on either side of the substance to be analysed is said to improve the result.

Also a mixture of equal parts of sodium thiosulphate, sodium acetate, and soda-lime, instead of soda-lime alone, appears to give even better results.

Diastatic Activity of Malt.—This may be estimated and classified by Lintner's method. A solution of soluble starch is prepared, of which 10 cc. represent ·2 gramme, *i.e.*, a 2% solution. It is prepared in the following way. Pure potato starch is covered with hydrochloric acid of 7·5% strength, and allowed to stand for seven days at ordinary temperature or for three days at about 104° Fahr., whereupon it loses its property of forming a paste. It is then repeatedly washed with cold water (by decantation) till litmus paper shows no acid, then drained and dried in the air. The product gives a clear solution with warm water, and of this, as required, 2 grammes are taken and dissolved in 100 cc.

In ten test-tubes, containing each 10 cc. of this solution, are added varying quantities (viz., ·1, ·2, ·3, ·4, ·5,

·6, ·7, ·8, ·9, and 1 cc.) of a malt extract prepared as given below, in brackets. [An aqueous extract of 25 grammes of finely powdered malt is made, by allowing the mixture to stand for 6 hours at ordinary temperature of the air, filtering and refiltering, if necessary, on the same filter-paper till quite clear. It is then made up to 500 cc.]

The ten test-tubes after the addition of the malt-extract then stand for one hour—" at ordinary room temperature," Lintner says, but a *uniform* 70° Fahr. is better, after which 5 cc. of Fehling solution are added to each, and all are placed in boiling water for 10 minutes. [The student who has worked through this chapter will not require the rationale of these steps.]

Then the test-tubes are looked at. If there be one in which the blue colour is exactly discharged that may be taken for classifying, but probably the exact cupric-reducing power will not exactly coincide with the amount of maltose existing in any one of the test-tubes; but there will be one still showing a faint trace of blue, while its neighbour, that had more malt-extract, shows the yellowish tint indicative of its being "overdone." In that case small additions (·02 cc.) of the malt-extract may be made, successively if necessary, the rest for conversion of course being allowed; but if rapidity be an object the mean may be taken.

The standard adopted is that when the maltose produced by the action of ·1 cc. of the malt extract, under the condition prescribed, exactly reduces 5 cc. of Fehling, the diastatic power = 100.

But suppose ·46 is found to be the exact quantity which precipitates *all* the copper, then $\frac{100}{4\cdot 6} = 21\cdot 74$, or correcting for moisture, say 3%, it becomes $\frac{21\cdot 74 \times 100}{97}$ = 22·41 for diastatic value of the malt.

This is a low value. A range between 45 and 30 might be looked upon as average. Higher than 45 might imply under-curing, a lower value than 30 might mean insufficient germination. A much over-cured, scorched malt had, in a series of experiments elsewhere referred to, a value of 16·8.

Analysis of Beer—(i) **Original Gravity.**—Take a sample of the beer, and pour from one large beaker to another for a considerable time in order to get rid of the carbonic acid. When the latter has been got rid of, take 250 cc. and distil (in the Liebig's glass condenser, as arranged by Dr. Graham). Let two-thirds distil over, catch this in another 250 cc. flask, and make both it (the distillate) and the residue up to 250 cc. with distilled water.

Then cool both flasks carefully down to 15·5°C., and fill the specific gravity bottle so that when the stopper is dropped into its place a tiny bead of the liquid just makes its appearance on the small perforation through the stopper. [It must not be a distinct drop, nor must there be any moisture outside the specific gravity bottle.]

With these precautions we weigh successively the specific gravity bottle filled with (1) the beer itself, freed from gas; (2) the distillate (made up as directed); (3) the residue, care of course being taken to rinse out the specific gravity bottle first with the liquid which is being weighed, and to use the counterpoise for bottle, as empty.

Let us suppose that the weights of the bottle filled with the respective liquids are :—

Distillate 49·549; residue 51·222; and beer 50·793 all in grammes.

It will be remembered that at the outset we weighed our specific gravity bottle filled with distilled water at 15·5° C. and recorded it to hold 49·983 grammes.

Accordingly the calculation will proceed thus :

$$\text{Distillate} = \frac{49\cdot549 \times 1000}{49\cdot983} = 991\cdot3.$$

$$\text{Residue} = \frac{51\cdot222 \times 1000}{49\cdot983} = 1024\cdot78.$$

$$\text{Beer} = \frac{50\cdot793 \times 1000}{49\cdot983} = 1016\cdot2 \,(\text{Final attenuation} = 5\cdot8 \text{ lb.})$$

Then we subtract the found specific gravity of the distillate, viz., 991·3, from 1000, which gives us 8·7, whereupon we refer to a book of tables generally supplied with the specific gravity bottle, and in one of the tables (Table I. opposite) we find that 8·7 = 37·5 degrees of gravity lost.

We then add the 37·5 to the specific gravity of the residue, viz., 1024·78, which gives us 1062·28 as the original specific gravity (= 22·42 brewers' lb., with a final attenuation, as stated above, of about 5·8 lb.).

Original Gravity by the Evaporation Process.—This is easier than the distillation process, though, if the other be carefully performed, probably a trifle less exact. It does not, for instance, involve taking any exact quantity of the beer. Any convenient quantity can be partially evaporated (enough to drive off the alcohol) in a beaker, cooled and weighed as before, the difference between the weight of the residue and that of the beer before evaporation providing the required *data*. We can of course use the weights already got for the purpose of illustration, thus:

Deduct gravity of the residue from that of the beer + 1000.

2016·2 − 1024·78 = 991·42, which in turn deducted from 1000 = 8·58. Or, what is simpler, deduct the beer gravity from that of the residue, 1024·78 − 1016·2 = 8·58.

On referring to the evaporation process table (Table II.) this will be found to show 37·7 degrees of gravity represented by alcohol, etc. This gives 1062·48 as the gravity of the wort before fermentation, against 1062·28 shown by the distillation process.

ORIGINAL GRAVITY DETERMINATIONS.

TABLE I.

Spirit Indication with corresponding Degrees of Gravity lost in Malt Worts by the "Distillation Process."

Degrees of Spirit Indication.	·0	·1	·2	·3	·4	·5	·6	·7	·8	·9
0		·3	·6	·9	1·2	1·5	1·8	2·1	2·4	2·7
1	3·0	3·3	3·7	4·1	4·4	4·8	5·1	5·5	5·9	6·2
2	6·6	7·0	7·4	7·8	8·2	8·6	9·0	9·4	9·8	10·2
3	10·7	11·1	11·5	12·0	12·4	12·9	13·3	13·8	14·2	14·7
4	15·1	15·5	16·0	16·4	16·8	17·3	17·7	18·2	18·6	19·1
5	19·5	19·9	20·4	20·9	21·3	21·8	22·2	22·7	23·1	23·6
6	24·1	24·6	25·0	25·5	26·0	26·4	26·9	27·4	27·8	28·3
7	28·8	29·2	29·7	30·2	30·7	31·2	31·7	32·2	32·7	33·2
8	33·7	34·3	34·8	35·4	35·9	36·5	37·0	37·5	38·0	38·6
9	39·1	39·7	40·2	40·7	41·2	41·7	42·2	42·7	43·2	43·7
10	44·2	44·7	45·1	45·6	46·0	46·5	47·0	47·5	48·0	48·5
11	49·0	49·6	50·1	50·6	51·2	51·7	52·2	52·7	53·3	53·8
12	54·3	54·9	55·4	55·9	56·4	56·9	57·4	57·9	58·4	58·9
13	59·4	60·0	60·5	61·1	61·6	62·2	62·7	63·3	63·8	64·3
14	64·8	65·4	65·9	66·5	67·1	67·6	68·2	68·7	69·3	69·9

TABLE II.

Spirit Indication with corresponding Degrees of Gravity lost in Malt Worts by the "Evaporation Process."

Degrees of Spirit Indication.	·0	·1	·2	·3	·4	·5	·6	·7	·8	·9
0		·3	·7	1·0	1·4	1·7	2·1	2·4	2·8	3·1
1	3·5	3·8	4·2	4·6	5·0	5·4	5·8	6·2	6·6	7·0
2	7·4	7·8	8·2	8·7	9·1	9·5	9·9	10·3	10·7	11·1
3	11·5	11·9	12·4	12·8	13·2	13·6	14·0	14·4	14·8	15·3
4	15·8	16·2	16·6	17·0	17·4	17·9	18·4	18·8	19·3	19·8
5	20·3	20·7	21·2	21·6	22·1	22·5	23·0	23·4	23·9	24·3
6	24·8	25·2	25·6	26·1	26·6	27·0	27·5	28·0	28·5	29·0
7	29·5	30·0	30·4	30·9	31·3	31·8	32·3	32·8	33·3	33·8
8	34·3	34·9	35·5	36·0	36·6	37·1	37·7	38·3	38·8	39·4
9	40·0	40·5	41·0	41·5	42·0	42·5	43·0	43·5	44·0	44·4
10	44·9	45·4	46·0	46·5	47·1	47·6	48·2	48·7	49·3	49·8
11	50·3	50·9	51·4	51·9	52·5	53·0	53·5	54·0	54·5	55·0
12	55·6	56·2	56·7	57·3	57·8	58·3	58·9	59·4	59·9	60·5
13	61·0	61·6	62·1	62·7	63·2	63·8	64·3	64·9	65·4	66·0
14	66·5	67·0	67·6	68·1	68·7	69·2	69·8	70·4	70·9	71·4

Method of Using the foregoing Tables.—In our example of the Distillation Process we find the "spirit indication" (*i.e.*, 1000—specific gravity of distillate) to be 8·7. We then refer to Table I., and taking the first column we find the whole number 8; next we look for the column which has ·7 at the head, and observing the place where these two columns, the one horizontal and the other perpendicular, meet one another, we find 37·5 given as the degrees of gravity lost, or solid extract which has been fermented away. Where the "spirit indication" is in two places of decimals the nearest single decimal is taken; thus for 8·58 take 8·6, which on Table II. gives 37·7 (8·58, however = 37·6, which gives a result very close to that of the Distillation Process).

[**Improved Alcoholmeter (Field's Patent).** This ingenious apparatus, of which Mr. J. Long of Eastcheap is the sole maker, may just be referred to here, although its proper sphere is rather the brewing-room than the laboratory. It has been found very useful for the rapid and accurate estimation of "waste" or "returns." It consists of a body or boiler with a spirit-lamp underneath, and a specially graduated thermometer, having a condenser attached, which has to be inserted into the boiler. Advantage is taken of the fact that spirituous liquids boil at lower temperatures than water, consequently the larger the quantity of alcohol in any beer the lower will be its boiling point. But as there is no exactly constant boiling point for water, which in fact varies with barometrical pressure, a preliminary operation has to be made by charging the boiler with water, lighting the spirit lamp, and noting the point at which the water boils, continuing the boiling for some seconds so as to be sure of getting the highest point. Then a movable ivory scale has to be adjusted so that the 0 (zero) exactly faces the highest point of ebullition, which makes the necessary adaptation of the thermometer to the boiling-point of the day. While the heating and boiling are progressing, a constant stream of cold water must run through the condenser.

ACIDITY IN BEER.

Then the boiling operation has to be repeated with the beer which is to be tested, and as soon as the liquid is in full boil the highest point which the quicksilver reaches must be carefully noticed, and there, instead of the temperature as in ordinary thermometers, can be read off the " lbs. per barrel," or " degrees of specific gravity," the former on the right hand, the latter on the left of the scale, corresponding to the lbs. or degrees of gravity " lost " during fermentation. This, added to the present gravity as found by a small saccharometer, gives the original gravity of the beer.]

Beer showing a Marked Degree of Acidity.—The beer in question was an actual sample of stout, bottled by a large firm, but palpably sour. Special care being taken to get rid of the carbonic acid, the respective gravities are found to be—

$$\text{Beer before distillation} = \frac{50 \cdot 899 \times 1000}{49 \cdot 983} = 1018 \cdot 32.$$

$$\text{Distillate} = \frac{49 \cdot 484 \times 1000}{49 \cdot 983} = 990 \cdot 0.$$

$$\text{Residue} = \frac{51 \cdot 389 \times 1000}{49 \cdot 983} = 1028 \cdot 12.$$

Then subtract as before the distillate 990 from 1000 = 10, which it will be seen, on referring to Table I. above, shows 44·2 degrees of gravity lost.

So that, as far as we have got, the strength of the beer appears to have been 1028·12 + 44·2 = 1072·3 degrees; but owing to the large quantity of acid, acetic (volatile) and lactic (fixed), present, it will be necessary to determine these, and calculate how much " gravity lost " they represent.

We avail ourselves of the following table:—

TABLE III.

For ascertaining the Value of the Acetic Acid.

Excess per cent. of Acetic Acid in the beer.	Corresponding degrees of "Spirit Indication."									
	·00	·01	·02	·03	·04	·05	·06	·07	·08	·09
·0	—	·02	·04	·06	·07	·08	·09	·11	·12	·13
·1	·14	·15	·17	·18	·19	·21	·22	·23	·24	·26
·2	·27	·28	·29	·31	·32	·33	·34	·35	·37	·38
·3	·39	·40	·42	·43	·44	·46	·47	·48	·49	·51
·4	·52	·53	·55	·56	·57	·59	·60	·61	·62	·64
·5	·65	·66	·67	·69	·70	·71	·72	·73	·75	·76
·6	·77	·78	·80	·81	·82	·84	·85	·86	·87	·89
·7	·90	·91	·93	·94	·95	·97	·98	·99	1·0	1·02
·8	1·03	1·04	1·05	1·07	1·08	1·09	1·10	1·11	1·13	1·14
·9	1·15	1·16	1·18	1·19	1·21	1·22	1·23	1·25	1 26	1·28
1·0	1·29	1·31	1·33	1·35	1·36	1·37	1·38	1·40	1·41	1·42

N.B.—It will be observed that all the acid is virtually expressed in terms of acetic, which of course involves a slight inaccuracy. One per cent. of acetic acid (or acid equal thereto) is allowed for as being normally present.

The Process.—Take 50 cc. of the beer freed from carbonic acid (by dashing repeatedly from one large beaker to another), and warm over steam, stirring with a glass stirring-rod. But do not boil, because acetic acid would evaporate. Then cool and put into a porcelain dish, adding $\frac{N}{10}$ ammonia gradually, trying the mixture with litmus papers of both colours, and noting the point at which neutrality is reached. In the case of the acid beer, above mentioned, 27·2 cc. was required to produce neutrality.

Then 50 cc. having been taken, 100 cc. would take 54·4, the *datum* for *total acidity*.

We next proceed to get the fixed acid, and shall then be able to arrive at the volatile acid by difference.

Evaporate 50 cc. of the beer over a water-bath to dryness, make up to about the original bulk, and test with $\frac{N}{10}$ ammonia. Supposing it takes 20·6 cc. to neutralise the acidity, this = 41·2 for 100 cc. (50 cc. having been taken).

Subtracting 41·2 from 54·4 we get 13·2 (as representing the acidity due to volatile acid), and arrange the following Rule of Three sums:—

1000 : 41·2 :: 9 = ·370, fixed or lactic acid.
1000 : 13·2 :: 6 = ·079, volatile or acetic acid,

or ·449, total acid. Upon referring to Table III., taking the nearest index figures given, viz., 45, *i.e.*, looking first *along* the ·4 column and then *down* the ·05 column to the point where they meet, they will be seen to correspond to a "spirit indication" of ·59, which on reference to Table I. (and taking the nearest decimal, viz., ·6) is seen = 1·8 degree of gravity lost. So that we now have 1072·3 (found by distillation) + 1·8 = 1074·1 degrees, or 26·7 brewers' lb., original gravity.

Analysing the Solid Residue (Dry Extract) of Beer.—We will now go back to the beer first dealt with, and separate the constituents of its solid residue. The first step is to take 25 cc. of the beer, evaporate it to dryness, cool in desiccator, and weigh. Say we evaporated in glass basin No. 2, the weight of which = 23·203. If we now find the residue + pan = 24·715, the weight of the residue = 1·512. Multiplying this by 4 (to bring to a percentage, 25 cc. having been taken) we get 6·048% for the solid residue.

Next we proceed to get the maltose and dextrin, for which determination we make use of Fehling's solution, proceeding as before and in two stages.

(*a*) Before inversion.

Take 50 cc. and make up with distilled water to 100 cc. Suppose that 9 cc. precipitates 10 of Fehling. Then as 50 cc. were made up to 100, 100 cc. would be made up to 200, so the Rule of Three sum is—

9 : 200 :: ·05 = 1·11 as glucose = 1·11 + ·55 = 1·66 maltose.

[It will be remembered that maltose has only two-thirds the cupric reducing power or K of glucose, but as it is ·05 of glucose which exactly reduces 10 cc. of Fehling, the correction into maltose, where the sugar is maltose, has to be made by adding the half.]

(β) After inversion (to determine dextrin).

50 cc. are taken and 50 cc. of water added with 3 cc. of sulphuric acid, and the whole is boiled for 3 hours. After being neutralised, it is warmed and shaken up with animal charcoal to decolorise, filtered, and the filtrate, care being taken to wash the residue carefully, made up to 250 cc.

Suppose 5 cc. reduces 10 cc. of Fehling; then 50 cc. having been made up to 250, at the same rate 100 cc. = 500, and the Rule of Three sum will be—

5 : 500 :: ·05 = 5·0 maltose and dextrin expressed as glucose.

The next step is to multiply 1·66 by $\frac{100}{95}$ = 1·74, which means that the 1·66 of maltose determined is now represented by 1·74 of glucose.

Then 5 − 1·74 = 3·26. From this $\frac{1}{10}$ must be deducted to get the dextrin equivalent; thus 3·26 − ·32 = 2·94, the percentage of dextrin in the dry extract.

[Owing to there being sometimes a difficulty in reading the exact point of precipitation, the gravimetric process, as before described, may give closer results than the volumetric here used.]

To determine the Albuminous Matter.—10 cc. of the beer is made up to 100 cc. with distilled water, and of this 10 cc. only (= 1 cc. of the beer) is taken to be "Nesslerised." It is added, as in the case of malt, to a good-sized flask two-thirds full of water, and connected with the condenser. The first distillates are Nesslerised, to ensure that the water is free from ammonia, and then the permanganate-potash solution is added as before. After this addition successive distillates of 100 cc. are obtained, the first of which we will suppose to be diluted to 500 cc., the others being Nesslerised undiluted.

In each case 50 cc. are Nesslerised.

(1) 100 to 500.	50 took	3·5	=	35·0
(2) 100 undiluted	50	,,	7·0	=	14·0
(3) 100	,,	50	,,	3·5	=	7·0
(4) 100	,,	50	,,	3·0	=	6·0
(5) 100	,,	50	,,	2·5	=	5·0
(6) 100	,,	50	,,	1·75	=	3·5
(7) 100	,,	50	,,	·50	=	1·0

$$71·5$$

The calculation then proceeds on the basis that as each cc. of the ammonic-chloride solution = ·00001 gramme of ammonia, and as 71·5 cc. thereof were required to produce the tints which the distillates from 1 cc. of the beer gave with Nessler, each cc. of the beer = ·000715 gramme of ammonia, or 100 cc. = ·0715 gramme of ammonia, which × 5·2 (the constant factor) = ·371 albuminous matter per cent.

Acidity has also to be taken into account, but as its determination has already been described, we will assume it to stand at ·169 fixed and ·012 volatile.

Then we have—

Maltose	= 1·66
Dextrin	= 2·94
Acidity	= ·181
Albuminous matters	= ·371
Undetermined (ash, etc.)	= ·896
	6·048

[N.B.—The albuminous matter is higher than it should be: ·01 per brewers' lb., *i.e.*, ·22 per cent. for a 22 lb. beer, is allowable. The ratio of dextrin to maltose is also higher than is usually found in the dry extract of an average beer.]

Water Analysis.

We can now proceed to the analysis of one average sample of water.

(i) The first step is to get the **Total Solids.**

Take two portions of the water (100 cc. or 70 cc. each) and evaporate over a water-bath to dryness (finally drying the residue in drying-oven at 115° to 120° C.).

[70 cc. is a "miniature gallon" in which milligrammes correspond to grains of the full gallon. If 100 cc. be taken, then $\dfrac{\text{solids in milligrammes} \times 7}{10}$ = grains per gallon.]

The water not being very saline we will operate upon 100 cc., and evaporate *two* portions each of 100 cc. in our evaporating basins [the best things, however, are platinum dishes, but large ones are costly], which, when empty and properly dried, weigh, let us say, 31·063 and 31·42 respectively.

Then, if the first weighing gives 31·09; 31·09−31·063 = ·027, and the second shows 31·447, which − 31·42 = ·027, *i.e.*, in each case 27 milligrammes.

Then $\dfrac{27 \times 7}{10}$ = 18·9 grains of total solids per gallon.

[One residue can now be tried with a drop or two of hydrochloric acid; effervescence will indicate **carbonates.**

The other is kept for the **Qualitative test for nitrates and nitrites.** Or the first may be kept for "**soluble solids.**"]

(ii) Meantime 4 beakers, each containing 500 cc., should have been placed on a sand-bath to partially evaporate. Two of these will be used to determine the sulphuric acid present as **sulphates**, the second pair for determining the **lime and magnesia.** We will return to these later. [It is recommended to do these operations

WATER ANALYSIS.

in duplicate, as they check one another, at all events, till accuracy in manipulation is obtained.]

Nitrates and Nitrites, Qualitative Test for.—Wash the total solids of one dish with distilled water (very little, as they are very soluble), and put into two small test-tubes (about half an inch depth in each).

(a) To one test-tube add sulphuric acid, rather more than the liquid already in the test-tube. (This is done in order to concentrate the minute quantity of nitric acid, which it does by uniting with the water; and it must be done under the tap to prevent the nitric acid from being volatilised).

This being done, add very gradually and carefully, *drop by drop*, ferrous sulphate, so that *it rests upon the surface of the mixture*. Then, if a brownish ring appears at the point of contact, this indicates nitrates. If the nitrates are high, the ring is *blackish*.

(β) To the other test-tube add one drop of ferrous sulphate without sulphuric acid. Similar rings indicate *nitrites*.

We now return to the four beakers, evaporating on the sand bath (step ii).

(a) The two sulphate beakers are to be acidified with hydrochloric acid, a few drops, until the precipitate of carbonate of lime is dissolved. When reduced to one-fifth, add saturated solution of barium chloride. Go on heating till the precipitate settles. Filter through Swedish filter paper. Dry precipitate (with the filter-papers) in drying-oven; ignite over Bunsen in platinum dish; cool as usual. [N.B.—The baric chloride must be slightly, but only slightly, in excess; that it is in excess can be ascertained by testing the filtrate with silver nitrate solution, and then, if barium chloride be present, *i.e.*, not converted into barium-sulphate, which remains on the filter paper, there will be a curdy precipitate of silver chloride. After this the filtrate may be thrown away. If there is any difficulty in getting a clear filtrate, it is recommended to introduce a minute quantity (half a milligramme) of pure starch immediately after the barium chloride, which conglomerates precipitate, and adds practically no inorganic residue.]

For brevity's sake we only calculate out one beaker here. Suppose the total weight = 14·238, from which we have to deduct 14·216 for platinum dish + ·003 for the filter paper, then ·019 of barium sulphate remains, *i.e.*, (500 cc. having been taken) ·019 × 2 = ·038 in litre, which is the same as ·038 grains in 1000 grains. Seeing that a gallon = 70,000 grains, ·038 × 70 or 2·66 represents the barium sulphate in *grains* per gallon.

We have now to get at the amount of anhydrous sulphuric acid which this sulphate represents, the equivalents being baric sulphate $BaSO_4 = (137 + 32 + 64) = 233$; $SO_3 = (32 + 48) = 80$.

Then the Rule of Three sum will be—

$$233 : 80 :: 2·66 : x = ·913 \text{ grains } SO_3 \text{ per gallon.}$$

(β) The two lime (and magnesia) beakers.

Add a few drops of hydrochloric acid to dissolve the precipitate, then a few drops of strong solution of ammonia, enough to render it just ammoniacal (which will prevent the solution by HCl of the oxalate of lime, which is formed later).

Add a few drops of oxalate of ammonia (saturated solution), and heat gently for half an hour. When the precipitate has settled slope the beaker, and run a drop of oxalate of ammonia down its side; if a precipitate forms at the point of contact, add more oxalate of ammonia until no such precipitate occurs.

Filter through Swedish paper, but the *filtrate* is *to be kept* to test for magnesia.

The precipitate is to be ignited in the platinum dish (where two beakers have been taken, each filter paper should be ignited separately and the results averaged) until reduced to whitish ash. The oxalate of lime will now have been converted into carbonate of lime (and some oxide of lime, from loss of carbonic acid). Therefore

WATER ANALYSIS. 257

treat with a few drops of carbonate of ammonia solution to restore the carbonic acid, using gentle heat. Weigh, then again add a little more carbonate of ammonia solution till the weight is constant.

Suppose the first weighing gave 13·241 and the second and third 13·240, we take the last, viz., 13·240 − 13·140 (weight of platinum dish) = ·1 gramme of carbonate of lime in 500 cc.

·1 × 2 × 70 = 14 grains per gallon *as* carbonate of lime (*i.e.*, total lime in terms of carbonate). But as we do not yet know how much lime is really present as carbonate, the $CaCO_3$ will have to be calculated into calcic oxide CaO, to which end it must be multiplied by 56 and divided by 100, or shortly × ·56, on the equivalent principle. Ca = 40, C = 12, O_3 = 48 = 100, and Ca = 40, O = 16 = 56. Then 14·0 $CaCO_3$ corresponds with 7·84 CaO.

Testing for Magnesia.—The filtrates kept from the lime beakers are first concentrated by boiling, then cooled. About 5 cc. of a saturated solution of phosphate of soda is now added, and the whole made strongly ammoniacal by the addition of about its own bulk of strong ammonia (if, however, it is made faintly ammoniacal at first the precipitation will be better). Filter again after twelve hours' stand, and wash the precipitate with ammonia solution (made of $\frac{1}{5}$ strong ammonia and $\frac{4}{5}$ water). It may be a wise precaution to test the filtrate from the washing with a few drops of silver nitrate to show freedom from ammonium chloride; if there is any white precipitate (of silver chloride) the washing should be continued.

Then the filter-papers containing the residues, after being dried in the drying-oven, are to be burnt in the platinum dish (calcined to whiteness). Very careful weighing is required, as a single milligramme makes an important difference. We will suppose that two precipitates have been ignited, of which we take the average. One weighs 13·148, the other 13.149, which, less 13·140 for the platinum dish and ·002 for the filter-paper, leave

17

·006 and ·007 respectively. Then ·006 × 2 × 70 = ·84, and ·007 2 × 70 = ·980, of which the mean is ·91.

This is pyrophosphate of magnesia, $Mg_2P_2O_7$, or structurally $\left\{ \begin{array}{l} MgO \\ MgO \end{array} \right\} P_2O_5$.

$Mg_2 = 48$, $P_2 = 62$, $O_7 = 112 = 222$, and $\left\{ \begin{array}{l} Mg = 24, \\ Mg = 24, \\ O = 16 \\ O = 16 \end{array} \right\} = 80$.

Therefore $\dfrac{·91 \times 80}{222} = ·32$ grains magnesic oxide (MgO) per gallon.

Chlorine (Chlorides).—This is estimated by using a standard solution * of silver nitrate of such a strength that each cc. corresponds to one grain of chlorine per gallon of the water under inspection, if 70 cc. of the latter be operated on.

The presence of chlorine is immediately indicated by a white precipitate of silver chloride, but to ascertain the exact point at which all the chlorine has become combined with the silver, use is made of the fact that silver forms a red precipitate with chromic acid (chromate of silver), though less readily than it forms silver chloride, giving a white precipitate, with chlorine.

The process is as follows. 70 cc. of the water is rendered yellow with a crystal, or a few drops of solution of chromate of potash. Then the nitrate of silver solution is run in from a burette till the red colour just begins to be permanent.

We will suppose 1·2 cc. is run in before that point is reached, and this = 1·2 grains of chlorine per gallon.

[Care must be taken that neither water nor silver-nitrate solution is acid, as acid dissolves the silver chromate. Acidity should be neutralised or rather more than neutralised with carbonate of soda.]

---

* 4·79 grammes of nitrate of silver (dried in air-bath at 100°C.) dissolved in 1 litre of water.

Soluble Solids.—The determination of "Soluble Solids" and of the "Insoluble Solids" (by difference) affords a valuable clue to the general constitution of the water. The "soluble solids," in fact, comprise generally the alkaline salts, the salts of magnesia and the sulphate of lime (which is far more soluble than the carbonate).

The insoluble solids are almost identical with the carbonate of lime, probably + a little silica.

When the soluble solids are likely to be fairly high, wash with distilled water one of the pans containing "total solids" (evaporated in the first operation), being careful to rub round the pan thoroughly with a glass stirring-rod, which has a short piece of india-rubber tubing fitted to its stirring end. Filter and evaporate filtrate in a tared glass dish, or platinum dish. Dry in a drying-oven, and weigh with the usual precautions (cooling in desiccator, etc.).

When, however, the soluble solids are not likely to be high, it is better to make a fresh evaporation, taking 500 cc., which we will suppose done in the present case. Otherwise the manipulation as before.

Then suppose the weight deducting that of pan = ·03 gramme (30 milligrammes).

$\cdot 03 \times 2 \times 70 = 4\cdot 2$ grains per gallon.
  i.e., Insoluble solids   14·7
         Soluble do.   4·2
                             ———
         Total solids   18·9 (found in Operation i.).

Precipitate on Boiling.—Boil 500 cc. for one hour, keeping the beaker filled up to the original level with distilled water. Filter and dry precipitate between watch-glasses at 105° C. [We will assume the weight of the watch-glasses, thoroughly dried, = 12·723, and the weight of the filter paper, unignited, = ·64.]

Cool in desiccator and weigh.

Then suppose gross weight = . 13·454
Deduct glasses 12·723 }
Filter paper   ·640 } . 13·363
                                    ———
                                    ·091 (from 500 cc.)
·091 × 2 × 70 = 12·74 grains per gallon.

(This corresponds with temporary hardness.)

Tabulating the above Results.—Many analysts content themselves with stating results got as above, on the ground that such a method states actual facts and does not lend itself to cookery; but, on the other hand, it does not enable even the practised chemist to see at a glance what the exact character of the water is, and, of course, is utterly valueless to the inexperienced.

Therefore it seems preferable to combine acids and bases in the form of the most probable combinations, and this we may now proceed to do with the results before us. These results (all in grains per gallon) are—

Total solids	18·9
Soluble	4·2
Precipitate on boiling . . .	12·74
Total lime as CaO. . . .	7·84
Magnesic oxide, MgO. . . .	0·32
Chlorine	1·2
SO_3	·913

Then, as there is too much SO_3 (anhydrous sulphuric acid) for saturating the MgO without overplus (80 parts SO_3 take 40 parts MgO), the acid may be combined with some of the lime. [And note that, speaking generally, the tendency is towards the most insoluble compounds, viz., to a combination of SO_3 with lime rather than magnesia, if both bases are present.]

Then ·913 SO_3 will combine with ·639 CaO (80 : 56 : : ·913) to form sulphate of lime, of which we accordingly have 1·55 grain per gallon.

Then dealing with the rest of the lime; 7·84−·64 (taken as sulphate) = 7·2.

$$\frac{7 \cdot 2 \times 100}{56} = 12 \cdot 86. \quad \text{Lime as carbonate } (CaCO_3).$$

[Or it may be calculated thus, $\overset{CaO.}{56} : \overset{CO_2.}{44} :: 7 \cdot 2 = 5 \cdot 66\ CO_2$ carbon dioxide to combine with the CaO (to form calcic carbonate $CaCO_3$). $7 \cdot 2 + 5 \cdot 66 = 12 \cdot 86$].

The ·32 MgO is to be expressed as carbonate. Then as 40 MgO unites with 44 CO_2, ·32 will unite with ·35 CO_2 = ·67 $MgCO_3$ (carbonate of magnesia).

The chlorine 1·2 is multiplied by the factor 1·647 to bring it into common salt (sodic chloride), its most probable combination, and = 1·97.

[The factor 1·647 is got on the equivalent principle. Chlorine = 35·5. Sodium = 23. NaCl (sodium chloride) = 58·5. Then $58 \cdot 5 \div 35 \cdot 5 = 1 \cdot 647$.]

So we have—
Sulphate of lime	1·55
Carbonate ,,	12·86
Carbonate of magnesia	·67
Chloride of sodium	1·97
Silica and undetermined (water of hydration)	1·85
	18·90

In the above analysis the silica, etc., is perhaps somewhat high, but as it and the carbonate of lime together agree remarkably closely (the analysis was an actual one done by the writer) with the "insoluble solids," while the other constituents total up very closely to the "soluble solids," the analysis may be taken as substantially correct.

In applying the qualitative test for nitrates and nitrites, the water had appeared free from the latter, and with only a trace of the former, so that it hardly seemed necessary to **combine any of the lime with nitric acid.** But if the nitric acid should be considerable (see Indigo process, p. 213), note that it combines more readily with lime and magnesia than with soda, and that the

Rule of Three sum (to get the amount of CaO or MgO to be added to the ascertained amount of nitric acid) would be—

108 : ascertained nitric acid :: 56 (or 40 for MgO),

and the result + the ascertained amount of nitric acid = nitrate of lime or magnesia, as the case may be).

Seeing that nitric anhydride N_2O_5, as compared with sulphuric anhydride SO_3, combines in the proportion of 108 : 80, and as compared with carbonic anhydride CO_2 in the proportion of 108 : 44, a given quantity will obviously saturate less lime than either of the other acids; consequently, if an appreciable quantity of those bases be combined as nitrates, the result will be an increase of the total solids actually determined. In other words, the carbonates of lime and magnesia will not be decreased by nearly the total of the nitrates.

Carbonates of Soda and Potash.—Generally, if determined, they are calculated as the former, though really, if potash be present as carbonate in any quantity, a considerable numerical error is introduced by so doing. This simpler, but hardly correct process, is as follows.

500 cc. is evaporated to dryness, washed and filtered, though if carefully ignited, the magnesic carbonate, if present, is rendered insoluble, while the carbonate of soda passes through the filter after successive washings.

Then to the filtrate $\frac{N}{10}$ sulphuric acid is added, and the excess titrated back, after rewarming, with $\frac{N}{10}$ ammonia, which gives greater accuracy. Suppose, then, to a filtrate of a considerably alkaline water, prepared as above, 11·5 cc. of $\frac{N}{10}$ sulphuric acid is added, and after the warming of the mixture, 6 cc. $\frac{N}{10}$ ammonia is required to produce neutrality.

ALKALINE CARBONATES—SOAP TEST.

Then 5·5 cc. $\frac{N}{10}$ sulphuric acid will have been neutralised.

$5·5 \times 2 \times 70 = 770 \frac{N}{10}$ or 77 cc. normal acid per gallon. But a litre (1000 cc.) of normal acid = 53 grains carbonate of soda (because 53 grains, half the total atomic weights of Na_2CO_3, as in the case of oxalic acid, makes a litre of normal Na_2CO_3). Accordingly the sum is,

1000 : 77 :: 53 = 4·081 grains per gallon, reckoned as Na_2CO_3.

[Note that cochineal is a much more delicate reagent than litmus, because carbonic acid does not mask its indication; however, the evaporation to dryness should have got rid of all carbonic acid.]

The Hardness of a Water is generally determined by the **"Soap Test,"** originally devised by Dr. Clark, of Aberdeen, a test which, though sometimes decried because of the instability of the standard solution, is yet capable of giving very useful, and probably accurate results, if the solution be frequently standardised. This it is one of the easiest things possible to do.

The test rests upon the basis that salts of lime and magnesia react upon soluble soap to form insoluble oleate, stearite, or palmatite of lime or magnesia, or, in other words, that it is only after those salts have become saturated that a *permanent lather* (one capable of lasting five minutes) is obtainable upon shaking the water in question up with a solution of soap. To make the test quantitative, the soap solution is made of such a strength that each cc. contains exactly soap enough to be neutralised by 1 milligramme (0·001 gramme) carbonate of lime. The quantity of water used is the miniature gallon, 70 cc., in which milligrammes correspond to grains in the actual gallon. Thus, by reading off the number of cc. of soap solution required to produce the permanent lather (less 1 cc. as a correction for that which even distilled water requires) we arrive at the degrees of hardness—*i.e.*, grains per gallon reckoned as carbonate of lime.

Before making the soap-solution it is necessary to have for standardising it a stable solution containing exactly ·001 gramme (1 milligramme) of carbonate of lime in each cc.

Standardising Solution for Soap Test.—Pure calcic chloride is heated just to redness in a platinum crucible, cooled in the desiccator, and 1·11 gramme taken (= 1 gramme carbonate of lime) and dissolved in a litre of distilled water; or 1 gramme of powdered marble or Iceland spar may be taken and dissolved in slight excess of dilute hydrochloric acid, which is afterwards neutralised with a slight excess of ammonia. Whichever is taken, it is to be made exactly up to a litre with distilled water.

The Standard Soap Solution.*—10 grammes purest Castile soap are dissolved in a litre of weak (35%) alcohol (methylated spirit will do). This should make a solution corresponding very nearly with the test solution. To try it, a measured quantity of the lime solution (say 10 cc.) is put into the "miniature gallon," which is then filled with distilled water to the 70 cc. mark. This 70 cc. is then put into a larger flask of say 200 cc. capacity, and the soap solution added; then the flask is shaken and laid upon its side. If the soap solution is accurate, exactly 11 cc. (= 10 cc. for the standardising solution and 1 cc. for the distilled water) will be required to produce a lather capable of persisting for five minutes. Obviously, it is best to try with less of the soap solution to begin with, as it may require dilution to make it exactly correspond.

The testing of the actual water is performed in the same way (the soap solution having been ascertained to be correct) and similarly the number of cc. of the water taken, *minus* 1, will represent the degrees of hardness reckoned

---

* Another recipe is given at the end of this chapter, one which is said to keep better.

as carbonate of lime. Note, however, that if 70 cc. of the water require more than 16 cc. of soap solution (*i.e.*, with all water more than moderately hard) it will be advisable to dilute the water with exactly twice, thrice, or four times its bulk, as the case may be, and then to take 70 cc. of the diluted fluid, of course multiplying the cc. of soap solution taken by the figure of the dilution.

Hardness after Boiling.—If some of the water be boiled and 70 cc. of the cooled filtrate be tried with the soap solution, the degrees of hardness after boiling will be ascertained, by deducting which from the total the hardness which disappears on boiling is found by difference. These are otherwise known as the **Permanent and Temporary Hardness**, the former being due to sulphates of lime and magnesia, the latter corresponding fairly closely, though not exactly, to their carbonates.

Objections made to the Soap-test and Precautions— Magnesic Salts.—Apart from the instability of the soap-solution itself, objections have been made on the ground of the very different behaviour of salts of lime and magnesia (the two chief factors of hardness) towards the soap-solution, as well as because of the obvious fact that expressing one in terms of the other would lead to error. But it is really in the different way in which the salts behave respectively that the chief safeguard is found. Thus lime salts re-act immediately, magnesia salts only after a lapse of time, so that it is quite possible to produce a persistent lather before all the magnesia salts are decomposed. But on letting the mixture stand a little and shaking it up again, the lather, in the presence of magnesia salts in quantity enough, will vanish. [At 70° C. = 158° Fahr. this difference is not apparent.]

Professor Wanklyn gets at the magnesia salts in this way, precipitating the lime salts by adding powdered oxalate of ammonia to the water (about 1 gramme per litre), which is then shaken up for a minute and filtered. He tests the filtrate to ensure the absence of free acid, and likewise with a little of the oxalate to ascertain that all the lime salts have been got rid of (precipitate otherwise of oxalate of lime), and then titrates 70 cc. with soap-solution in the usual way. But owing to the fact that approximately $1\frac{1}{2}$ equivalents of magnesia consume the same quantity of soap as 1 of lime, the result got (number of cc. of soap solution − 1) has to be multiplied by the fraction $\frac{42}{75}$ to give the actual quantity of magnesia in terms of carbonate of magnesia.

Free and Albuminoid Ammonia in Water.—This process is conducted on somewhat similar lines to that given for determining the albuminous matter in malt, which is indeed only an adaptation of the water process. Only in the case of water the determination is made in two parts. First, the ammonia already existing in the water in the form of " free ammonia " is ascertained and recorded ; then, the residue is boiled with a solution of potassic permanganate and caustic potash (the latter immensely in excess), whereby the organic matter is converted into ammonia, which can then be distilled over and estimated as the free ammonia was.

It will be remembered that the test depends upon the depth of the tint produced by adding a small quantity of Nessler's solution (very sensitive to ammonia) to the liquid, this tint being matched by Nesslerising side by side with it an equal bulk of water to which a standard ammonia solution has been added. Then the quantity of ammonia added being calculated from the amount of ammonia solution taken to produce the match-tint, this gives the amount in the original liquid. [Note that, as the Nessler does not react immediately to its full extent, the 50 cc. cylinders in which the distillate is caught, as well as the comparison cylinder, should stand an appreciable time, say two minutes, and that before the operation begins the apparatus should be copiously washed, seeing that all surfaces long exposed to the air are liable to attract traces of ammonia therefrom ; but ordinary good tap-water will do, though it is recommended to rinse out the retort first with strong hydrochloric or sulphuric acid.

Of course the subsequent water-rinsing must then be continued till no trace of acidity remains.]

The Process.—500 cc. of the water is taken and placed in the retort (carefully poured through a funnel). The retort is then connected with the Liebig's condenser (or Dr. Graham's glass arrangement of it), and when all the connections are properly made, the flame of a Bunsen burner applied to the naked retort, so that it plays upon the surface of the latter up to, but no higher than, the surface of the liquid. The cold water connections are made, and cold water started flowing through the outer tube of the condenser, in order to condense the vapour which comes over. This liquid is now caught in the measured 50 cc. cylinder, and Professor Wanklyn recommends that this first 50 cc. should alone be Nesslerised for free ammonia, because although the next 150 cc. may also contain some and is therefore to be distilled off (to concentrate the liquid as well), the first 50 cc. invariably, he says, contain 75% of all the free ammonia, the total of which can accordingly be got by adding one-third of that shown by the first Nesslerising to the said result. If the free ammonia is likely to be higher than is consistent with fair purity (above ·08 parts per million is " a sign that the water in question consists of diluted urine in a very recent condition "), yet not in great excess, it may be better to distil over 150 cc. into a measured flask, Nesslerise 50 cc. of it, and multiply the result so got by 3. If the free ammonia is in great excess the water must be diluted in carefully ascertained proportions with *ammonia-free* distilled water (distilled water boiled with some carbonate of soda and ferrous sulphate to get rid of the ammonia).

We will, however, suppose that only the first 50 cc. is Nesslerised, the next 150 cc. distilled over being thrown away. At this point the flame is removed temporarily, and to the 300 cc. left in the retort (half a litre was originally taken) 50 cc. of the potash-permanganate solution is carefully added. The flask is now not unlikely to bump violently enough to cause a fracture sometimes, which bumping a few pieces of well-ignited tobacco-pipe (clay) put into it will tend to moderate. At least three successive quantities of 50 cc. each must be caught and Nesslerised (for albuminoid ammonia); in fact, the Nesslerising must be continued as long as the Nessler when added to 50 cc. distillate strikes a decided tint.

We will suppose, then, that in the first Nesslerising (before the addition of the potash-permanganate) a tint was produced which it required 2 cc. of ammonia solution in the comparison cylinder to imitate. [Then as 500 cc. is operated on all results must be multiplied by 2, and it will be remembered that each cc. of the ammonia solution corresponds with $\frac{1}{100}$ milligramme or ·00001 gramme of ammonia.]

Then 50 cc. took 2 cc. and 2 cc. × 2 = 4 cc. = ·00004 gramme ammonia, but add one-third. Then ·00004 + ·0000133 = ·0000533 gramme or ·0533 milligramme or parts per million. [N.B.—A litre contains a million milligrammes.]

We will suppose that 3 cylinders (of 50 cc. each) are Nesslerised after the boiling with potash-permanganate, a fourth giving no coloration, and that

1. 50 took 2·25, then 2·25 × 2 = 4·5
2. 50 ,, ·75, ,, ·75 × 2 = 1·5
3. 50 ,, ·5, ,, ·5 × 2 = 1·0

(50 free) 7·0 c.c.

= ·00007 gramme ammonia, or ·07 part per million albuminoid ammonia.

The Oxygen Process (Oxygen required to Neutralise Organic Matter) is performed in different ways. Thus the moist combustion process, as Professor Wanklyn calls it, is carried out by means of four solutions—viz., (1) permanganate solution, each cc. of which contains 1 milligramme of active oxygen (*i.e.*, ten times the strength

OXYGEN PROCESSES.

of the solution subsequently given); (2) protosulphate of iron solution, of which 1 cc. absorbs 1 milligramme of active oxygen; (3) solution of caustic potash; (4) solution containing sulphuric acid.

The same retort as was used for the ammonia process having been cleaned and mounted, is charged with 1 litre of the water. Before the distillation begins 5 cc. of the caustic potash solution is dropped into the flask or retort, and then 5 cc., very carefully measured, of the permanganate solution is also dropped. Distillation is then rapidly carried out until about $\frac{9}{10}$ of the water has distilled over. Then 10 cc. of the sulphuric acid solution is dropped into the retort and shaken up with the remaining 100 cc. of water therein. Then 5 cc. of the protosulphate of iron solution is dropped in, and very soon the liquid, which before was pink, will become colourless from absorption of oxygen by the iron solution. Now more of the permanganate solution is dropped from an accurately graduated burette, and the quantity which is *just* sufficient to bring back a permanent pink noted. This quantity 2·6, 3·6, or whatever it may be, represents the quantity consumed by the organic matter in a litre of water, and as each cc. represents ·001 gramme, 3·6, for instance, would be ·0036, which $\times$ 70 = ·025 grains oxygen required per gallon.

A more elaborate plan is the so-called **Forchammer Process,** which necessitates several standard solutions, *e.g.*, potassic iodide, hyposulphite of soda, and starch solutions, the latter two being, especially the hyposulphite, very unstable. Permanganate of potash solution of such a strength that 1 cc. = ·0001 gramme oxygen (the strength used in the next modification) is also required, and the test turns upon the fact that, after the pink colour has been established in a manner very like that adopted in the first example, it is again discharged by the addition of potassic iodide (2 drops of the solution are first added) in favour of a yellow coloration by free iodine. Just so much iodine is set free as corresponds with the permanganate previously undecomposed, and this is measured by employing the hyposulphite of soda solution, which parts with some of its sodium to form sodic iodide. A comparison is then made between the results got with the actual water and those got with an exactly parallel one made with distilled water, and the quantity of oxygen calculated from the difference. The starch solution mentioned has been used to ensure the disappearance of the last trace of free iodine, the presence of which it will show by the characteristic blue iodide-of-starch tint, and the hyposulphite is accordingly cautiously added until the exact point is reached at which this tint no longer appears on the addition of starch.

This process being, for an oxygen process, both complicated and lengthy, and being equally, with others, open to the charge of inaccuracy (protosalts of iron and nitrites into the bargain, see pp. 104, 105, affect its determinations), exact working details are not given, and we will proceed to—

The Permanganate and Oxalic Acid Oxygen Process.—Take ·3955 gramme of powdered potassium permanganate, dried at 100° C.; dissolve in distilled water and make up to a litre. Then 1 cc. of the solution contains ·0001 gramme oxygen.

Test solution for the above. Dry between blotting-paper ·7875 gramme of pure oxalic acid. Dissolve and make up to a litre.

Two burettes should be filled, one with the permanganate, the other with the oxalic acid solution. Into a beaker containing about two teaspoonfuls of distilled water and 12 drops of sulphuric acid run 25 cc. of the oxalic acid solution and warm on sand bath. Add about 2 cc. of the permanganate solution, and warm up again till the colour goes. Then run in gently, drop by drop, more permanganate, of which 25 cc. ought to produce a faint pink colour. The correctness of the permanganate solution having been thus tried and proved, the water may be tested.

Take 500 cc. of the water, add 2 cc. strong sulphuric acid, warm over sand bath, and run in permanganate gently till the tint becomes permanent. Suppose that 2 cc. of the permanganate solution produce a permanent pink tint.

We now run in an excess of the permanganate solution (say 5 cc.) and heat the mixture up to nearly boiling, after which enough oxalic acid solution is added just to destroy the pink. [N.B.—Be careful not to add the oxalic acid solution too fast, otherwise a brownish coloration will be produced.] Suppose it takes 4·9 cc. of the oxalic acid solution, then ·1 cc. more of the permanganate has been required by the organic matter, or 2·1 cc. together.

But 2·1 cc. = ·00021 gramme oxygen, and ·00021 × 2 × 70 = ·0294 *grains* of oxygen required *per gallon*.

Testing Hops for Sulphur (Sulphurous Acid).—A portion of the suspected hops, mixed with some distilled water, is placed in an ordinary chemical flask, fitted with an india-rubber stopper perforated for a funnel and delivery tube, and a piece of pure zinc is added to the contents of the flask. The stopper is then replaced, and the delivery-tube connected with a second flask containing a solution of acetate of lead (sugar of lead). Sufficient hydrochloric acid is now poured down the funnel to re-act upon the zinc and set hydrogen free, which if sulphurous acid be present takes the form of sulphuretted hydrogen. This, passing into the flask containing the lead acetate solution, causes the formation of a black precipitate of lead sulphide, whereas, of course, if the gas evolved be simple hydrogen no such precipitate occurs.

Alternative method. Owing to the fact that zinc not unfrequently contains traces of sulphur sufficient to vitiate the result with unsulphured hops, the following method has been recommended. 10 grammes of hops are placed in a 20 oz. flask with 200 cc. of distilled water and a stick of caustic potash. Boil until the hops are thoroughly mixed, then remove flame, and add half a wineglassful of hydrochloric acid gradually. Replace the flame, and let the steam pass into a flask with a foot, containing 50 cc. of a solution of lead acetate (made by dissolving 500 grammes lead-acetate in 2 litres of water).

A third method adopted by Dr. Griessmayer requires sodium-amalgam and hydrochloric acid. [The sodium-amalgam is prepared as follows.* 100 grammes of mercury are taken, and into them are thrown gradually 4 grammes of well-dried sodium, from which any white crust that forms has been removed. As each particle of sodium combines with the mercury a slight explosion takes place, sometimes sufficient to throw the mercury out of the mortar. When working them together with the pestle it is well to protect the face and hands; the best plan perhaps is to pass the handle of the pestle through a stiff sheet of paper, which serves to cover the mortar.] The process is as follows.

The hop-liquor (got by steeping a portion of hops for some hours in water) is filtered, and about 100 cc. of it placed in a flask or test-glass. From ·5 to ·7 gramme (as much as will lie on the point of a knife) of the sodium amalgam is now thrown in, and a strip of paper moistened with an alkaline lead solution suspended in it, after which a few drops of hydrochloric acid are poured in. The flask is now quickly closed, *but not hermetically*, with a cork or glass stopper, and within five minutes, if the least quantity of sulphurous acid be present in the sample of hops, the lead paper will be blackened.

An easy plan of detecting sulphuring, if one possess some long silvered pins, is to thrust one or two up to the head in a pocket of the suspected hops, and to leave them there for some time. If the suspicion was well-grounded the silvered surface of the pins will blacken.

"**Constants**" are factors used to convert one (acid or) salt into terms of another salt (or acid). A few of the more useful for the foregoing tests are annexed.

---

* But it can be bought ready prepared for about 1*s.* 6*d.* per oz.

"Constants."

$CaCO_3$ (Calcic Carbonate) ×	·56	to obtain	CaO (Calcic Monoxide or Lime).
$Mg_2P_2O_7$ (Pyrophosphate of Magnesia) ×	·6396	,,	P_2O_5 (Phosphoric Anhydride).
SO_3 (Sulphuric Anhydride) ×	1·7	,,	$CaSO_4$ (Calcic Sulphate).
Cl (Chlorine) . . . ×	1·647	,,	NaCl (Sodic Chloride or Common Salt).
$CaCO_3$ (Calcic Carbonate) ×	1·36	,,	$CaSO_4$ (Calcic Sulphate).
$CaSO_4$ (Calcic Sulphate) ×	·41176	,,	CaO (Calcic Monoxide).
AgCl (Silver or Argentic Chloride) ×	·4076	,,	NaCl (Sodic Chloride).
SO_3 (Sulphuric Anhydride) ×	1·775	,,	Na_2SO_4 (Sodium Sulphate, Anhydrous).
$BaSO_4$ (Baric Sulphate) ×	·343347 (or $\frac{80}{233}$)	,,	SO_3 (Sulphuric Anhydride).
$BaSO_4$,, ,, ×	·58369 (or $\frac{136}{233}$)	,,	$CaSO_4$ (Calcic Sulphate).

Standard Solutions :—

Nitrate of Silver (for Chlorine), 4·79 grammes nitrate of silver (dried in air-bath at 100° C.) dissolved in 1 litre of water.

Nessler's Solution.—35 grammes iodide of potassium, 13 grammes corrosive sublimate (mercury perchloride).

Dissolve separately, with heat (N.B.—The corrosive sublimate dissolves with difficulty), and mix. Add distilled water, but not more than 800 cc. and 160 grammes caustic potash, or 120 grammes caustic soda, making up to a litre. Before the potash is added, a cold saturated solution of corrosive sublimate in water is to be added till a permanent red precipitate is formed. The "Nessler" should be *yellowish* in colour.

Ammonia Solution (for Nessler Test).—Dissolve first 3·15 grammes ammonium chloride in 1 litre of ammonia-free water. Then take 10 cc. of the above and make up to 1 litre (*i.e.*, the second litre contains ·0315 gramme, and each cc. of it = ·01 milligramme of ammonia).

N.B.—This dilution of the stronger solution is likely to be more accurate than making up the solution with ·0315 gramme would be, but that can be done at once if preferred. The weaker solution is the one used.

Potash and Permanganate of Potash.—200 grammes of stick caustic potash, 8 grammes permanganate of potash. (Made up to a litre.)

If dissolved in about 500 cc. first, and then evaporated almost to dryness in a porcelain dish before dilution to a litre, all ammonia will be expelled.

Soap Solution (another in text). 40 parts of dry potassic carbonate rubbed in mortar with 150 parts of emplastrum plumbi (British Pharmacopœia), methylated spirit being afterwards added, and the whole triturated to a cream. Filter, washing residue several times with methylated spirit, and dilute with same to the required standard (to be standardised as before with calcic chloride).

Litmus Solution :—

I. About 10 grammes of the solid material are digested with 500 cc. of distilled water in a warm place for a few hours. The clear liquid is decanted from the sediment and a few drops of nitric acid added—enough to produce a violet colour. If at any time the colour should partially disappear it may be restored by exposing the fluid to the air in an open dish.

II. "A purer solution," Sutton says, " may be prepared as follows : Boil the litmus, previously reduced to coarse powder, two or three times with alcohol of about 80 per cent., and throw the liquid so obtained away (this treatment removes some colouring matter which is a hindrance to the proper reaction), then digest the litmus repeatedly with cold distilled water till all soluble colour is extracted, let the mixed washings settle clear, decant, and add to them a few drops of concentrated sulphuric acid until quite red, then heat to boiling ;—this will decompose the alkaline carbonates and convert them into sulphates ;— now cautiously add baryta water until the colour is restored to blue or violet; let the baric sulphate settle perfectly, and decant into a proper vessel for use.

"Litmus prepared and kept in this way is very sensitive to dilute acids and alkalies. With the slightest excess of oxalic, sulphuric, hydrochloric, or nitric acids it gives a pink red, and with caustic soda or potash, a blue colour; with ammonia or the bicarbonated alkalies it retains its violet colour."

Barfoed's Solution.—[Though this solution is not indicated for use in the present chapter, its mode of preparation is given below, because it is claimed that it indicates *dextrin* and glucose—the former after a somewhat prolonged boiling but glucose on a short boiling—but that it is not reduced by *maltose* or lactose.]

One part of crystallised neutral acetate of copper is to be dissolved in 15 parts of water, and 200 cc. of this solution are mixed with 5 cc. of acetic acid, containing 38% of anhydrous acid. The solution contains about 1% of free acid, and was used by Barfoed in the place of Fehling's solution, the mode of preparing which has been given at the beginning of the chapter.

CHAPTER VIII.

MASHING, SPARGING, AND BOILING.

Objects in Mashing—Restatement of General Principles—Axioms applied to Practice—Noting Acrospire Growth of Malt—Malt of Average Diastatic Capacity—Mode of increasing Dextrin Ratio—Starch—Granulose—Amylo-cellulose—Dextrin—Amylo-, Achroo-, and Erythro-dextrins—Maltose—Equations of Mash-tun Changes—Malto-dextrin Theory—Evidence on which the Theory is based—Isolation of Malto-dextrin — Formula — Modification of Equation Series — Percentage and Type of Malto-dextrins, and their Influence—Limited Decoction—Semi-prepared Raw Material—Hot Grist-mashing—Stout and Porter Grists—Brown and Patent Malt—Substitute for—Raw or Return Wort—Dead Mashes—Sparging—Underback—Stewing—Boiling—Adding the Hops—Steam-boiling and Fire-boiling—Open or closed Coppers—Hot Aëration of Wort.

THE objects that the practical brewer, consciously or unconsciously, keeps in view when standing by the mashtun, are to get as large an extract from his malt as is consistent with quality; to secure spontaneous clarification to a fair extent in running beers, and to the point of absolute brilliancy in store beers; to supply his yeast in the fermentation stage with sufficient suitable food to keep it vigorous, a condition which has a good deal to say on the question of clarification, without over-feeding it; and finally, so to regulate the ratio of maltose to dextrin (or according to the newer lights, the proportion and type of malto-dextrins) in his wort, that the resulting fluid shall be what the taste of his customers demands—viz., either a clean alcoholic (vinous) beer, or one which is "fuller in the mouth," even, it may be, to an extent that

QUALITIES OF GOOD BEER.

makes the product taste somewhat mawkish and cloying to those who are accustomed to a more stimulating, alcoholic drink.

And in truth, between the two possible extremes lies the region of safety. A beer brewed so as to develop the maximum proportion of alcohol (on the lines of a distiller's "wash"), far from being stimulating, would taste poor, flat, and thin; while, on the other hand, the retention of a large proportion of unfermented matter does not, as might perhaps be expected, necessarily give the impression of "body,"—often indeed the reverse. The palate, in fact, demands a certain balance of qualities, variable within somewhat restricted limits. There must be "vinosity," *i.e.*, a generous percentage of alcohol, but there must also be body to back it up; there must be, albeit this is a question with which mashing, as such, has nought to do, more or less hop-flavour; and there must be such a degree of saturation with carbonic acid as produces, in conjunction with the other good qualities, what is known as "a bite upon the tongue." Yet all these things are as vanity if the beer will not go bright, either spontaneously or upon the employment of finings; for so close is the connection between eye and palate in estimating the quality of that article, that it is difficult to say which sense takes the lead. Certainly, as far as the general body of consumers is concerned, the eye seems to be gaining the preponderance in the partnership.

I trust I shall not seem ungrateful if I venture to suggest that gentlemen to whose scientific researches the principles which underlie the mash-tun changes owe so much of their development, are too prone to consider malt as being of one unvarying quality. They speak as if malt digested at a certain temperature (or between certain temperatures), and for such and such a space of time, will produce an absolutely unvarying ratio of maltose to dextrin, each computed to the second place of decimals. At least—though, stated thus, the absurdity seems evident—this is what they have the air of doing.

However, the operative brewer has grounds for suspecting that although the factors which he, standing by the mash-tun, is able to influence, viz., the heat of the liquor used (the "striking heat"), the degree of liquidity of the mash, and the length of "stand" after mashing, will have considerable influence on the constitution of his wort, yet that those factors, too, which he cannot then influence, viz., the degree of growth of the malt and specially the temperatures it underwent in drying and curing, as well as the character of the original barley, are not less potent. And as practical uniformity of growth, year by year, is the most easily observed, it appears that varying, perhaps widely varying, kiln-temperatures and subtle differences in the character of barley, must be made responsible for such modifications of the mashing-process as are needed to attain a sufficiently uniform result.

But whatever the modifications, they are modifications which have to be made upon certain lines, and I, for one, cannot agree with an assertion, which lately caught my eye in a responsible publication, to the effect that the diastatic power of malt had now become so extreme that it was hopeless to try to limit it by any variations of temperature. This is "throwing up the sponge" with a vengeance; but fortunately practical experience demonstrates that it *is* possible to do so. Such an assertion is only the crystallised expression of generalisations as to the persistent flatness of beer nowadays; uncontrolled diastatic energy and extreme flatness standing, as has been said above, in the relation of cause and effect. That such a tendency to persistent flatness is universal I can, of my own knowledge, deny; that it is even general I find it hard to believe, seeing that it is quite possible for a brewer, using material of no especial quality, to produce beers, even of the lightest gravity, capable, when poured into a glass, of carrying a head which will last for half an hour or more.

But to do this he must be prepared to modify any hard and fast rules which he may have previously formulated, still, however, paying due regard to the general principles on which his earlier system was fashioned.

Restatement of General Principles.—These general principles are based on a series of facts: (1) that an active principle, which is known as diastase, exists in malt, and that it is capable (the malt being ground and mashed, and the heat of the mash kept within a certain range of temperature) of converting all the soluble starch of the grain (and even of large quantities of added starch in the form of gelatinised rice, etc.) into a type of sugar known as maltose, and another body—or mixture of bodies—of a more gum-like and less fermentable nature, known by the generic name of dextrin.* (2) That this diastase, though more readily extracted in an active condition by water of comparatively low temperature, requires heats higher than those most favourable to its own solution— heats which will ensure the solution of the starch, in order that its influence may be brought to bear upon the latter to the utmost possible extent, or even to the extent desired by the brewer. [Yet if all the starch be dissolved Baszwitz's investigations appear to have shown that a temperature of 112° Fahr. determines the largest percentage of maltose. *Zeitschrift für Spiritus-industrie*, 1879, p. 321.]

(3) That the ratio of maltose to dextrin may vary between 2 parts of maltose to 1 of dextrin, and 2 parts of dextrin to 1 of maltose—but not beyond these limits (though careful digestion at or below 140° Fahr. may produce maltose in the ratio 4 : 1 of dextrin). (4) That the nearer the initial heat † approaches the lowest permissible limit of 140° Fahr., being subsequently gradually raised by underlet or other means some 10° or 12°, the higher will be the ratio of maltose to dextrin, and conversely, the nearer it approaches 160° (not that the writer has ever known quite so high an initial heat as this), the higher will be the ratio of dextrin to maltose.

---

* But see pp. 294-302 for statement of malto-dextrin or amylöin theory.

† "Initial heat" is always used to express the heat of the mash, directly it is all in the mash-tun.

(5) That the liquidity of the mash affects the ratio in a less degree—*e.g.*, that a stiff mash (one made with less than two barrels of "liquor" to the quarter of malt) lessens the normal proportion of maltose; while a "free" mash (one made with over two barrels to the quarter of malt) increases it. (6) That a wort rich in maltose is one that "attenuates," *i.e.*, which has its solid extract broken up during fermentation readily and rapidly, tending to yield, in consequence, a thin beer, and one in which, when the attenuation is extreme, the unpleasant symptom of "greyness" is apt to appear. That a dextrinous wort, on the other hand, does not attenuate very rapidly, and that a large proportion of its solid extract remains unbroken up during the primary fermentation, remaining as nutriment, gradually yielded, for those types of yeast which carry on the secondary or cask fermentation. Consequently, that dextrinous beers drink "full," and if properly fermented, and if the dextrin proportion be not overdone, have condition with a reasonable amount of pungency and "a bite upon the tongue" (owing to their being saturated with carbonic acid). [This should also be read in the light of the more recent malto-dextrin theory as stated on pp. 294-302.]

(7) That for the subsequent nourishment of the yeast, certain albuminoid (nitrogenous) bodies are required (peptones and amides), differing from ordinary nitrogenous or proteid bodies in that they have undergone some alteration of character (*e.g.*, the peptones are such bodies which have undergone hydration, *i.e.*, have taken into combination the elements of water through the agency of peptase), whereby they are rendered diffusible, *i.e.*, capable of passing through the thin but continuous envelope enclosing the yeast-cell, a property which the unaltered albuminoids did not possess. That amides appear to be even less definitely known, but possibly are more stable and less assimilable by yeast than peptones are (forming perhaps a reserve store of nutriment), and that peptones are very slightly, if at all, precipitated by heat or by tannin in

a slightly acid medium, such as wort is, but that the coagulum observed after boiling, and the precipitated tannate of albumen, mainly consist of unpeptonised albuminoids.

The subject-matter of the foregoing seven sections being looked upon as axiomatic, the brewer will apply them to practice. Knowing very well what class of beer he wishes to produce, he will consider the quality of the malt he has to deal with (and generally the character of the whole season's make). If he finds that the malt has a good, bold, well-developed acrospire, and as a consequence of this and of proper kiln treatment is altogether tender and floury when bitten, he knows that the diastase, and probably the peptase, will be in a pre-eminently active condition, that moreover the starch, being relatively in a very soluble state, will be immediately acted upon and the conversion be very prompt, the maltose—under ordinary conditions—reaching a high proportion.

In such a case he knows that he must limit the action of the diastase, and this he does by either a high "striking heat," and consequent high "initial," by making a stiffer mash, by considerably reducing the customary two hours' rest after the mash is finished, or by a combination, maybe, of all three. And if he uses a circulator (see Introductory Chapter) by working it for a short time only, say fifteen minutes, just long enough for the wort to run bright. Circulating, as such, unless very high heats are reached, distinctly assists diastatic action, consequently its adoption renders some curtailment of the "rest" after mashing essential. [A plan, which has been found to answer, is to circulate for fifteen minutes, starting the circulation ten minutes after the mash—including underlet, if used, and one revolution of the rakes—has been finished, and to set taps one hour after the circulating is over.]

The extreme limit to which the initial heat may be allowed to rise can hardly be stated—so much do circumstances alter cases—but it is limited, first of all, by the paramount necessity of providing the yeast during fermentation with peptonised food. [156° to 158° Fahr. may be mentioned as high "initials," in result of which no starvation phenomena appeared, and this with a rather large proportion of invert-sugar used in making up "length," which of course reduced the amount of peptonisable matter.]

This deficiency of peptonised food, it may be mentioned here, will manifest itself by signs (bladdery heads, etc.) during fermentation, which will be further referred to in one of the chapters dealing with that subject; but such a fact as that the initial heat quoted above was possible, without such manifestations, renders it probable that the activity of peptase increases with the solubility of the albuminoids, just as that of diastase appears to increase with the solubility of the starch. Both, therefore, largely depend upon the friability of the malt, the result of acrospire development.

Dealing with Ill-vegetated Malt, perhaps containing an Appreciable Quantity of Idlers.—With an ill-vegetated malt, on the other hand, a malt in which possibly 50% of the grains have the acrospire only half, or less than half up their length, with an appreciable quantity of totally ungerminated corns, a much more coaxing system will be necessary. A low initial, say 140°, raised gradually by successive underlets to 150° Fahr. or thereabouts, will go some way towards achieving what is desirable—namely, the extraction of the diastase (and peptase) and the gradual solution of the starch, which is in a much less tractable condition than that of well-grown and properly dried malt. The starch of that part of the endosperm to which the acrospire has not reached approximates in fact to the starch of unmalted grain, although more soluble than that (which requires a temperature approaching 212° Fahr. for *its* solution); indeed, as has been mentioned, the starchy portion even of "lie backs" or "idlers," although they have not grown at all, has been somewhat modified in the direction of solubility.

Noting Acrospire growth in Proportions per cent.—

To notice the quality of the malt systematically is a useful habit, and the following way of recording it may be recommended. Take 100 grains from the sample haphazard, and proceed to separate them into a number of little heaps, representing "grains fully grown," acrospire three-quarters "up," acrospire two-thirds "up," acrospire half "up," acrospire less than half "up," and ungerminated. The numbers in each heap will then give the number per cent. of the particular degree of growth which the heap represents, and this percentage may be registered in the brewing-book. With very freely grown, in fact overgrown malt, it may be necessary to have one heap containing grains, in which the acrospire is actually through, but this ought not to be; indeed, a uniform acrospire growth of three-quarters the length of the grain is about the ideal.

Readers of this will probably be familiar with the old-time test, made by throwing a number of the grains on to a surface of cold water, which is then slightly stirred. Those which float are the well-malted grains, those which sink are the ungerminated, while those which float point upwards are imperfectly grown. It is obvious that such a mode of estimating value is very crude, and far inferior in exactness to the count per cent., which moreover has the merit of stimulating a habit of exact observation.

Malt of Average Diastatic Capacity.—Hitherto we have taken as examples either malt of such extreme diastatic capacity that special measures have to be taken to keep that action within bounds, or malt so exactly opposite that equally extreme measures, in the opposite sense, have to be adopted to secure a wort capable of attenuating sufficiently during fermentation; but it may very well happen that the bulk of any given season's malt will be of medium character, having, perhaps through some climatic conditions which we cannot easily gauge, a normal diastatic capacity with the starch of the endosperm in a sufficiently soluble condition.

Such a malt is of the type most desirable, being the easiest to deal with. The brewer using it will be able to obtain a wort in which either the maltose or the dextrin preponderates, according to the description of beer he may wish to produce, by using in the one case low to medium initials (say 145° to 147°), and then bringing the heat up some five or six degrees, and that not too rapidly, or by a rather high initial (150° to 152°) in the second, an initial which is simply maintained or not raised to any great extent.

Generally speaking, in running beers the maltose ratio will be high as compared with the dextrin, the reverse being the case with stock beers, and to some extent with the light bitter ales which pass rapidly into consumption, and therefore are not entitled to be classed as stock ales, but which may yet be occasionally kept (for bottling or other purposes), or which often remain for some weeks on draught when sold to small private families, and accordingly ought to be brewed somewhat on the lines of a stock beer.

Ales of medium gravity, say from 24 to 26 brewers' lb., and practically running beers, will be, generally speaking, better if the maltose ratio be somewhat higher than in the worts of running-beers of lower gravity; for if the wort be too dextrinous its fermentation is not unlikely, as skimming or cleansing point is approached, to become somewhat sluggish, and the resulting beer will then drink heavy (with perhaps a marked tendency to "kick up"), and yet without giving the impression of body, and be lacking in vinosity (but refer as before to pp. 294-302 for recent views on malto-dextrins.)

Method of increasing Dextrin Ratio, but one requiring a Special Arrangement.—One specific method of increasing the dextrin ratio may be mentioned. It has met with distinct success in the brewing of certain kinds of competition beers, but it needs a special, though simple kind of steam-inlet, and a plentiful supply of uncontaminated free steam for the mash-tun. A metal ring, into which the steam-pipe from the boiler is led, is fitted beneath the false bottom. At its lower curved surface, the one facing the *real* bottom, a number of small holes are drilled, so that when the steam is let in it is to some extent spread abroad by the ring, around which it has to make its way, instead of rushing upwards in jets, as would be the case if the perforations were on the upper surface.

The plan, then, is to mash low, say at 140° to 142°, and almost directly after the mash is finished, to raise the temperature very rapidly by letting in steam till 160°, more or less, is reached. Probably 7° or 8° more would be necessary to reduce diastatic action to a minimum. It is evident that by this method, properly carried out, two important factors in the production of a full "round" beer would be brought into play—namely, a rather high proportion of sufficiently peptonised albuminous matter coupled with a distinctly dextrinous character of wort. As a matter of fact, the ales brewed in this way were able to compete with fair success against rival beers of higher gravity.

We will now postpone for a short time the further consideration of purely operative details such as the effect of mixed grists, limited decoction, hot grist mashing, etc., and proceed to consider rather more fully than there has been a chance of doing hitherto, starch, the dextrins and maltose [the albuminoids have been referred to on pp. 204-208], with the reactions which take place in the mash-tun. Nor must we in this connection overlook the latest view, which has already been briefly referred to in Chap. I and elsewhere, that of the formation, in greater or less quantity, of certain compound bodies known as malto-dextrins.

Starch $(C_6H_{10}O_5)_n$ is fairly ubiquitous in the cells of plants, being found everywhere therein except in the tip of a bud, or the ends of rootlets; it consists of a substance called granulose, enclosed in an envelope of amylo-cellulose, or starch-cellulose. This amylo-cellulose is unaffected by the action of diastase, which, moreover, being what is known as a colloid, cannot penetrate the intact membrane composed of the former, and accordingly can only get at the contained granulose upon the said membrane being ruptured, either by heat or by trituration with something rough like sand, in a pestle and mortar.

Upon the application of sufficient heat to a mixture of starch and water, the previously opaque mixture becomes nearly transparent, the starch is gelatinised, or forms a starch-paste. If a dilute starch-paste be filtered, the granulose passes through the filter, as can be observed by applying the iodine test, but the amylo-cellulose remains behind. It is even then doubtful whether real and complete solution of the granulose has taken place; at all events, if a trial can be made of its ability to pass through the walls of plant-cells, only a negative result will be obtained. Hence the necessity of diastase, or of some such factor in germination, to render the starch stored up in the mature seed available for the nourishment of the growing plant.

The prefix amylo- is not a superfluity, seeing that amylo-cellulose does differ from ordinary cellulose in so far that the former is insoluble in Schweitzer's reagent, which first gelatinises and then dissolves the latter. One marked result of the malting process has been to considerably lower the temperature requisite to rupture all the amylo-cellulose envelopes, and to bring it accordingly well below the maximum at which diastase is capable of action. There is no doubt, I think, that the so-called diastase consists of a group of nitrogenous bodies, rather than that it is a distinct individual body, and that of these bodies the most powerful degraders of the starch molecule are those which are the most easily coagulated by heat. Perceptible coagulation occurs at 167° Fahr. or thereabouts, and several degrees below that temperature would be sufficient to greatly restrict diastatic action.*

---

* To be more precise, Messrs. Brown & Heron have shown the proportion of albuminoids coagulated in malt-extract to be as follows: At 122° Fahr. = 19%; at 140° Fahr. = 53·5%; at 150° Fahr. _ 67·4%; at 169° Fahr. = 80·8%; while at 176° = 178 Fahr., all the coagulable albuminoids are precipitated. This is probably not absolutely true for all malts, but is a useful approximation.

What precisely the nature of this action is we do not yet know for certain, although its results are tolerably clear; but possibly it may be referable to molecular vibration, inducing a break-up of the molecules of starch upon which the enzyme acts. It is generally accepted that heat is an outward and visible sign of intense molecular vibration, and seeing that starch heated with water under a sustained pressure of four or five atmospheres (say at 302° to 320° Fahr.) is ultimately hydrated into some form of fermentable sugar, either maltose or glucose, there is analogy to support that view.

The starch granule varies in size and shape according to its source. Barley-starch granules appear roundish or oval under the $\frac{1}{4}$ to $\frac{1}{10}$ objective, and show no markings unless it be " the pitting " which appears as germination advances. The markings and concentric stratification which some starch granules show more conspicuously than those of barley, are supposed to be due to water not absorbed into the body of the granule. On addition of strong alcohol the water is removed, and the stratification vanishes. On the other hand, chromic acid and dilute alkalies intensify the stratification, the granules swelling up in those liquids. These markings will be noticed surrounding the nucleus or hilum, which is sometimes central as regards the granule itself, but often more or less distant from the centre, especially in the case of potato starch. Potato starch shows the largest granules; the granules of wheat starch, which greatly resemble those of rye and barley in shape, are noticeably smaller.

The micromillimetre or μ ($= \frac{1}{25400}$ inch, nearly) is used to designate the diameter of these granules, and accordingly taking the largest and the smallest granules, wheat approximately ranges from 50μ to 2μ; barley from 39μ to 13μ; potato starch from 100μ to 60μ. The size of the wheat and potato starch granules is very variable; in barley-starch there is greater uniformity, but its granules would not be readily distinguishable from those of wheat starch in a mixture of the two. Very conflicting statements, however, are made, both as to the diameter and the relative proportion of large and small granules. The above measurements are from a leading English text-book, but Thausing, quoting Wiesner, states that the smallest granules are found in barley, and that in wheat and rye the number of small and large granules is nearly equal, while in barley the small granules outnumber those of larger size. The subject evidently wants study, but is complicated by the difficulty of getting a microscopic field of unruptured granules.

The average amount of starch in the more usual types of raw material containing it is:—

Potatoes (fresh)	18%	Starch meal.
Barley	57·7%	,,
Wheat	63·2%	,,
Maize	65·0%	,,
Rice	74·0%	,,

From this the value of rice as a brewing material can be seen.

The Dextrins—2 ($C_6H_{10}O_5$) or $C_{12}H_{20}O_{10}$—have already been spoken of, as a collective whole, more than once, both in respect of their influence on the beer in which they preponderate, and of the method of securing a sufficient proportion of them in the wort. But as there are several recognised varieties and sub-varieties of dextrin, it will be useful to set down at a little greater length the indications which serve to distinguish them.

W. Nägeli (and others) have identified

> Amylo-dextrin I.
> Amylo-dextrin II.
> Erythro-dextrin.
> Achroo-dextrin (a, β, γ, δ, ϵ, ζ, and η).

Amylo-dextrin I. and II. If starch granules are allowed to stand at an ordinary temperature for two or three weeks in dilute hydrochloric acid (for 1000 grammes of starch, Nägeli used 6 litres made by adding 12 parts of concentrated hydrochloric acid to 88 parts of water, a 12% solution) no external change takes place in the granules, but an internal chemical change occurs, which is evidenced by the behaviour of the unswollen residue with regard to iodine. Whilst ordinary starch, if so tried, is coloured blue by the iodine, the starch which has been digested in the above-mentioned way is coloured *yellow*. Moreover, the fluid covering the altered starch contains sugar and a body which is precipitable by iodine and alcohol. That portion which is turned yellow by iodine is Amylo-dextrin I., enclosed in the unaltered envelopes of the starch granules, and that body which is precipitable by iodine and alcohol out of the supernatant fluid is Amylo-dextrin II.

It does not appear, however, that the yellow coloration is a characteristic reaction of Amylo-dextrin I. with iodine, when the former has been obtained in a state of purity. Then a solution of it gives a blue-violet coloration with iodine, while a solution of pure Amylo-dextrin II. gives a red-violet. It appears that neither of these dextrins is one uniform homogeneous substance, but that they consist of two separate substances in varying proportions. These Nägeli claims to have isolated, and has found that one constituent is coloured violet and preponderates in Amylo-dextrin I., whilst the other constituent which preponderates in Amylo-dextrin II. is coloured red by iodine. As both are equally precipitated by alcohol, and as their polarimetric dextro-rotation is the same, it is doubtful whether they should be classed as distinct varieties or merely sub-varieties of the same dextrin.[*]

Amylo-dextrin I. can be got by washing the granules, from which the liquid containing the Amylo-dextrin II. has been filtered, with hot water, whence, upon the solu-

---

[*] Amylo-dextrin is now considered (by Brown & Morris) to be a member of the same series as malto-dextrin (*q.v.* pp. 294-302), being identical in most respects, *e.g.*, being unfermentable by *S. Cerevisiæ*, though reduced by malt-extract to maltose. Unaltered, *they say*, by fractional precipitation, it has optical and cupric-reducing powers corresponding to a mixture of dextrin and maltose.

tion being cooled down to 32° Fahr., it crystallises out in the form, as the microscope shows, of circular discs—flat circular plates, although at first, unless some movement be imparted to the liquid, the crystals may appear to be of globular form. It has also been obtained in needle-shaped crystals, and there is ground for supposing that the discs are formed by a radiated grouping of these crystalline needles, although the needles are soluble in cold water, but the discs not.

Amylo-dextrin II. falls as a voluminous white precipitate from the fluid which covers the altered starch in the above-described experiment, if a four or five-fold volume of 93% alcohol be added to the filtrate. To purify it further the second precipitate is collected in a filter, washed with alcohol, and afterwards dissolved with water, and the solution brought to freezing-point, whereupon it crystallises out, like Amylo-dextrin I., in flat plates, though occasionally it forms needle-shaped crystals too.

Erythro-dextrin ($\grave{\epsilon}\rho\upsilon\theta\rho\acute{o}\varsigma$ = red) and **Achroo-dextrin** ($\breve{\alpha}\chi\rho oo\varsigma$ = colourless) are also distinguished by their behaviour with regard to iodine, the former giving a *red* reaction, the latter *none*. Boiled with dilute acids both dextrins are converted into glucose, the erythro-dextrin passing through the intermediate stage of achroo-dextrin in the process; or, if digested with cold, aqueous malt-extract they are hydrolised into maltose.

If Nägeli's experiment be carried on a little further, a time comes when the acid fluid covering the altered starch gives no further reaction with iodine. If the fluid then be neutralised, first with milk of lime and afterwards with calcic carbonate, and then filtered and evaporated to a small bulk, on alcohol being added to the concentrated filtrate, an amorphous precipitate forms, which, upon being filtered and deprived of its water by absolute alcohol, and subsequently dried over concentrated sulphuric acid (in a desiccator), is found to be a white powder, a solution of which gives no colour with iodine, and has accordingly been named achroo-dextrin. It is equally soluble in hot

DEXTRIN A COLLOID.

and cold water, and even at freezing point no turbidity of the solution, *i.e.*, no precipitate, occurs.

Erythro-dextrin, as far as the writer is aware, has not been prepared in a state of purity. It is, however, a constituent of commercial dextrin, which, under the name of "British Gum," is used in calico-printing for thickening colours, and is prepared by heating starch up to a heat ranging between 410° and 520° Fahr., or if it be moistened with very dilute nitric acid, say water containing 2% of the acid, up to one ranging from 230° to 300° Fahr. In practice it is done in two cylinders, one within the other; the inner one having an arrangement for stirring the contents, the interspace between the outer and the inner cylinder being filled with rape-seed oil, which conveys the fire-heat steadily to the contents of the inner cylinder.

The above-named dextrins have this in common, that they show no organised structure, that they are colloids, *i.e.*, unable to diffuse through membranes either vegetable or animal, and that they are more or less soluble in water but not to any extent in alcohol. Erythro-dextrin is, however, less soluble than achroo-dextrin in alcohol, solubility in fact increasing as the scale (*vide* the series of equations on p. 293) is ascended. They differ in their optical power on a ray of polarised light, though all have a right-handed rotation (*dextra* = the right hand), less than that of starch, but exceeding that of maltose, that is to say, as hydrolysis advances the specific rotatory power decreases.

Dextrin, as such, has no reducing action upon Fehling's solution, though there is a possibility of a partial conversion into glucose occurring through the agency of tartaric acid (from the Rochelle salt) if boiling be prolonged (*vide* the test in laboratory chapter), and of a consequent over-estimation of the co-existing maltose. But on the other hand, Barfoed's solution, which is practically normal acetate of copper acidified with acetic acid (the solution contains about 1% of free acid), is said to be reduced by *glucose* after a short boiling, but not at all by *maltose*, and by dextrin after a more prolonged boiling.

Maltose ($C_{12}H_{22}O_{11}$), identified by the distinguished French chemist Dubrunfaut in 1847, and rediscovered by C. O'Sullivan in 1874-76, is the final product of diastatic action upon starch. Before the latter's epoch-making communications it was generally supposed that this ultimate product was glucose (Dubrunfaut's view having been completely lost sight of), but from this sugar maltose has now been clearly differentiated, both by its greater rotatory power and its lower reducing action upon Fehling's solution (66·6 parts of glucose, or according to other investigators 61 parts of glucose, precipitate as much cuprous oxide from the solution as 100 parts of maltose are capable of doing). Though the action of diastase, however prolonged, effects no change in maltose, yet boiling with sulphuric acid does bring about an alteration, in the shape of a reducing power corresponding to that of glucose. Possibly this change is the result of a hydration process, whereby the maltose is changed into two molecules of glucose (dextrose).

$$C_{12}H_{22}O_{11} + H_2O = 2 (C_6H_{12}O_6).$$

Maltose crystallises in hard, white, needle-like crystals, containing a molecule of water of crystallisation, which is lost in an air-bath at 212° Fahr.

Equation dealing with the successive Changes which take place when Diastase acts on Starch.—We may now proceed to consider the equations which indicate the changes taking place when diastase acts upon starch at a jointly favourable temperature (140° Fahr.), although, as will be seen (p. 298), this somewhat elaborate series will require modification if the malto-dextrin theory be definitely accepted.

It must be observed, too, that the unknown n of the formula for the starch molecule—$(C_{12}H_{20}O_{10})_n$—must have the value of 10 *at least* assigned to it, and that the changes appear to take place as the result of successive hydrations, maltose and dextrin being formed *simultaneously* at the first hydration, during which and the succeeding hydration steps one molecule of maltose after another separates, leaving constantly diminishing quantities of dextrin, which as hydration proceeds also alters into higher types.

		*Specific Rotation. 216·0 (for Starch).	Cu_2O (reduced).
(1)	$\begin{cases} \text{Soluble Starch.} & \text{Water.} & \text{Maltose.} \\ 10\,(C_{12}H_{20}O_{10}) + H_2O = C_{12}H_{22}O_{11} + \end{cases} \begin{cases} \text{Erythro-dextrin } \alpha. \\ 9\,(C_{12}H_{20}O_{10}) \end{cases}$	209·0 :	6·4
(2)	$\begin{cases} \text{Erythro-dextrin } \alpha. \\ 9\,(C_{12}H_{20}O_{10}) + H_2O = C_{12}H_{22}O_{11} + \end{cases} \begin{cases} \text{Erythro-dextrin } \beta. \\ 8\,(C_{12}H_{20}O_{10}) \end{cases}$	202·2 :	12·7
(3)	$\begin{cases} \text{Erythro-dextrin } \beta. \\ 8\,(C_{12}H_{20}O_{10}) + H_2O = C_{12}H_{22}O_{11} + \end{cases} \begin{cases} \text{Achroo-dextrin } \alpha. \\ 7\,(C_{12}H_{20}O_{10}) \end{cases}$	195·4 :	18·9
(4)	$\begin{cases} \text{Achroo-dextrin } \alpha. \\ 7\,(C_{12}H_{20}O_{10}) + H_2O = C_{12}H_{22}O_{11} + \end{cases} \begin{cases} \text{Achroo-dextrin } \beta. \\ 6\,(C_{12}H_{20}O_{10}) \end{cases}$	188·7 :	25·2
(5)	$\begin{cases} \text{Achroo-dextrin } \beta. \\ 6\,(C_{12}H_{20}O_{10}) + H_2O = C_{12}H_{22}O_{11} + \end{cases} \begin{cases} \text{Achroo-dextrin } \gamma. \\ 5\,(C_{12}H_{20}O_{10}) \end{cases}$	182·1 :	31·3
(6)	$\begin{cases} \text{Achroo-dextrin } \gamma. \\ 5\,(C_{12}H_{20}O_{10}) + H_2O = C_{12}H_{22}O_{11} + \end{cases} \begin{cases} \text{Achroo-dextrin } \delta. \\ 4\,(C_{12}H_{20}O_{10}) \end{cases}$	175·6 :	37·3
(7)	$\begin{cases} \text{Achroo-dextrin } \delta. \\ 4\,(C_{12}H_{20}O_{10}) + H_2O = C_{12}H_{22}O_{11} + \end{cases} \begin{cases} \text{Achroo-dextrin } \epsilon. \\ 3\,(C_{12}H_{20}O_{10}) \end{cases}$	169·0 :	43·3
(8)	$\begin{cases} \text{Achroo-dextrin } \epsilon. \\ 3\,(C_{12}H_{20}O_{10}) + H_2O = C_{12}H_{22}O_{11} + \end{cases} \begin{cases} \text{Achroo-dextrin } \zeta. \\ 2\,(C_{12}H_{20}O_{10}) \end{cases}$	162·6 :	49·3

The same series of changes may be expressed more concisely as follows:—

$$10\,(C_{12}H_{20}O_{10}) + 8\,(H_2O) = 8\,(C_{12}H_{22}O_{11}) + 2\,(C_{12}H_{20}O_{10}),$$
$$\text{Starch.} \qquad \text{Water.} \qquad \text{Maltose.} \qquad \text{Dextrin.}$$

which expressed as percentage = 80·8% of maltose and 19·2% of dextrin [worked out as follows: The atomic total of 8 $(C_{12}H_{22}O_{11}) = 342 \times 8$; that of 2 $(C_{12}H_{20}O_{10}) = 324 \times 2$, consequently dividing the 324 by 4 will preserve the ratio = 342 : 81. Then $342 + 81 = 423$, and this divided by 100 = 4·23. Then $\dfrac{342}{4\cdot23} = 80\cdot8$ (nearly), and $\dfrac{81}{4\cdot23} = 19\cdot2$ (nearly)].

* It may be well to mention that the optical activity (dextro-rotatory power) stated refers to the actual products of the starch-transformations, not to the wort itself. They are $[a]_J$. The cupric-oxide reducing power is expressed shortly as K.

Dr. Squire, in the course of an admirable paper read before the London section of the Society of Chemical Industry, suggested the following equation for the reaction taking place at 167° Fahr., which he says is tolerably constant:—

$$10\ (C_{12}H_{20}O_{10}) + 3\ (H_2O) = 3\ (C_{12}H_{22}O_{11}) + 7\ (C_{12}H_{20}O_{10}),$$

or expressed in percentage as above = 31·15% of maltose to 68·85% of dextrin.

The dextrin produced at such a temperature is, he says, achroo-dextrin, giving no reaction with iodine; but if the temperature be raised, or the mixture be rendered slightly alkaline, then the quantity of maltose produced is lowered, and the dextrin would be an erythro-dextrin, giving a red reaction with iodine.

Malto-Dextrin Theory.—If the theory of the formation of certain definite compounds of maltose and dextrin, malto-dextrins or amylöins, be established beyond reasonable doubt, then the equation setting forth the mash-tun reactions will require readjustment, or, at any rate, will have to be taken with the qualification that certain molecules of maltose either effect a fresh combination with free dextrin to form the bodies above-named, or—which is the accepted view—that the converse takes place —viz., that certain complex groups of which the starch molecule is assumed to consist are split up as to four-fifths of the groups, and, if the most favourable conditions exist, are successively hydrolised into maltose *through* a series of amylöins (malto-dextrins). I shall deal a little more generally with these malto-dextrins before giving the formula invented to explain all the ascertained facts, it being a somewhat complicated one.

It will be clearly understood that the theory states these malto-dextrins to be *compounds* and not mere mixtures, having indeed properties varying either from those of their constituents, or from mixtures of them, as is the case with other chemical compounds.

The maltose is readily fermentable in the primary fermentation by ordinary yeast (*Sacch. cerevisiæ I.*). Dextrin is now alleged to be absolutely unfermented in the primary, and practically unaltered in the secondary fermentation (being found in the beer unchanged, and in the same proportions after some months' storage). Consequently the malto-dextrins, unfermentable in the primary fermentations, alone remain to produce the necessary brisk cask condition by their gradual conversion into alcohol and carbonic acid gas, through the agency of some secondary yeast type or types, one of them being Hansen's *Sacch. pastorianus* II. in all probability.

It is held that there are different types of these malto-dextrins, the higher types (those most suitable for stock-beers) containing more dextrin and less maltose, while the lower types, containing a larger proportion of maltose to dextrin, are less resistant to converting agencies, and therefore, determining more or less rapid condition, are adapted to beers of short storage.

The tenet is that even the lower malto-dextrins are, as such, unfermentable, but that in their case the preliminary stage of the conversion of the whole into fermentable maltose is speedily passed through, when rapid condition follows as a matter of course. A necessary sequence of the unfermentability of malto-dextrin, as such, is that the breaking up must always be effected in successive stages.

(1) The higher types being converted into lower types.
(2) Conversion of the lowest type into free fermentable maltose. (3) Splitting up of the maltose molecule into alcohol, carbonic acid, etc.

The lowering of type is possibly effected by a diastase-like enzyme secreted by the secondary yeast named above, or some other.

Evidence on which the Malto-dextrin Theory is based.—When it chanced to be found that the higher dextrins, especially up to Conversion No. 7, yielded larger quantities of maltose when degraded with malt extract than the lower dextrins (albeit associated with less free maltose), the conclusion seemed inevitable that it was in some way in *combination* with the maltose. Further, a substance having been prepared (by acting upon starch with malt-extract, and subsequent repeated treatment with alcohol) soluble in alcohol of 70 to 80%, and giving the analytical results of maltose 39·8, dextrin 58·1 : inactive matter 2·1%, an aqueous solution of this substance was made by dissolving 12·663 grammes of it in 100 cc. of water, which thus corresponded to 5·039 maltose (100 : 12·663 :: 39·8). This being set to ferment with a little Burton pressed yeast, the fermentation which ensued stopped at the end of three or four days, with the result that on the ninth day 3·687 grammes of maltose still remained.

Pure crystallised maltose was now added, upon which a brisk fermentation ensued, and after a time ceased, whereupon more maltose was added, and the fermentation started again. Examined when fermentation had finally subsided, the increase of alcoholic strength corresponded very nearly to the added maltose, and the cupric reducing power of the liquid was but very slightly reduced. In other words, the added maltose had entirely disappeared, but the 3·687 grammes of the original maltose was only reduced to 3·577.

Again, the dextrin, acted upon by malt-extract, gave 70% of maltose, just as the dextrin of the liquid before the free maltose was added had done, showing that no degradation of the dextrin had occurred. The question then arose why this 3·577 grammes of maltose had not disappeared, when the brisk fermentation which ensued on the addition of free maltose showed that its survival was in no way due to the defective power of the yeast, or to other unfavourable conditions.

Moreover, if, instead of the free maltose, a few drops of cold-water malt-extract were added at the close of the first fermentation, it was also found that fermentation was vigorously renewed, and in the result not only did the apparent maltose (3·687 grammes) practically disappear, but also some of the dextrin, *the action being accompanied by a degradation of the dextrin.*

Considering these facts, there seem very strong grounds for concluding that the "apparent maltose," as it has been called, is not "free" maltose, but is held in close chemical combination with dextrin in the form of the bodies now called amylöins or malto-dextrins; and this conclusion is strengthened by what is found to take place when a mechanical mixture of fairly pure dextrin and pure maltose is likewise set to ferment. In the latter case nearly all the free maltose disappears after a rapid and vigorous fermentation.

Isolation of Malto-dextrin.—Messrs. Brown and Morris proceeded to effect it in the following way. Making a starch conversion at 140° to 149° Fahr, with very active diastase, the conversion was stopped at a point very nearly corresponding with Conversion 3 of the series on p. 283. The solution, after boiling, was set to ferment with a little Burton yeast, and after the free maltose was thereby fermented away the liquid was filtered, concentrated to a syrup, and digested for some hours with 90% alcohol to remove the non-volatile products of fermentation. The strength of the alcohol having been reduced to 85%, the alcoholic extract was, after digestion, poured off the residue. The alcoholic extract was distilled, and the residue again treated with 85% alcohol. The extract was again distilled to remove the alcohol, and the residue thus obtained was very nearly pure malto-dextrin (absolutely unfermentable by ordinary *Sacch. cerevisiæ*, though treatment with malt-extract converts it completely into maltose), corresponding in optical and cupric-reducing power to a mixture having the percentage composition of maltose 33·9, dextrin 66·1.

Formula for Malto-dextrin.—Accordingly the simplest formula assignable to it is $\begin{cases} C_{12}H_{22}O_{11}. \\ (C_{12}H_{20}O_{10})2, \end{cases}$
i.e., one maltose or amylon group united to two dextrin or amylin groups.

Modification of the Equation Series.—Messrs. Brown and Morris have come to the conclusion that the starch-molecule is not less than five times $(C_{12}H_{20}O_{10})_3$, and, as a matter of fact, they now take it to be $5\,(C_{12}H_{20}O_{10})_{20}$, or as five times the size of the dextrin molecule $(C_{12}H_{20}O_{10})_{20}$. They suppose that four of these amylin groups are arranged round the fifth and similar group; that the inner group resists hydrolising influences, and constitutes the stable dextrin corresponding to that of Equation 8. This involves the view that the dextrins are not, as previously supposed, a polymetric series, but are uniform in character, the so-called higher dextrins being in no wise different from that found at the conclusion of the mashing operation. The four outer amylin groups, however, are held to be incapable of existing, as such, when hydrolising influences are at work upon them, being, in fact, theoretically capable of undergoing rapid conversion into maltose by a succession of hydrolisations through a series of amylöins, at first, of what are known as the higher types, and afterwards, of less and less complexity (in the sense that, as the series advances, the worts containing them, or rather the beers containing them, are less persistently obdurate to the fermentative agencies which determine " condition ").

In an interesting article which appeared in the *Brewing Trade Review* (September 1st, 1890) Dr. Morris writes that " the action may be graphically expressed by the following equations where n represents the number of amylin groups converted into amylon groups and m the number of unchanged amylin groups " ($n + m$ must $= 20$, the number of amylin groups in each complex). " In the first instance we may express the very earliest stage of hydrolysis thus :—

$$\begin{cases}(C_{12}H_{20}O_{10})_{20}\\(C_{12}H_{20}O_{10})_{20}\\(C_{12}H_{20}O_{10})_{20}\\(C_{12}H_{20}O_{10})_{20}\\(C_{12}H_{20}O_{10})_{20}\end{cases} + n\,H_2O \quad \begin{array}{c}(C_{12}H_{20}O_{10})_{20}\\ \text{Stable dextrin.}\end{array} + 4\begin{cases}(C_{12}H_{22}O_{11})_n\cdot\\(C_{12}H_{20}O_{10})_m\cdot\end{cases}$$

Starch Molecule.

At an intermediate point in the hydrolysis the following probably represents the reaction:—

$$\left\{\begin{array}{l}(C_{12}H_{20}O_{10})_{20}\\(C_{12}H_{20}O_{10})_{20}\\(C_{12}H_{20}O_{10})_{20}\\(C_{12}H_{20}O_{10})_{20}\\(C_{12}H_{20}O_{10})_{20}\end{array}\right. + xn\,H_2O = (C_{12}H_{20}O_{10})_{20} + 4 - x\left\{\begin{array}{l}(C_{12}H_{22}O_{11})n\cdot\\(C_{12}H_{20}O_{10})m\cdot\end{array}\right.$$

Starch. Dextrin. Amylöin Group.

$$+ x(C_{12}H_{22}O_{11}).$$

Maltose.

"This theory," he adds, "appears to embrace and explain all the known facts in connection with starch-transformations; it enables us to understand why it is impossible to separate the whole of the maltose of a limited conversion either by solution in alcohol or by fermentation; it also offers a complete explanation of the observed facts in connection with fractional degradation, and other questions of a like nature." My excuse for transporting this paragraph bodily must be the impossibility of putting the theory, as expressed by equations, more concisely, and the general importance of the question.

Evidence for the Opinion that Secondary Yeasts hydrolise Malto-dextrins.—One experiment out of many, devised by the investigators, was to ferment away the free maltose from a conversion made in the usual way. Then after freeing the fermented liquid from alcohol, a solution was made of the residue (containing, be it remembered, no *free* maltose), but still showing on analysis the proportion of

6·986	grammes	Maltose.
16·792	,,	Dextrin.
0·315	,,	Inactive Matter.
24·093	,,	in 100 cc.

The solution had a specific gravity of 1093 and the dextrin yielded 66·8% of maltose.

Yeast was again added, and the preparation kept at 30° C. (=86° Fahr) and closely watched, and the sediment examined daily under the microscope. Gradually the yeast-cells (*Sacch. cerevisiæ*, — primary yeast) finding no free maltose, shrivelled up and apparently died. *At the end of* six *or* seven *days* a few cells of *Sacch. pastorianus* and *ellipticus* began to appear and, concurrently, fermentation started, at first extremely slowly, but by degrees progressed much more rapidly as the newer forms of yeast became more abundant. It was continuing slowly, even at the end of forty days, when the experiment was concluded.

The amount of maltose which had undergone fermentation being determined (1) from estimation of the alcohol formed and its calculation as maltose, and (2) the decreased specific gravity of the solution (after such distillation), was found to be 14·41 and 14·398, practically 14·4; and, as the experimenters say, " when we consider that the original solution only contained maltose = 6·986 grammes per 100 cc., it is evident that the remaining 7·414 grammes must have been produced at the expense of the dextrin."

Factors determining (1) Percentage and (2) Type of Malto-dextrins.—These factors are three in number—viz., extent of germination, extent of kiln-drying, and mashing heats. As regards (1), the result of undergrowing is based upon what has been insisted upon before—viz., that the starch of badly germinated malt approximates to that of the original barley, and may even be to a great extent insoluble at ordinary mashing temperatures. Accordingly it is only as the heat of the mash rises under the influence of hotter sparge temperatures that the starch gets gelatinised, and this only arriving at a time when the power of the diastase is much weakened (both by the withdrawal of the first worts and the higher temperatures), the conversion of such starch is very far from complete, and probably only dextrin and *malto-dextrins of an abnormally high type* are produced in the later runnings. Consequently, though the first copper wort may be of fairly normal constitution, the later worts will contain a high percentage of abnormal malto-dextrins, fermenting with exceeding slowness even in the cask. (In such cases, if anything like early condition is wished for, the use of aqueous malt-extract is indicated.) (2) High kiln-heats, and (3) High mashing heats, both of which, as compared with lower heats, determine an increase in the amount of malto-dextrin; although in respect to No. 3, this is more marked when the temperature rises above 150° Fahr. than below it; and in fact, as long as it keeps within the usual range, the type of malto-dextrin does not vary much, and indeed is far more influenced by germination and kiln-drying.

And here, in these experimental mashes, a curious discrepancy—as stated by Dr. Moritz—occurs between laboratory experiments and samples taken of actual brewery worts. While the laboratory experiments (at all events, a series on which he relied) showed, with heats rising from 140° to 155°, a very marked increase in the *quantity*, but no alteration in the *type* of the malto-dextrin, which to begin with was rather high (maltose 1 : dextrin 4), the brewery samples, in the preparation of which the heats ranged from 146° to 156° initial, not only showed an increase in the proportions of malto-dextrin, but the type rose also (from M. 1 : D. 1 up to M. 1 : D. 2·9).

Kiln-drying, on the other hand, has a marked influence both on quantity and type. Thus in the case of malts mashed under identical conditions, with one which was undercured, the type was low (2 M. : 1 D.), while the quantity was very small; but as soundly cured malt was reached, both quantity and type rose, and continued to do so the higher the curing, up to 1 M. : 2 D. When, however, the permissible limit was passed and overcured, scorched malt was used; though the quantity markedly increased, the type somewhat strangely did not (remaining at 1 M. : 2 D.).

Comparing the influence of kiln-drying and mashing heats, Dr. Moritz states that a pale malt and a high-dried malt, the latter being mashed 9° lower than the former, gave an almost exactly equal quantity of malto-dextrin, but with the high-dried malt the type was lower, and he therefore makes the practical recommendation that for pale (and store) ales, a malt relatively lightly cured and mashing heats relatively high should be employed, while for running beers high-dried malt and relatively low mashing heats should be the aim. [The theory is, it will be remembered, that the high types of malto-dextrins are gradually degraded into lower and lower types, and finally into maltose, as which alone they are fermentable—*i.e.*, amenable to the influence of the yeasts, which bring about *cask condition*.]

"Fretting" explained by the Malto-dextrin Theory.— If we accept the view, also propounded, I believe, by Dr. Moritz, that beer at the time of racking may contain malto-dextrins of such abnormally low type as not to be far removed from free maltose (19 M. : 1 D.), then it is easy to see that such bodies (which might even have been fermented by a young and vigorous yeast during the primary stage in the fermenting vessel, *had such young and vigorous yeast been present*), having escaped fermentation before the racking, may undergo it shortly after, either by the agency of the primary yeast stimulated by aëration, or more probably by secondary yeasts, the germs of which have been absorbed and developed in the interim.

Although we may not be disposed to accept implicitly all the conclusions of the investigators who have, of necessity, been so often referred to in dealing with the question of malto-dextrins, their researches are certainly of the highest importance in a technical sense, and it is gratifying to think that they form a contribution to brewing science, made by this country alone, although the name "malto-dextrin" was proposed by Professor Herzfeld of Halle for a substance stated to be intermediate between achroo-dextrin and maltose. This substance, however, was fermentable by primary yeast, and this, as well as its optical and cupric-reducing power, suffice to

LIMITED DECOCTION.

distinguish it altogether from the malto-dextrins which the English observers claim to have identified.

A few operative details remain to be considered.*

Limited-Decoction Process.—The so-called " Limited-Decoction Process" is an attempt to get some of the results of the German system of mashing, without the expensive and cumbrous plant which that system requires. Something has been said about it already in Chap. I., but the *modus operandi* is as follows. An arrangement for letting free steam into the mash-tun having been provided—a $1\frac{1}{2}$ inch pipe will do for 50 lb. pressure, but should branch into two pipes of the same diameter when just through the bottom of the mash-tun, and the false-bottom plates of the latter must be fastened down securely with bolts and bands, or they will be likely to shift—the mash is made with 2 barrels to the quarter, which may be made first with $1\frac{1}{2}$ barrel at 164° Fahr., the remaining half-barrel at 187° being let in, with steam if necessary, to bring the mash temperature up to 155° or thereabouts for mild ales, and higher for bitter ales. These proportions of liquor may be modified, and probably it would be found generally advisable to use a larger quantity for the actual mash, and less for the underlet.

In 75 minutes from beginning mash, taps may be set, and wort at the rate of half a barrel per quarter is run off and pumped into a suitable vessel (with steam coil) commanding the mash-tun. The heat of the " goods " is now raised to boiling, gradually up to 170° or 175° at first, then rapidly. After the mash has been kept at 212° or nearly that for ten minutes, it is cooled down to 165° with sparged cold liquor, after which the strong wort previously run off—and which of course has not been allowed to get much over 160° Fahr.—is returned to the mash-tun, the rakes going all the time.

* The formula for ascertaining the striking heat required to attain any given initial, being of the nature of a calculation, will be found in Chap. V., p. 169.

The mixture must, on no account, exceed 165°. A short stand of 15 minutes will probably be enough, and then taps can be set and the coppers made up without further delay.

If the iodine test be applied after the boiling of the goods, it will appear that much fresh starch has come into solution. This disappears when the strong wort, which has been held back, is returned to the mash-tun. After this, almost any heat, however high, can be used for sparging, there being no risk of unconverted starch being carried into the copper in solution.

Over-fine crushing of the malt should be specially avoided for limited-decoction mashes, and the use of Conron's patent mashing rakes (those with india-rubber ends, which sweep the false-bottom plates) have been found useful, though for the ordinary system they are scarcely to be recommended. Probably the inrush of free steam somewhat prevents that forcing of fine particles through the apertures of the plates, which brewers, using those rakes in the ordinary infusion process, have found to be their most trying fault. Rakes, at any rate, should revolve while boiling, cooling, and mixing are going on. The extract got from malt, and that factor's malt, in fair years by the limited-decoction method will average 90 or over, but the difference of extract and the benefit is most apparent when dealing with hard and steely malt. The drainage gives no unusual trouble, and it may fairly be claimed that a remarkable brightness of the racking sample usually results. I have seen limited-decoction beers bright in the round at four days.

Limited Decoction with 25% of Unmalted Grain.—The experience of an energetic experimenter in this direction and his mode of applying it was as follows, and without alteration of plant he obtained very bright beers with most brilliant worts. Mashing 25% of whole grist maize, flour, or rice with two-thirds of the malt of which one-fourth was Algerian, so as to get an initial of 125°, he then gradually raised the heat—taking an hour—to 165°, with the rakes revolving all the time; then he raised the mash rapidly to the boil. After boiling for ten minutes he cooled down to 165° (with cold liquor as before), mashed in the remaining third of the malt, and set taps after 60 to 90 minutes' stand. This time about half the contents of the mash-tun was run off without sparging. Then the boiling being repeated and continued for ten minutes, the mash was again cooled down to 165°, and the large quantity of strong wort last drawn off and held back was returned to the mash-tun, and taps set again after fifteen minutes' stand. The copper lengths were then made up without further delay.

In the narration this seems a troublesome process, but it must be remembered that in the ordinary way, if raw grain material be used, the process is a troublesome one, and additional plant—a Pigeon's converter, or what not—is absolutely required.

Semi-prepared Raw Material—" Flaked Malt."—But I do not advocate the use of raw and untreated grain, seeing that we have so excellent a material as the so-called flaked malt (really gelatinised rice) of Messrs. Gillman & Spencer, Limited, and another so easily used as the torrefied malt (grain) of the same company. Of the gelatinised rice in its present flaked form, and when carefully prepared, it is difficult to speak too highly; in the granular form, in which it was originally manufactured, the mash, of which it formed a part, often left much to be desired in respect of drainage. In the more recent form, however, that difficulty does not occur, and it may be mixed with the grist easily enough. The best plan is to have a special hopper, with adjustable slides, so that it can be fed into the ground malt, a small portion going up with that grist in each cup of the elevator.

In the preparation of this material the starch of the rice is ruptured by steaming the grain, which is afterwards dried and rolled or otherwise pressed into its present convenient shape. Latterly, I understand, superheated steam has been used.

Torrefied Grain (barley or maize) is made by admitting those grains, down a shoot, into a cylinder revolving over what is in effect a row, extending the whole length of the cylinder, of combined Bunsen burners, and the result of the sudden blast of heat to which they are subjected is to rupture the starch-cells most effectually, and in fact "to pop" the grain. Smallish foreign barley goes in at the higher end of the cylinder (which revolves on an incline), and emerges from the lower end markedly larger in bulk than the finest malt, so that there is no difficulty whatever in grinding this preparation concurrently with the malt. If I may speak from a limited experience, there appears to be no drawback to its use unless it be a distinctly *sui generis* and somewhat empyreumatic smell which the worts running into the copper possessed, but which afterwards passed off, and even had it remained, would not have been disagreeable.

Other preparations of unmalted grain or meal there are, which may give good results in the miniature mashes of a laboratory, yet often fail—owing to some difficulty of drainage—to give their proper extract in operations on a larger scale.

Hot Grist Mashing.—This has been made the subject of a patent by Mr. Charles Clinch, whose method is to pass heated air into the crushed malt for some hours, whereby he imparts a uniform heat (within a few degrees, say a variation of 12° at the outside) to the whole bulk. The benefits claimed for this system are that a distinctly malty aroma is brought out in the grist and remains in the beer (some analogous results may be observed on toasting, or even warming, a slack biscuit before the fire); that defects in kilning, notably undercuring, are made good; and that the heated air coming into contact with the crushed particles of malt does this very effectively and without imparting the slightest increase of colour; and that the employment of relatively low "striking heats" (no higher, in fact, than the initial heat desired) instead of heats 12° or 15° higher, with perhaps an underlet besides at a much more considerable temperature, not only results in speedier conversion owing to the non-coagulation of diastase, but secures the attainment of a large proportion of dextrin (or malto-dextrin if the view as to the absolutely uniform quantity of dextrin resulting from a starch-transformation be correct), with much greater yeast-feeding property than such highly dextrinous worts, obtained on ordinary lines, as a rule exhibit. A great tendency to fobbing, necessitating careful boiling of the worts, is evidence of the presence of much dextrin, whether free or combined, while the possibility of reducing the pitching-yeast by some 20%, which is said indeed to be advisable, will show the yeast-feeding character that the wort possesses.

Stout and Porter Grists.—A proposition advanced in some treatises dealing with the practical side of brewing, namely, that for black beers a low initial heat is to be recommended, seems to me to refute itself. The writers allege that palate fulness is thereby produced, whereas there can be no doubt that the tendency would be exactly the reverse. I will even go so far as to say that, if no raw or return wort is used for the mash (p. 311), a higher heat than that used for running ales is required. I am now speaking of black beers brewed in the comparatively small quantities in which country brewers, having no very large local demand for that class of beer, have to produce it.

More than in any other beer is a good firm persistent head a desideratum in black beers, and from what has been said before it will be understood that this is attainable solely by ensuring the presence of a good proportion of dextrin, whether it be combined as malto-dextrin, or free, as was at one time supposed.

And although there is no diastatic capacity in the black or roasted malt, which forms part of the grist, and very little, if any, in the brown malt, there is equally no starch in the former, and very little in the latter to undergo hydration, so that the question of the wort's relative poverty in diastase does not come into play, and indeed has no foundation in fact.

I have no doubt that the extraction of a large proportion of albuminous matters, especially in the form of peptones, also tend to give softness and body, if their presence can be secured without the extreme degree of conversion into maltose, which, unless special precautions be taken, they will determine. This, I should say, might be done by working on lines laid down in an earlier part of this chapter, *i.e.*, by getting a low initial heat and rapidly and considerably raising it (to diastase-crippling point) by free steam, or by some specific modification of the limited-decoction system, or by the employment of the hot-grist process. But failing facilities for these, my own experience makes for higher heats than those used for ales. Similarly, I hold that the " rest " or " stand " after mashing should, if anything, be curtailed.

Black beers are brewed from a mixture of pale, brown, and patent, or black, malts, though in Dublin, and I believe in Cork, the brown is omitted. The Irish brewers' patent malt, however, is not the over-roasted *black* stuff (giving a rough and burnt flavour) which so often does duty for that material in England. It is rather of a rich chocolate brown, and being used in large quantities easily escapes the extreme slackness which samples taken from the country breweries here would often exhibit. Also, as I am given to understand, the brewers in Ireland depend largely, if not solely, upon malt, while in England sugar is considerably used, and that often of very inferior quality, under the questionable idea that anything will do for stout, as the colour covers a multitude of sins.*

Brown or Blown Malt is made by subjecting well-

---

* Also it may be added that another characteristic of the Irish system is attenuation pushed to an extreme that the English brewer, who rather aims at keeping a high proportion of unattenuated matter in beer of this class, never dreams of, body and condition being afterwards secured by " worting," *i.e.*, by adding strong wort in incipient fermentation (what the German brewers know as Kräusen, *anglice Kreising*) instead of priming with dissolved sugar, as is general in England.

vegetated barley—after the moisture has been duly got rid of—to a sudden blast of intense heat generated by heaping up the kiln fire with oak or beechen faggots or billets. The result is an increase of bulk averaging 25%, if all the conditions are favourable. Owing to the risk and the high rates of insurance demanded in consequence, this malt is generally made at certain centres by maltsters, the large London breweries being alone able to profitably make for themselves.

Patent, Roasted, or Black Malt.—The first name was given because a "patent," or licence, was required for its manufacture when the malt-duty was in force. It should be plump and not too black; the malt exhibiting a brownish fracture is the best. It is roasted in a large revolving cylinder.

Owing to the necessity of buying these malts in larger quantities than are required for one operation, they are generally used in far too slack a condition for perfect success. A large part of the aroma certainly gets lost, and accordingly, Mr. Stopes points out the advisability of using patent malt fresh, giving the following detailed method of producing it on a small scale.

The apparatus consists of a perforated cylinder, turning easily on bearings, and fitted above a fireplace enclosed in sheet iron, which is extended upwards, so as to form a chimney to carry away smoke, steam, or fumes. The cylinder holds one or two bushels of corn, and should be kept revolving steadily. There should be a low coke fire at first, and afterwards, as the steam passes away, a brighter one. In thirty minutes a fine aroma steals from the malt, which should be inspected five minutes later, by which time a good chocolate tinge ought to have been acquired. In forty minutes the operation will be completed, and the charge may be turned out to mellow. Mr. Stopes also points out that slack pale malt may be more advantageously used in this way than by redrying it for ordinary use.

This plan certainly involves trouble, but the advantage

of using the roasted malt fresh is very great. Manual labour for turning would perhaps prove somewhat expensive, but moderate hydraulic power would perhaps do better than power got from the ordinary shafting.

Substitute for Patent Malt.—A very effective substitute for patent malt—at least in part—is the "intense caramel" of Messrs. A. Boake, Roberts, & Co., and it not only gives colour (about 14 lb. to 16 lb. = a bushel of patent in colour-giving power) but also adds to the non-fermentable extract, and thus helps the production of a full-bodied article. Its tendency, too, is to increase the permanence and brownness of the head.

The following grist of 30 quarters has been recommended for porter—

Pale Malt (and equivalent in sugar)	24
Brown Malt	4
Patent Malt	2
	30

And for stout 4 bushels less of patent and 4 more of pale malt, the required length being shorter.

For some districts, *e.g.*, where blending with ale is done, this stout might be too pale. I myself, in a case where deep colour is required, have found the following proportions answer for single stout of between 24 and 25 lb. gravity.

25 quarters pale, 4 quarters brown, 2 quarters patent (in mash) and 6 bushels ditto (in copper); 8 cwt. (approximately) of cane-sugar, and 140 lb. of intense caramel. (N.B —The latter is sent out in iron drums holding exactly that quantity *nett.*) This grist will produce about 110 barrels at the required gravity in the fermenting round. It may be mentioned that before the patent is added to the copper the wort will be perfectly black, but as the addition involves no burnt taste, seeing that part of the colour is got from the intense caramel, it is used as a safeguard. Much larger proportions of caramel are

employed by some brewers, and I have heard of a case in which it has entirely replaced black malt.

I hold that the mashing liquor should, if possible, be boiled for stout, and that common salt should be added to the maximum extent formulated in the chapter on water.

Raw or Return Wort.—The latter is the better name, seeing that all such worts ought to be *boiled* before use, and they are either a portion of the last runnings from the mash-tun, which are too strong to be wasted, or a sparging of the hops in the hop-back, or a compound of both, which is held over from one day to the next, and used instead of ordinary water to mash the malt with. They, and especially the hopped return worts, tend to make the mash what is called "dead"—*i.e.*, the goods do not rise, and are not in that spongy condition in which they are said "to take the sparge liquor well," and which is most favourable to full extraction.

It has been suggested that the tannin extracted by the sparged water, which is a much better solvent than wort, acts upon the coagulable albuminoids in the mash-tun, and thûs considerably limits diastatic action. For this reason, which implies that worts mashed with them do not show such a tendency towards attenuation as those mashed with simple liquor, apart from the obvious economy of using up the latter runnings of a strong wort, return worts have been found very useful for stout and porter, where very free attenuation is not desired. Of course where these worts are employed lower striking heats will be the rule, for not only do they restrict diastatic action, but the initial heat which results from using simple water at a given temperature can be obtained by using return wort of $1\frac{1}{2}°$ to $2°$ lower.

Dead Mashes (and flooding of Goods).—Besides the possible influence of return worts, other factors which determine deadness of mash are over-fine grinding of the malt, the separation of the heavy flour from the lighter husk, which otherwise tends to keep it buoyant, perhaps intensified by jarring in the elevator cups, and an excessive fall into the grist-case, steely malt, or the use of too much huskless malt substitute. Knocking about of the mash with the rakes has also some influence in the same direction. In the first two, and probably in the last two cases, a layer of pudding-like starchy matter will, when the grains are thrown out of the mash-tun, be found to have formed midway between the top and the bottom, or lower. This layer, obdurate at first, may partially, if not entirely disappear, owing to the solvent action of the diastase, and thus, as is generally found to be the case when the taps make a bad start, drainage gradually improves. At higher temperatures, be it noted, the liquefying action of diastase is even more rapid than its saccharifying action.

Sparging has also a good deal to say about deadness of mash and consequent flooding of the goods, if it be carelessly performed. The sparge-liquor should flow on evenly and lightly, a three-armed sparger being better than a two-armed for a large mash-tun. Messrs. Wilson & Co. of Frome arranged a simple but ingenious appliance for testing the evenness with which spargers work. It is, in effect, a shallow vessel made of copper or tinned iron, the bottom forming a sector of the mash-tun circle—*i.e.*, occupying an angle enclosed by two radii, and the arc they cut off. This vessel is then divided by partitions, as shown in the annexed outline, and placed upon a level corresponding to the surface of the goods. The sparger being then made to revolve with liquor in the usual way, if its action is correct, obviously all the divisions of the test-vessel will be filled simultaneously.

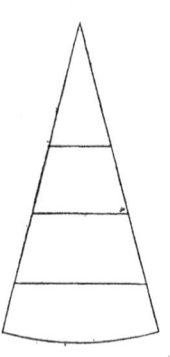

The heat of the sparge-liquor should be so regulated that the temperature of "the taps" shall not, at any time, exceed 162°, and an even lower temperature may sometimes cause the extraction of starch. Not

SECOND MASH.

that the unconverted starch, as such, is specially injurious, only that a heat high enough to liquefy starch and cripple the diastase involves the extraction of certain nitrogenous bodies (*e.g.*, mucedin) more soluble at the higher than at lower temperature, especially in a saccharine wort, and that these accordingly getting into the worts in a state of semi-solution will tend to cause, if the quantity be large, a persistent turbidity of specially obdurate character. Moreover, towards the end of the sparges the tap temperature should show a decided drop. As a general rule, sparges beginning at 170° to 175°, and finishing at 160°, would be within the limits of safety. If the sparger acts correctly, and if it is not a question of brewing beers of extremely high gravity, I see no advantage in point of extract or otherwise in having a second mash, preferring indeed to sparge on the whole length of liquor required for making up the copper lengths. In that case the sparging should begin ten or fifteen minutes at least before the taps are set, so that the goods may be kept "well up" in the earlier stages. Of course towards the conclusion of the sparge they will be drawn down, but to get them down too early is fatal to extract. Where, however, for any reason it is desired to get a concentrated wort at first, it may be necessary to draw off the larger portion of the wort which the mash contains (roughly speaking, 40 quarters mashed with 80 barrels, will yield 50 barrels, *i.e.*, $1\frac{1}{4}$ times the number of quarters of malt), without or with very little sparging. In this case a second mash will be a necessity, the liquor required, the temperature of which should hardly exceed 160°, being run in by underlet, and the rakes set going. When the drainage is very bad, it may also be found necessary to do the like, not, however, drawing off the wort quite so closely, and underletting less. In such cases the "wort-circulator" already spoken of is invaluable, shortening the time of rest by its use for a few minutes before running into the copper, and securing an absolutely bright tap from the beginning.

The Underback.—In some of the newer plants attempts have been made to dispense with the underback, the mash-tun taps running directly into the coppers. Although it is convenient to be able to run straight into either copper, without the wort passing through the underback, yet the latter should not be suppressed. It should be adjoining the coppers and like them of copper, and at a level higher by a few inches than the rim of the copper, so that the wort can flow easily into those vessels. The underback should certainly have a steam coil; and a convenient size, having regard to the necessity of sometimes keeping back strong wort for the purpose of bringing up the gravity of later coppers (especially in the case of parti-gyles), would be one capable of holding fully one-third of the maximum amount which can be boiled in the largest copper. I may say from experience that one holding only one-fourth is sometimes found inconveniently small.

For example, a brewer is, let us say, in the habit of brewing 200 barrels at a time, of which 130 barrels are pale ale and 70 barrels XX. We need not enter far into his reasons for arranging his brewing thus, which may be complex; suffice it to say, he is able to return his good pale-ale hops (*i.e.*, boil them a second time in the XX), and thereby economise hops, or the arrangement may be dictated by some consideration of convenience in racking, while, owing to the pale ale being more or less of a running character, or certainly not stock in the full sense of the word, the mashing conditions which suit the one kind of ale will not be unsuitable for the other. Well, in brewing the above quantity, he finds perhaps that it does not do to habitually get *more* than 25% of his XX extract from sugar, within which limit an underback holding 20 to 24 barrels of strong wort (of 30 to 35 lb. gravity) will enable him to keep; but supposing that, owing to some extra pressure, he wants to brew 80 barrels, which his larger copper is quite capable of turning out at one boiling, then he will find, having only an underback of the above size, that he must exceed the percentage of sugar which he finds most satisfactory.

I am perhaps arguing rather from a particular case to cases in general, but my own experience is dead against exceeding a certain limit, which of course may vary with circumstances and in different plants. Once in a way an excess of sugar beyond the usual maximum may do no harm, but persisted in it will tend to yeast-weakness and to the necessity of skimming at lower attenuations if a clean yeast-outcrop be insisted on. Special measures, however, such as aëration and continuous rousing, to free the fermenting wort from all the carbonic acid gas which can be so disengaged (in itself a wasteful aim), and the employment of some form of peptonised or mineral yeast food, may facilitate the use of even larger percentages of sugar; an instance is even within my knowledge where beers of considerable repute have been brewed with as much as 50% of sugar, the yeast being at the same time of rather exceptional purity and vigour.

The reasons for and against this continuous rousing and knocking out of carbonic acid belong to another portion of our subject, but enough has perhaps been said to show the advisability of having a sufficiently large underback.

Stewing the Wort in Underback or Copper.—This practice, which consisted in keeping the worts while gathering, or for part of the time, at a uniform (and converting) temperature of 170°, or somewhat under, was at one time advocated, either with the idea of securing the conversion of any soluble starch, or from some misty notion of peptonisation. Brewers however, I think, came to the conclusion that whatever the benefits of the system might be, and they were not very apparent, they were heavily discounted by a thinness of palate developed thereby. Thick-and-thin upholders of the amylöin theory maintain that diastase in the underback has no power of degrading to a type lower than that of the malto-dextrins already co-existing in the wort (though this is arguable with the above experience), and they would stew (if they did it at all) the later runnings, in which both percentage and type of malto-dextrin are generally very much higher, with some of the diastatic first wort kept back at a suitable temperature.

Boiling.—The objects of boiling are fourfold :—

1. Sterilisation of wort in regard to therein-existing organisms.

2. Coagulation or precipitation of certain albuminoids.

3. The extraction of as much of the hop-aroma as possible.*

4. To obtain the full effect of any directly antiseptic influence which the hops (probably in their resins) possess.

As to 1, some very interesting researches by Dr. G. H. Morris have shown that absolute sterilisation is secured—almost universally—by 15 minutes' boiling with hops in the copper. In one case only out of several, and that when the malt was apparently a very bad specimen, did a sample of wort, taken after a 15 minutes' boil in the copper, and then submitted to the ordeal of the forcing tray for 7 days, show a few short *bacilli*; others showed none after 21 days of the same treatment.

Dr. Morris thinks that the temperature of the boiling wort, which he fixes at about 215° Fahr. for the lower part of the copper, is greatly aided by the acidity of the medium, due partly to the lactic acid incidental to the malt and partly to acid (tannic) derived from the hops. (Acid liquids are much more easily sterilised than alkaline, as Pasteur showed long ago.) Also it is aided, he thinks, by an antiseptic property which the hops possess, and which is supposed to reside in some of the resins. He quotes Hayduck's experiment as showing that the extract of 1 gramme of hops in 500 cc. would be sufficient to entirely stop the action of the lactic ferment, and to restrict, more or less, that of the other disease-ferments except *Bacterium aceti*. Hayduck's extraction, though the fact is not stated, was probably an aqueous one, so that the conditions are not quite on all fours with those

* Methods of working out proportions are given on pp. 167 168.

which obtain in the brewer's copper; but, on the other hand, seeing that the proportion 1 : 500 only means about ¾ lb. of hops per barrel, the brewer's position is in respect of quantity more favourable.

As to 2, the albuminous matters affected by the boiling divide themselves into two groups, those coagulable by boiling (or, indeed, by a temperature of 180° Fahr.), and those precipitated by the action of the hop-tannin, which combines with them, forming insoluble tannate of albumen. The former separate as a flocculent coagulum in very minute flakes, and though partially redissolved in the boiling wort help to form the cooler sediment. They are easily precipitated, so much so that a sample of first-copper wort, taken almost directly after the length has been made up (I refer to one which has been at, or near, boiling-point when gathering), will often filter bright and remain bright, and even if boiled in a beaker will give little or sometimes no further precipitate.

The case is different with the tannate of albumen. This is only formed after somewhat prolonged boiling (necessary, of course, to extract the hop-tannin), whereupon it shows as a somewhat coarsely flaked coagulation, forming the portion of the wort-constituents which separates when the so-called "break" occurs.

A patent has been taken out by Messrs. Valentin and F. Faulkner for an apparatus to remove the albuminous matter which is coagulable by heat, before its re-solution in the boiling wort. The wort in its passage to the copper is first heated, then cooled, and then passed through a cellulose-filter, which removes the albuminous coagulum, and the patentees claim that thereby a good deal of potentially harmful matter is removed, matter which, they allege, does come out of solution again slowly both in cask and bottle, and forms a considerable part of the sediment in both.

No. 3 is not always very intelligently aimed at. I have heard it stated that some brewers—it is to be hoped not many—boil all their hops in their first copper, returning them all to the second. This is about the worst plan that could be adopted. Another plan, also open to objection, is to add the hops, which have been apportioned for each copper, entirely while the copper length is being made up, *i.e.*, to have them all in before the copper boils. This, if the object is to extract as much as possible from the hops without regard to the risk of obtaining a harsh, bitter flavour, or of dissipating much of the volatile essential oil, might pass muster; but such is not the way in which fine-flavoured ales are produced. Another way, a somewhat niggling one, but with a good deal to recommend it, is to divide the hops for each copper into fractional parts, say, for argument's sake, into tenths, and then as each tenth of the copper length is got, to add one portion of the hops, save as regards the last tenth, which is to be of the best hops used in the day's brewing, and which is only put into the copper half an hour or so before "turning out."

I myself, however, at all events when dealing with a somewhat extractive water, do not care about having any of the hops in before the copper length is made up, and then I should divide them into three portions, boiling one portion all the time, and the other portions less; the last portion, which consists of the best hops used, being only in the copper 30 to 40 minutes. And I have known good results in point of flavour come from *simmering*, but not boiling (the copper, if a fire one, being actually "damped down"), this last portion of the hops, and this is especially to be recommended where circumstances allow of *all* the first copper hops being returned. That is not always the case by a very long way, even when there is no apparent reason to account for the fact.

Hops, when added to a boiling copper, should be roused in to prevent the volatilisation of their essential oil before they get submerged. Volatile as this oil is, there seems reason to suppose it less readily driven off when diffused through the wort.

As to No. 4, although it has been suggested that any

antiseptic properties possessed by the hop reside in the resins, this is by no means certain. At any rate, a good boil is necessary to dissolve these resins, and as they seem somewhat intimately bound up with a portion of the essential oil, it is probable that a strong boil, by dissolving more of the latter out, will retain as much in the nett result as a slack boil which causes less volatilisation. It is remarkable, however, that no apparatus has been devised for general use to secure the retention of *all* the essential oil (so much of which now scents the air for furlongs' distance when coppers are boiling) without losing the advantage of vigorous ebullition.

Steam-boiling v. Fire-boiling—Closed v. Open Coppers.
In spite of the increasing use of steam-jacketed coppers, there is still a feeling in many quarters that they are only a convenient makeshift, far inferior to fire-coppers for producing a keeping and brilliant beer. One who has seen ales quite up to the average in the former respect and inferior to none in the latter, produced in a brewery where the only boiling vessel was an iron square back, with a coil, which only succeeded in keeping up the semblance of a boil for the greater part of the time that the wort was supposed to be boiling (sometimes not more than 80 minutes), may well feel somewhat sceptical about this.

The notion appears to be that as the heat of steam is not more than 212°, or, say, not more than 240° when at considerable pressure, whereas the heat of a furnace will be several times this, the heat from the latter must be much more searching and effective, it being forgotten that if this were so, if in fact the wort were not protected from such extreme temperatures by an impalpable cushion of vapour between itself and the inner surface of the copper, and which probably absorbs all the heat above 212°, or, say, 215° (for the temperature will vary with the depth of the liquid, being higher at the bottom of the copper where the pressure is greater), the brewing of a pale beer in a fire-copper would be impossible, owing to the caramelisation which must ensue. That a fire-copper, closed at the manhole, and in which boiling takes place under some amount of pressure, will be the best for black beers, may be readily believed.

Open coppers are credited with causing less coloration of the wort than closed coppers. If this be correct it may be due to a larger extraction of colouring matter from the hop owing to the boil under pressure, as well as to caramelisation. Pale enough beers can be brewed with a dome-and-pan copper.

Hot Aëration of Wort.—Of late years a great deal of importance has been attached to this, on the grounds that it not only affords a supply of free oxygen to give the yeast, subsequently added, a good start, but that also some oxygen enters into combination with some of the nitrogenous matter, and eliminates it in the form of cooler sediment. The alleged necessity of such aëration is made the excuse for the retention of the old-fashioned coolers, which otherwise afford such scope for the infection of the wort by disease and other organisms. Huge numbers of these organisms, neutral or hurtful, have been estimated to impregnate the wort during its exposure on the coolers. They are reckoned by tens of millions, and were it not for the great preponderance of the yeast cells (estimated, by a modest computation, at about three quarters of a *billion* per lb. of pitching yeast), they would soon be masters of the situation.

There is not much to say about refrigerating, and it has been touched on in the opening chapter.

CHAPTER IX.

FERMENTS IN GENERAL.

ORGANISED AND UNORGANISED FERMENTS—SO-CALLED INORGANIC FERMENTS—ENZYMES—TABLE OF FERMENTS WITH FUNCTIONS—DEFINITION OF FERMENTATION—GERM THEORY *V.* SPONTANEOUS GENERATION—PROFESSOR TYNDALL'S DEDUCTION—FUNGI—WHY FERMENT-ORGANISMS MUST BE CLASSED AS VEGETABLE ORGANISMS— PASTEUR'S SOLUTION — *Aspergillus Niger* AS AN EXAMPLE — RAULIN'S LIQUID — PROTOPLASM — HYPHA—MYCELIUM—SEPTATION—CORRELATION OF GROWTH ABORTIVE MYCELIA—MODES OF REPRODUCTION—POLYMORPHISM AND PLEOMORPHY—SCHIZOMYCETES—HYPHOMYCETES AND SACCHAROMYCETES—THE MICROSCOPE—HINTS ON SELECTION AND MANAGEMENT OF MICROSCOPE—ANGLE OF APERTURE—ITS PARTS—MAGNIFYING COMBINATIONS—EXAMINATION OF YEAST.

A GENERALISATION founded upon imperfectly understood premises has classed together as "Ferments" a number of widely different agents, whose spheres of action are on such varying planes that it is no easy thing to bring them into one scientific focus.

But though it seems better to reserve the name of ferment for those factors, which by their life-processes bring about certain changes or degradations in organic substances or fluids containing them, changes with which their own reproduction is closely connected (*e.g.*, yeasts, bacteria), and to class by the newer title of **enzymes** or **zymases** those other agencies which, although secreted by organised structures, yet have their sphere of action, or at any rate are capable of having it, when once secreted, outside or independently of those organisms (*e.g.*, diastase, invertase, pepsin, peptase, etc.), yet it will

Table of Ferments, Organised and Unorganised (Zymases).

Group.	Represented by	The action consists in
I. Diastatic Ferments.	Diastase of malt. Ptyalin of the saliva. Pancreatic juice.	(α) Liquefying and (β) splitting-up the starch molecule and turning it into dextrin and sugar with the co-operation of water (hydrolysis, hydration). In accordance with an equation resembling— $C_{18}H_{30}O_{15} + H_2O = C_6H_{10}O_5 + C_{12}H_{22}O_{11}$. Starch and Water. Dextrin. Maltose. [N.B.—Ptyalin requires an alkaline or neutral medium, but diastase a slightly acid one—less than ½% solution which coagulates it. Alkalinity is fatal to diastase.]
II. Glucoside-splitting Ferments.	Emulsin (found in bitter almonds).	Splitting glucosides (see Glossary) into sugar and compounds which mostly belong to the aromatic group, with aid of water. $C_{20}H_{27}NO_1 + 2\,H_2O = 2(C_6H_{12}O_6) + C_7H_6O + CNH$. Amygdalin. Water. Glucose. Oil of Bitter Almonds. Prussic Acid.
III. Inverting Ferments.	The Invertin or Invertase of beer yeast.	Converting the molecule of Cane-sugar into a mixture of dextrose and levulose, with co-operation of water. $C_{12}H_{22}O_{11} + H_2O = C_6H_{12}O_6 + C_6H_{12}O_6$. Cane-Sugar. Water. Dextrose. Levulose.

TABLE OF FERMENTS.

IV. Peptonising Ferments.	Peptase of malt. Pepsin of gastric juice. Trypsin of pancreas.	Changing the albuminoids (sparely diffusible in themselves) of plants and animals into easily diffusible peptones. The trypsin forms not only peptones but simpler compounds—leucin and tyrosin. N.B.—Acid medium for peptase and pepsin—the gastric juice secretes hydrochloric acid; but trypsin prefers an alkaline one. The pancreatic juice contains carbonate of soda.
V. Alcohol-forming Ferments.	Saccharomyces (yeasts) of various kinds (not *S. Glutinis*). Mycoderma vini (when submerged, *i.e.*, acting as anaërobic ferment).	Splitting the molecule of the fermentable substance (glucose, maltose, etc.) with the co-operation of water, whence chiefly result alcohol (ethyl), fusel oil, glycerine, succinic and carbonic acids. [Anaërobic *M. vini* seems to have an action on succinic acid and glycerine, which *S. cerevisiæ* does not possess.]
VI. Acid-forming Ferments.	Mycoderma aceti. Bacterium aceti. Bacterium lactis. Bacillus subtilis. Bacillus amylobacter *alias* Clostridium butyricum.	The *M. aceti* conveys oxygen to the alcohol, dehydrogenates it into aldehyde, whence it is oxidised into acetic acid. *B. subtilis* and *B. amylobacter*, otherwise *C. butyricum*, produce butyric acid.
VII. Putrefactive Ferments.	Bacteria (vibrious) Moulds.	Some (moulds) act as oxygen-carriers to the organic substances; others, as anaërobic ferments in a medium deprived of oxygen disengage hydrogen, which combines with the sulphur and phosphorus of the compound to form sulphuretted and phosphoretted hydrogen (putrid smell). Probably the bacteria have a more directly active *rôle*.

be more consistent with general practice to group together in the first instance all which have any pretension to interest the brewer, however remotely.

And some writers even include, under the name of inorganic ferments, those mineral acids which are able by their presence, and without themselves undergoing any change or loss in the operation (by catalysis, as it is called), to determine, under suitable conditions, changes like those of starch into dextrin and dextrose, or of canesugar into invert, but these surely ought to be rigorously excluded.

The foregoing table, accordingly, has been drawn up to show at a glance the groups into which the zymases and the ferments, properly so called, are divided, and to give a general notion of their mode of action. It may also serve to show how Nature adheres to leading ideas, albeit modified in details.

Having now made the preceding concession to usage, we will henceforth use the term "fermentation" only in connection with the action of organised ferments (Groups V., VI., and VII.), by which are meant those microscopic forms, one or more of which are always to be found in fluids undergoing change. That these forms are the causes and not the effects of these changes has been proved beyond the possibility of doubt, and equally that their functions are specific, viz., that one, a rounded organism (yeast), produces alcohol, carbonic acid, etc., at the expense of the sugar, that others, either short and rounded, or elongated rods, produce acid, lactic or butyric, and that a third form of bacterium, constricted in the middle, is associated with putrefaction. Certain organisms take up the work where the others leave it, and act upon their residues, bringing the originally complex bodies nearer and nearer to an elemental condition. Let us now define fermentation in this sense.

Fermentation (from *fermentum*, a ferment, short for *fervi-mentum*, from *fervēre*, to boil), so called from the internal movement moderately resembling that of ebullition which wine-must and beer-wort undergo, is the name applied to all those processes wherein certain microorganisms, as a result of their nutrition and multiplication, effect the degradation of complex matter into simpler forms. And though we are accustomed to look upon wine or beer as the ultimate aim of fermentation, it will not be overlooked that those products really only represent a stage of arrested degradation. Whether they enter into consumption at that stage or not, their inevitable lot is to be converted into the simplest derivatives, of which water and carbonic acid form the major part.

That these fermentations—from the highest to the lowest in the scale—were the work of distinct microorganisms, Pasteur's experiments some score of years ago conclusively proved, but the opinion which he felt justified in publishing, that, under no circumstances, could such or such a fermentation take place without the introduction, designed or accidental, of some member or members of the specific ferment, did not meet with such ready acceptance.

Against this opinion "*omne vivum ex vivo*," or **Germ Theory,** as it was called, certain learned pundits rose up and propounded the **"Spontaneous Generation" Theory,** to the effect that the introduction of an actual predecessor was not necessary to secure a crop of micro-organisms, seeing that decomposing organic matter developed within itself (spontaneously, so so speak) yeast, bacteria, bacilli, etc., according to circumstances.

They were fortified by the fact that on several occasions flasks of fermentable matter sterilised (*i.e.*, boiled for a certain time) and hermetically sealed in accordance with Pasteur's suggestions had undoubtedly undergone fermentation, whereas Pasteur had said they would not; and it was not until Pofessor Tyndall took the matter up that the spontaneous generation theory practically collapsed. Himself observing that certain liquids, apparently sterilised and closed with due precautions, showed fermentative changes, and especially in proximity to a store for hay (infusions of which soon teem with bacteria, or rather bacilli), he made the brilliant deduction* that "indurated germs," as he then called them, "spores," as they are now styled, must exist capable of withstanding much more adverse conditions than the fully developed organisms to which they belonged, and which Pasteur had studied and classified.

And he found experimentally that intermittent boiling, *i.e.*, short periods of boiling with an interval, say, of one day between, was quite destructive of spores, as well as of the fully developed organisms, whereas a continuous boil of even greater extent had only destroyed the latter. Accordingly, it is now found to be a simple matter to sterilise infusions so that no fermentative changes shall take place within any measurable time, nor is it necessary to seal the flasks hermetically. If only they are closely plugged with previously sterilised cotton wool (which filters the air and arrests the spores), and subsequently sterilized in the manner described, the absence of any fermentative change, in the vast majority of cases, almost conclusively disproves spontaneous generation, the very few exceptions being referable to imperfect sterilisation and manipulation.

All ferments—limiting the term to those organic forms which can be handled or, at all events, seen in the mass with the unassisted eye or individually with the microscope (yeasts, moulds, or bacteria)—belong botanically to the group of **Fungi**.

That they are to be assigned to the vegetable rather than placed low down in the animal realm is made clear by the fact that they are able to draw all the nutriment required for their growth from a suitable mixture of mineral matters. This is typical of vegetable life. The most lowly organised animal must have its food prepared for it in some way or other, must have the mineral or elementary constituents, into which that food could be

---

* This deduction was later on confirmed inductively by microscopic observation, the sporulation of bacteria, and the tenacious vitality of their spores, being now ascertained facts.

resolved by analysis, got ready for it by some previous agency, and this is necessarily the agency of some vegetable organism or organisms.

On the other hand, all plants—except those which deliberately elect to live a parasitic existence on the juices of other plants (amongst which parasites the dodders may be instanced)—can and do draw all their nutriment from the mineral constituents of the soil, or extract the carbon which they require to build up starch or its kindred carbohydrates from the carbonic acid gas which the air contains. Plant-life, in short, using the term in its widest sense, is the agency which bridges the great gulf fixed between the inorganic and organic realms.

It must be added that the fungi, and notably the bacteria and moulds, co-operate in this destructively rather than constructively; although they may be capable of building up organic structures (their own) out of mineral matter, their most important function is the breaking down of complex organic substances into simpler and simpler forms, in which they are again available for plant nutrition. In fact, it is not too much to say that it is these minutest organisms, formidable only in their numbers—a bacterium reproducing itself once in an hour is theoretically capable, and given suitable conditions may be really capable of developing into over 16,000,000 individuals at the end of twenty-four hours—which alone render the earth habitable. Were it not for them, dead plants and animals would lie where they fell, and in no long time the surface soil would be cumbered with *débris*.

Again, were it not for the fact, of the utmost importance to brewers, that each separate kind of organism, such as we are speaking of, secretes, while performing its special functions, matter which acts as a **specific poison** to itself, there would be practically no limit to their reproduction, and all creation would become their prey.

To come to particulars—yeast is capable of converting into alcohol, carbonic acid, etc., sugar which is in a sufficient degree of solution, but as sugar contains no nitrogen which (as well as phosphoric acid and potash) is essential for the growth of the ferment, there would come a time when yeast sown in such a solution of pure sugar would cease to act as a ferment—long before all the sugar became converted—simply because the necessary food for its development was absent. But add to the sugar and water ammonic tartrate, potassium phosphate, calcic phosphate, and magnesic sulphate in the following proportions (**Pasteur's Solution**)—

Potassic phosphate	20 parts
Calcic phosphate	2 ,,
Magnesic sulphate	2 ,,
Ammonic tartrate	100 ,,
Cane-sugar	1500 ,,
Water	8376 ,,
	10,000

the growth and development of the yeast goes on *pari passu* with the splitting up of the sugar into the usual products of fermentation, just as readily and thoroughly as it would in the most perfectly prepared malt-wort. Nor is the presence of the organic sugar in the solution even necessary to the growth of the yeast, apart from the exercise of its fermentative functions. That is to say, the yeast can split up the salts, getting its needed phosphoric acid from the phosphates, its nitrogen from the ammonic tartrate, the hardly less necessary potash from the potassic phosphate, and so on.

Aspergillus Niger—Raulin's Solution.—A still more minute study has been made of the requirements of a certain mould, known as Aspergillus Niger, by M. Raulin, a disciple of M. Pasteur.

Although this mould grows readily enough on bread moistened with vinegar, on slices of lemon or other acid fruits, M. Raulin has found that the medium which in the shortest space of time produces the largest weight of the plant (in which, in fact, it chokes all rival growth) is composed as follows,—

	Grammes.
Water	1500
Sugar Candy	70
Tartaric Acid	4
Nitrate of Ammonia	4
Phosphate of Ammonia	0·6
Carbonate of Potassium	0·6
Carbonate of Magnesia	0·4
Sulphate of Ammonia	0·25
,, ,, Zinc	0·07
,, ,, Iron	0·07
Silicate of Potassium	0·07

The culture to take place in shallow porcelain basins, open to the air, the liquid being an inch or less in depth. The temperature required is about 95° Fahr.

Complex as this solution may appear, it has been found that even trifling deviations produce most marked diminution of the crop. Thus, the phosphate being omitted, instead of each gramme produced with the full solution, only ·005 gramme is found, and the omission of the ammonium nitrate causes almost as great a fall-off; the withdrawal of the potassium salts brings each gramme down to ·04 gramme, and, what is perhaps the most remarkable of all, the mere traces of zinc and iron contained in their compounds also have a most potent influence.

Again, in the case of yeast, every cell under the microscope is observed to be bounded by **a continuous cell-wall or membrane,** without any orifice, either for the absorption of food or the excretion of waste products, and this involves the necessity of its food supply being in such a state of thorough solution as to be capable of passing into the cell by **Osmosis** or **Diffusion.**

This is a distinctly vegetable characteristic, considering which, in conjunction with their power of assimilating mineral food and the total absence—except perhaps in sundry bacteria—of chlorophyll, and the consequent inability of yeast and its kindred organisms to utilise the atmospheric carbon as nutriment, we can see why botanists have placed these organisms firstly among the great division of the **Cryptogamia,** then amongst one of its subdivisions the **Thallophytes** (see Glossary), and finally amongst a subdivision of the latter—viz., the **Fungi.** To the most commonly known species of the latter a considerable resemblance is shown indeed by yeasts in the rapid multiplication of their cells; and the fact that the cells of yeast rapidly separate, as a rule, while those of a mushroom adhere together is only a distinction and not an essential difference. Indeed, in one species of yeast, the caseous yeast of Pasteur, a certain amount of coherence may be observed, and the mushroom, as we know it, is a complex form of what will be mentioned later, **a Sporophore.**

It does not appear of vital consequence to consider whether these fungi are plants which have degenerated from plants of higher organisation, that is to say, plants in which, consequent upon some lapse of the ability to secrete chlorophyll, there has been that degeneration of structure which is observed to take place on disuse of functions in other organisms, or whether they are plants whose race has never known aught but development of cell on to cell by some sort of gemmation or budding process.

The fact, however, that the same cell is capable of two methods of reproduction, fairly analogous to those, for instance, of a potato, viz., by shoot (bud) and by seeds (spores), points to a merging of root and stem into a single cell—*i.e.*, a degeneration. These may be interesting problems in evolution or its converse, but to consider them in full would take us too far afield.

All the fungi with which we have to do, whether they be yeasts, moulds, or bacteria, may be referred, as regards their first appearance, to separate **hyphæ.**

A hypha is a tube-shaped membrane of cellulose, charged with the mysterious nitrogenised-carbon substance known as **Protoplasm.*** The protoplasmic contents are

* **Protoplasm** is so called because it is the primary substance found generally in all organic structures, though itself appearing to be a clear

sometimes watery in appearance, sometimes finely granular. When certain moulds, where hyphal growth has its most extended development, are observed under the microscope (though so exceedingly delicate are they that to get a fairly perfect specimen is no easy matter), the hypha is seen to be a tube of relatively considerable length, which at intervals branches out just below thin transverse divisions of cellular matter (**transverse septa**), which form at right angles to the direction of the tube's growth. These branches branch out again in their turn, so that before long a much-branched tree-like organism (though of course of microscopic dimensions) appears—especially with the mould styled *Mucor Mucedo*—which is known as a **Mycelium**.

Very rapid growth is rendered possible by the action of the protoplasm, which plasters on to the inner surface of the enclosing membrane fresh layers of cellular matter, whereby the membrane, continuously expanded as it is, is kept from becoming too attenuated. Although layers of cellular matter are spoken of it will not be forgotten that we are referring to an organism so minute that a single mycelium under a less magnification than 300 diameters would scarcely be discernible; it is only indeed the enormous aggregate of the mycelia which renders the

and structureless jelly-like substance, except under the highest microscopic powers, under which it assumes the aspect of a very fine network of delicate fibres, whose interspaces are filled with minute particles and fluid, yet even then no trustworthy evidence of structure is obtained. As Professor Huxley says, "Protoplasm, simple or nucleated, is the formal basis of all life. It is the clay of the potter."

Some scientists regard it as a form of proteid + water. A late writer says, not contradictorily, "Now protoplasm is one of these carbon compounds, and perhaps the most complex of them all. In fact, it seems to have reached the utmost limit possible in this respect, and the chemical equilibrium is so unstable that it is ready to break down at the least touch. We can regard protoplasm as occupying the summit of chemical changes: the elements of food are by their mutual affinities gradually built up into more and more complex structures, until they reach the form of protoplasm, when they can go no further, but begin to break up under certain conditions into less and less complex forms, until they reach the final stage of CO_2, H_2O, etc., which all organic matter comes to."

mildews, with which we are familiar, visible to the unassisted eye.

Harking back again to hyphæ, we shall see that in the case of other fungi—for instance, yeasts and bacteria—the initial stage of growth is similar to that of moulds, though this growth stops short of the development of mycelia.

In the case of yeast, for example, which in an ordinary nutritive medium like wort develops by budding, that is to say, by small cells growing out of the parent-cells, and which, having reached a sufficient stage of growth, separate, and soon proceed to put forth cell-buds of their own, or may even do so before the separation occurs—the cell is, in effect, a hypha,* the new cell is the hyphal branch, which instead of forming part of a mycelium, growing on to the original hypha, separates as soon as it is sufficiently developed, the septation, if such it can be called in the case of yeast, showing the greatest variation from the original type, seeing that instead of occurring above the branching-point and preceding such branching or budding as with mildews, in the case of yeast it occurs at the point where the bud is formed and subsequently thereto.

In the mildews the formation of a transverse septum appears to be the cause of branching, impelling, as it does, the ever-growing protoplasm to seek a new outlet; in the yeasts it is—if a true septation at all—a consequence of it.

Nor need this variation be any obstacle to considering these two methods of growth as simple developments of one original scheme. What is known as "**correlation of growth**" is an accepted principle in respect of organic nature; one which means that all the parts of an organism are so intimately connected and bound together that when one part is made to change, some other parts are not unlikely to undergo modification as a consequence of the first change.† The artificial conditions, then, under which

---

* This is most obvious to any one looking at the illustrations of film formation of *S. Cerevisiæ*, given by Hansen, as to which see Chapter XI.

† This question of correlation of growth may have a closer interest

the yeast-fungus has been cultivated for centuries has most probably brought about enough variation from the original type to account for the divergences of the two methods of growth.

The bacteria, schizomycetes, or "splitting fungi," also increase in a similar way "with a difference." This difference is that, instead of budding as yeast does, they multiply by repeated transverse subdivision, following the formation of a fine diagonal membrane at the place of fission. As soon as this membrane has thickened sufficiently, separation of the one organism into two occurs.

Abortive Mycelia.—And the view that these methods of reproduction, both in yeasts and bacteria, may be looked upon as an abortive tendency to form mycelia, is strengthened by a converse tendency which has been observed in organisms, which normally develop a mycelial growth. For instance, in the case of *Mucor Mucedo*, a mould of common occurrence, forming a white mass on bread, fruit, etc., and in that of *Mucor Racemosus*, it has been observed that the filamentary tubes of the mycelia sometimes get divided by relatively close transverse partitions, and that these divisions then bud, the buds and the divisions themselves thereupon becoming so rounded that there is actually a difficulty in distinguishing them from yeast cells.

I do not mean to say that these mucors take entirely to the formation of what I have styled "abortive mycelia"—indeed, the phenomenon appears to be due to unfavourable conditions, principally a limitation of the needful amount of air, which being corrected, the bud again develops mycelial threads, or erect hyphæ, which eventually terminate in the usual spore-bearing heads.

The fact, however, that budding is occasionally substi-

for us than that stated in the text, which indeed is somewhat academic. When yeast strives, as it will and as other organisms do, to get into correspondence with its environment, which may vary much within the limits offered by actual malt-wort and other fermentation conditions, it is conceivable that other physical changes may occur not obviously connected with that attempt at self-adaptation.

tuted for branching, even to such a limited extent, is a connecting link between the two vegetative modes, as they may be called to distinguish them from the mode of propagation by special reproductive arrangements.

The Two Distinct Modes of Reproduction.—As has been hinted above, the fungi, with which we have been dealing, have two distinct modes of reproduction, both analogous to those double methods met with in some more highly organised plants. Just as the potato can be propagated either from tubers or from seed, or strawberries either from runners or seed, and other plants from bulbs, which grow on to the original bulb, or from cuttings, and as a rule likewise from seed, so these lower organisms have their double method of reproduction, the one distinctly vegetative, the other by special reproductive arrangements.

The vegetative mode occurs by the formation of cell on to cell, which either separate rapidly, as in the case of yeast, or remain connected, albeit parted by septation, as in the case of moulds, and is one in which the analogy even gets closer to the vital conditions of higher organisms (*e.g.*, the potato) in that, nutritive conditions being suspended—as, for instance, when the yeast is skimmed from the wort, or the potato removed from the soil—the cell (yeast) or agglomeration of cells (potato) passes into a quiescent condition, wherein the potential vitality of the single cell, with its cell-wall thickened by protoplasm, does not yield in permanence to that of the tuber.*

The second mode, viz., that by special reproductive apparatus (organs one cannot well say without limiting the ground too much, though the process is analogous in one of its aspects to the reproductive one of higher

---

* Some readers may remember that a year or so ago some old bottled beer, brewed in the eighteenth century, was found at Messrs. Worthington's Brewery, and of which it was stated that the yeast cells in its deposit still showed signs of vitality. And it is not an unknown practice in country places, where a store of yeast is not easily got, to dip a quantity of twigs into yeast, which being carefully dried, are competent to start a fresh fermentation many months after.

SPORES. POLYMORPHIC FORMS.

organisms, and in the other has its counterpart in the parthenogenic births known to occur with certain lowly animal forms), manifests itself by the formation of **spores,** which are generally **asexual,** *i.e.*, produced without the co-operation of any external protoplasm, but which may also be, as in the case of some of the moulds, of apparently **sexual** origin, where two mycelial threads join together, the conjunction resulting in the formation of a so-called **zygospore.**

The asexual spores of moulds are known as **gonidia** or conidia, and are borne upon short branching finger-like joints known as **sterigmata,** the branching being sometimes simple, sometimes complex, but (when a microscopic specimen can be secured, which however, is difficult) forming a tassel-like head—the **sporophore**—to the hyphal ends of the mycelium.

The spores of yeast, which are endogenous and asexual, are called **ascospores,** but these will be more fully referred to in Chapter XI.

But whether the spores be sexual or asexual, they are obviously a resource for the maintenance of the species under extremely adverse conditions, being, as they are, much more resistant to hostile influences (heat, drought, etc.) than the vegetative cell ever is, and yet when favourable conditions recur, readily originating a new growth—the ascospore budding, and the gonidium or zygospore sending out a hypha in the usual way.

Polymorphism and Pleomorphy.—Before touching on the classification of the fungi, incidental to our industry, let us understand the meaning of these two terms, which, though sometimes confused, may well be kept distinct. In the classification which follows, and looking at Division I., the schizomycetes, *i.e.*, the bacteria, in the widest and popular sense of the term, we shall find that very considerable variations of shape are mentioned (*e.g.*, micrococcus, bacterium, bacillus, leptothrix, spirillum, etc.); and though these differences of shape often indicate organisms, which are far from being identical in function, and which may therefore be looked upon as individually distinct, yet it has been shown (by Zopf) that the same organism can, under certain circumstances, assume either of these forms. This variation, known as **polymorphism,** or **alternation of generation,** naturally detracts somewhat from the value of any classification on morphological lines, which, however, is the only basis open to us at present.

Polymorphism should however be distinguished from what de Bary calls the **Pleomorphic craze,** in which view, according to A. G. Salamon, an organism might begin as a yeast, then, if it chanced to be swallowed by a fly, would develop into a totally different organism, pathogenic to the fly. And again, if the fly chanced to fall into water, that the organism, totally changed once more, would become a mucor, which on being wafted into a fermentable fluid, would become a yeast again, and so on in a continuous circle.

The fungi, with which the brewer is mostly concerned, may be marshalled in three divisions—

1. The **Schizomycetes** (fission-fungi, or bacteria).
2. The **Hyphomycetes** (or moulds).
3. The **Saccharomycetes** (sprouting-fungi or yeasts).

The **Schizomycetes** multiply in two ways—viz. (1) By subdivision, which sometimes occurs in three dimensions of space, the parts which separate developing each into a fresh schizomycete; or (2) By spores formed endogenously.

[The schizomycetes are the smallest fungi known. Some are **Chromogenic,** *colour producing*, others **Pathogenic,** *disease producing*, and others **Zymogenic**, *producing fermentation*. Many of these organisms are motile forms, *i.e.*, showing a spontaneous movement, actuated, as very high microscopic powers show, by one or more hairlike appendages at either end known as a **cilium** or **flagellum.** Their interior is charged with a pasty mass of protoplasm differing in no way, as far as the present

THE SCHIZOMYCETES.

means at command enable us to judge, from that of yeast.

That this active, but apparently identical, protoplasm should in one case produce lactic acid, in another butyric, in others putrefactive ferments, and yet again, alcohol and carbonic acid, is a mystery as yet unfathomable.

Bacteria perish in pure water from lack of nutriment, which fact differentiates them from *algæ*, with which they are often confounded. Though frequently isolated, they sometimes exude a gelatinous matter which causes a number of them to adhere together in a mass. Such a colony is called a **Zoogloea,** or resting-stage.

The importance of the *rôle* they fill in breaking up complex matter into simpler forms has been dwelt on before. Many forms appear to have a **peptonising** influence; indeed, the liquefaction produced by bacterial colonies on gelatine-stiffened wort is a peptonisation.]

Various forms found amongst the schizomycetes are—

(i) **Coccus forms.** Micro- and macro-coccus, simple or compound.

[Spherical bodies, some of which, the **micrococci,** are extremely minute, even for microscopic objects, as small as 0·5 μ (see Glossary under M.), though *Micrococcus crepusculus*, the one associated with all sorts of putrefaction, is 2 μ. The macrococci are, of course, the larger spherical forms. Among compound cocci is **Tetracoccus** (four cells joined together, but in pairs), supposed to be a **Sarcina**, but hardly showing the characteristic package-like shape of other Sarcinæ. A long chain of micrococci is called a **Streptococcus.**]

(ii) Bacteria (in limited sense).

[Short rods. Amongst them are **Bacterium termo,** *the* ferment of decay; **B. lactis,** a ferment which forms lactic acid in milk and beer; **B. aceti,** which oxidises alcohol into acetic acid. The latter collectively, *i.e.*, when forming a wrinkled film, is known as **Mycoderma aceti,** and the individual organisms assume various forms, appearing both as bacteria and bacilli, in irregularly swollen forms and in curved forms. **Bacterium xylinum**, myriads of which organism constitute the gelatinous membrane known as the vinegar plant, its action being similar to that of *B. aceti*, *plus* the production of an appreciable quantity of cellulose.]

(iii) Bacilli.

[Longer rods, which grow till twice their original length, then split into two transversely, although even then the separation is not always apparent without staining;* the latter, however, makes the articulations visible.

Among the bacilli which affect the brewer injuriously are **B. subtilis,** or bacillus of hay-infusion, causing a butyric fermentation, and said to be the agent concerned in the ripening of cheese. Length 6 μ.

B. amylo-bacter, an anaerobic ferment causing butyric fermentation too, is morphologically very like *B. subtilis*, but may sometimes be distinguished from it, when it contains starch in its cell, by staining with iodine. Its size, too, is greater, length 10 μ width 2 μ. The two bacilli are also said to sporulate differently, *B. subtilis* forming its spore at the end of the rod, while *B. amylobacter* forms it at the centre.

B. ulna.—Also morphologically very like *B. subtilis* (unless it be that the cells are broader), found in putrefying white of egg infusion, and is therefore an indicator of *uncleanliness*, though apparently itself unhurtful in beer. A magnification of 3,000 diameters by Dr. Dallinger showed it to have a flagellum at each end. The plasma within appears dense and fine grained.

B. panificans.—Supposed by Laurent to act as the "leaven" of rye-bread, just as ordinary yeast (or, according to Engel, *Sacch. minor*) does for wheaten bread.]

---

* Staining is done in various ways (methods of Kock, Ehrlich, Prideaux, etc.). Koch, for instance, treats fluid from diseased tissues (tuberculosis) with strong tincture of methylene blue and potash, afterwards adding vesuvin, which discharges the blue from everything except the special bacilli (even other micrococci), which remain blue on a brown field. It has been objected that such violent treatment alters the proportions (length and breadth) of bacteria.

(iv) **Clostridium forms.**

[A bacillus enlarged in the middle or near it and drawn out towards the ends.

Bacillus amylobacter is sometimes called **Clostridium butyricum.**]

(v) **Leptothrix forms.**

[Unbranched thread-like forms which are frequently parasitic. Very similar to them (though the freely oscillating threads enveloped in a gelatinous envelope are somewhat thicker) the **Beggiatoæ**, which certainly set free sulphuretted hydrogen in sulphur-containing water, and have solid granules of sulphur within their structure.

Another noteworthy example is Leptothrix, or more generally **Crenothrix kühniana**, a tough, slimy fungus which partially clogs water-pipes (noticeable in attemperator outlets), and which, under the microscope, appears to consist of unbranched hyphal tubes, straightish or curved, visibly articulated at the base, but primed towards the apex with spores ready to escape. The spores seem to take the *coccus* shape, passing into *diplococci*, before developing into a fresh tube-like process, or sometimes they cluster together, forming a *Zooglœa*; and sometimes the spores develop new threads before leaving their original hyphal home, the threads making their way through the gelatinous sheath of the latter.]

(vi) **Cladothrix forms.**

[Quasi-branched forms, very similar to Leptothrix. High magnifying power shows the apparently ramified structure to be what is known as "false branching."]

(vii) **Spirillum (Vibrio, Spirochœta, Spirulina) forms.**

[Curved spiral. Probably an alternative form of otherwise-shaped schizomycetes. There is especially ground for supposing that **spirillum amyliferum** is only a phase of *bacillus amylobacter*, it being found in the latter's company, and apparently storing up starch (its contents, except where a spore afterwards develops, are coloured blue by iodine, *but only when growth has ceased*) within its cell-wall.

Further than this spirilla do not appear to be of particular interest to us, the *habitat* of this form of schizomycete being generally brackish or putrefying water.

(viii) **Involution forms.**

[Irregular shapes difficult to classify. *Bacterium aceti* assumes one such form, thus differentiating itself from *B. xylĭnum*, the organism of vinegar plant, which does not.]

Hyphomycetes, or Moulds.

These form a growth with which all are familiar; but the patches of them, visible to the naked eye, consist of innumerable mycelial tubes, of microscopic dimensions, intertwined in every possible way, the mass being sprinkled, as it were, with spore-bearing heads formed at the terminals of the branches.

Although, when compared with bacteria, they may be looked upon as only being in the second line of attack, they are yet of great import, not alone on account of the ill effects which they undoubtedly bring about, but also because a definite growth of mildew is generally a cover for a horde of bacteria.

The greatest field for mischief which they have in connection with brewing is that afforded by the malting floor, where, given a number of broken, "tipped," or cracked corns, mould is certain to appear, infecting a proportion even of the sound grain.

Here the degradation of nitrogen-compounds by these powerful oxidising and putrefactive agents, not to speak of that of the carbohydrates affecting profit, is greatly conducive to unsoundness of product. An indirect, but no less certain, evil is that the enormous number of spores and mycelia, however thoroughly they may be themselves destroyed during the brewing process, nevertheless afford a suitable nutriment to similar organisms finding their way into the fluid after sterilisation-influence has ceased.

A few of the more important moulds, classified as Saprophytes or Parasites (see Glossary), are:—

(a) **Saprophytic Moulds.**

(i) **Penicillium Glaucum.**—The commonest mould of all, forming masses, whitish at first but afterwards greenish-grey, upon the green malt, or in empty casks and neglected brewing vessels, and consisting of innumerable mycelia tangled together. The hyphal branches of the mycelia terminate in a number of short irregularly branched tubes which end in the so-called **sterigmata**, elongations of the tube which bear the conidia, the whole spreading out in a somewhat fan-like way. The conidia, however, do not hang on alternate sides of each sterigma, but are formed by a globular swelling-out of the sterigma at short intervals, so that the actual tube appears to pass through the centre of each conidium. One conidium forms at the tip of each sterigma, and this is actually the first to appear, the one nearest to it being next oldest, and so on.

This mould, like *Aspergillus niger*, grows well in Raulin's liquid, but better with addition of a little gypsum. It, with *Aspergillus* and with *Oïdium lactis*, are classified as Ascomycetes (see Glossary).

(ii) **Aspergillus Glaucus (Eurotium Aspergillus Glaucus)** is perhaps the next most frequent mould; it grows freely on green malt,* where it feeds on the latter's saccharine constituents, and forms a felt-like greyish mass (white, however, when young), the greyness of which is due to conidia separated and settling down as a dust of that colour.

Its conidia are borne on numerous sterigmata, shorter and spreading out more radially than those of *P. glaucum*, and forming on a hyphal tube in which elongation has extended further than usual without septation.

Also, it develops a somewhat circular-shaped ball fruit,

---

* According to Hansen, however, though *A. glaucus* was the most often found in trial flasks infected by the *air* of malting floors, it was comparatively rare on the floors themselves, where *Penicillium glaucum* was most frequent.

the **sporocarp,** supposed to be sexual (see Glossary), and interesting because of its ascospore formation, not unlike that of yeast.

(iii) **Aspergillus Niger.**—The mould referred to on p. 329 as the one studied by Raulin. As the name implies, the colour of the mildew in mass is black. It may sometimes be found on broken, damp rice, even when the latter has been subjected to heat, if sterilisation-influence has been imperfect, as when it has balled into lumps during careless gelatinisation.

(iv) **Mucor Mucedo.**—Found on decaying fruits, bread, meat, also on yeast, grains of corn and malt, but growing most freely on horse excreta. When the oval spores are placed in nutritive fluid they rapidly swell, their homogeneous protoplasm becomes granular, and crowds up to the cell-wall, leaving a large vacuole. Shoots, developing from one or more points, form a much-branched mycelium (branching without septation), from the midst of which arises a thick branch (sporophore) with a sort of elongated knob-shaped head. With the length of this knob as a radius, a round, yellow-coloured sporangium forms, and within the latter a large number of the oval spores develop. This mould also forms zygospores (p. 335).

One of its functions appears to be the secretion of calcic oxalate, but the importance of the mucors to us is that under some conditions they can act as alcoholic ferments, though to a less extent than yeast.

(v) **Mucor Racemosus.**—Found on stale food, fruits, etc., and *fæces*. It resembles *M. mucedo*, but is altogether on a smaller scale. Its sporophores throw out side branches, each terminable by a sporangium, which then appear to cluster together, whence the name (*racemosus* = clustering, *racemus* = a bunch of grapes). Its chief interest consists in a habit peculiar to itself of forming propagative buds (as well as sporangia and zygospores) within the mycelial tube (cell-wall forms and separates them off), which can bud like yeast-cells, although formed on a larger scale than the latter.

(vi) **Mucor stolonifer.**—Found in warm seasons of the year on sourish soft fruits, where it forms a woolly white growth with black-stalked heads.

(vii) **Mucor erectus.**—Habitat on decaying potatoes; said to be capable of forming 8% alcohol in beer wort.

(viii) **Fusarium hordei.**—Forming the red mildew seen on germinating barley of low quality, but apparently does not spread rapidly. Develops crescent-shaped spores, very characteristic under microscope.

(ix) **Oïdium lactis.**—A mould fungus producing lactic acid, and whose hyphæ form a thick white felt, somewhat resembling that of *Mycoderma vini*, but whiter and thicker. The hyphæ, generally in their upper portion, are transversely septated at brief intervals, so that short pieces, resembling conical cells and with granular contents, freely separate off (a connecting link between yeasts and moulds?). Sometimes found in beers of low alcoholic strength, but growing more freely on the surface of yeast or stale milk. The terminal cells (conidia) are colourless. It is suspected of being pathogenic (certain forms of skin disease). [Another oïdium, *O. albicans*, is associated with the infantile disease called "thrush." *Oïdium vini*, or *Tuckeri*, is the too-well-known scourge of vineyard proprietors.]

(x) **Monilia Candida.**—A mould occurring on ripe juicy fruits, etc., which at certain stages forms cells, closely resembling those of yeast, especially when added to wort, in which it can excite alcoholic fermentation. It also appears to have the faculty of fermenting saccharose *as saccharose*—*i.e.*, without previous inversion, it being unable to secrete invertase.

(xi) **Dematium Pullulans.**—A mould developing yeast-like cells in freely septated divisions of hyphæ. The cells show budding processes but otherwise are not of much importance, seeing that they incite no alcoholic fermentation, unless Lintner's idea that it is a factor in ropy fermentation were established.

(xii) **Aspergillus or Eurotium oryzæ.**—See "Koji" in Glossary.

(xiii) **Botrytis cinerea** (see Glossary), also a facultative parasite (*e.g.*, on snowdrop).

β. **Parasitic Moulds.**

(xiv) **Ustilago Carbo or Segetum.**—The "smut" on barley, oats, etc., where it forms black patches. Dark coloured hyphal growth, somewhat like *O. lactis* in form.

(xv) **Tilletia caries** and **lœvis.**—On wheat.

(xvi) **Fumago salicina.**—On hops.

(xvii) **Sphœrotheca castagnei.**—On hops.

Saccharomycetes.—[Fungi which propagate by budding, and also, under less favourable conditions, forming spores. They generally act as degraders of saccharine bodies into alcohol, etc., or affect the alcoholic product favourably or unfavourably. Amongst them are—

(i) **Sacch. Cerevisiæ.**—The real alcoholic ferment; now supposed incapable of acting except as a primary ferment—*i.e.*, to be unable to effect degradation of malto-dextrins, on which cask conditioning depends. Average diameter 8 μ.

Three sub-types at least have been isolated. See p. 370.

(ii) **Sacch. Pastorianus** [Reess].—Cells of elongated form, some very much so. Found in bottle deposits of even sound ale. Suggested as the ferment which breaks up malto-dextrins, reducing them first into lower and lower types, and finally into maltose, in which form *Sacch. cerevisiæ* can deal with them.

Three sub-types isolated, one of which causes a strong, harsh bitter, another turbidity. See pp. 400, 401.

(iii) **Sacch. Ellipsoideus** [Reess].—Otherwise *Sacch. ellipticus*. The yeast of wine. Cells about 6 μ long and elliptic in shape. A sub-variety, *Sacch. ellipsoideus II.*, is supposed to cause turbidity.

(iv) **Caseous Yeast.**—A form described by Pasteur, resembling ordinary high yeast, except in its tendency to agglomerate in a curdy mass. In water, he says, it falls at once to the bottom like a curdy precipitate, and the supernatant water is scarcely dimmed by the few suspended globules. He thinks it can survive a heating (in bottle) of 122° Fahr., which suffices to kill the pure high yeast left in the alcoholic fluid. Length of long axis about 10 μ.

(v) **Sacch. Coagulatus**, otherwise **Caseous Yeast No. 2** (Matthews).—Apparently an agglomerating variety, distinct from (iv), observed and named by Mr. C. G. Matthews, and said to have an activity hardly inferior to that of *Sacch. Cerevisiæ* at 60° to 70° Fahr. and greater above 70 Fahr. Further it is said to take up little or no resin from the worts, and consequently to produce a beer with a marked resin bitter. The beer has also a high ratio of acidity, and is stubborn in brightening. The average diameter of cells is given as 5 to 6 μ.

(vi) **Sacch. Conglomeratus** [Reess].—Cells united in clusters, produced by budding from one or more parent cells. In wine-must and decaying grapes. Diameter 5 to 6 μ.

(vii) **Sacch. Exiguus** [Reess].—In after fermentation of beer and said to cause turbidity, floating, as it does, on account of its low specific gravity. According to Hansen it cannot ferment maltose, and therefore only yields about 1% alcohol in beer wort, but excites vigorous fermentation in solutions containing saccharose (which it inverts) and dextrose. Cells about 5 μ × 2·5 μ.

(viii) **Sacch. Minor** [Engel].—Said to be the active factor in the fermentation of bread. Diameter 6 μ; of another kind, according to Matthews and Lott, 3 to 4 μ.

(ix) **Sacch. Apiculatus.**—A ferment occurring freely in wine-yeast, on succulent fruits and sometimes in spontaneously fermented (Belgian) beer. The cells are lemon-shaped as a rule, but decidedly smaller than *Sacch. Cerevisiæ* (4·5 to 7 μ long × 2 to 3 μ wide). Its power of dealing with maltose or saccharose is *nil*, hence in beer wort it does not produce more than 1% by volume of alcohol. In dextrose-solutions it excites vigorous fermentation. Its chief interest to us lies first in the fact that it became the object early employed in Hansen's brilliant inductions, for which its typical shape adapted it, and again, which may seem contradictory but is not, in the great variety of forms it can assume, (oval, sausage-shaped, bacterium-like ?) in addition to its typical one.

(x) **Sacch. Mycoderma** or **Mycoderma vini** (or *M. cerevisiæ*).—The organism whose cells densely crowded together form the greyish, wrinkled, greasy-looking film on exposed beer or wort. The cells are sometimes like those of *Sacch. Pastorianus* (elongated with one or two large vacuoles), but more translucent, and by close observation minute granular bodies may usually be seen moving about, apparently in the fluid contents of the vacuole. It has been classed among the Saccharomycetes, because, according to Pasteur, although naturally aërobian, it is capable, when submerged, of acting as a somewhat feeble alcoholic ferment. According to Hansen, however, this is not so. This is the organism which may sometimes be seen in bottled ales of light gravity, forming a filmy growth just at and above the level of the liquid. [Those troubled in this way should note Pasteur's advice, p. 437.]

There are sundry other sorts of so-called Saccharomyces, *e.g.*, **S. Marxianus, S. Membranæfaciens, S. Coprogenus, S. glutinis**, etc., which are of little or no practical interest —even stretching that expression to its widest extent—as far as brewers are concerned.

The Microscope—Selection and Management.—Seeing that all the organisms, whose changing aspects form the subject matter of this chapter hitherto, are only to be studied by aid of a microscope, it appears that a few pages may be profitably devoted to that instrument. And though the chapter headed "The Brewing Room" might seem the appropriate place for those hints, that apartment, in consequence of rarely ceasing vibration, is so seldom adapted, without special precautions, for microscopic work, that they come in quite as fittingly here.

The good qualities of a microscope are partly **mechanical,** partly **optical.**

The mechanical qualities consist in stability and smooth movement of the working parts, with just that amount of rigidity which ensures the maintenance of a focus once obtained.

The optical good qualities are (1) Freedom from chromatic and spherical aberration. (2) A fairly large and well-illuminated "field." (3) Good definition. (4) Good penetration. (5) Resolving power. (6) Flatness of field.

The mechanical qualities explain themselves. As to the optical, **Chromatic aberration** means the tendency to split up a compound ray of white light into its component coloured rays, so that the object under observation appears fringed with colour. The correction of this tendency in objectives and eyepieces will be referred to again, but it may be mentioned incidentally that perfect achromatism, *i.e.*, the avoidance of any coloration with every object and when used with *oblique* light, is sometimes attained at the expense of definition.

Spherical aberration, also due to imperfect correction, or to the lenses not being ground in true spherical form, is evidenced by putting under the objective a glass slide on which are drawn a number of fine lines, crossing one another at right-angles, whereupon the lines, especially at the edges of the "field," will appear curved, either towards one another at top and bottom or the reverse (in the former case like the lines of longitude on the map of a hemisphere).

Fair size of the field (other things being equal) and **good illumination** of every part are obvious advantages, and only need be insisted on because some makers endeavour, by reducing the diameter of the optical tube, or by fixing in the objective with a rim of metal (a continental practice, as opposed to the English maker's method of fixing with Canada balsam), to give a factitious quality to their objectives, which the contraction of the field (the outer portion, which is generally most defective, being cut off') enables them to do. [The size of the field should however not be so great as to fatigue the eye, *i.e.*, the eye must be able to take in every part of it at one time.]

Good definition is perhaps the most important point of all; it means clearness of detail, in other words, absence of mistiness.

Penetration is the power of giving a good idea of an object (or a fluid) possessing appreciable depth, without alteration of the focussing adjustment; thus a microscope giving at the same time a *clear* view of yeast and bacteria (which, extremely thin as is the pressed-out droplet of liquid in which a mixture of them would be examined, float, generally speaking, at different levels) would have a penetrative power not easily obtained.

Resolving power.—This is the power of resolving or separating the component parts of minute objects, striations, close lines, etc., instead of fusing them into an apparently entire surface, and accordingly is akin to good definition, except that it largely depends on a wide angular aperture (and is thus a somewhat antagonistic property to penetration, which is characteristic of medium angular aperture), whereas definition seems to depend on a proper balance of constructive precautions.

Flatness of field is, practically, absence of spherical aberration; and though absolute flatness is rarely to be got in objectives over $\frac{1}{4}$ inch, the more closely they approximate thereto the better.

The angle of aperture is strictly that angle formed with the focus as one point and the two opposite extremes of that part of the objective which is used in the magnification* as the other two points—*i.e.*, the angle within which rays of light can pass from any part of the object, which is in focus, into the objective; but practically it is measured in the following manner.

A semicircle of wood, marked at the circumference with the angular degrees (180°), and technically known as a

* Therefore if the outer defective portion of the field be cut off, as has been stated to be the case sometimes, the angular aperture is reduced.

ANGLE OF APERTURE.

Protractor, is used. On it is a flat, narrowish piece of wood moving freely on a pivot fixed in the centre of the straight side of the semicircle. This piece of wood has two uprights, deeply grooved at top to receive the tube of the microscope placed horizontally, and the end furthest away from the pivot, in its circular movement, just touches the line outside of which the angles are marked off. The microscope tube, detached from its stand, is then placed in position, lying down upon these grooved uprights, and exactly in a line with it (at a distance of some 8 feet from the objective end) is a lighted candle.

On looking now through the tube, the field of course appears perfectly illuminated, but if the wooden support be now rotated on its pivot, either to right or left, the illumination will gradually vanish. This is accordingly what is done. The eyepiece end of the tube is rotated, say first to the right, until a thin *crescent* of light alone remains, and then similarly to the left.

The number of angles passed over from right to left is then noted and taken as the angular aperture, though in reality the angle through which image-forming rays pass is often not more than two-thirds of the tabulated angle, especially when the aperture is high. This can be got as high as 170°, and when it is remembered that 180° equals two right angles (so that two rays proceeding from a common point and 180° from each other would be in the same straight line, and therefore could not possibly pass through the same lens) the difficulty of getting beyond this will be seen.

But, as has been said before, penetration, with which wide angular aperture is inconsistent, is of importance in a brewer's microscope.

Magnifying power depends primarily upon the **Objective**, which is a combination of lenses, forming one whole, which is screwed into the bottom of the tube (closest to the object), " the nose " of the microscope; and secondarily, upon the **Eyepiece**, used in conjunction with it, the A eyepiece giving less magnification but a wider field than the B eyepiece with the same objective, while the C is more powerful than B.

A and B are the eyepieces most frequently used, "deeper" eyepieces, except with objectives of very wide angular aperture, losing in illumination and definition more than they gain by amplification. Hence it is a good, though severe test of the excellence of a microscope to look at some test object (*e.g.* the Podura scale *) with an objective and a shallow eyepiece, and then again after replacing the latter by a "deeper" eyepiece. If there is no appreciable loss of definition, the instrument has come triumphantly through the ordeal.

Objectives, or object-glasses, are classified according to their powers, and the names $\frac{1}{5}$, $\frac{1}{4}$, $\frac{1}{10}$ (inch), etc., approximate to their focal distance; and the shorter the latter is, the greater the magnifying power. Thus—

Low powers are: The inch, the two-thirds inch, and any of greater focal distance.
Medium powers are: The half-inch, four-tenths, quarter-inch, and fifth.
High powers are: All of shorter focal distance than one-fifth, *e.g.*, $\frac{1}{6}$th, $\frac{1}{8}$th, $\frac{1}{10}$th, $\frac{1}{12}$th inch, etc.

Approximate magnifying power of certain combinations—

$\frac{2}{3}$ inch about 60 diameters with A and 90 with B eyepiece.
$\frac{1}{5}$,, 250 ,, ,, A ,, 400 ,, B ,,
$\frac{1}{10}$,, 400 ,, ,, A ,, 600 ,, B ,,

Magnifications of 1000 and 1200 (expressed × 1000, × 1200 when the magnified object is sketched) and even more are obtainable, but necessitate very high-class instruments.

[The **Immersion Principle** is adopted with some of the highest powers—*i.e.*, a drop of water is interposed between the lower lens of the objective and the object or its cover glass. Less light is lost thereby because some of the

* The scale of an insect found in timber-stacks. But the slide should be procured from one of the few *practical* microscope makers.

oblique rays of light, instead of passing onwards in the same line of obliquity, are, in accordance with a well-known optical principle (because passing from a rarer medium, air, into a denser medium, water), deflected from their course, and travel upwards in a more or less parallel direction. This system is not, however, adopted to any extent, if at all, by English makers, who rely upon superior methods of illumination.]

High power objectives have their definition much affected, according to the thickness of the cover-glass usually interposed between them and the object, and accordingly most of them have a screw-collar, by rotating which the necessary correction can be made; but Mr. Crouch gets over this necessity in his brewer's cheap microscope by adjusting his objective (a $\frac{1}{10}$th) to one particular thickness of cover-glass, which he supplies in small squares.

Each objective consists of three pairs of lenses, each formed of a double convex of crown-glass and a plano-concave of flint-glass (sometimes even of eight lenses), this arrangement being necessary to cure chromatic aberration, and the eyepieces, also corrected, consist of two plano-convex lenses with their convexity downwards.

The eyepieces should further be inspected for **scratches** on the surface of either lens, or for minute **air-bubbles**, technically known as "seeds," imprisoned in joining the lenses.

To detect these, screw on a medium or moderately high power objective, and let subdued light through from the mirror. If this be properly done, these and adventitious specks may be located by turning the eyepiece round, then by unscrewing the top lens and turning it round alone first, and afterwards the bottom part. The specks, etc., will of course move with the part on which they are.

Compound microscopes are either **Monocular** or **Binocular** (with two eyepieces), the latter, although the most comfortable for general work, not being adapted for use with the high powers which the study of yeast and bacteria requires, and which, for even moderate ambition, should reach a combination × 600, though undoubtedly for yeast alone a distinct magnification of 200 to 300 diameters is better to work with than a hazy one of 600.

Other parts of the microscope include **the Stand**, with its base in tripod form, the two front feet having a good wide spread, and the hinder one (near the observer) being U shaped and with a broad bearing, widely curved, at bottom, to secure steadiness, if the tube is to be pulled down into a horizontal position. There are variations in form, some microscopes having, for instance, a wooden stand, but the above arrangement in iron is as workmanlike as any.

The Tube is that portion of the instrument into which the objective is screwed below, and the eyepiece slipped above. The extreme length between these points should not exceed $8\frac{1}{2}$ inches, and for brewer's work one of less length, but with a draw-tube (like that of a telescope) enabling it to be lengthened if desired—this increasing magnification—is useful.

The tube is connected with the tripod part of the stand by " a limb," which works upon pivots or trunnions at the apex of the tripod, and can be moved through an angle of 90°, or more, and so stand vertically or horizontally.

Beneath the tube is the **stage,** on which the object to be examined is placed, and there is generally, as part of it, a smoothly moving object-holder, which can be made to slide either by two small projecting brass handles, or, as in the more highly finished microscopes, is made in two parts and fitted with two milled heads, one of which moves the upper portion (of the object-holder) from right to left and back again, the other moving the whole object holder, virtually the greater part of the stage, at right angles thereto.

Underneath the stage is sometimes a **substage** in which the **Diaphragm** is placed. The important part of this is a round blackened plate pierced with circles of different diameter for regulating the admission of light to the

FOCUSSING. THE MIRROR.

object, but better for high powers is the **Achromatic Condenser,** which in its simplest expression is a planoconvex lens, with the convexity undermost, rimmed with brass to enable it to be fitted to the stage or substage, and covered with a removable cap pierced with a small round hole. This arrangement not only concentrates upon the object the rays of light thrown upwards by the **Mirror** beneath (which should be of at least two inches diameter, and moving on trunnions, as well as on a crank-arm fixed to "the limb"), but cuts off peripheral rays of the pencil.

The focus is got by means of the **coarse** and **fine adjustments,** both milled heads (the former generally actuating a rack and pinion, though a draw-up arrangement instead is practicable and cheaper), the coarse adjustment serving to get the approximate focus, the fine adjustment (one *turn* of which only moves the objective upon which it acts $\frac{1}{1000}$ inch) being finally used to get a sharp definition.

It is more convenient to have the light, especially when a lamp is used, on the observer's left hand than upon his right, as his right hand will be wanted, more or less, for moving the slide and the adjustments, and so might intercept some of the illumination.

It is impossible to lay down any short general rule for tne position of the mirror with reference to the object, the path of the reflected rays depending not only on the direction whence they come before impinging on the mirror, but also upon the concavity of the latter or its absence. The mirror will accordingly be moved about until ample light to view the object is obtained.

Direct sunlight, falling on the mirror, is not to be recommended, for it often causes the object to appear fringed with a prismatic ring of colour. Sunlight reflected from a white wall or from a white cloud is the best natural illuminant. Microscopists, however, generally prefer artificial light, and to fulfil their requirements special lamps, burning mineral oil (which must be of the best), are constructed, the wick portion of which is easily raised or lowered, and which have a chimney for cutting off all light except in the required direction.

Great cleanliness is necessary, and the microscope must be kept out of the damp. It is more convenient to have one which can be taken out of its box ready for use, without screwing the parts together; if, however, the microscope is one which must be taken apart before it will go into the case, it is better not to use the latter habitually, but to have the instrument ready for action and protected by a glass shade. Be careful to wipe off all dust, and to use the cleanest and softest (old) handkerchief that can be got for finishing the wiping of lenses, cover glasses, etc.

To protect it from the vibrations of the brewery, Messrs. Matthews & Lott recommend that the feet of the table on which it is wont to stand should rest on four thick india-rubber pads.

The most perfect way of keeping a supply of clean glass slides and covers, especially the latter, is to wash them after use in dilute nitric acid, rinsing two or three times afterwards with fresh distilled water, and then to drop them into a stoppered wide-mouthed bottle of alcohol. From this they can be removed as required by aid of a clean pair of forceps, and carefully wiped.

Or they may be put away, ready wiped, in a receptacle made of wash-leather and having divisions, each of which takes one glass. But practically it is generally enough to wash with some friction under a hot water tap, letting the moderately hot water run on long enough to rinse the glass thoroughly.

To examine yeast, etc., it should be diluted freely with water (tap water of good quality will do) till the fluid has a milky, or rather "sky-blue" appearance, because the details of crowded fields cannot be well observed. Put the smallest possible drop upon a clean glass slide, and for this the best thing is a short bit of platinum wire fixed into a handle of glass tubing (this is done by causing the end of the tube to contract upon the wire by the heat of a gas flame), and with its (the wire's) end bent into a fine hook. The platinum hook can be thoroughly rinsed in a stream of hot water before use, without causing any tendency to rust, or may be sterilised by heating to redness in the flame of a Bunsen. Over the droplet so placed upon the glass slide one of the clean thin glass covers is gently put, so that the liquid spreads evenly, without intermixture of air-bubbles, nearly to the edge of the glass cover. For moulds, alcohol is a better medium than water.

The only thing remaining to caution the novice about is to be careful not to ram down the objective on to the object, which might result in a breakage of the slide and even injury to the objective. The best plan is to get the objective down *within* the focal distance, first, by means of the coarse adjustment, looking while doing so, not through the tube, but at the objective and object themselves, and then focussing upwards—*i.e.*, away from the object.

Possibly, however, he may be puzzled by a sort of to-and-fro movement of apparent particles; but this is merely optical, and will cease to trouble him with practice.

There is also the so-called **Brownian movement**—that is, an apparent vibratory or dancing movement of inanimate, but real particles, which might lead to a hasty inference of the presence of vibriones. The movement is, however, different, and the simplest way of getting an idea of it is to rub a trace of the water-colour pigment, known as gamboge, upon a slide, diluting slightly with water, and after putting on the glass cover, inspecting in the usual way.

Without making invidious distinctions, it is right to name two makers who have successfully endeavoured to satisfy the demand for a trustworthy microscope at a moderate cost. These (naming them in the order of acquaintance) are Mr. Crouch of the Barbican, several of whose microscopes have come under the writer's observation, and Messrs. James Swift & Son, at whose establishment (81, Tottenham Court Road) visitors are not only certain to have all their questions courteously answered, but may have the opportunity of seeing the various lenses in process of manufacture before purchasing.

CHAPTER X.

FERMENTATION WITH COMMERCIAL YEAST— ITS SCIENCE AND PRACTICE.

Liebig and Pasteur—Conflicting Theories—Prof. Huxley's Simile — Traube's Hypothesis — Brefeld's Researches — Adolf Mayer's—Yeast Reacting on its own Tissues—Nägeli's Theory—Dumas—Bourquelot and "Selective Fermentation"—By-products (Glycerine and Succinic Acid)—Inevitable Contamination of Industrial Yeast—Number of Aërial Spores Varies—High and Low Yeast—Three Varieties of the Former—Microscopic Appearance of the Cells—Ordeals which Yeast can Survive—Analysis of High Yeast—Effect of Aëration—Alcohol Percentage and Maximum Density of Wort—Heat Generated—Concurrent Action of Disease Ferments—Attenuation—Heads—Foxy Smell—Sluggish Fermentations—Fiery Fermentations—Baker's Yeast.

We shall not attempt to peer into the mists of antiquity in the hope of discerning the birth of the primitive yeast-cell, or even do more than mention the respected names of Leuwenhoek, Willis, Stahl, and Schülze. Their researches, important as they were, have now merely an historical interest.

Rather more than thirty years ago, **Pasteur** began his epoch-making publications, and proved that certain forgotten discoveries (particularly those of Cagniard-Latour and Schwann) were based on facts, and that yeast is not a dead mass, as Liebig (to select a great name) supposed, but that it consists of living and multiplying organisms, that yeast germs (spores, as such, were of course unknown till later) occur in the air, and that fermentation is bound up with the presence, the reproduction, and the nutrition of these organisms.

Then the battle raged. **Liebig** had enunciated as early as 1839, with all the weight of his authority, his theory that yeast was a lifeless albuminous body, the molecules of which, being altered in composition by oxidation, imparted a similar disturbance of equilibrium to the adjoining sugar molecule, causing it, in consequence, to break up into alcohol and carbonic acid.

Pasteur, on the other hand, maintained that yeast, like all living things, takes oxygen from the air, giving out a corresponding quantity of carbon dioxide, and that accordingly no fermentation is induced in the presence of *free* oxygen. But if access of free oxygen were prevented, the yeast, he said, would take the required oxygen from the oxygen-containing compounds (*e.g.*, sugar), whereupon equilibrium being destroyed, the sugar splits up into alcohol and carbonic acid, by-products being formed in the shape of succinic acid and glycerine. He accordingly constructed the definition **"Fermentation is life without air."**

Professor Huxley illustrated the difference of these opinions by the simile of a card-house, to which he likens the sugar, comparing the yeast to a child coming near the card-house. "Liebig's hypothesis is," he says, "that the child comes by, shakes the table and tumbles the house down," while that of Pasteur is that "the child pulls out the bottom card, and thus tumbles the house down."

Liebig would never entirely give up his mechanical theory, though forced to own that yeast is no lifeless mass; the most he would do in the way of concession was to suggest that an enzyme (like invertase) was secreted, or perhaps excreted, from the yeast capable of splitting up glucose into the products of fermentation.

The chemical hypothesis was supported by **Traube,** whose views deserve to be cited as an example of perverted ingenuity in its main contention, though in details there

TRAUBE'S VIEW. BREFELD'S RESEARCHES.

may be fact to support them. He contended, first of all, that the ferment itself is a chemical compound, which cannot be separated from the yeast-organism without loss of activity (consequently not an enzyme), and that its action was as follows: Sugar consists, he said, of two complex atoms, a reducible (A) and an oxidisable (B). The ferment in the yeast takes oxygen from the group A, and conveys it to group B, whence arises on one side alcohol, on the other carbonic acid. And seeing that the oxygen-conveyer (the ferment) never became saturated, but by surrender of the oxygen taken up was constantly qualified again for fresh reduction, so it was clear that a small quantity of ferment could split up a very large quantity of sugar.

Traube later on modified this view so far as to assign to the water of the fermenting fluid a part in the fermentation, contending that by the affinity of the ferment for oxygen on the one hand, and of the atom-group A for hydrogen on the other, the water was first of all decomposed, then that its hydrogen was taken up by the atom-group A, while its oxygen was taken up by the ferment and conveyed to the atom-group B. The atom-group A was thereupon transformed into alcohol, the atom-group B into carbonic acid.

This extremely fanciful view is ingenious but further removed from demonstration than when enunciated. It takes no account of the by-products formed in every alcoholic fermentation, in greater or less quantity. Nevertheless, we, who have seen the resuscitation of many ideas once consigned to the limbo of neglect, may hesitate before branding this as nonsense.

Traube traversed Pasteur's view that the sugar serves as a source of oxygen for the yeast, maintaining as the result of experiments so late as 1874, that the albuminous bodies of the fermenting fluid have to supply that requirement, when air is excluded.

Brefeld was the next, whose investigations claim notice, with his experiments aimed at Pasteur's statement that yeast can grow even without free oxygen. He hermetically sealed up a fermenting fluid sown with two or three yeast cells (say a droplet of fermenting beer-wort) in small lenticular-shaped glass chambers, with almost air-free carbonic acid gas, and then followed the growth of the yeast-cells microscopically. He found that growth of the cells only lasted for two days with the temperature at 13° to 14° C. (= 55·4° — 57·2° Fahr.), their appearance at the end of fourteen days being completely that of dead cells.

Relying upon his experiments, Brefeld thought himself (1874) justified in concluding, in opposition to Pasteur and Traube, that yeast cannot grow without free oxygen, and that Pasteur's theory (that yeast, unlike all living organisms, can live and grow without other oxygen than the *combined* oxygen of the sugar) was completely without foundation in fact.

Brefeld further asserts, on the strength of other experiments, that the yeast growing in a fermentable fluid and having a constant supply of free oxygen, cannot cause fermentation. In this he is in practical agreement with Pasteur, as will appear later on; he differs, however, in holding fermentation of sugar by yeast to be the expression of incomplete co-operation of all the conditions necessary to maintain the growth of the cells—in other words, that "Fermentation is a pathological phenomenon, which begins at the moment when the yeast in the unexhausted nutritive fluid can grow no longer, and which stops with the death of the yeast-cell."

Brefeld's standpoint, accordingly, was that the growth of yeast and fermentation are two separate processes. In breweries, according to his position then, both stages go on side by side in different parts of the fermenting wort. On the surface, where the oxygen of the air has access, the yeast grows without being able to cause fermentation; in the lower depths, on the contrary, where all quasi-free oxygen has been consumed by the yeast, *fermentation* occurs. Then the yeast absorbs sugar (maltose or glucose) out of proportion to other nutritive bodies, and splits it up into alcohol, carbonic acid, and other products. This abnormal life-process, Brefeld said, will last for weeks, the vitality of the yeast getting less and less, and finally the fermentation dies away, even though the supply of sugar outlasts the vitality of the yeast.*

The practical outcome of Brefeld's conclusions, supposing them to be accepted, is that air must be allowed access to promote the multiplication of the yeast, while exclusion of the air and consumption of such oxygen as has been already admitted, seems necessary for fermentation, as such, to start. The aëration of the wort should then take place once and thoroughly for the yeast to gain strength and multiply, whereby it is eventually able to decompose a larger quantity of sugar; but a further introduction of air would be not only undesirable, but even injurious.

A natural corollary of Brefeld's views as to fermentation being the expression of an arrested development is that he inclines to Liebig's opinion, holding that the nitrogenous substances exuding from the yeast-cells during fermentation (an emission whereby, he says, the yeast becomes poorer in nitrogen as fermentation is prolonged †) are, in all probability, the actual exciters of fermentation, and that fermentation is therefore a purely *chemical process*.

Adolf Mayer now turned his attention to the matter, and repeated Brefeld's experiments in the glass chambers, at one time enclosing carbonic acid, at another hydrogen, in order to determine the possibility of an injurious influence due to carbonic acid, so poisonous to some other

* Such a residue of undegraded sugar in a malt-wort would be explained by the advocates of the malto-dextrin (amylöin) theory, with great probability, as being due to the fact that it originally existed, and still exists, not as free maltose, but as the definite compound (though the type may vary) malto-dextrin, which is, until degraded by some other agent, obdurate to the attack of primary yeast (see pp. 295-299).

† This statement is hardly borne out by Hayduck's experiments, to be mentioned later.

forms of life; he worked, however, with larger quantities of fermentable fluid (4 litres of beer-wort), and with most careful exclusion of air. He found no marked difference of appearance, whether carbonic acid or hydrogen had been introduced before the closure of the vessel. It further appeared that, in the majority of cases, budding of the yeast-cells occurred in spite of the most careful exclusion of atmospheric oxygen, but that the growth died away always on the second or third day, before the sugar of the nutritive solution was exhausted.

Further, the majority of the samples, totally freed from oxygen as they were, showed cloudiness and yeast deposit, a fact which pointed to growth and multiplication of the yeast.

Mayer accordingly confirmed Brefeld's experimental results to the extent of allowing that the growth of yeast is hindered by exclusion of oxygen, but did not think himself justified in concluding that absolutely no growth of the cell occurs when oxygen is excluded.

He also draws attention to the discovery made during his researches that the lactic bacteria entering in very small quantity (in company with the yeast) into fermentable fluids, multiply very vigorously in spite of the exclusion of oxygen; therefore Brefeld's strongly enunciated law that "*all* organisms must breathe free oxygen" cannot claim to be universal.

Brefeld's second assertion, that growing yeast, with an ample supply of air, causes no fermentation, was tested by Mayer, and this investigator found that very considerable quantities of air can be introduced into fluids containing budding yeast without stopping the yeast-fungus from acting as a ferment. "This much," he says, "is at any rate established, that under certain conditions of oxygen-introduction simultaneous fermentation and growth *can* occur, and that, not in the intermittent way imagined by Brefeld (viz., that here one cell which finds itself favourably situated with regard to oxygen will grow, and that there another, lying at the bottom, will act as a ferment), but that the selfsame cell will simultaneously grow and excite fermentation. He considers that the existence of a stage, intermediate between the two states, which Brefeld hypothetically argued for, is demonstrated, and that this stage, in which yeast simultaneously grows and ferments, appears to be a very wide one.

Pasteur again returned to the charge, and by use of a large flask, containing a fermentable fluid, and from which oxygen was rigorously excluded (entire absence of free oxygen was shown by there being not the faintest blue coloration of indigo carmine, reduced with sodic bisulphite), proved, on very slightly impregnating the contents of the flask with yeast, that fermentation can occur in the absence of free (*i.e.*, not combined in sugar) oxygen, the extraordinarily small quantity of the ferment developing immediately, and the fermentation continuing to completion, although somewhat more slowly than when air was admitted.

And, finally, Brefeld renewing his experiments with yeast (from wine) and with the *gonidia* of *Mucor Racemosus*, in a solution prepared from the purest inverted sugar-candy, ammonia salts, and mineral constituents derived from cigar ash, air being rigorously excluded, satisfied himself that his former contention was incorrect, and that Pasteur's statement, that the growth of yeast cells in a medium free from oxygen was due to the oxygen of the sugar, had been verified. The results also, as far as they went, knocked the bottom out of Traube's theory (that the oxygen demanded by the yeast in a medium where no atmospheric oxygen was present would be wrested from albuminoids and not from sugar), seeing that there were no albuminoids admitted into Brefeld's solution.

Brefeld was still disinclined to acknowledge absolute uniformity; he still distinguishes between (1) Fermentation with growth; (2) Fermentation without growth or loss of substance; and (3) Fermentation with loss of substance to the point of extinction. And many will admit the possibility of these processes going on contemporaneously.

A curious fermentation-phenomenon, observed by M. Pasteur, throws some light upon the way in which the latter process may occur, though of course his experiment —equally with all the others—was not on actual brewing lines.

·424 gramme of pure sugar-candy was set to ferment with an amount of damp yeast = 10 grammes of dry yeast, and this mixture furnished by the end of two days 300 cc. of CO_2, whereas the sugar alone would only be capable of yielding 110 cc. of the gas. The liquid then, being carefully distilled, gave rather over ·6 gramme of absolute alcohol, or a weight of alcohol greater than the total weight of the sugar employed and proportionate to the volume CO_2 formed. Whence came this?

This experiment shows that very large excess of yeast mixed with sugar will first decompose the latter, and then go on reacting energetically on its own tissues and carbonated constituents. And it was found upon stopping the fermentation at a moment when the CO_2 formed corresponded to, or was but little in excess of that corresponding to the amount of sugar employed, that *all the sugar had disappeared.* This is a point of some importance, as tending to show that as long as a fermentable sugar-body is present, the ferment will not begin to consume its own tissues, although there is reason to suppose that the soluble nitrogenous matter,* of which yeast contains considerable quantities, is utilised to form fresh protoplasm for new cells, otherwise how could cell-multiplication in a pure sugar solution be possible?

What is the reason why yeast, mixed with a feeble

* Fresh yeast, dried at 212° Fahr., shows a loss upon being washed, which may be estimated at about 23%, calculated on its weight when dried. Yeast, which has been softened by being kept in a warm place, say at 80° Fahr., for two days, will show a loss of weight = over 50% calculated similarly. [100 grammes fresh yeast dried at 212° then weighs 30 grammes, after the washing 23 grammes: the softened yeast weighs after washing 14 grammes. Schützenberger.]

proportion of sugar, after it has decomposed the latter, proceeds to act with such energy upon its own tissues when, as far as we know, no such action takes place with the brewer's "store-yeast," which is generally kept—often in considerable bulk—for three or four days after collection? Can it be that in the former case a molecular vibration is set up, which does not immediately subside at the point when the sugar is all decomposed? If this could be proved it would furnish an argument for the last general theory of fermentation—apart from that which is, in the main, Pasteur's—to be mentioned in this chapter.

Nägeli's Fermentation Theory.—As Liebig's was the **chemical theory,** and Pasteur's is the **vitalistic theory,** so Nägeli's may be called the **molecular** or perhaps the **catalytic theory.** According to his view, the action of the yeast-cell is due to the molecular vibration of the protoplasm which it contains: further, in consequence of this molecular action, the decomposition of the sugar takes place outside the cell, and not inside, as Pasteur's theory requires. The action is supposed to extend to a minute but (having regard to the extreme smallness of the objects we are speaking of) sensible distance from the cell.

Dr. Squire, in a lecture referred to in another chapter, pointed out that the formation of acetic ether, which contributes to the scent of fermenting wort, and which occurs, as far as we can see, by the combined action of the alcoholic and acetic ferments, tells strongly for Nägeli's view, because we know that "acetic ether is produced when alcohol and acetic acid are brought together in the nascent state. Now if acetic acid be formed *inside* the acetic-ferment cell, and the alcohol produced *inside* the yeast-cell, no acetic ether could be produced, but if a zone of molecular vibration, in which the work is done, surrounds each cell, it is clear that, whenever these zones cut one another, acetic ether would be produced.

Further, **Nägeli's** theory also explains—what is not easily explicable otherwise—the suppression of one ferment, present in small quantity, by another ferment, present in large quantity. More powerful vibrations tend to suppress less powerful vibrations, which are not in unison with them; and if we suppose each ferment to have a peculiar vibration of its own, by which it sets up a specific decomposition in the surrounding medium, we can easily understand how the predominating vibrations tend to suppress the rest."

However, the following facts demonstrated by Dumas, though prior, I believe, to the publication of Nägeli's hypothesis, especially the first, rather militate against that view. The third aims at the chemical theory.

(1) That saccharine liquids are not influenced by a ferment, even through the shortest columns of liquid or *the thinnest membranes*. (2) That sonorous vibrations have no influence on the movements of fermentation. (3) That no chemical action amongst the great number of those which have been tried has been able to effect decomposition of sugar into alcohol and carbon dioxide.

Again, Bourquelot's experiments on **"Selective Fermentation,"** if their results could be shown to be constant for every species of yeast, would go far to prove that the decomposition of the sugar takes place within the yeast-cell, as Pasteur said, and not outside of it, as Nägeli maintained. For he claims to have established that the rate with which any fermentable sugar is decomposed stands in a close ratio to its diffusibility through membranes (*i.e.*, by dialysis), *i.e.*, that dextrose is more rapidly fermented away than levulose, and levulose than maltose, their diffusibility standing in the same order.

The By-products of Fermentation (Glycerin and Succinic Acid).—The French chemist, Gay-Lussac, formulated an equation to explain the fermentation of cane-sugar, which, reconstructed by MM. Dumas and Boully, stood—

$$C_{12}H_{22}O_{11} + H_2O = 4(C_2H_6O) + 4(CO_2).$$
Cane-sugar and Water.   Alcohol.   Carbon Dioxide.

According to which, taking the equivalent weights of each multiplied by the factor 4 (viz., 4 (24 + 6 + 16) = 184, and 4 $(12 + 32) = 176$), alcohol and carbon-dioxide are formed in the proportions of 184 parts of the former to 176 of the latter, or expressing them as a percentage, 51·11 of alcohol to 48·89 of carbon dioxide.

And although Dubrunfaut discovered, shortly after, the impossibility of making the equation of fermentation with alcohol and carbonic acid gas alone, it was left for M. Pasteur to prove that about 5% of the fermentable sugar was diverted into the formation of by-products and of tissue for the newly formed yeast (say 4% for the by-products, and 1% for the yeast).

His conclusions, summarised by Schützenberger, and a further development of them, are as follows:—

Pasteur endeavours to represent by an equation the decomposition of the 4 parts of sugar which yield succinic acid and glycerine. This expression is very complex.

$$49\,(C_{12}H_{22}O_{11} + H_2O), \text{ or,}$$
$$49\,(C_{12}H_{24}O_{12}) + 60\,H_2O = 24\,(C_4H_6O_4) + 144\,(C_3H_8O_3) + 60\,CO_2.$$
$$\text{Succinic Acid.} \quad \text{Glycerine.} \quad \text{Carbon dioxide.}$$

This equation can only be considered, as Pasteur himself says, as a very approximate expression of the numerical results of the analysis, and not as a mathematical expression of the reaction.

M. Monoyer (*Thèse de la Faculté de Médicine de Strasbourg*) proposes a much more simple equation to represent Pasteur's analysis.

$$4\,(C_{12}H_{22}O_{11} + H_2O), \text{ or,}$$
$$4\,(C_{12}H_{14}O_{12}) + 6\,H_2O \quad 2\,(C_4H_6O_4) + 12\,(C_3H_8O_3) + 4\,CO_2 + O_2.$$

He supposes, at the same time, that the excess of oxygen serves for the respiration of the globules of the ferment, a very plausible interpretation, as we shall presently see.

Nor are the proportions of these two by-products, as it appears, absolutely constant for a given weight of sugar. With a slow, *i.e.*, probably a sluggish fermentation, and where the yeast is either weak, or vegetating under unfavourable conditions, the proportion of alcohol produced seems to decrease, and that of the glycerine and succinic acid to increase. On the other hand, a good store of assimilable nitrogenous food, and of suitable mineral matter, increases the amount of alcohol, and lessens that of the by-products. A slight acidity of the medium is also somewhat unfavourable to them, the reverse being noticed if the medium be neutral.

In the present chapter, be it understood, we have been and are discussing **Commercial or Industrial Yeast,** which though nominally consisting of the cells of *Sacch. cerevisiæ* (the true alcoholic ferment), really consists of an admixture of yeast-types, infected, however slightly, with a few of the other organisms, known as bacteria or bacilli, and classed by Pasteur under the name of *ferments de maladie*.

But in any fairly good yeast there is an immense preponderance of the cells of *Sacch. cerevisiæ*, and under conditions favourable to its growth it will develop so much more rapidly than the undesirable organisms, that the mischief wrought by the latter is much restricted, and except when ales are being brewed for long storage is hardly of practical significance. Whether there is any "crowding-out" of "wild yeasts," with a restriction of the evil influence of some of them (for which see next chapter) by conditions favouring a vigorous growth of *Sacch. cerevisiæ* is less clear, but assuredly, if absolutely pure yeast could be employed to excite fermentation and all access of bacteria prevented, there need be no limit to the keeping quality of the product.

But this ideal state of things is impossible with the ordinary arrangements of a brewery plant. The prolonged exposure of worts, on the coolers and in other vessels, gives ample chance for spores of bacteria and mildews to fall into the fluid, and these spores or germs are capable of resisting the heat of the wort, after it has left the copper, whatever it may be, a heat which would be often sufficient to destroy the fully developed organisms.

So it is here that the question of sound material and good manipulation becomes important; if the ideal state of things—absolutely pure yeast and exclusion of bacteria—could be secured, the soundness of the material would be a minor matter; but in the actual state of casual contamination unsound malt and hops tend to give bacteria the upper hand; with badly contaminated yeast, no malt, however sound, and no manipulation, however skilful, will suffice to produce a stable beer; it is only when malt and hops of first-rate quality are skilfully manipulated, and the wort produced from them is set to ferment with yeast free from visible contamination, that the casual bacterial contaminations, numerous as they are, get so pressed in the background, that the final product can be relied upon to withstand the forcing-tray test, or support the ordeal of consignment to the tropics.

Undoubtedly the number of aërial spores varies greatly.—Prolonged rain, as Miquel showed, greatly purifies the air from bacteria, and so long as the earth keeps moist their number continually diminishes. As the air dries their number proportionally increases. The contrary holds good with the spores of mildews.

Such being the enemies to whose attacks beer-wort lies exposed, an important thing to do is to assist, as far as possible, the survival and predominance of what is fittest from the brewer's point of view—viz., the alcoholic ferment, *Sacch. cerevisiæ*. What the most favourable conditions are we shall in a short time consider.

High and Low Yeast.—Of the ordinary alcoholic yeast, *Sacch. cerevisiæ*, there are two distinct varieties (without counting sub-varieties, of which two at least, *Sacch. cerevisiæ I.* and *Sacch. cerevisiæ II.*, have been isolated), viz., high yeast, and low yeast. The high yeast (surface or top-fermentation yeast) is used to ferment infusion beers, and is the variety known to English brewers; low yeast is the variety which brewers of Lager beer employ in the fermentation of decoction-worts.

That they are simply deviations from a common stock,

started and made stable by the persistently different conditions under which their vital activity is exerted [amongst which need only be cited the frequent aëration which high yeast undergoes and the very much higher temperature at which it works], few will be disposed to doubt, though it is more questionable whether either variety could, by suitable treatment, be changed into the other in the course of a few fermentations.

An authority of great weight, Jörgensen, says: "In spite of many assertions to the contrary, it has hitherto been impossible to bring about an actual conversion of top yeast into bottom yeast, and *vice versâ*; according to the investigations of Hansen and Kühle, it is easily possible to produce transitory top fermentation phenomena with a bottom fermentation yeast; these, however, quickly disappear with the progressive development of the yeast. Therefore, when it is stated that bottom yeast, for instance, can be converted into top yeast by continued cultivation at an elevated temperature, we must first assume that the bottom yeast employed was impure, and had contained admixed top yeast, which slowly developed by cultivation at an elevated temperature at the expense of the bottom yeast, until it finally constituted the chief portion of the yeast."

It was stated above that at least two varieties of *Sacch. cerevisiæ* had been isolated. To be strictly correct, according to Jörgensen, there appear to be at least three distinct races of bottom-fermentation and the same number of races of top-fermentation yeasts, which have been prepared in a pure state. Dealing with the latter class only, their characteristics are—

No. 1. Slight attenuation, quick clarification. The beer has a sweet taste.

No. 2. Great attenuation, quick clarification. The beer has a more pronounced taste.

No. 3. Slow clarification, but *giving normal after-fermentation*. Flavour more wine-like. The beer resistant to yeast turbidity.

The importance of the words in italics will be seen in connection with the subject-matter of the next chapter, and with the latest view of "cask-conditioning," dealt with elsewhere (pp. 47, 295).

Neither of the above sub-varieties are wild-yeasts, and consequently may be expected to co-exist in the very purest specimen of commercial yeast; if then the results produced by pure cultures of them in *identical worts* are so markedly different, this may help us to see why the beer from one brewery will have a flavour and *cachet* quite distinct from that produced in another, however much the materials and systems employed may be alike, and to attribute the fact to one or the other of the sub-varieties having gained the preponderance.

It may also help to explain why a modification of mashing-heats designed to bring about a change in the character of the product (say in the direction of more or of less attenuation) does not always bring about that change at once with mathematical certainty, because maybe, in the pitching yeast used, the sub-variety, unfavourable to the desired alteration, preponderates.

It will of course be understood that it is impossible to differentiate these sub-varieties by aid of the microscope, and in many cases even the cells of wild-yeasts are only distinguishable by the Hansen method of analysis (ascospore and film formation) to be touched upon in the next chapter. With this reservation we will proceed to describe

The Appearance of the Cells under the Microscope.—
In outward shape the cells of the top fermentation or high yeast are rather larger and more globular than those of low yeast, but in any microscopic "field" some of the cells will appear oval, others round, according as they are observed sideways or "end-on."

In the very young cells, such as may be found in a drop of wort taken from a tun in incipient fermentation, a portion of which is examined under the microscope, the contents have a clear appearance almost like water—*i.e.*, they contain clear and homogeneous plasma; in the more developed cells careful observation may detect a finely granulated condition of the contents, while in the cells which are germinating there will be distinctly visible in the protoplasm one large **vacuole**, or two (or more) smaller ones, which appear to consist of clear liquid isolated in the form of drops.

These are the most vigorous cells, which, probably on account of the great abundance of nitrogen in their protoplasm, are the heaviest and the best fitted to effect reproduction. Later still the internal plasma may contract still more, and one abnormally large vacuole be discerned, but generally the contents of the old cells will be darker and more coarsely granulated and without vacuoles. They are then enclosed by a *thickened* membrane, which occasionally is compressed in such a way as to give the cells an irregular shape. [N.B.—A slight alteration of the fine adjustment causes these vacuoles to look lighter or darker than the surrounding part of the cell, and the cell itself than the surrounding medium according to the focal distance.]

Nuclei (in the Cells) and Rejuvenation of Old Cells.—Further cell-nuclei are observable on staining with certain reagents,—*e.g.*, osmic or picric acids,—and there are sometimes spherical bodies within the vacuole, occasionally moving with some activity in the clear plasmic fluid; this, however, we have most clearly noticed in a "field" of *Mycoderma vini*. If mature cells, in which the protoplasm has shrunk towards the cell-wall or membrane, be placed in a fermentable liquid, they present, says Jörgensen, "a highly characteristic picture during the short period which precedes the phenomena of fermentation. The granulations disappear, and numerous fine threads of plasma occur in the clear cell-sap and gradually mark out rounded vacuoles; finally these disappear, and the cell is again filled with a clear homogeneous plasma."

Detection of Old and Effete Cells.—The best way for those who are not as yet very expert in observing yeast, if not for all, to enable them to detect old and effete cells in a sample of pitching yeast, is to add a little aniline blue to the water with which the yeast is diluted in preparing it for the microscopic slide. The colouring matter very soon penetrates into the interior of the aged cells and stains them, but the young and vigorous cells, being able to resist it, remain uncoloured. A weak solution of iodine has a similar effect, the worn-out cells being stained brown.

Regularity of Size is also a desirable feature, so that, other things being equal, a yeast in which the cells appear uniform, though only of moderate size, might be expected to give better fermentation results than one in which a portion of the cells are larger and a portion smaller.

As a rule, high fermenting temperatures, if continuous, tend to determine irregularity of size, and so will cultivation in strong worts, as compared with those of medium gravity, when they serve as the fermentation medium, the abnormally large cells consisting of over-fed, gorged specimens, which are on the point of losing their special functions. Hayduck's researches—to be referred to again in the chapter containing the section on yeast-turbidity—showed pretty conclusively that fermentative vigour increases with the amount of nitrogen present *up to a certain point*, after which a loss of assimilative power in respect to the nitrogenous constituents of the wort rapidly occurred; a discovery which furnishes one reason why **store-yeast, taken from fermentations of wort whose original gravity was only medium, say 18 to 20 lbs., gives better results than that taken from worts of much greater density,** though the latter would, at first sight, be expected to show greater fermentative and reproductive vigour.

We say one reason because repletion of the cells is not the only one why yeast taken from high-gravity worts tends to weakness instead of strength. In such worts the fermentation itself loses much of its original vigour as attenuation advances, the yeast being, as it were (and as happens to other ferment-organisms) hampered, if not poisoned by its own excretion-products, notably the alcohol, and as a consequence, only producing a relatively degenerate offspring.

Severe Ordeals which Yeast can survive.—Although an alteration in the constitution of a wort, which is relatively very slight, will destroy that delicate equilibrium of reproduction and fermentation which is essential for the brewer, yet yeast will retain its vitality under conditions, the rigour of which would kill higher organisms instantaneously. According to well-known observations by Melsens,—

(1) Fermentation *can* proceed in melting ice, *i.e.*, at a temperature too low for grain to germinate in.

(2) Its vitality is not destroyed by a temperature of $-100°$C., say, or $148°$ Fahr. *below zero*.

(3) Yeast immersed in water and enclosed in strong vessels can resist the pressure caused by the water being frozen, even when the pressure is of the intensity of 8,000 atmospheres.

[If this be so, it is by no means wonderful that yeast can resist the pressure applied by an ordinary yeast press, without any rupture of its elastic cell-walls.]

Further, it is stated, that yeast, when carefully dried, will withstand heating up to $212°$ Fahr., although a much lower temperature will destroy the activity of ordinary moist yeast.

Its Limitations.—On the other hand, all alcoholic fermentation, even the feeblest, is stopped when the temperature is maintained for some time at $120°$ Fahr.; indeed the maximum temperature for genuine alcoholic fermentation may be looked upon as about $92°$ Fahr.

Similarly, fermentation only reaches a point short of the normal, in a closed vessel; and when the pressure of the evolved carbonic acid exceeds 25 atmospheres, the yeast perishes.

Analysis of High Yeast.—Concordant analyses of yeast are hardly to be expected. The following are given by

Thausing, as the results determined from high yeast, apart from its ash.

	Dumas.	Mitscherlich.	Mulder.	Wagner.
Carbon	50·6	47·0	50·80	45·5
Hydrogen	7·3	6·6	7·16	6·2
Nitrogen	15·0	10·0	11·08	9·4
Oxygen (and Sulphur)	27·1	36·4	30·98	38·9
	100·0	100·0	100·02	100·0

The sulphur according to Mitscherlich being ·6%,

The Nitrogen is of course in various Combination.—Von Nägeli made the proteids (separable into (i) those in the form of ordinary albumen, and (ii) those in the form of phosphated compounds, analogous to casein) 36 and 9 respectively, and peptones (precipitable by lead acetate), 2%, or 47% in all, which, taking the usual divisor of 6·37, gives a lower percentage of nitrogen than any of the high-yeast analyses show.

The Ash (representing the Mineral Constituents) varies from 2·5% (Schlossberger) to 8·9% or more. It is supposed that Schlossberger's low percentage was due to his having experimented with freely washed yeast, which had accordingly parted with an appreciable quantity of its mineral constituents. And the mineral constituents, or ash, may be taken upon the average to be made up as follows:—

50 to 59% of phosphoric acid, 29 to 39% of potash, 4% of magnesia, and 2% of lime.

Consequently we see **the necessity of mineral constituents,** chiefly phosphoric acid and potash, in any medium intended to nourish or be fermented by yeast. And hence, as well as owing to the absence of nitrogenous food, yeast cannot carry on a prolonged fermentation in a pure solution of sugar.

For a short time fermentation—given a suitable temperature—can progress, the adult yeast giving up some of its own nitrogenous matter to supply the young cells, but this is a process of impoverishment which can be only temporary. The overlooking of this has probably been the cause of apparently contradictory experimental results.

Of each of the two groups (mineral matter and nitrogenous food) fairly prepared malt wort contains more than a sufficiency, but the replacement of a large proportion of the malt-extract by saccharine substitutes—and the more so perhaps, the purer the latter are—tends to reduce them below the quantity desirable. In such a case, accordingly, the desirability of the utmost possible "peptonisation" of the existing nitrogenous matter, in order to make it available for yeast nutrition, is obvious.

Some brewers, where the wort shows a deficiency in those constituents, advocate continuous rousing as a stimulant to the yeast, but this is a treatment which cuts both ways.* Indubitably both the resultant aëration and the elimination of some carbonic acid are measures calculated to give a decided fillip to the yeast, but in reality one stimulating its propagative rather than its fermentative faculty.

In the majority of cases the course indicated is to use a larger initial proportion of pitching yeast when the medium is likely to be below the proper nutritive value—*i.e.*, to depend for the due attenuation rather upon the mature cells of the pitching yeast than upon the cells which they may give birth to. If such a course be adopted without excessive aëration the yeast will assert its presence rather in the fermentative than the propagative sense.

Effect of extreme Aëration.—This was investigated in connection with M. Pasteur's dicta upon **Aërobic** and **Anaërobic** ferments, *i.e.*, ferments which require air in

* In one large brewery within the writer's knowledge the early "heads" are systematically knocked in every hour or two, often enough, at any rate, to prevent the necessity of boarding up the tuns. Another has a costly apparatus of shafting and permanent rousers. Dr. Graham, too, a good many years ago, designed an apparatus for pumping in filtered air, and thus combining aëration and rousing. He claimed that by its use very strong beers intended for vatting, which in the usual way would not attenuate below say 8 or 9 lbs., could, if desired, be attenuated to a third of that.

order to perform their function and those which only act as a ferment when air is excluded, and as far as the writer knows, the conclusions come to by him and his school have not in one respect been controverted, namely, in regard to the influence exercised by the oxygen upon the increased crop of yeast on the one hand, and the decrease of alcohol, etc., on the other.

These conclusions may be formulated thus.—Yeast, though it *can* exist and act as a ferment without air (deriving its necessary oxygen from the sugar which it breaks up), does not like to do so; and it is, in fact, less able to support the absence of free oxygen, or more correctly atmospheric oxygen, than many disease organisms are—*e.g.*, the butyric ferment, which was once supposed to be quite anaërobic. Therefore, though yeast is capable of fermenting sugar in the absence of air, such fermentation goes on with dangerous slowness, but in one sense very profitably, seeing that only 1% of the sugar is abstracted for the necessities of the growing ferment, the other 99% being available for the production of alcohol, carbonic acid, etc.

But if, on the other hand, the operation were to be conducted with thin layers of wort and in such very shallow vessels that any gas evolved, which might otherwise prevent the readiest access of air, easily passes off, then not only will yeast, amounting in weight to some 25% of the sugar and probably representing that weight of it, be formed (instead of a weight approximating to 1%), but the remaining 75%, or thereabouts, of the sugar will be burnt up by the atmospheric oxygen and resolved into water and carbonic anhydride(CO_2), giving almost absolutely no alcohol at all. *

This being so, we may doubt the wisdom of excessive and indiscriminate aëration of worts after the fermentation

---

* This hypothetical case of the unprofitable combustion of all the saccharine matter is, of course, an extreme one, unless as regards a very small proportion of the constituents of any given wort; but it may indicate an explanation of the unpleasant experience of most exporters of

is well established. More yeast will be clearly produced, but it will be at the expense of the matters which were intended to yield exhilarating and palatable products.

These facts have their analogues amongst plants more highly organised. To name one instance only, beetroot, which is capable (after being lifted from the ground and given free access of atmospheric oxygen) of forming fresh leaves, *i.e.*, fresh cells at the expense of the sugar stored up in its root tissues, will, on the other hand, says Duclaux, produce alcohol from the same store if placed in carbonic acid gas so that air is excluded.

Alcohol percentage.—Highest Allowable Density of Saccharine Wort.—Probably in no case can any yeast, however pure or vigorous, raise the proportion of alcohol beyond 14 to 15%, nor is fermentation likely to progress in a solution containing more than 20% by weight of fermentable matter (water 4 : sugar 1)—say in a gravity of over 51 brewers' lb.—perhaps owing to the reason assigned by Helmholtz, viz., that in solutions of greater density the excess of alcohol formed, by precipitating nitrogenous matter hindered the fermentative vigour of the yeast, but quite as probably to the fact that the alcohol and carbonic acid produced act as specific poisons. Moreover, in solutions of great concentration the excess of sugar tends to diminish the amount of water within the yeast cell to a point below that essential for its vitality.

Heat generated during Fermentation.—The reader knows that fermentation is always marked by a rise in temperature, which is fairly close to a rise of 1° Fahr. for each brewers' lb. of gravity disappearing from the ken of the saccharometer. What is the source of this heat?

We know that in chemical decompositions and combi-

---

beer—viz., that occasionally the samples taken at the shipment port are affirmed to show, on analysis at Somerset House, a gravity lower than that which was declared for drawback. It is of course annoying for the shipper, who knows he was charged upon the higher scale, to be mulcted perhaps in two or three degrees, but his first impulse to condemn the analyst of inaccuracy is probably unjust.

HEAT GENERATED IN FERMENTATION.

nations generally heat is evolved, and a German scientist, Fitz, explains the greater part of the heat which becomes free in fermentation to be due to the difference of expansive force between the sugar on the one hand and the bodies into which it is broken up on the other. Some again refer it to a combustion process, and make it dependent on the amount of carbon oxidised into carbon dioxide. Further, Thausing says, no inconsiderable amount of heat —nearly one-fourth of the whole—is set free by the mixture of the alcohol formed with water.* But on the other hand, part of the warmth set free is absorbed by the multiplication of the yeast-cells and part is translated into work, whereby the resulting carbonic acid gas is enabled to overcome the pressure of the atmosphere.

But the heat actually generated in a normal fermentation is estimated at only one-tenth part of that which the combustion of the sugar, with free access of air, would yield (Bertholet says one-fifteenth part only), and this limitation is explained, on a simple combustion theory, first, by the fact that only one-third of the total carbon is consumed instead of the whole, and secondly, because the alcohol, which is formed in the case where air is excluded, is itself combustible, through the agency of certain ferment-organisms other than yeast, and therefore —until these other organisms come into play—that it locks up a not inconsiderable amount of heat.

Concurrent Action of Acetic and Lactic Ferments.— In pre-scientific times brewers used to find it gravely stated in their text-books that acetous fermentation began at a certain temperature—77° if I remember rightly, neither more nor less. There is, however, reason to suppose that no definitely fatal temperature exists, but that the action of the acetic as well as of the lactic ferment is generally to some extent concurrent. The formation

* It is well known that on mixing absolute alcohol with water a very considerable rise of temperature occurs, though the combined quantity shrinks below those of its component parts. This may account, too, for part of the loss of bulk which occurs between that of the gathered wort and that of the racked beer.

of acetic ether (ethyl acetate), which contributes to the pungent smell of tuns in strong fermentation, not only points to some activity of an acetic ferment, but, as has been said, supports Nägeli's view that the fermentative influence is exercised outside the cell, but within zones of molecular vibration.

It is true that the formation of acetic acid chemically by oxidation of alcohol is a possibility (though in a laboratory only effected when platinum black is added), and it is perhaps conceivable that such acetic acid, at the moment of its formation, might penetrate the cell-membrane of the nearest yeast-cell (yeast is not averse to moderate acidity, indeed is stimulated by it), and there combine with its equivalent of *nascent* alcohol to form acetic ether.

We believe the range of fermentative power to be fairly covered by the following table:—

	Action Begins.	Maximum Activity.	Action Destroyed.	
Yeast	a little over 32° F.	92° F.	122° F.	Vitality destroyed as well.
Acetic Ferment	54° F.	97° F.	122° F.	
Lactic Ferment	50° F.	112° F.	122° F.	But vitality can support a much higher temp.

Fortunately, however, the lactic ferment develops with difficulty in the presence of even 1% lactic acid, while 2% kills it; yeast, on the other hand, *prefers* a degree of acidity approaching 1%.

Growth of Moulds.—If a mixture of yeast, bacteria, and moulds were to be introduced (and they always are introduced, though the former enormously preponderates) in anything like even quantity into—

(*a*) A neutral wort. Bacteria would gain the upper hand.
(β) Wort with 1% acid. Yeast would gain the upper hand.
(γ) Wort with 5% organic acids. Mouldiness would gain the upper hand.

(Dr. Squire.)

ATTENUATION, APPARENT AND ACTUAL.

Other Fermentation Phenomena.—Attenuation.—At first sight it might be supposed that the lowering of gravity indicated by the saccharometer as any fermentation proceeds, would show the actual amount of saccharine matter converted into alcohol, carbonic acid, etc., + the 1% of sugar and albuminous matter abstracted for the food of the growing yeast plant. But this is not so.

The apparent degradation of solid matter is greater than the real one, owing to the fact that the great specific lightness of the alcohol formed (displacing an equal quantity of heavier water) masks a certain amount of unaltered matter. Let us assume a case.

A beer whose final attenuation = 1016 ·2 (say 5·8 lb.), might if a measured quantity were distilled and the distillate and residue then made up to the original bulk in the way described on p. 245, have a residue (i.e., when all the alcohol was away) = 1024·7 and a distillate of 991·4 (= 10·9% of proof spirit, or over 5·3% of absolute alcohol?*

Obviously, then, the alcohol present hid 8·5 degrees of specific gravity, or a percentage of solid extractive matter which may be got approximately by dividing the excess of degrees over 1000 (viz., 24·7 and 8·5 respectively) by 3·95. [3·85 is sometimes recommended, but 3·95 is considered the more correct divisor for starch transformation products in solutions of low density.] Then $\frac{24·7}{3·95}$ = 6·25% of solid extract and $\frac{18·5}{39·5}$ = 2·15 of the same covered or hidden by the alcohol present.

Nor is the alcohol, though by far the most influential, the only factor in what we call attenuation. Caramelised sugar bodies are formed, having only the gravity 5 : 6 compared with that of the maltose which yielded them.

* The spirit indication 8·6 (1000—991·4) shows 37 degrees of gravity lost ; 37 + 1024·7 = 1061·7 (= 22·2 brewers' lb.). So that this beer attenuated to nearly an (apparent) fourth, has nearly ½% proof spirit per lb. of original gravity, and seeing that proof spirit contains 49·24% absolute alcohol *by weight* (or at least alcohol containing not more than 1% water), there will be nearly half the quantity of absolute alcohol that there is of proof spirit.

They are, however, not produced beyond the limit of 5%, and generally less than that of the total sugar, but remain in the residue, and thus affect final gravity. Glycerine and succinic acid also have a lighter specific gravity than the sugar which yielded them, and the farther fermentation is pushed, the higher will be the proportion of these by-products at the expense of the alcohol.

Albuminous matter is, moreover, eliminated to the extent of at least one degree of gravity.

The latter considerations can hardly be taken account of; they are at most mentally averaged by the practical operator. The hiding effect of alcohol is more important, but only requires to be stated for its significance to be grasped.

Perhaps a more important point is **the influence exerted by hops in preventing the loss of gravity in a wort.** Nettleton (p. 22 of his very detailed "Original Gravity") says: "It appears that hops tend to prevent the loss of gravity in a wort, *although the same amount of alcohol may be produced.* To do this, some compensating action must be going on in the wort during fermentation, say by the building up of some heavier body; by the prevention of the formation of some lighter body, which would, if hops were absent, be formed, and consequently give lightness to the beer; or the action of hops in retarding the loss of gravity may be by their preventing the precipitation of some otherwise insoluble body.

"The mixing together of pale and brown malts to form a wort has a similar effect to that of hops, in partially preventing the loss of gravity."

[This action is distinct from and more recondite than that exerted by hop-extract, derived from heavy hopping, and especially from the introduction of a large proportion of new hops, upon the rate and extent of fermentation. In this latter case it seems probable that the resinous and oily matter of the hop either coats the membranes of the yeast-cells, rendering them less permeable, or makes the wort too viscous for the easy separation of the maltose.

Whatever the explanation may be, the fact is within the experience of most brewers that heavy hopping—and the rule applies in some measure to the use of new hops also—retards the fermentation and tends to check attenuation. The course indicated, then, is naturally the employment of a larger quantity of pitching-yeast.]

Influence of Cane-sugar on Attenuation.—Some brewers, though not many in this country, use uninverted sugar in quantity, and the author of "Original Gravity" points out an interesting fact in connection therewith—viz., that if it were practicable to prepare a wort entirely from cane-sugar, it would be found two or three hours after the wort had been pitched, that the gravity had become higher, instead of lower, owing to the change of cane-sugar into invert-sugar [$C_{12} H_{22} O_{11} + H_2 O = 2 (C_6 H_{12} O_6)$—*i.e.*, 19 parts, or say lb. into 20 parts or lb.], and he says that a cane-sugar wort might even rise from 1055 to 1058 under these circumstances.* Or to put it in another form. Suppose a wort containing 7·5% of cane-sugar, *i.e.*, 3·158% of carbon with a gravity of 1030·2. This, by inversion, will rise to 1031·3—*i.e.*, there would be an increase of 1·1 degree of gravity, albeit the same quantity of carbon would be present.

Now, as the quantity of alcohol producible depends on the amount of carbon, it is evident if the carbon of these sugars were all fermented equally, that an invert-sugar wort of 1031·3 would lose a full degree of its original gravity more and yet produce no more alcohol than a cane-sugar wort of 1030·2, and this holds good throughout for any invert-sugar wort as compared with a cane-sugar wort of equal gravity, except that the higher the gravity, the more the divergency increases.

Moreover, this point not only applies to glucose or

* 1055 degrees = 19·8 brewers' lb. Now, 2·6 lb. cane-sugar dissolved in a barrel of water give it 1 lb. gravity (see p. 159), consequently it would require 52·6 lb. to produce a gravity of 19·8 in a barrel. This increasing on the 5% ratio would become 55·2 of invert (by hydration), the extra 2·6 lb. being enough to give an extra lb. (nearly) of gravity, which is *nearly* 3 degrees.

invert-sugar worts as compared with cane-sugar solutions, but (in a somewhat less degree) as compared with all-malt worts. Of course very few brewers get more than one-third of their extract from invert or other sugar, but in respect of the part they do so get, an invert-sugar wort having say a gravity of 1055 would lose quite 1·5 degree more than the corresponding malt-wort, so that, assuming one-third of the extract to be derived from invert or glucose, the beer on analysis would show an original gravity of 0·5 less, a point worth the attention of exporters, who leave no margin in their declarations for drawback.

"The Head."—"Foxy" Smell.—It was hinted in the opening chapter—where fermentation from its practical side was rather more fully treated than other operative processes—that picturesque names are not wanting for the different appearances of the "heads"; thus "rock," "bold rock," "cauliflower," "curl," "fair silvery head," and so on are all descriptive terms within the writer's experience, and a great deal may be gathered from a close observation of these heads and from the smell coming over with the carbonic acid gas.

For instance, a faint and rather "foxy" smell may at some time or other be noticed, and this, if allowed to get round all the fermentations, would be a very serious matter, for the contaminated yeast carries on the taint. The elimination of the contaminated yeast is an obvious precaution, but no time should be lost in treating the wooden vessels (the writer believes the cause of infection to lie in the wooden vessels, especially the fermenting vessels) with bisulphite.

A periodic dressing of the fermenting tuns, or wherever they chance to be empty for a day or two, with calcic monosulphite applied in the form of thin whitewash and left on until the tuns are cleaned for use, will prevent the recurrence of this faint smell. Monosulphite is much less disagreeable to apply than bisulphite.

The Rise and Fall of the Head.—In a normal fermentation, the head, soon after the "rocks," or irregular, pointed masses of yeasty froth, have "come through" and covered the entire surface, begins to rise (of course, in a degree varying with the depth of the F. V., etc.), the individual rocks meantime rising up with the pressure of carbonic acid gas beneath, until they curl and finally topple over; and this rise of the whole head continues up to a certain point, say till the temperature has risen 5° or 6°, more or less, when it again subsides gradually, changing from the frothy "fobby" head into a yeasty one, after which stage, unless the said head be removed by skimming or otherwise dealt with when ripe for it, it will again begin to rise.

What are the Causes of these Phenomena?—Probably, that in the first stage, when cell-multiplication goes on more freely than fermentative action, the carbonic acid gas which is generated pushes up some of the newly formed cells, wherever resistance is least, finally forcing upward and raising the head as a whole, and continuing to do so until such time as the generated gas can get away more easily, on account of the original density of the wort having been considerably reduced, or when fermentation rather than propagation having become predominant, there is not that rapid formation of new cells of light specific gravity which at first occurred. [It will be observed that, other things being equal, the greater the original density of the wort the longer will the first rising of the head last.]

Finally, when fermentative action slackens, the yeast agglomerates at the surface (possibly its activity enabled it before to resist the upward impulse of the carbonic acid gas; and this will seem more likely if we accept Nägeli's theory), and presenting more of an obstacle than before to the passage of the gas, still being generated, is accordingly carried upwards. That this is so, viz., that the gas, hampered in its passage upwards, is the determining factor, is rendered the more tenable by the fact that the yeasty head begins, if left untouched, to sink again as the gas gradually disengages itself.

Poverty of the Yeast Outcrop, (*a*) **Sluggish Fermentation.**—The normal crop of yeast should amount to five or six times the quantity of pitching-yeast, and if it falls much below this it should set the brewer inquiring where the screw is loose. Primarily, the scanty development of yeast is due to the formation of protoplasm not keeping pace with cell-formation, or in other words to a want of balance in the wort constituents.

Probably the albuminoids, though not deficient in point of quantity, are so in respect of the quality of diffusibility; that is to say, the yeast cannot assimilate enough of them to correspond with its normal degree of growth whilst degrading the free maltose. The latter, relatively speaking, will not be very high (*excess* of maltose as a factor in poverty of outcrop, will be touched upon in the coming paragraph on "fiery" fermentations), but the compound bodies, known as malto-dextrins, and those too of high type, and therefore utterly beyond the power of the primary yeast to break up, will probably show an unduly high percentage in the wort-extract. The superabundance indeed of high-type malto-dextrins would alone be sufficient to account for a much-reduced yeast-crop, even if there were not reason to suppose that restricted peptonisation is concurrent.

This degeneration of the ferment is generally attended by more than the usual discoloration of the head, and that too persisting to a lower point of attenuation than usual, so that the *clean* yeasty head is a long time in coming. For this discoloration the passing of the hop-resin out of solution, as its solvent maltose gets broken up, is partly responsible, as in other cases; but it is very probably also due to the action of oxygen upon the relatively large number of weakened cells, which are exposed to it for a longer time than usual—an action which occurs, more or less, when any yeast is exposed for some time to the air, and which may be a sort of combustion-process, exercised by its most energetic element upon the tissues of the older and weaker cells of the outer layer.

In such a case the remedy indicated seems to be (apart from the more thoroughgoing one of reforming the mashing system), **"dressing"** either **with malt-flour** (*i.e.*, mixing some with a little wort, and rousing into the tun), or adding **cold-water (filtered) malt extract.** The reason of this is that the new diastase introduced is capable of setting to work very energetically in degrading the maltodextrins into free maltose—*i.e.*, from an obdurate to a readily fermentable constituent, while peptonisation is probably effected to some extent simultaneously. [In the type of degeneration commencing with a "fiery" fermentation dressing with wheaten flour seems preferable, for reasons hereafter given.]

Nor must we overlook the possible influence upon sluggishness of fermentation, of **nitrites** in the brewing water, as set forth by M. Emile Laurent. In a series of experimental fermentations he used a partly uniform medium (1000 grammes water, 50 grammes saccharose, ·75 grammes potassium phosphate, ·1 gramme magnesium sulphate), and of this he set a check-flask, impregnated with a trace of high yeast, to ferment. To five other flasks he added various salts, each, however, *supplying nitrogen in the proportion of 1 gramme.* [These salts were respectively sulphate of ammonia 4·71 grammes, phosphate of ammonia 4·71, nitrate of potassium 7·22, nitrate of sodium 6·07, and *nitrite* of potassium 6·07.*] These were also "set" with a trace of high yeast.

The results were interesting. The sulphate of ammonia flask took the lead, but the one containing ammonia phosphate showed the largest crop ultimately (·174 gramme : ·110 gramme). The nitrate flasks yielded hardly more than the check flask, while the nitrite flask yielded *nil.*

* The nitrogen yielded is arrived at as follows : adding up the atomic weights, and taking the Sodium Nitrate $NaNO_3$ and Potassium Nitrate KNO_3 as examples, we find the first $= (23 + 14 + 48) = 85$, the second $= (39·1 + 14 + 32) = 85·1$, or practically 85. Dividing this by 14 (atomic weight of nitrogen) we get 6·07, the quantity required to yield 1 part of nitrogen.

Although Laurent suggests that the nitrates are reducible to nitrites by yeast—in fact, proved it by showing that the liquid originally containing the former subsequently answered to the test for the latter—he does not think that the former do much harm in actual fermentation, but that nitrites, *nearly always co-existing*, do the harm. Even these would be innocuous in a neutral wort, for it is the **nitrous acid** set free by the acidity of the medium which does the mischief; but under normal conditions yeast secretes acid products enough (in conjunction with the normal acidity of the wort and possible products of lactic ferment) to set nitrous acid free.

From these conclusions it appears that brewers troubled with persistent sluggishness of fermentation, combined with scanty yeast outcrop, would do well to look closely into the character of their water-supply, even before making drastic changes in their mashing system.

(β) **Fiery Fermentations.**—In these, although they also determine poverty of yeast-crop, the want of balance is generally in the opposite direction. Excess of free maltose, inducing such a rampant fermentation that the whole fermenting vessel appears to be in a boil with the continuous rush of gas to the surface, is one factor; another is an unusually low percentage of assimilable nitrogenous food, caused probably by unduly high mashing heats, which for some reason or other have not the usual marked influence, at least to the usual extent, in raising the quantity and type of malto-dextrin.

The indication of the former cause has been given a few lines back; the latter will be rather manifested by the formation of bubbles, sometimes of considerable size, and full of gas, which finally burst on the surface. In neither case is any yeast formed unless it be at a somewhat late stage, when, for instance, in the first case the excess of maltose has been fermented away, and so the balance is restored, or when in either case the beer is "cleansed,"[*] when the effect probably of working under pressure

---

[*] See Introductory Chapter.

causes a certain amount of yeast to be ejected. But the yeast from such fermentations can never be recommended for pitching purposes, albeit the beer from the second class of fiery fermentations, the one characterised by "bladdery heads," frequently is excellent, being "round," full, and limpid, and, maybe, superior to the average product of the brewery.

As this case is somewhat exceptional, involving the employment of extremely diastatic malt, seeing that with ordinary malt the high mashing temperature which limits the assimilable nitrogenous matter also increases the high-type malto-dextrin to an extent incompatible with early "conditioning," we shall limit our consideration of "fiery" fermentation to the first case, an altogether undesirable state of things, seeing that the resulting beer will be thin and poor, and often "grey."

In a previous case dressing with malt-flour or treatment with malt-extract was recommended, but in the present case it would be obviously incorrect, seeing that conversion has already been pushed to an extreme. If the plan of dressing be adopted it should be with wheat or bean flour—using from one-fourth to one-third per barrel—and some add half that quantity, or less, of salt. It is not very easy to see how the flour can supply nutriment for the yeast, its nitrogenous matter not being, as far as we know, in a diffusible form, and we must therefore suppose that any resulting benefit comes from the increased viscosity of the wort, and perhaps from its mechanically assisting the yeast to conglomerate.

It has also been suggested that the fresh atmospheric air introduced with the whisked-up mixture acts as a stimulus to the yeast; but this in such a case as we are now considering, where the activity is already too great, would be a questionable benefit. [One disadvantage of flour-dressing is that a certain degree of haziness generally characterises "dressed" gyles, a point which is of much more moment now, when glasses have ousted the "straight quarts" and pewters of yore, than it was twenty or thirty years ago. Then, as I am informed, some brewers dressed *every* gyle just before cleansing.]

The predisposing Causes of Fiery Fermentations.—Of these of course errors in the mashing system stand first, and amendment may be tried in the direction of limiting the amount of mashing liquor, or of raising its heat (tentatively by a degree or two at a time), or by both combined. Again, as to underlet, a small quantity of liquor so applied at a high temperature is less favourable to free-maltose formation than, and should consequently be employed in preference to, a larger quantity at lower temperature, but containing the same number of units of heat as the former. The said underlet, if used, should be put under as early as possible, and the "stand" after mashing might be somewhat shortened.

Other predisposing causes are slackness and probably acidity of malt. (Slackness apparently greatly enhances diastasic activity.) The use of old or of an insufficiency of hops, the oil and resin of which seem to promote the cohesion of the ferment; the use of stale and impure yeast, and perhaps, to a limited extent, barometric variations.

The following **Table of yeast-cell increase, etc., during the course of fermentation,** based on Mr. Adrian J. Brown's experiments, will be interesting as a standard, though probably only approximately exact for any given fermentation.

Hours after fermentation began.	Yeast-cells present for each one added at pitching.	Grammes Alcohol per cent. (by weight).	Mean number of yeast-cells present during the interval before time named.	Grammes of Alcohol per cent. formed in each such interval.
12	7·4	0·654	4·2	0·654
24	18·5	1·933	12·9	1·279
36	23·5	2·975	21·0	1·042
60	24·4	4·237	23·9	1·262
84	24·3	6·187	24·3	1·950

The experiments, it should be said, were made with a liquid containing 18% of dextrose, a medium probably of greater density than the one most favourable to yeast production.

Surplus Yeast.—The disposal of this is a problem sometimes not easy to solve, and the following method of preparing **Baker's Yeast,** as given by Thausing, may prove useful.

The fresh yeast is passed through a fine hair-sieve in order to remove the coarser contaminations. Then it is brought into eight or ten times its quantity of the coldest possible water, in which some carbonate of ammonia, soda, or potash (the first salt is preferable) has been dissolved, and mixed therewith in a deep vessel, which has sundry openings, closed with taps, one over the other. The quantity of the salt may be reckoned at 100 to 120 grammes per hectolitre (= 22 gallons) of yeast. The salts act as solvents of the hop-resin, remove the bitter from and purify the yeast at the same time, and that better than water alone can do.

When the yeast has settled, the separated and dirty water above it is allowed to flow off; cold water is again added, and the mixture thoroughly stirred. If the yeast is still not clean enough, a third lot of water is used, or a small quantity of ammonic carbonate (or one of the other salts) is added to the second water. The yeast, by frequent and continuous washing, gets weakened and loses its power ("*Trieb*") in baking. The washed yeast is wrapped up in pressure cloths (*Presstücher*), moderately pressed, and kneaded up with dry starch, so that it becomes fairly dry, and yet can be formed into quadrangular pieces. The separate pieces are packed in paper and preserved until sold in a cool and dry place.

It is essential to have the water for washing very cold, the best plan being to throw some ice into the vessels, and let the latter stand in a *cold* cellar.

[A suggested explanation of the fact that **one brewer's yeast finds favour for baking, whilst another's, appa-**

rently stronger and better, does not. The active ferment in bread-raising is supposed to be *Sacch. Minor* (Engel), which Messrs. Matthews & Lott say they have noticed in racking beers to the extent of 1% to 2%. Now, a high proportion of this, which would be an impurity in pitching yeast, seeing that it sometimes causes cloudy fret, would greatly enhance the value for baking purposes.]

CHAPTER XI.

CULTURE FROM A SINGLE CELL—WILD YEASTS.

Pasteur's Methods of Purifying Yeast—Survival of the Fittest—Hansen's Theory—Wild Yeasts—Dilution and Gelatine Methods of Isolating a Single Cell for Cultivation—Ascospore Formation; Film or Pellicle Formation—Table of the Preceding, serving for Analysis of Yeasts—Pure Culture on an Industrial Scale—Trials of " Pure Culture " Yeast in North of France—Experience of a Brewer there—" Pure Culture" Yeast in Australia.

Pasteur's and Hansen's Methods of Obtaining Pure Yeast compared.—Until M. Hansen's most important researches at Carlsberg were made public, the utmost that the scientific brewer hoped to do was to secure pure yeast by the culture system, recommended by M. Pasteur, and which may be said to have been based upon the law of "the survival of the fittest." That is to say, the ferment was to be cultivated under conditions which, though unfavourable to its own development, were still more unfavourable to the development of the disease-ferments. Consequently the latter might be expected to perish, whereas the yeast would survive.

Summarised, Pasteur's recommendations (see *Études sur la Bière*, 1876, pp. 225, 226) resolve themselves into the following alternatives:—

1. To cultivate yeast in a 10% solution of sugar, boiled and cooled with access of filtered air only, and in shallow vessels covered with plates of glass.

2. To cultivate it in wort to which $1\frac{1}{2}$% of tartaric acid, and from 2 to 3% of alcohol, have been added.

3. Or in wort to which a 10% solution of carbolic acid

has been added in the proportion of 1 part solution to 100 parts of wort.

Obviously, however, these plans are scarcely available on a large scale, and Pasteur himself admits that the second of them is equally favourable to the growth of *Sacch. Pastorianus*, to which he attributed a detrimental *rôle*, though were it only the determination of a vinous flavour, as he specially states, English brewers might afford to disregard and even welcome its presence.

He also relates that the use for pitching in the *Brasserie Tourtel* at Tantonville, of a yeast which he had obtained of remarkable purity by the carbolic acid method, resulted in the production of a beer of remarkable stability, compared with the other products of the same brewery, but which unfortunately always developed a yeasty flavour and want of brilliancy (*une cassure défectueuse*).

Therefore he admitted the possibility of the yeast undergoing some change, which would unfit it for practical use, albeit its purity from his point of view could not be questioned.

Other plans, based on the same leading idea, have been advocated—notably to use a certain proportion of salicylic acid, either in the fermenting wort—it being alleged that such an addition in moderation inhibits the growth of bacteria whilst allowing the yeast to flourish, or, to wash the yeast with an aqueous solution of the acid containing not more than one part acid in 10,000 of water, and not less than one part in 20,000.

Even now, **M. Velten of Marseilles**, a distinguished practical and scientific brewer, zealously maintains that some such method, based on Pasteur's recommendations, would be amply sufficient, and therefore preferable to the more novel system, which we will now consider—the system based upon the researches of Hansen, the Danish *savant*.

He, although admitting the incalculable harm done by bacteria and Pasteur's *ferments de maladie* generally, is quite as strongly of opinion that yeast, apparently pure to ordinary microscopic observation, may contain within itself the causes of much evil, that, in fact, unpleasant flavours, turbidity, and so on, effects which are only second, if second at all, to the development of acidity, are due to certain types of yeast, which he has classified as "wild yeasts."

To avoid the detrimental influence of these wild yeasts, he advocates the cultivation of a crop of pitching yeast from a single cell, selected and isolated in a way to be described later on. It has yet to be shown that yeast, the progeny of one single cell, jealously preserved from contamination and therefore of one single and uniform type, can give the results, in point of flavour and condition, which the English brewer desires; the possibility is strenuously denied by many, and indeed certain experiments which have been carried out at Burton-on-Trent are understood to have tended to negative it, nor can the results of practical experience on a larger scale in the north of France—to which reference will be made at some length later on in this chapter—be held to confirm it absolutely, as far as the information actually at hand enables a judgment to be formed.

But for bottom-fermentation beers there is positive evidence that pure yeast—*i.e.*, *Sacch. Cerevisiæ*, without intermixture of "wild yeasts"—answers extremely well, proper precaution being taken against over-attenuation. The contradiction, if one it be, between this successful result in the one case and its very questionable success in the other, may perhaps be explained by the fact that the low temperature, at which bottom fermentations are conducted, enables a large amount of carbonic acid, developed in the primary fermentation (and which would be lost in a top-fermentation) to be retained—the beer being, in fact, already saturated with it; whereas a secondary fermentation (complementary cask fermentation), impossible, as it seems, to be got with *Sacch. Cerevisiæ* alone, is requisite for the due conditioning of top-fermentation beer.

If, however, we admit the undesirability of having any type of yeast except *Sacch. Cerevisiæ*, the true alcoholic yeast and the main constituent of every good commercial yeast, and even if we do not admit it *in toto*, few will be disposed to question the immense interest and value which M. Hansen's discoveries have for intelligent brewers.

Hansen's investigations, in so far as they aim at differentiating yeasts not only into types—which Pasteur and still more Reess had done to some extent before him—but into sub-types, though foreshadowed in 1878, only took the present definite direction in 1881, when he conceived the idea of obtaining growths, each cultivated from a single cell and therefore uniform, and of observing the characteristics of each separate culture, when enough had been obtained for that purpose. The problem—which seems simple enough now it has been solved—was to ensure the derivation of the growth from a single cell, and from a single cell alone.

He had, ready to his hand, two methods of isolation, neither of which, however, was altogether satisfactory from his point of view—

(1) **The Dilution Method of Nägeli** and

(2) **The Gelatine Plate Cultivation Method of Dr. Koch.**

The Dilution Method briefly consisted in taking a definite quantity of liquid containing the class of cells to be experimented on, and counting the number of cells therein (which may be most conveniently done by aid of a hæmatometer), then diluting an *equal* quantity to such an extent, that it might fairly be assumed that a certain small volume of the diluted fluid contained only one cell. For instance, suppose that in 1 cc. (cubic centimetre) of the undiluted fluid 750 organisms were counted, then if 1 cc. were taken and made up to 750 cc. with *sterilised* water, there would probably be 1 cell in each cc. of the diluted fluid.

Each centimetre, then, put into a flask with some *sterilised* nutritive fluid, would give rise, *in all probability*, to the required growth from a single cell. But the absolute certainty so essential was wanting, for it was impossible to distinguish between flasks which might have received several cells and those which had only received one, so that the method had to be modified to make it of scientific value.

The Gelatine Method of Dr. Koch also begins by a free dilution with sterilised water of the growth, whatever it may be, which is to be investigated. A small quantity of this diluted fluid is then transferred to a flask containing nutritive fluid and gelatine, which at its then temperature of 86° Fahr. does not stiffen. The flask is then vigorously shaken so as to disseminate the introduced cells evenly throughout the flask, which being done the contents of the latter are at once poured out upon a large plate, and immediately covered with a bell-glass.

As it cools, the mixture becomes solid, whereby the cells are isolated from one another, and in a few days whitish specks appear which are with great probability taken to be colonies derived from a single parent cell. Each speck is then removed to a culture flask of sterilised wort or other nutritive fluid, and a growth from each obtained. Still even here absolute certainty is not secured. Moreover, comparatively simple as the manipulation is, it is found that the addition of the gelatine decreases, as far as the saccharomycetes are concerned, the nutritive value of the wort to which it is added, and that therefore few but the more vigorous cells thrive in it.

Hansen's Modification of Nägeli's Dilution Plan is as follows :—

Having counted the number of cells in one drop of the fluid (and having been careful, with that object, to keep it from overflowing the outermost square of a number of fine lines engraved on a glass-slide, and crossing one another at right angles), he proceeds to dilute a similar drop with such an amount of sterilised water that, on shaking up the flask, a certain measurable quantity (say 2 cc.), of which the half can be conveniently taken, ought to contain one cell. Then if quantities of 1 cc. be withdrawn (the flask being well shaken before and between the withdrawals), and placed into flasks containing sterilised wort, and if these be then properly protected from the access of adventitious germs, the probability is that, not only will one flask out of every two have been impregnated, but that the growth, when it does occur, will have had its origin in a single cell. But Hansen is not content with probability; his method requires the largest measure of certainty possible.

Accordingly, having impregnated the series of flasks as above, each of the series is vigorously shaken, so that in the event of more than one cell having found their way into any one flask, they may be separated and settle upon a different part of the bottom or sides of the flask. This it is practically certain they do, and that the entrance of more than one cell into any particular flask will be revealed by the appearance of more than one of the white specks, which are evidence of the position of a yeast (or other culture) centre.

If, then, careful examination of the flasks at the end of several days discovers only one such speck in any of them, there is the strongest ground for concluding that one cell only entered those particular flasks, and when these single colonies have been used for the impregnation of fresh flasks, containing sterilised nutritive solution, the pure culture is started.*

This, however, is only a first step; it is only clearing the ground for that analysis of yeast which has been rendered possible by Hansen's labours alone. There are two steps further:

(1) To investigate and note the effects produced in regard to flavour, soundness, condition, and brightness, by each variety of yeast, which had been isolated, and (2) To devise some plan of differentiating yeasts

* Of course these cultures are not on a scale adequate for commercial use, and a special apparatus has been designed by the experimenter for the production of large crops.

ASCOSPORE AND FILM FORMATIONS.

which, though apparently alike, have yet shown themselves dissimilar by inducing good or harmless changes in the one case, and positively hurtful changes in the other.

The former is comparatively simple, though lengthy; it obviously requires a series of actual fermentations to be carried out on a relatively large scale—one at least for every culture of yeast isolated—and finished so that eye and palate together may judge what the result has been. For the latter the course was by no means so plain; but the final outcome of much thought and patient research was that two means of differentiating yeasts, morphologically alike but otherwise unlike, existed which depended, first, on the length of time taken to form **ascospores,** under conditions covering a wide range of temperature, but constant for each set of experiments; and secondly, on their mode of **film or pellicle formation** also under varying conditions.

It has previously been mentioned that the yeast-cell under certain circumstances—and the fact was noticed by Reess, Engel, and others before Hansen—unfavourable for propagation in the way we now consider normal, viz., by budding, provides for its reproduction by developing endogenous spores, the protoplasm dividing itself generally into four separate masses, which being surrounded with a cell-wall are known as **ascospores** ($\dot{a}\sigma\kappa o\varsigma$ = a skin or bag).

Accordingly Hansen, or those associated with him, arrive at these appropriate conditions conveniently by the use of small blocks made from plaster-of-Paris, on each of which, after they have been sterilised in a flame or otherwise, a small portion of the pure culture is smeared, the block being then placed in a small vessel of water provided with a cover, so that the water absorbed into its pores suffices to keep the surface just moist. The series of blocks, so arranged, are then placed in a thermostat, and kept at a uniform temperature, say of 18° C. (= 64·4° Fahr.), or of 25° C. (= 77° Fahr.), etc., as the case may

Synoptic Table for Yeast Analysis by Variations in Ascospore and Film Formations at Various Temperatures.

	\multicolumn{7}{c}{Ascospore Formation.}	\multicolumn{7}{c}{Film Formation.}
	Max.	Min.	\multicolumn{5}{c	}{At Degrees Fahrenheit.}	\multicolumn{5}{c	}{Feebly developed flecks at degrees Fahrenheit.}	Max.	Min.
			62·6–64·4	77	81·5	86		42·8–44·6	68–71·6	91·4–93·2	100·4		
Sacch. Cerevisiæ I. The true alcoholic yeast of top or bottom fermentation. [*Sacch. Cerevisiæ II.* is a variety of the same type, both are in use at the Carlsberg Brewery.]	96·8 to 98·6	51·8 to 53·6	Hours 50	Hours 23	N.D.	Hours 20		Months 2–3	Days 7–10	Days 9–18	None	91·4 to 93·2	42·8 to 44·6
Sacch. Pastorianus I. As observed, is a "bottom" ferment, which gives a strong, bitter taste to beer.	86·0	37·4 to 39·2	35	25 (about)	Hours 24	30		1–2	8–15	None	None	78·8 to 82·4	37·4 to 41

SYNOPTIC TABLE FOR YEAST ANALYSIS.

Sacch. Pastorianus II.	81·5	37·4 to 39·2	36		25	34	None	1-2	8·15	None	None	78·8 to 82·4	37·4 to 41
As observed in top fermentation. Produces no evil result in beer.												
Sacch. Pastorianus III.	81·5	47·3	44		28	35	None	1-2	8·15	None	None	78·8 to 82·4	37·4 to 41
Another top-fermentation form, which produces turbidity in beer.												
Sacch. Ellipsoideus I.	88·7	44·6		33	21	N.D.	[86·9 to 88·7] 36	2-3	10-17	8-12	None	91·4 to 93·2	42·8 to 44·6
The yeast of grapes. [Otherwise *S. Ellipticus*.]												
Sacch. Ellipsoideus II.	92·3	47·3		42	27	N.D.	23	1-2	4-6	3-4	**Days** 8-12	96·8 to 100·4	37·4 to 41
As observed, is a "bottom" fermentation form, causing yeast turbidity.												

[*N.B.*—In the third column of the above list the time taken is placed on the left or the right of the *dotted line*, according as the lower or higher temperature of the range (62·6° or 64·4°) was used. The letters N.D. = *no data.*]

be, and the *exact time* at which ascospores develop is in each case noted.

It will be observed from the preceding table, which has been drawn up with the aid of the lucid work by A. Jörgensen,* that the former temperature allows of a very ready differentiation of *Sacch. cerevisiæ* from all the wild forms there given, while again a temperature of 81.5 enables a distinction to be made between the injurious *Sacch. Pastorianus I.*, and the harmless, if not useful, *Sacch. Pastorianus II.* Other differentiations will occur to those looking at the table, which might have been made larger, but has been purposely kept within comparatively narrow limits in order to make it synoptic.

The Film or Pellicle Formation observed as a second means of differentiating yeasts, are small flecks of (aerobian ?) yeast, which are formed towards the close of flask fermentations, in periods that vary with the conditions, as the foregoing table will show. The wort becomes lighter in colour, and the cells obtained are often elongated and approximate to the mycelial growth referred to in Chapter IX. Access of filtered air is necessary, and the flecks of the film can be distinguished from those of the ordinary aerobian ferments (*M. vini* and *M. aceti*), when the formation has advanced further by a difference of colour, the former being usually a distinct greyish-yellow, the latter grey.

It has been quite recently pointed out by Jörgensen that all top-yeast is by way of forming stronger and more numerous spores than cultivated bottom-yeast does; that the spores of the cultivated variety of the former, though larger and with better-defined cell-walls than those of the uncultivated variety, have not the clear and homogeneous structure which the latter has when young.

He also points out that at the temperature of 25° C. (=77° Fahr.), the sporulation period of each variety is too close for a satisfactory analysis, and accordingly 59° Fahr

---

* Translated by Morris & Brown, published by F. W. Lyon, Eastcheap, at 5*s.*

and even 53·6° Fahr. are preferable, as giving much more marked divergencies.

Cultivation of the Yeast in sufficient quantity for Pitching.—The method of culture from a single cell has hitherto only been described as far as the first stage—the introduction of the minute, almost microscopic colonies into small Pasteur flasks of sterilised wort. It is next advisable to introduce the small crop from each of these into larger flasks of sterilised wort, and crops having been secured in the latter, it is possible to proceed to the cultivation on a larger scale.

For this Hansen has devised a special apparatus which, without entering into minute detail, may be stated to consist of four parts—viz., **(1) An air-pump, (2) An air reservoir, (3) A wort receiver, and (4) A fermentation cylinder.** All parts in contact with the wort are of well-tinned copper, and all, as well as those of the air-pump and air-receiver, are so arranged as to be thoroughly sterilised at any stage by the admission of superheated steam. The air-pump, which of course only pumps in filtered air, has been made an adjunct because of the proved necessity of aëration for the pure cultures, and the air-receiver, which contains air at a pressure of 3 or 4 atmospheres, enables the air to be introduced with greater uniformity than would be possible with an air-pump alone.

The wort-receiver may be connected by a tube with the copper, but this is hardly necessary if wort can be introduced into it at an absolutely boiling temperature without the admission of contaminated outside air. The wort-receiver has a jacket, between the walls of which cold water can be made to circulate, in order to cool the wort to the desired temperature, and it is connected with the air-receiver so that the wort may be efficiently aërated before being mixed with the yeast. Then the fermentation cylinder is partially filled with wort, some of the pure culture introduced with precautions against infection, and the fermentation cylinder is then filled up to the highest advisable level. [Of course, the fermentation-cylinder has an outlet for carbonic acid gas; it is also provided with a stirring apparatus, actuated from the outside, for mixing wort and yeast thoroughly.]

There is a tap for drawing off the liquid mixed with the new yeast at the right moment; and in the arrangement at Carlsberg the fermentation cylinder is once partially emptied and once totally emptied (except for a small quantity of yeast, sufficient to start a fermentation in a fresh charge) every 10 days, enough yeast being got in that time to pitch 8 hectolitres (*i.e.*, 176 gallons) of wort.

Thus it will be seen that the production of a full crop of pure pitching yeast is not a very speedy affair, but from this point—up to which it has been conducted with precautions for absolute sterilisation—the cultivation is carried on in fermenting vessels of the ordinary type. Undoubtedly, even in the purest air, infection by wild yeasts, bacteria, etc., now begins, but it is found in practice that sufficient purity is maintained for a considerable time, and that, for operations on an industrial scale, the culture does not require to be begun again *de novo*, in respect to the whole crop of pitching yeast, but that it is sufficient, when once a pure crop has been obtained, to reinforce it from time to time with fresh yeast developed on the pure culture system recently described. [Hansen found—it may be mentioned—that, when the proportion of wild yeasts was less than 2·44%, or perhaps we may say 2.5%, no evil results ensued.

Experiments with Pure Cultures in Top-Fermentation Breweries (France).—These experiments have been mentioned earlier in the present chapter, and as detailed accounts from one point of view have come to hand, and as the writer was further enabled to get some first-hand information from the owner of a brewery on the spot and a letter from another gentleman connected with the trade there, which qualify those accounts somewhat, he thinks it would be interesting, before concluding this section, to give a *résumé* of what has been done in that locality, and extracts from the letters he has received.

The expert who presides over these pure-culture fermentations is M. Kokolinski, analytical chemist of Lille. The following is an abstract of his method, and what he claims for it. [It is stated that fifteen breweries in the Département du Nord have regularly adopted it, since its first introduction into a top-fermentation brewery at Lille in 1888.]

To Select the Desirable Type.—A sample is taken from the yeast in general use, rather than from the first heads thrown up during fermentation. [First heads are found to contain fewer species of yeast than the pitching yeast, some of the best types being occasionally missing.]

A trace of the sample taken is submitted to gelatine culture, the individual cells being thus separated [?]; then the colonies from at least 12 isolated cells are carefully observed—*e.g.*, the time is noted in which ascospores are formed, the same with pellicles, besides numerous details of fermentation and of the resulting beer, primary and secondary fermentation, etc.

The materials used, type of beer wanted, and the method of fermentation must be taken into account; even then there is no certainty of succeeding at the first attempt. Often three or four sorts of yeasts have to be tried before a satisfactory result is obtained.

When the desirable type is found, the cultivation on an industrial scale begins.

1. In Pasteur flasks.

2. In tinned copper flasks, or covered copper cans of 24 litres' (nearly 5 gallons') capacity, capable of containing 16 litres (nearly $3\frac{1}{2}$ gallons of wort, in active fermentation. [In these cultures M. Kokolinski attaches great importance to perfect sterilisation of wort, and he always operates in an Autoclave at a temperature of 115° to 120° C. (=239° to 248° Fahr.).

3. The quantity produced by 2 is enough to prime a Hansen's apparatus if there be one, or to pitch 150 litres (about 32 gallons) of wort.

4. The yeast from the Hansen's apparatus (or from the

150 litres) is used to pitch 8 hectolitres (176 gallons) of fresh wort.

5. The yeast obtained from 4 suffices to pitch 37 barrels.

The beer got from the wort used in yeast-production, though a little flat, is perfectly sound, and can be used either directly or blended; and though the first fermentations are sometimes not very active, M. Kokolinski says it is a mere question of acclimatisation, and that after the second or third generation the fermentation will resume its normal activity. He also finds—as has been stated before—that it is unnecessary to replace the whole yeast-store with pure yeast when a pure-culture store has once been obtained. Additions of pure yeast from time to time will do.

Never More than Two Types are blended.—A single type of yeast is easier to work and gives more regular fermentations, but it is sometimes necessary to select two types. The admixture of two types, however, has hitherto been found sufficient.

Commercial Yeast of North of France.—More than 60 different types (!) have been differentiated, of which 40 have been carefully studied and classified in M. Kokolinski's collection. Many of these types, the so-called "wild yeasts," are absolutely bad.

The alleged advantages are (1) That beers so brewed have the special flavour desired. (2) The flavour is regular, uniform, and well defined. (3) Clarification is easier and more rapid. (4) The beers resist bacterial agencies better and keep longer.

Moreover, M. Kokolinski claims that the advantage of using "pure culture" yeast is greater with high-fermentation beers than with those brewed on the low-fermentation (bottom fermentation), because the former have not the advantage, which the latter have, of cold to check the action of hurtful ferments, and to keep their growth down.

Of my two correspondents, who so kindly wrote to me, No. 1, the Brewer, says, "I have made some trials of pure fermentation with Hansen's apparatus for about a year, and without having been completely successful, I may say that it has given me much satisfaction. There is, in effect, a very appreciable result in the regularity of the flavour of the beer and in the purity of the fermentation. Formerly, when I had a change of yeast the flavour of my beer was altered, and my customers did not find the uniformity indispensable to successful manufacture. It is a point of great importance to be able to re-establish the dominant yeast of a brewery at will.

"In the second place, this regeneration has, as corollary, the production of a pure yeast free from bacteria. I do not insist on this point, because it is beyond disproof that bacteria and sometimes wild yeasts are our worst enemies.

"Thus far the advantageous side of pure yeast. But now I must confess that in my case the reconstitution of a store of industrial yeast has been less easy to obtain than in other breweries. I have sometimes, according to the season, required 4, 5, or even 6 industrial cultures, before seeing the yeast recover the qualities of odour, colour and agglomeration. I repeat that other breweries have not experienced the same difficulties, and I ask myself why the yeast which I use is so difficult to set going.

"My opinion is that, for certain races, the mode of selection proposed by M. Hansen, viz., by gelatine culture,* takes the nature out of the cell (*dénature la cellule*). The cell becomes sick, and no longer secretes the sort of mucus which agglomerates it to the other cells. Moreover, the beer produced by the first generation often has a yeasty taste.

"Have I perchance experimented badly? Have I lighted on a bad kind of yeast? One or the other of these hypotheses must be correct, because my colleagues have been able to obtain commercial yeast at the first attempt.

---

* The dilution method, previously described, is preferable, it will be remembered, on ground of accuracy.

"Then I tried a mixture of two varieties, and succeeded better, but one of the two varieties stifled the other, which was less resistant.

"Whatever the cause may be, I have never since beginning my attempts had any bad flavours due to manufacture. My beers have not been flat, the attenuation has been constantly the same, and there has been no occasion to dread that which the detractors of Hansen's system everywhere proclaim.

"To sum up. This question has many obscure points, which time and practice will make clear; but a progress there is, and in my opinion (who am only a very modest practitioner, with no intention of posing as a learned experimentalist) the system will one day or other become very practical for top-fermentation beers.

"I believe that the brewers of 'bottom-fermentation' beers have a better chance than we of succeeding, because their yeast rests at the bottom of the vessel, and accordingly its alteration is less frequent and less probable. But we shall succeed after them, I doubt not."

My other correspondent does not take an optimist view, though he is unaware from sampling or trustworthy information how the change of ferment has modified the product. But he has not heard, he says, that the brewers working with yeast cultivated from a single cell have achieved any dazzling success. He is inclined, however, to attribute any want of marked success less to any inherent unfitness of the system for top-fermentation beers than to the light gravity of the beers in the North of France (worts of 9° to 10° Balling), conjecturing that such beers, exempt from all acidity beyond that normal to the malt they were made from, might easily taste insipid.

The "Pure Culture" in Australia.—Mr. de Bavay has placed upon record that his employment of a pure culture of *Sacch. Cerevisiæ* has been successful in Australia, his ales in bottle developing all the "condition" so essential to high quality. To this it has been objected that brewing conditions in Australia are very different to those which obtain in England. The employment of as much as 50% of high-class cane-sugar is not infrequent, and this might very well account for matter being left after the primary fermentation had apparently finished—either invert or maltose—which the primary yeast cells would be capable of degrading. The famous French chemist, Dumas, found that it takes twice as long to ferment cane-sugar as it does to ferment inverted—*i.e.*, the inversion takes as long as the fermentation, and where yeast has to ferment as much as 50% of sugar, it is far from unlikely, unless the primary fermentation were to be unduly prolonged, that primarily fermentable matter would pass into cask, and even into bottle, before being altogether split up into alcohol and carbonic acid.

Moreover, where the wort is exposed on open coolers, and especially in regions whose temperature is on the average high, it is not easy to see how an absolutely pure " store," free from secondary yeasts whose germs are of necessity floating about the brewery, can be maintained. But if there is any weight in the latter contention it cuts the ground from under those who maintain that the so-called pure-culture yeast is unfitted for top-fermentation brewing, on account of the absence of " cask-conditioning."

Such are a few of the various opinions on what must for some time remain an open question, but the suggestion, elsewhere advanced, may be reiterated, that it will ultimately be found feasible to have a pure culture of *Sacch. Cerevisiæ* for the primary fermentation, and a distinct pure culture of some secondary yeast, say of *Sacch. Pastorianus II.* (if that be what determines " condition "), to be added at the time of racking.

CHAPTER XII.

TREATMENT OF BEER.

TURBIDITY OF BEER—(i) FROM DEFECTIVE YEAST—(ii) FROM BACTERIA—(iii) FROM ALBUMINOIDS—(iv) FROM HOP-RESIN (AND HOP-SICKNESS)—(v) FROM AMYLÖINS OF ABNORMALLY LOW TYPE—(vi) FROM MINERAL MATTER IN SUSPENSION—ROPINESS—YEAST-BITE — ANTISEPTICS — FININGS — DIFFERENT METHODS OF FINING — STORAGE OF PALE AND BITTER ALES —POROUS SPILES — SAMPLING — BOTTLING — FORCING TRAY—SIMPLER TEST FOR STABILITY IN BOTTLE.

A TOLERABLY accurate idea of the causes of acidity in beer has been obtainable since the publication of Pasteur's *Études sur la Bière*, but the causes of turbidity and yeast-bite are always further to seek, being involved in possible complications which make them obscure. We will, however, try to get some light thrown upon the causes of turbidity first. These are :—

(1) **Defective Yeast.**—And this defect may be due either (a) to insufficient nutrition or (β) to over-nutrition; and this not only in the wort actually in course of fermentation, but during the past history of the yeast, which is the head more immediately under consideration.

Apart from the so-called "wild-yeasts," *Sacch. Ellipsoideus*, *Sacch. Pastorianus III.*, and *Sacch. Exiguus*, which definitely cause turbidity, it is easy to see that ill-nourished yeast, being only capable of reproduction and fermentative action in a modified way, will be less able than stronger yeast to deal with such factors of turbidity as are mentioned in some of the succeeding paragraphs. The aged cells, which are relatively very numerous in yeast of this description, with their thickened membranes through which

TURBIDITY FROM YEAST.

the fermentable fluid does not readily pass, are, even if their vitality be only dormant, manifestly less able to break such fermentable matter up within a reasonable time.

And whether the young cells which such an enfeebled stock does produce be *Sacch. Exiguus*, as used to be supposed, or whether the latter belongs to a distinct type, to be classified with wild yeasts, there can be little doubt that a number of cells are produced of relatively light specific gravity, a quantity of which remain in the wort, and either do not subside at all, or easily rise to cloud the beer upon the slightest increase of temperature or vibration.

On the other hand, over-fed yeast, yeast clogged with nitrogen, is equally, without some special stimulation, incapable of performing those reproductive and fermentative functions which are so essential. Hayduck, who made exhaustive researches on this question, determining the nitrogen percentages most carefully, came to the conclusion that (1) The amount of nitrogen in pitching yeast increases with each fermentation; (2) Increase of nitrogen up to a certain point increases the fermenting power of the yeast; but (3) The capacity of the pitching yeast for assimilating the nitrogenous nourishment decreases as the yeast is repeatedly used—*i.e.*, as it becomes itself richer in nitrogen.

He accordingly recommended pitching at a higher temperature than ordinary (he himself set his experimental worts to ferment at $63\frac{1}{2}°$ Fahr.) and aëration, especially the latter, seeing that the admission of atmospheric air into worts during fermentation stimulates vigorous budding (as does the higher temperature to a less extent), and it is clear that the more vigorously yeast grows in a fluid containing a given quantity of nitrogenous matter, the more of the latter will then be absorbed, seeing that every yeast-cell formed requires some of it to form its protoplasm.

The course indicated to remedy this phase of turbidity, short of using acclimatised yeast derived from a pure culture, is to select yeast carefully (1) according to observed previous results—*i.e.*, eliminating for pitching purposes the yeast-crops of any gyle which has shown a marked tendency to yeast turbidity; and (2) by aid of the microscope, viz., to use those yeasts only which show cells of regular size (this is much better than cells, some abnormally large, others below the average) with well-defined vacuoles and practically free from worn-out cells with dark and granulated plasm. Particularly should the absence of small cells of *Sacch. Exiguus* be ascertained. Of course, too, relative freedom from bacteria is essential, and this indeed is, to some extent, a corollary of yeast-vigour.

It has been suggested that in the washing of yeast we have a means, generally satisfactory in result, of sorting out the small cells and other impurities, and this applies, not only to the small cells of *Sacch. Exiguus*, but to others of a larger type which are weakened or dead, or to bacteria. [It will be noticed that even in the extremely thin layer of a microscopic " field " the latter float at a higher level than the yeast cells do.]

The success of the operation depends upon the greater specific gravity of the more desirable cells. The *modus operandi* recommended is as follows. The yeast is to be mixed with a fairly large quantity of water at 32° Fahr., in a special receptacle, with a tap (or taps at different levels) in its side. As soon as the largest and heaviest cells have settled to the bottom of the receptacle, the turbid water above must be drawn off before the myriads of light cells and other impurities in suspension have time to settle. The precise temperature of the water is of importance; the yeast settles less readily in warmer water, and if suddenly chilled has a tendency to mass together, so that its cells cannot be sorted according to their specific gravity.

Two objections to this treatment occur: (1) If it be the practice to use uninverted cane-sugar to any extent, the yeast being deprived of its invertase, degradation of the sugar might possibly not take place. (2) The washing will lower the nitrogen percentage of the yeast (the said constituent in its compounds being very soluble) on which, up to a certain point, its vigour largely depends.

[Should this be the case a remedy may be found in a preliminary treatment of the selected yeast—*i.e.*, before pitching with it, but after the sorting-out process—with unhopped wort of fair gravity and in a shallow vessel. As a general rule, the wort should be *boiled* and filtered; unboiled wort, so added, might have too stimulative an effect in some cases, determining, as it probably would, some amylöin-degradation as well. Its proper sphere seems to be in a certain form of stubbornness to fining influence—hardly turbidity in the strict sense of the term, but referred to under that due to albuminoids.]

Turbidity from Sacch. Pastorianus, according to Hansen, is specially due to the sub-variety isolated as *Sacch. Pastorianus III.*, but it appears that where either sub-variety is in excess, the light specific gravity of the cells may cause a cloudiness more easily provoked (by vibrations, atmospheric changes, etc.) than allayed.

Matthews and Lott say that a distinctly unpleasant smell and flavour, especially the former, which often accompany a *Pastorianus* fret, may pass off and be succeeded by a normal fining, with gas production and the disappearance of the unpleasant symptoms of *Pastorianus* growth. They point out that, beyond casual impregnation of the store yeast by wild yeasts, predisposing causes to an undue growth of *Sacch. Pastorianus* probably are :— Insufficient attenuation and yeast-production, and further a combination of fineness and flatness at racking in conjunction therewith.

Turbidity from Sacch. Exiguus.—The cause of this has already been indicated as the lighter specific gravity of this elongated yeast. The turbidity is prolonged and (according to the writers lately referred to) accompanied by marked flatness, which is probably not unconnected with its inability to ferment maltose.

Turbidity from Sacch. Ellipsoideus.—This saccharomyces, according to Matthews and Lott, " is associated with cloudy frets and sickness," which are often, but not invariably, accompanied by " a stench." Conversely, they say, a bad stench is generally marked by the presence of *Sacch. Ellipsoideus.* Their opinion is that a beer, which has gone through a bad *Sacch. Ellipsoideus* fret, may, if otherwise sound, become quite palatable.

(2) **Turbidity due to Bacteria.**

The turbidity due to bacteria generally, unless in very aggravated cases, manifests itself in the secondary, rather than in the primary stage of fermentation, and oftenest, perhaps, after a beer has been bottled without full preliminary storage. The turbid fluid, examined under the microscope, then appears to be swarming with *micrococci* and *sarcina-like* forms (*diplococci* and sometimes *tetracocci*), generally associated with *Bacterium termo* and rod-like organisms. It is quite possible for such a beer, *i.e.*, one in which *micrococci* predominate, to remain, as it will, persistently turbid, and yet without developing excessive acidity; to be, in fact, apart from its appearance, which always influences the palate, rather pleasant in flavour than otherwise.

This form of turbidity, should it occur in bulk, is very difficult to deal with, the very slight specific gravity of the organisms keeping them suspended, while their extreme minuteness enables them to elude the coagulated network of finings.

(3) **Turbidity due to Albuminoids.**

The knowledge of the nitrogenous bodies or albuminoids, possessed even by the best-informed, is confessedly meagre and wanting in exactness, but there is reason to suppose that the fact of its total nitrogen being either below or above an arbitrarily fixed percentage does not necessarily decide the fitness or unfitness of a malt for brewing. It could not be known without a series of difficult tests how that nitrogen is distributed, how much of it exists in the form of diffusible compounds, or compounds easily rendered so (amides, peptones), and which would therefore at a later stage be assimilable and therefore eliminated by the yeast, and how much in forms, which will always be non-assimilable, and are therefore not removable in the same way. Of course in a finished beer the percentage of albuminoids, determined as such, would be more of an index, representing the non-assimilable bodies much more closely.

Albumen we are accustomed to consider as that portion of the nitrogenous bodies which is either coagulated at a temperature approaching boiling (though a recent patentee, Mr. Valentine, holds that much of the albumen coagulated at 160° to 170° Fahr. is redissolved at 180° or over, and not being eliminated again causes fret and turbidity), or precipitated as **tannate of albumen.**

Identical with the latter perhaps is a modification of albumen, for which the name of **albumose** has been suggested, from its analogy with the albumose of animal digestion. It is alleged that the non-removal of this substance (and it is not assimilable by yeast) may be a cause of turbidity, and that, when this is so, the fact may be ascertained by saturating the liquid with ammonium sulphate, which will cause it to precipitate.

The albuminoids other than albumen found in barley are gluten-fibrin, casein, and mucedin. The latter is known to be more soluble in hot than in cold water, in which it is but very slightly so, and therefore the same conditions which are likely to extract free starch (high sparge heats) are likely to extract mucedin too. The last runnings from "the goods" probably owe their greyness, *which cannot be removed by finings*, to mucedin, and therefore over-sparging is as unadvisable as high sparge heats. Trials made by shaking up mucedin with water have shown that it falls into such a fine state of subdivision that its precipitation is a very lengthy affair.

The percentage of gluten and mucedin will of course depend on natural causes, but a good deal depends on malting operations being carried out in unison with these conditions—*i.e.*, to counteract their influence, when unfavourable, as far as possible.

A good development of acrospire and rootlets are undoubtedly favourable indices, connoting relative elimination of albuminoids; but the writer thinks that the brewer is not without a further means of judging—viz., by observation of the wort's saturation point with regard to the above-mentioned bodies.

Seeing that these bodies are but slightly soluble in boiling water and insoluble in cold, it is probable that of two worts of equal gravity, the one which remained clear (after being boiled) when reduced to say 160°, would be less rich in them than one which clouded at 170° or 180°, that is to say, that **the saturation point** (the temperature at which these albuminoids go out of solution) is in proportion to and in fact rises with the quantity of albuminoids present.

A saturation-point, relatively high in temperature, accordingly indicates the necessity of replacing some portion of the malt, over rich in gluten and what not, by non-albuminoids, rice (flaked malt) and invert-sugar. It is a fact that light worts brewed with such materials, and under conditions such that no mucedin due to sparging could have possibly found its way into the copper, can after a very short boil be filtered (just to remove coagulated albumen) into a test-tube, perfectly bright, and that they will remain so when quite cold.

There is one type of turbidity, characterised by incomplete fining action—*i.e.*, when upon addition of finings to a sample in glass, a sort of break readily begins but does not continue to brightness, or at least takes a long time about it, smeary-looking particles attaching themselves to the side of the glass, while a powdery rather than a flocculent precipitate falls to the bottom. Even upon keeping, probably the resulting beer gets very little brighter, but responds to the action of finings in carriage casks, with, however, a large quantity of "bottoms" or "pitchings."

This is the sort of turbidity that one is inclined to attribute to albuminoid influence, and perhaps to those albuminoids once coagulated but afterwards re-dissolved on boiling, the more so that it is characteristic rather of stronger beers, in which yeast reproduction is comparatively crippled, than of weaker qualities. Moreover, where such beers are of running character it is often necessary to use a lower mashing heat than the corresponding weaker beers would require (in order to limit the amount of malto-dextrin of high type), and the tendency of this is of course to increase the amount of albuminoid extract as well as that of the free maltose. Thus the fermentation is made more rapid, just when, as regards the removal of fine albuminoid particles, it ought to be steadier.

Any real difficulty from this source might be met by very distinctly raising the mashing temperatures, so as to reduce the amount of albuminoid extract, subsequently adding (if too large a quantity of malto-dextrin were likely to be present in the wort for early condition) either cold aqueous malt extract (ref. p. 49), or treating the yeast before pitching with cooled unboiled wort of energetic diastatic quality, which will not only give it a good start, but will also, as the malt-extract does, help to degrade the malto-dextrins into primarily fermentable maltose.

Aëration, by stimulating yeast-growth, may have some good effect.

The above suggestions will perhaps serve as a clue to causes which, as yet, cannot be formulated with precision.

(4) **Turbidity due to Hop-resin.**

That hop-resin may be a factor in the turbidity of beer, albeit only a secondary one, there is good reason to believe. That is to say that, in a perfectly brewed and fermented beer, a slight increase in the normal amount of hop-resin would have no detrimental influence, nay, probably might facilitate the action of finings, but in beer brewed so that cask-condition does not readily set in and then only feebly, any excess or even the normal amount of hop-resin may lead to a turbidity difficult to eradicate.

The hop-resin appears to be in solution in the earlier stages of fermentation, but to pass out of it to a great extent afterwards, some holding that the closely associated essential oil determines its solution, others, with more apparent probability, thinking that maltose is the determining solvent, and that, as this is fermented away, so the resin passes out of solution, helping to form, as it does so, the discoloured mass of amorphous matter seen upon the surface of fermenting tuns.

If this be so, there are more reasons than one why this form of turbidity should occur, as it does, in beers produced from a wort in which the ratio of free maltose was high; for not only will more than the normal amount of resin pass into solution and then be thrown out of it, owing to the excess of solvent maltose present at first and then rapidly fermented away, but it will have less yeast to adhere to, and a lessened opportunity of doing so, because the yeast in a wort, with a high ratio of maltose, is so vigorously engaged in breaking up that readily fermentable constituent as to have little tendency, comparatively speaking, to reproduction, and moreover, on account of this fermentative activity, the yeast which is produced is more rapidly evolved than is the case when the wort-constituents are better balanced.

According to any view too, including the latest theory of cask-conditioning, a wort in which free maltose was originally in excess, implies deferred and feeble secondary fermentation, just where a good secondary fermentation is wanted to get rid of the hop-resin turbidity, which has remained over from the primary fermentation.

Accordingly, the plan to adopt where trouble of this sort occurs, is to endeavour to decrease the ratio of free maltose by using higher mashing heats, which will have the effect too of determining a less rapid fermentation, and the presence of those bodies which play a leading part in a satisfactory secondary fermentation.

[Although the above seems the sounder view, certain authorities, as has been said, suspect the hop-oil of being the predisposing cause of trouble; Balling holding that the resin is dissolved under the influence of the ethereal oil, and that, if the latter were absent, the hop-resin would be completely thrown out by fermentation, Habich supposing that, as the hop-oil becomes volatilised in fermentation and storage, the resin, deprived of its decomposing agent, separates in fine particles, which remain suspended in the liquid.

There would be more ground for adhering to this view if it were found that ales with the most hop-flavour at racking were specially liable to this form of turbidity.]

To satisfy himself as to hop-resin being the cause of turbidity, the brewer may make a sample of his turbid beer alkaline with caustic potash or shake it up with ether; in either case a removal of turbidity indicates hop-resin as the cause, these reagents having no effect upon yeast-turbidity.

[Messrs. Matthews and Lott, however ("On the Action of Finings," *Trans. Inst. Brewing*, iv. No. 8), do not consider hop-resin turbidity so productive of trouble in beer-fining as is commonly supposed, because although an apparently stubborn opalescence ensued if a drop or two of alcoholic solution of hop-resin were added to distilled water, yet on finings being added, perfect clarification, as their experiments showed, usually resulted.

Decoctions of hops in water were for the most part stubborn in behaviour with finings, which the authors attribute to the hop-oil in a state of minute subdivision. The same decoction added to beer, however, caused the finings to separate in a more bulky form, the beer above being brilliant.]

(5) **Turbidity from Dry Hopping (Hop-Sickness).**— Though only transient with well-brewed, sound ales, it may be far otherwise with those of less satisfactory character. This form of turbidity should not in strictness be classed by

itself, being partially due to some of the actual hop-constituents passing into the ale in a state of semi-solution, but even more to fermentative organisms, introduced with even the best of hops, and which accelerate the secondary fermentation. This acceleration, if excessive, may take the form of a persistent "fret," frequently attended with a disagreeable "nose," which, however, passes off under favourable conditions.

(6) **Turbidity due to Amylöins of abnormally Low Type and Free Maltose.**

This form of turbidity is most likely to occur in summer, when wild yeasts are plentiful. These break down the amylöins (malto-dextrins) violently, not quietly as in winter, and accordingly fretfulness results even where the amylöins, though of rather low, are still of perfectly normal type.

It is supposed, however, that amylöins are sometimes formed of such abnormally low type (Maltose 19 : 1 Dextrin) that they are nearly as unresistant to the influence of primary yeast as is maltose itself. Consequently the impetus given to any primary yeast remaining in suspension by the inevitable aëration at the time of racking will be quite sufficient to induce a tumultuous fermentation, without the usual pause for the secondary ferments to begin.

Again, it may happen that owing to some defect in the yeast, or more probably to undue viscidity of the wort (malto-dextrin of abnormally *high* type being present), which would hamper the yeast in its action, all the *free maltose* is not degraded at the time of racking, and thus when the suspended primary yeast is invigorated by aëration, there is a constituent at hand very susceptible to its fermentative influence.

The presence of the low type amylöins referred to above would seem to be indicated when the primary fermentation is unduly prolonged, *i.e.*, when instead of the last head (in the case of skimmed beers) being taken off thirty hours, or at most thirty-six hours from the time of the first skim, the skimming has to be continued nearly till the usual time of racking.

In any case the immediate remedy should be to use larger quantities of pitching yeast (so that the low-type amylöins may be broken up more speedily) and to postpone, as far as possible, the time of fining, but rolling the casks about in cellar as often as possible by way of preliminary. The writer is inclined to think that the "working-out" system of fining would be better adapted than the ordinary method for this kind of turbidity, where early consumption is desired, but on this point he lacks practical experience.

The cure of course is to be sought earlier, and should turn, for running beers, on the employment of higher but evenly dried malts, albeit higher mashing heats are supposed to be an even more potent factor for raising *type* of malto-dextrin.

(7) **Turbidity possibly caused by Mineral Matter in Suspension.**

Messrs. Matthews and Lott, in their valuable and suggestive paper on the action of finings, pointed out the possibility (of which they have strong evidence, though not enough to prove it actually) of the turbidity of certain stubborn ales being due to the presence of very minute crystals of phosphate of lime and magnesia.

Such crystals, they say, are discernible in some cloudy beers, and they find that obdurately dim beers are rendered much less so by applying a pressure of carbonic acid gas. The clearing that occurs cannot be due to solution of hop-resin or nitrogenous substances, the solubility of these bodies being lessened by acidity of the medium, but on the other hand, the phosphates spoken of are remarkably soluble in carbon dioxide.

This view is countenanced by the fact that a dull beer, on becoming brisk, will often concurrently brighten, and they suggest, "as a rider," that the turbidity which bright beers acquire upon free exposure to the air may possibly be due to these same phosphates being thrown out of solution, in consequence of the escape of carbonic acid gas, and the thereby reduced acidity.

Ropiness. The Ropy Ferment.

This very unpleasant phenomenon—which, at its worst, makes the ale infected with it pour out like castor-oil, or even hang in strings, as it were, from a stirring-rod that has been dipped into it—seems to be the work of an organism or organisms which convert the fermentable sugar of the wort into **Mannite** and a gum-like body known as **Dextran**, but not in any precise proportion.

What these organisms are can hardly be unhesitatingly laid down, but Dr. Van Laer, Professor at the Brewing School of Ghent, has identified two kindred ferments which he names respectively *Bacillus viscosus I.* and *Bacillus viscosus II.*, in the sphere of which sugar, contrary to the accepted view, plays an unimportant (?) part. We will return to these presently.

Another organism which produces an analogous result in sugar refineries (whence its spores may easily be introduced into breweries) is *Leuconostoc mesenteroides*, an organism which occurs in twining chains of colourless minute spherical cells, each chain being enclosed in a relatively thick gelatinous sheath of toughish character.

This may be the chaplet form, which those following the earlier researches of M. Pasteur describe the ropy ferment to be. Others attribute the disease to *Pediococcus cerevisiæ*, a sort of sarcina, which at any rate appears to be frequently present in beer so infected. And, according to Lintner, the mould *Dematium pullulans* grown in beer-wort has the same effect.

All we can say with any degree of certainty is that beers in bottle are more liable to the malady than those in wood, consequently it is a fair inference that pressure stimulates the activity of the organisms, and that whatever the organism may be, it is capable of an anaërobic existence.

Further, we find that ropy beers lose their excessive viscosity if kept till acidity develops, and with ropy beers there is generally a tendency towards excessive development of lactic and butyric acids, so we may conclude that acidity, as such, is unfavourable to ropiness.

Again, lightly hopped beers are more liable to ropiness than those which are heavily hopped (well-hopped pale ales, perhaps, never go ropy), which may be connected with the general fact that an increase in the acidity percentage appears to discourage ropiness, or may be more due to the special type of acid, tannic, in which the hops are richest. The fact mentioned by Schützenberger, that white wines, which are poorer in tannin than red wines, are much more liable than the latter to be attacked by the malady in question, strengthens the latter view.

Beyond a doubt the disease is the work of some organism, which gains a foothold through some uncleanliness, possibly beyond the brewer's control (*e.g.*, the earthy matter attaching to pigeons' claws has been found teeming with *Sarcina* germs, and they and other birds not unfrequently use the brewery as a resting-place).

But **predisposing causes seem to be** the use of *slack* and inferior malt, insufficient hopping, and a degree of acidity below the normal, whether the latter be reduced by a large proportion of sugar used in brewing, or (as is sometimes done) by the addition of relatively large quantities of unboiled liquor to the fermenting vessel for the purpose of making up "length," if a longer one than the coppers can effectively boil is wanted.

Possibly the vicinity of the hayloft may have some influence (chopped hay infusion stimulates growth of *Sarcina*, which also is encouraged by the neutrality or alkalinity of its medium), as it has in the providing of other disease-ferments.

To return to Dr. Van Laer. In submitting to plate-cultivation a ropy beer deposit, in order to isolate certain *micrococci*, which appeared to be identical with Pasteur's chaplet form, he found that these cultivated *micrococci* would not cause ropiness, but that certain slender rods (1·6 to 2·4 μ long and 0·8 μ in width) which were not at first suspected did cause it.

These organisms, whose behaviour he found to differ in wort, though it was similar in meat extract, he called respectively *Bacillus viscosus I.* and *Bacillus viscosus II.* Morphologically they hardly differ, unless it be that the former is a shade the more slender of the two.

Bacillus viscosus I., at the high temperature of $80\frac{1}{2}°$ Fahr., turned sterilised beer-wort ropy in 24 hours. In 48 hours it was as viscous as the albuminous part of an egg. Turbidity and a characteristic smell, with the liberation of much carbonic acid in the early stage, but lessening as viscosity increases, seem to be features of this fermentation. With *Bacillus viscosus II.* the evolution of carbonic acid gas was much less in amount.

Dr. Van Laer showed that a mixture of sucrose, peptone, and water in the proportions of 3 : 1 : 100, was rendered turbid and afterwards ropy by the No. 1 type, but that type No. 2 only made it turbid, unless the acidity due to peptone were neutralised by sodic bicarbonate, in which case type No. 2 was also capable of making the above-mentioned mixture ropy. He also found that gypsum in the brewing water promoted the vigour of the organism in question.

Jörgensen regards viscosity as a phenomenon nearly related to the commonly occurring zoogloea formation of certain bacteria.

E. Kramer (*Monatschrifte für Chemie*) says that the gummy body produced during the mucous fermentation —viz., the substance $C_6H_{10}O_5$—can be isolated by precipitating the liquid with alcohol. It is an amorphous white substance, quite insoluble in water, and capable of being drawn out into threads. Solutions formed by dissolving it with alkali are yellow in colour, but iodine has no action upon it, and from the alkaline solution fine white compound crystals can be precipitated by alcohol.

He maintains that the active ferment is a different one according to the constitution of the liquid in respect of acidity,—*e.g.*, (1) that liquids containing saccharose, having either neutral or feebly alkaline reactions, suffer it under the influence of *Bacillus viscosus sacchari*, an organism 2·5 to 4 μ long, and 1 μ wide; (2) That liquids containing glucose, and with acid reaction, suffer it from *Bacillus viscosus vini*, an anaërobic ferment 2 to.6 μ long and ·6 to ·8 μ wide; and (3) That sweet liquids, with merely neutral reaction—*e.g.*, milk—suffer it from a *coccus* about 1 μ in diameter.

Kramer's views require confirmation, but it is hoped that by their inclusion in the above abstract the ground will be fairly covered.

Yeast-bite and Good Hop Flavour.—" Yeast-bitten " or " Barm-stricken " beers have been supposed to owe their disagreeable clinging bitter to some action of the alcohol in the beer towards the end of its primary fermentation, upon the contents of the yeast-cell, an action mainly due to the high temperature at which it sometimes comes in contact with the latter; and it must be admitted that cautious cooling, as soon after skimming as is otherwise prudent, minimises the risk of its occurrence.

As a matter of fact, almost all beers, unless in very cold weather, may be attemperated twenty-four hours after the first skim, and pale and bitter ales somewhat earlier, without detriment; indeed, some brewers advocate a slight fall of temperature while the yeast is coming off, asserting, too, that a preferable hop-flavour is secured for that class of ale with a maximum of 68° Fahr.; and though it is difficult to lay down a hard-and-fast rule, the writer may state that his own practice is in general agreement with this view.

Further, absence of aëration is alleged to be a factor of some weight in yeast-bite, and the ales from one particular brewing centre are cited as characteristically affected in this way, as the writer believes without due warrant.

It is precisely stated that the oxygenation which the cleansing process brings about is sufficient to obviate yeast-bite, whilst skimming in one fermenting vessel without special aëration after the wort has left the refrigerator, is alleged to bring it about.

As to the value of this opinion, the writer can only say that he remembers a year or two since tasting a large number of samples, representing every style of store beer, from one of the most important breweries worked on the cleansing system, *every one of which was yeast-bitten*, whilst samples representing thousands upon thousands of barrels, in the production of which aëration after pitching is quite exceptional, come under his notice without being found to have a trace of yeast-bite.

Moreover, Hansen's pronouncements show the probability of yeast-bite being due not to ordinary yeast, but to one of the wild types associated with it (*e.g., S. Pastorianus I.*), in which case the presence or absence of that, or a similarly acting type, is the all-important point, albeit prolonged high temperature in the alcoholic fluid may give a degree of importance to quite a small proportion of it, which with more careful attemperation it would not possess.

Antiseptics.—These afford defensive weapons of undoubted value, and if used in the usual moderate proportions are, as far as we know, innocuous. They divide themselves broadly into salicylic acid on the one hand, and preservatives which owe their influence to combined sulphurous acid (*e.g.*, bisulphite of lime and kalium meta-sulphite or K. M. S.) on the other.

Salicylic Acid is the more difficult to use, in that being prepared in the form of a very light crystalline powder, it does not readily mix with a relatively large bulk of beer; in fact, it must be made into a paste with a small quantity of the liquid as a preliminary. It is much more soluble in alcohol or glycerine than in beer or water, and one of the former solvents has been used to permit of the acid being added in the more convenient fluid form.

Salicylic acid is more costly and less potent than bisulphite of lime. Used in excess it flattens beer, and this more permanently than the rival antiseptics. Many brewers have found that beers in which it has been used develop peculiar flavours on lengthy storage, probably owing to decompositions which the acid undergoes. [It has a very complicated formula, and is prepared synthetically from phenol—carbolic acid—or from benzoic acid, being thus allied to the benzene series, aromatic coal-tar derivatives. When heated it breaks up into phenol and carbon dioxide.] But that this is not always the case, even with storage of some duration, the writer can say from experience. It is the best preservative for "pressings" in summer time.

Bisulphite of Lime (see Glossary) and **K. M. S.** are both added at racking (the former at the rate of about half a pint per barrel), though it is sometimes recommended to use them, especially the K. M. S., in the mash-tun too. The latter is in the form of crystals, and for addition to casks Messrs. Boake, Roberts, & Co., the manufacturers, prepare it in convenient tablets of different sizes, the smallest being just the size required for a pin.

It is alleged that the potassic base with which the sulphurous acid is combined in K. M. S. is more stable than the calcic base of the bisulphite, and the recommendation to use either in the mash doubtless turns on the fact that a small quantity has a much more effective deterrent influence on disease organisms (lactic and butyric) before their prodigious multiplication begins, than a larger quantity later, but the quantity so used is dissipated by the time the fermentation stage is reached.

What is known as **the Bisulphite smell or stench,** probably brought about by the reducing action of bacteria upon its sulphurous acid, resulting in the evolution of sulphuretted hydrogen, is (if always attributable to bisulphite when it occurs) a drawback. But even then, paradoxical as it may seem, the smell may be caused by using too little, rather than too much, of the bisulphite; because as long as there is sulphurous acid, free or ready to be liberated, the reducing action is held in check.

Used in excess, of course, it has a similar destructive

influence on secondary ferments that salicylic acid seems to exert, and flattens the beer to which it has been so added.

The Action of Finings.—The fining of beer—that is the freeing it by artificial means of such suspended matter as interferes with its perfect brilliancy—is a necessary condition of modern competitive trade, and the demand for a beer free from any acidity beyond what is normal and absolutely bright. Capital must be turned over quickly, and it will be neither profitable nor safe to allow beers, except in comparatively limited quantity, to clarify spontaneously.

The action of finings is not very perfectly understood, but much valuable light has recently been thrown thereon by Messrs. Matthews and Lott in a paper read at a meeting of the Institute of Brewing. Although I cannot pretend to set forth all the results given in their paper, which should be read by every one interested in the subject, a few points summarised will supplement what was said under this head in Chapter I.

They first of all made **experiments to determine the best kind of acid,** and somewhat contrary to the general view, they found that sulphurous acid did its work (that of cutting the isinglass) rather more quickly than either tartaric or acetic acids, and confirmed what was known before, that finings made with it were the least liable to mildew. They also experimented with lactic acid, and found it markedly superior to acetic acid, whence they conclude that, in finings made with sour beer, the effective cutting agent is the lactic and not the acetic acid.

[In one respect, that of clearness of the finings themselves, those made with lactic and acetic were both superior to those made with sulphurous acid.]

The strength of the acid used appears to have a marked effect. Beyond a certain point (some ·7 to 1% of H_2SO_3) the effective cutting diminishes with the concentration of the acid. Undiluted commercial acid, for instance (7·4% H_2SO_3), cut very slowly and gave a very thin solution. The authors say that about 1% of acidity (one gallon of commercial acid per barrel) at starting, and a finish of ·2% is a good strength, *i.e.*, one gallon of commercial sulphurous acid, strength 7·4% H_2SO_3, diluted with 6 gallons of water at first and made up eventually to 36 gallons. The quantity of isinglass, they say, should vary with the quality, $2\frac{1}{4}$ lb. of best Russian being ample and $3\frac{1}{2}$ lb. of inferior kinds.

In a sample of properly made finings the isinglass appears to be in a state of true solution (finings thinned with distilled water will pass through a filter paper), but a very slight alteration of condition is sufficient to throw the isinglass out of solution, and it is upon this that its fining capacity depends. The specific gravity of the isinglass particles, as thrown out of solution, is very close to that of the fluid in which they are, and according to their degree of compactness, *i.e.*, according as they are just heavier or just lighter than the corresponding bulk of the liquid, so they will sink or rise in the liquid, carrying with them more or less of the suspended matter, which interferes with the brightness of the beer.

And I think most brewers will agree that the beers which give the most brilliant results are those in which the finings rise to the top of the fining-glass, after a very short stay at the bottom, carried up it may be by bubbles of carbonic acid gas; and if this be so, the more closely the specific gravity of the isinglass particles corresponds with that of the liquid, or in other words the finer and more widespread the mesh of the isinglass network (if the simile may be allowed) the better.

Probably this rise to the surface is followed by a fresh descent, as coagulation increases the density of the floating finings, otherwise unsatisfactory results would occur on draught, such as do sometimes occur with incomplete fining, when, for instance, the ale is drawn alternately brilliant and cloudy. This state of things, however, can hardly be due to the rise of the whole body of finings to the surface, and it may be taken for granted, from practical experience, that finings which rise *en masse* also settle in the same way.

This delicate and sensitive state of solution seems to depend upon the acidity of the finings, for if these are made slightly alkaline isinglass is thrown out of solution. This fact is of practical import, because it explains why a cloudy beer, with a high percentage of acidity, is not likely to fine readily. But it being manifestly impossible to make a beer alkaline, this separation of the isinglass (making it act as an extremely fine-meshed net collecting particles of suspended matter) depends upon other causes whose action appears to be of a physical nature.

For example, experimenting on the influence of suspended matter, Messrs. Matthews and Lott found that cooler grounds and beer grounds, diffused in water, ensured a rapid precipitation of the finings, their action being perfect if the finings were somewhat in excess. Ordinary pitching yeast, suspended in water, was also got to fine perfectly, but washed yeast, free from bitter, was found, when no other matter was present, to be partially left in suspension, although it always caused coagulation of the finings.

Clay, powdered glass, asbestos, powdered or animal charcoal and other chemically inert matters, suspended in water, were also found to cause rapid coagulation of the finings, followed by speedy clarification. Finely ground malt, they say, will cause a nice separation of finings from beer which does not take them readily, and it is their practice, in getting stubborn beers or worts ready for the polarimeter, to add powdered asbestos and a small quantity of finings before filtration.

The discovery of these facts is by no means without interest, because they help to explain why rolling about a cask—in fact, stirring up its sediment—of a beer which does not readily take finings, often assists the action of the latter materially. I say *helps* to explain, because carbonic acid as in solution, or even more so when just liberated from it, materially assists the action of finings.

With regard to the influence of mineral acids, they found that up to a certain point ·4% (over the normal ·1% of total acidity) of acetic acid did not hinder, but rather helped separation, whereas ·2% of lactic acid did affect the efficiency of the finings.

With regard to temperature, the experiments carried out show that finings cannot be expected to do their work effectively at a temperature below 50°.

The authors summarise the favourable and unfavourable conditions as follows:—

Favourable.	Unfavourable.
Dry hopping.	Unusual fineness at rack without true brilliancy.
Presence of a certain amount of suspended matter in the racked beer.	Flatness.
The presence of alcohol.	Greyness from imperfect or slack malt.
Presence of carbonic acid gas at small pressure, and in a state of liberation.	Presence of bacteria (active).
Normal acidity.	Fret. Abnormal or unusually vigorous secondary fermentation.
Soluble bitter and astringent hop derivatives.	Excessive acidity.
A rising rather than a falling temperature of the liquid to which finings are added.	Excess of suspended yeast.

Further, they state it as their opinion that finings, for which the isinglass has been "cut" with sulphurous acid, give the best results with hard-water beers, while for those brewed with soft water, especially when they are running beers, finings prepared with tartaric acid, and still more those made with sour beer, answer best.

Methods of using Finings.

Occasionally, one sees paragraphs or communications in the brewing papers referring to "fining in tank" (*i.e.*, settling or racking back); and where there is a very keen competition trade, and abnormal freedom from "bottoms" is looked for, some form of preliminary fining may be necessary. Beer so treated, however, cannot be expected to rack brilliant (owing probably to certain previously soluble matters being thrown out of solution by oxidation), consequently re-fining is essential, and the freshly insoluble matter, forming the slight haze, will be generally sufficient to cause the isinglass to go out of solution on the principle previously stated.

Besides this necessity of double fining, there is the risk of unduly flattening the ale, as a remedy for which the addition of a little of what the Germans call *Kräusen* (sometimes referred to in the English brewing organs as Kreising), viz., fermenting wort, may be found effective, but Thausing's caution never to take Kräusen from a weak fermentation should be borne in mind.

The strictly legitimate way of using finings is in the trade or carriage casks, and this, for running beer, divides itself into two methods; the first, adopted in the majority of country breweries, being the "**fining-in**" process, which means that a quart, or sometimes less, of finings per barrel is added to the carriage casks (the beer contained in which must be perfectly free from "fret"), and thoroughly mixed by stirring or rolling. This addition may be made either before the casks leave the brewery (whereby a quart of beer per barrel is saved, no inconsiderable matter in a large trade), or, what is better for the beer, if done in time and properly, in the retailer's cellar.

The **working-out, fining-out, or spurging-out method** is practised in some important centres, notably in London. It seems the one best adapted for a trade in which rapid maturity for delivery is aimed at (*e.g.*, four days from start to finish), a result arrived at by arranging the mashing conditions so that the fermentation would, under any circumstances, be vigorous, but by the avoidance of any early check with the attemperator—the heat perhaps running up to 70° Fahr. before the gyle is discharged into a finishing and racking back, where cooling influences are first brought to bear. Such beer is, as might be expected, sent out with the primary fermentation hardly completed, and the finings, added in the publican's cellar, and generally in excess, work out at the bunghole, bringing with them the sedimentary and suspended matter, which, if the " in-fining " method is adopted, must be got rid of before racking.

Fining Bitter and Pale Ales.—Although, with stock ales going out of vogue to some extent, the practice of fining these ales is growing, we cannot but think, where time allows, that spontaneous clarification should not be interfered with.

Certainly in the case of ales meant for bottling nothing of the sort should be attempted, unless it be with light bitter ales, vended at 2s. 6d. per dozen, a price which, with deductions, does not allow of the highest ideal being aimed at. And the ale should be allowed to go through all its cask-changes, spontaneous brilliancy at the end of them being the simplest criterion of ripeness for bottling.

Even with the cheapest beer intended for bottling, some short storage is advisable, for if finings are added before the secondary fermentation has properly begun, i.e., at the time of racking, perfect brilliancy cannot be expected, the flavour of the added dry hops will not have become diffused, and the result, even under favourable circumstances, will be a modified failure. Such beer, even if bottled bright, is less likely to remain so in bottle than a riper article would, and at any rate is certain to throw down a relatively heavy deposit which tells against it with consumers.

Daily rolling about of the casks stimulates secondary fermentation, and consequently accelerates condition; accordingly, fairly satisfactory results may be got with average well-brewed light beers, fined some fortnight after racking (though longer, of course, is better), provided spontaneous brightening have decidedly begun earlier, and especially if steps have been taken to secure quasi-maturity by rolling.

The foregoing considerations of course apply as well to casks intended for consumption from the wood (other than "running" beers); and though it is sometimes the practice to add finings, at the time of racking, to firkins of semi-stock bitter ale and all casks below that size, in order to avoid the necessity of drawing shives when they are sent out, it is not one to be much commended.

Besides, where hopped beers are rolled, as has been recommended, it seems better to do this before the casks are topped up for good, this allowing the hops to get saturated more speedily; the rolling may then be renewed with advantage after the topping-up and final shiving.

Before dealing further with the question of bottling, a few words on the storage and sampling of bulk beers will not be out of place.

The temperature of the store cellar should not vary much from 55°, especially for pale ales, though for running beers it may well be a degree or two higher. It was pointed out in Chapter I. that a due attention to storage temperature seems to determine flavour and condition in the most favourable sense.

A further *desideratum*, too often disregarded, is that the cellars should be dry. Damp air not only rusts the hoops of casks and causes the timber to perish, but, owing to its conductivity being greater than that of dry air, damp cellars are less uniform in temperature than those freer from moisture. Damp encourages the growth of mildews, and the effect of these, even if not so markedly detrimental as that of bacteria, is none the less in a destructive direction.

Porous Spiles and boring Casks (Spiling).—Porous spiles, inserted through the shive in order to let off excess of carbonic acid gas, not unfrequently get their pores clogged by the dried froth which has worked through them (and still more by dirt if the casks are rolled about with the porous spiles in them), and so cease to act. Sometimes, perhaps, it is fortunate that this is so, because porous spiles are frequently left in too long. They should be replaced by tight spiles directly the briskness of the complementary fermentation has subsided.

There is considerable difficulty in doing this when the

ales are stacked, the breaking down and remaking of stacks being just one of those sorts of work that there never seems time for. Probably large firms would find their account in adopting an arrangement on the lines of that described on p. 448, whereby the making of stacks of any height is much facilitated.

Sampling by boring and after-insertion of a spile is a crude method, which, apart from the inducement it offers thirsty persons of lax morality, when they see a cask-stave riddled with peg holes to insert one more spile, has the further disadvantages that the ends of the spiles not only afford a harbour for filth, but that the timber of the cask, made jagged inside by constant boring, serves the same ill end.

The boring is often very carelessly done, too, especially outside the brewery, for example, in the edge of a stave, where the imperfectly rounded hole that is made cannot so easily be stopped by a spile.

On the whole, the use of the little conical corks, known as "tit-corks," seems preferable with a view to sampling. One, or even two of these can be driven into existing spile-holes, and when it is desired to sample the cask, forced into the latter by means of a spile, just as a tap-cork is at tapping by the tail of the tap.

[When casks are habitually unheaded and scrubbed before refilling, the spile-ends can be cut off, but even then the objection to indiscriminate boring applies.]

More about Bottling—Temperature.—The temperature of the bottling cellar should not exceed 55°, and may well be lower, and a fair amount of ventilation, if it can be managed, with a uniform temperature, is desirable. When bottled, however, a higher temperature is required to ensure proper condition, say from 58° to 60°; but note that too speedy maturity is not to be wished for, pointing as it does to faulty brewing or incomplete complementary fermentation.

Messrs. Bass & Co. used to issue the following instructions to their agents:—

"The proper season for bottling pale ale commences in November and ends in June.

"Pale ale should not be bottled during the summer months, nor after hot weather has set in, even though the temperature should afterwards become cool.

"The ale should be placed bung upwards, in a cool, well-ventilated store, about 50° to 55° Fahr. temperature.

"If the ale should get into a brisk state of fermentation, a porous cane or porous oak spile should be inserted in the bung until the excessive fermentation has subsided, when a tight, close peg should be substituted.

"Ale should never be allowed to become flat.

"It should be bright and sparkling when bottled, but not fermenting. The bottles to be corked directly they are filled.

"In bottling, a tap with a tube reaching towards the bottom of the bottles should be used.

"When corked, the bottles to be piled standing upright, and not lying on their sides.

"When the ale becomes ripe, a sediment will be deposited in the bottles. In uncorking be careful not to disturb it, but empty the contents of the bottle into a jug, keeping back the sediment."

A more convenient filler of bottles than the tap recommended is the syphon arrangement, made by several firms, by which four or six bottles, or even more, can be filled at once, the filling going on continuously.

The piling of the filled bottles, standing upright, is of course necessary to avoid the formation of a sediment on the sides; but the recommendation to do this at once is only actuated by convenience and to avoid double handling. Where the latter is not objected to it is certainly preferable to let the bottles lie on their sides for two or three days, after which they may be stacked, standing upright.

I cannot do better than quote the words of M. Pasteur (*Études sur la Bière*, p. 15), premising that the precaution seems more necessary with lightly hopped, low gravity bitter ales than with the stronger pale ales. Perhaps, too, it is not unconnected with the manner in which the bottling store is ventilated. He says :—

"The bottles must be laid down at first after bottling for twenty-four or forty-eight hours, and then stood upright again. This is because the air remaining between the cork and the surface of the liquid might give rise to the production of a film of mycoderma (Pasteur says *fleurs* simply). By laying the bottles down, the oxygen of this air gets absorbed by certain oxidisable principles of the liquid, and there is no further occasion to fear the film when the bottles are stood upright. The latter, too, could not remain lying down longer without risk, because the complementary fermentation might burst the bottles. Moreover, if the bottles stand upright, the deposit forms on the bottom, and not on the sides."

I think, myself, that the benefit depends as much upon the fact that the aërobian mycoderma germs, which have begun to make good their footing on the moistened neck of the bottle, get submerged and killed, as upon absorption of the oxygen; but whatever the reason the remedy is good.

[For cleaning bottles a weak solution of potash is very useful. The water used to rinse them should be cold, as the vapour given off by hot water condenses on the inside and does not dry readily. There is also the risk of breakage to be considered. Better even than this, I should like to see all bottles dried by a blast of hot air. Far too many damp bottles are filled.]

The Forcing Tray * is a means of testing the stability of beer, which we owe to Mr. Horace Brown of Burton. Its usefulness comes in where large stocks have to be kept for prolonged periods; for a " hand to mouth " trade

* A forcing tray complete, enclosed in a polished wood case standing on four legs, can be procured from Mr. H. Manton, 29, Brighton Road, Moseley Road, Birmingham. The prices range from £7 upwards. This includes forcing bottles, and the necessary adjuncts, including Reichert's gas regulator, which keeps the temperature practically uniform, however much the pressure of gas may vary.

a simpler process of determining fitness (such as the one to be described hereafter) will amply suffice.

The mode of manipulation is briefly as follows:—

Sundry small bottles (Pasteur flasks), of which we will assume ten or twelve to be kept going at once, whose only available outlet is a glass tube bent downwards at right angles to its first direction, are partly filled with water, and the nozzles of the tubes being connected with a small pipette by means of gutta-percha tubing, are separately held over a Bunsen. Boiling water and steam soon rush out, whereupon the point of the pipette is introduced into a portion of the ale to be tried, sufficient of which, of course, enters the bottle to fill the vacuum produced on the egress of the boiling water.

The nozzles of the bottles, the tubing being disconnected, are then placed in a small basin of mercury, whereby they are, as it were, hermetically sealed.

The bottles themselves stand upon a water-tray, *i.e.*, a wide but shallow metal box containing water, and their temperature is maintained at a uniform heat, say 80° Fahr., for a fortnight, by means of a burner beneath. The supply of gas is regulated, as stated in a footnote, by a gas regulator (Reichert's or Page's).

At the end of a fortnight the deposits are examined with a microscope, and according to the proportion of faulty types of ferment found, the beer is sentenced to speedy consumption or kept for stock.

The above, albeit with risk of breaking some of the bottles, seems the better plan for insuring sterilisation of the apparatus, but some operators are satisfied to fill the trial flasks direct from the fermenting vessels at the time of racking, of course only after a *thorough* cleaning of the bottles, and a preliminary rinse out with the beer under trial itself. [For full details refer to Messrs. Matthews and Lott's microscope in the brewery and malthouse, pp. 128-137.]

The simpler test for bottling fitness referred to above is to catch a small portion, say a pint and a half, of the

SIMPLE TEST FOR BOTTLING FITNESS.

beer in a *thoroughly* clean, clear glass bottle and to put this in a water-bath, with a Bunsen burner beneath, regulating the latter so that the temperature keeps at a fairly uniform 90° Fahr. Beer so treated, and which then throws down no deposit in, say, four days, may, unless some exceptional probation is awaiting it, be bottled with all reasonable confidence.

CHAPTER XIII.

THE BREWERY AND PLANT.

Choice of Site—Purchase or Hire of Existing Brewery—Tower Principle—Semi-gravitation—Structural Essentials—Labour Savers—Stacking Apparatus—Flooring—Wells — Pumps — Transmission of Motion — Shafting — Coupling—Clutch—Keys, etc.—Wheel Work and Belting—Preserving Belts—Screws — The Boiler and its Fittings—Mechanical Stokers — Engine — Sack Hoists—Screens — Liquor Backs — Malt-Mills — "Jacob's Ladders" — Grist Cases — External Mashers — Rakes —Mash-Tuns—Coppers—Under Back and Hop Back—Coolers—Atomising Plant—Climax Aërator—Refrigerators—Ice-Making Machines (Compressed Air: Absorption Compression: Vacuum)—Fermenting-Tuns and Fittings — Cask-plant — Cask-cleaning—Hints on Cleanliness.

Although the undoubted tendency is for existing breweries to be closed rather than for new ones to be started, the latter possibility is not so inconceivable that a few truisms need be out of place. Let us "convey" a few of them.

The Choice of the Place in which a brewery is to be erected is one of the main points to be considered. A suitable locality is one where there is a demand for good beer, through the scarcity of breweries in the neighbourhood able to produce it. It is hard for a new concern to make its way when surrounded by long-established breweries of high reputation, with a connection already formed, and it is, in fact, only rendered possible by the production of an extraordinarily good, or a specially cheap article. Good means of communication, it is true, tend

SITE FOR BREWERY.

to neutralise the effect of this crushing rivalry, by enabling the brewer to send his beer to a distance and thus widen the field of his operations. But, on the other hand, the difficulties of management and the risk increase the more he has to depend upon distant markets.

The fact that raw materials of first-rate quality, especially barley, are to be obtained in any neighbourhood, may help to recommend it for the site of a brewery, but should never be made a consideration of paramount importance, as they can be conveyed much more easily from place to place than the beer that is made from them.*

Breweries constructed nowadays without a railway siding seem to be quite left out in the cold. Failing this, a canal is a great convenience; indeed, from the single point of view of cheap carriage, a greater convenience than even a railway siding.

I will now quote from myself words which will apply to the erection of a brewery for an existing trade.

"It may seem superfluous to insist on the necessity of a copious supply of pure water, yet how often is this essential left to chance!

"A dry and airy site should be selected, with a good natural fall for drainage purposes, and heed should be given to the configuration of the ground so as to utilise elevations for portions of the structure, whereby the advantages of what is known as the gravitating system may be attained at a lesser outlay in bricks and mortar. Cellarage may be made much more cheaply under certain circumstances than under others, for instance, by tunnelling into the side of a chalk hill, instead of excavating deeply into a piece of level ground."†

Chalk with its excellent self-supporting power is not always attainable, and therefore another relatively cheap

* Thausing, *Die Theorie u. Praxis der Malzbereitung u. Bierfabrikation*.

† "Papers on the Modern System of Brewing," *Brewer's Guardian*, 230.

way of forming effective cellarage, capable of supporting great weights, may be named. It avoids, too, the delay of excavation at the outset, and expense of building strong brickwork piers and arches. The material used is concrete.*

Deep trenches are dug, lower than the required depth of the cellarage, and these are filled with concrete. The surface of the spaces between is then rounded to form the curve of an arch, and the whole covered with a thick layer of concrete. The soil underneath can then be left until the cellarage is wanted, or excavated as soon as the concrete is thoroughly dry, the building proceeding all the time. A span of fully ten feet is safe; indeed, the writer has seen concrete arches, supporting considerable weight, of nearly twice that span.

Another useful way of employing concrete for cellarage is to construct the outer walls in $4\frac{1}{2}$-inch brickwork, with occasional rows of headers (*i.e.*, bricks placed endwise), filling up the interspaces between wall and earth outside with concrete and arching over by means of curved corrugated iron springing from transverse girders, the whole being finally covered in with a substantial thickness of concrete. This method will be found particularly suitable for cellarage under large malthouses.

What has been urged respecting the erection of new breweries also holds good in **the purchase or hiring of an already existing one,** with the additional necessity in the latter case of considering the producing capacity,

---

Concrete is an artificial stone (said, in fact, to be half as strong again as Portland stone) composed of a mixture of Portland or other cement with gravel, sand, powdered granite, etc., so tempered as to set in a hard mass. Concrete blocks, each weighing 330 tons, have been used, while bridges and houses have been made of it all in one piece.

For cellar floors the cement should be mixed with plenty of burnt brick; burnt brick-earth rather than broken brick-bats, or the clinkers from gasworks. This cement always dries rapidly, and when hot from the works does so with such speed that there is no time to apply it properly, and fresh water must be added, to the detriment of its cohesive strength. In such a case the addition of a little old beer materially delays the drying of the cement.

the condition of the buildings and machinery, whether the plan on which it is laid out is satisfactory and its several parts suitably arranged. The reputation of the brewery, moreover, is by no means a matter of indifference. A bad name is one of the most difficult things in the world to overcome, and prejudices continue rampant long after all justification for them is past.

If space allowed I should dwell on this important point at some length, albeit somewhat beyond the scope of this work. I must limit myself, however, to one hint—viz., that the *status* of any brewery may be gauged by the *status* of its "tied" houses, and accordingly intending purchasers should demand a complete history of *every such house*.

A flourishing brewery is one which has its tied houses let at reasonable rentals to responsible men, paying regularly for their goods and *at full local prices*. Strict inquiry should be made whether any house has been "under management," as this points (save in Liverpool or districts where it may be the rule) to a screw loose somewhere.

Further, the class of trade done by each individual house should be gone into; for it may be taken for granted that a public-house doing a low-class trade is generally (even putting it on the merest pecuniary grounds) worse than useless to a brewer.

For further suggestions I must refer my readers elsewhere.*

Finally, when a suitable site has been found and the question of ways and means duly debated and sifted, on what principle is a brewery to be built? **The gravitating, or tower principle** is undoubtedly the best for moderate-sized and small plants, though to enable, as its name implies, the whole process of manufacture to be conducted without the necessity of once pumping the wort, the

* A shilling pamphlet, "The Financial Elements of Brewing," by Mr. W. W. Ingall, of 22, Moorgate Street, Chartered Accountant, is instructive on this and other points.

buildings for a large brewery would have to be carried to such a height as to render its adoption there impossible.

The increased initial expense is also a drawback, so is the difficulty of afterwards enlarging a brewery constructed on this principle. On the other hand, its undoubted advantages are the entire suppression of wort and beer pumps, and indeed the relatively small amount of pumping required altogether.

Accordingly for large plants a combination of both plans is advisable,—viz., **the semi-gravitation principle,** where only one pumping of wort takes place. This involves in the case of a 60 or 70-quarter plant a height not exceeding 36 feet for the main walls of the brewery, and of 55 to 60 feet for the more elevated part where the cold-liquor back is placed.

An arrangement which seems as good as any is shown on the plan facing this page. This gives a good *façade*, with a line of rails running the whole length of the racking and loading-up cellar, and close up to the boiler house to enable coal to be easily unloaded. There will be a through draught across the coolers, and no great masses of brickwork to prevent the steam from getting away from the copper-side in certain states of the wind.

The cellarage beneath the racking and loading-out stage is supposed to be excavated some six feet, and the latter to be raised enough above the ground level to make it even with the floor of the trucks which come up alongside. There will, of course, be several doors for loading into the latter, and if the distance between the rails and basement is so arranged that the side flaps of the trucks are supported in the doorways, they will prove a convenience in loading.

The most crying essential is good drainage, and it is quite possible and much to be recommended in constructing a new brewery not to have *one single drain* within the structure, but to carry all the putrescible offscourings of the various vessels to the outside by means of very deep wooden shoots. This is quite feasible, and is done in one large brewery within the writer's knowledge.

The next thing is, insist on **all shafts, clutches, and mortise-wheels being made accessible.** Brewery architects apparently like to tuck these things, especially the latter, neatly out of sight; they are quite capable, for instance—incredible as it may seem—of so designing the shaft which drives the well-pumps, that if the wooden cogs of the mortise-wheel, which is keyed on to it, break (and they always go several at a time), it cannot be raised for the purpose of moving the wheel, but has to be drawn out bodily. This is an operation which consumes much time.

Haylofts and Oat-stores should on no account be anywhere near the fermenting-room, and it would be better if the prevalent winds did not blow from them towards the brewery. Hay teems with the spores of bacilli, and the light dust from corn is hardly less fertile, so that if stores for them adjoin the fermenting-room, pure yeast is not to be expected.

In constructing a malthouse connected with the brewery, **ample bin-room for malt** should be provided. For example, in a 60-quarter house, making a rather long season, four 350-quarter bins are not enough to keep different qualities of malt separate, especially if the season is begun with a bin or two of old malt in stock. And indeed if one hurries on to a just filled-up bin in order to get it empty, nine times out of ten it is not the oldest malt at the bottom, although the opening through which it passes is there, which is got, but a mixture consisting largely of hot malt from the top, the tendency being for a funnel-shaped depression to form, down which, after the first start, the upper part of the bin-contents comes down before the lower.

[As these bins will often be fitted up by a local carpenter, it will be well to have a formula for calculating the weights sufficient to break the supporting beams, premising that no beam ought to be subjected to more than one-fifth of its breaking weight.

The formula is $\dfrac{b \times d^2}{l}\, s =$ breaking weight in cwts. where $b =$ breadth (in inches), $d =$ depth (in inches), $l =$ length (in feet), and $s =$ the strain, the latter varying with different timbers, being as 5 for oak, and 3 for Riga fir.]

Bins are often made without due regard to the hygroscopic character of malt, and to the fact that slack malt—say malt containing over 5% of moisture—is very detrimental. Good sound well-stored brewing malt contains from 2% to 3%.

To prevent greater absorption of moisture than this, a precaution would be to line the bins with zinc or sheet-iron, but in reasonably dry positions wooden bins alone, made of seasoned material and well-tongued, give satisfactory results.

If **a Screw (Archimedean screw or "creeper")** is to be fitted up for bringing over from the malthouse the malt required for each brewing, care should be taken that the light metal blades, which are bolted on to the central revolving shaft, work with such accuracy against the bottom part of the cylindrical tube, which encloses the whole, that practically all the malt shot into the malthouse-hopper is brought over for crushing. Supposing only a depth of half an inch is left unground along a length of say 70 feet, that is an appreciable quantity, and a good portion of it is doubtless introduced into the next grist in an extremely slack condition.

The Malt-mills should be so arranged that the grist need not be carried up to a very great height, or have a great fall into the grist-case, the tendency in such cases being to separate the husks from the flour. If this separation is excessive it causes bad drainage from the mash-tun, and what are known as "dead mashes."

Fixed pipes, without facilities for admitting steam, or at any rate copious supplies of boiling water, into them, should be avoided; and wherever it is possible, there should be unions for the easy disconnection of lengths of piping.

Three-throw pumps are not supposed to stand steaming (and therefore rotary pumps have been recommended for moderate lifts), but this is mainly so when the buckets are of leather; there is no reason why with care (introducing steam fairly high up, and, if necessary, just covering pumps with liquor) the wort-mains, fitted with them, should not be steamed.

Where steam is used for boiling wort and liquor there should be **a sufficiency of check valves.** It is, for instance, most inconvenient to have only the ordinary steam valves attached to the liquor-backs available to shut off steam therefrom, for supposing that the thread of one of them gets so worn that all at once it will not hold, it will be impossible to remove the valve for repair, or to insert a new one until the entire brewing is ended.

Convenient Labour-saving arrangements are—

1. **A Descending Platform for Lowering Casks** from the racking floor, and in connection with this a light line of rails, laid on a gentle incline, so that the casks may roll away by their own momentum directly they are lowered. Directly the platform reaches the ground, a triangular block of wood juts up through a hole in the platform floor, and tilts the cask off. This triangular block of wood may be made to turn through a right-angle so as either to direct the cask on to the line of rails, which will probably carry it to some distant store (say under an adjoining malthouse) or to push it off into the cellar where the platform actually descends.

The platform itself works between guides, and is supported by strong chains passing over a roller and having a weight at their other end, just heavy enough to cause the platform to rise when unloaded, though of course the added weight of a barrel of beer is enough to make it descend. To prevent this descent being too rapid a brake is fitted to the roller, and from the lever-arm of this a rope hangs within easy reach both of the racking floor and of the platform itself, so that a man, standing on either, can with one hand stop the barrel midway, and so regulate the pace of its descent.

2. **A Cask Hoist,** consisting of two endless chains, inclined at an angle of 45° from the floor whence the casks have to be raised. Pairs of horns, one on each chain, occur at intervals, and as the latter revolve, come up from beneath a platform at the foot of the apparatus and catch up any cask which has been rolled there for that purpose, and convey it to the higher floor. The chains revolve round drums keyed on to short shafts, the upper of which has a "pulley" on it too. To this upper pulley motion is conveyed by a belt from a large shaft overhead, and of course, when the hoist is not in use, the belt is shifted on to a "loose pulley."

[Hydraulic lifts can be used if there is a good water pressure. One firm that the writer knows of utilises the company's water passing to their liquor backs in this way.]

3. **Stacking Apparatus in the Store itself.**—A long horizontal rod or shaft spans the entire width of the store, and has wheels at either end of it, which run smoothly on two rails, that, high overhead, skirt the longer walls of the store. A wheel of larger diameter, fixed on the centre of the rod, makes the latter revolve with it when set in motion by the pulling of an endless chain, which passes round its deeply grooved circumference. This central wheel can be kept in position by a number of light steel rods converging from its circumference to some point along the rod on either side.

When the endless chain, previously mentioned, is pulled one way or the other, the whole apparatus moves backwards or forwards with the greatest ease to any desired point. An arrangement of pulleys and ratchet-wheel then enables a man to raise a barrel, slowly but surely, to the required height. The writer has seen a storecellar where casks are "ridden" ten or twelve high by means of this appliance.

WALLS AND ROOFING.

[An adaptation of this apparatus has been found useful in malthouses, for moving green malt considerable distances.]

4. Traps in the bottom of the mash-tun for shovelling out grains, which are to be conveyed into a grain tank outside by an endless belt, or what is far more durable, by two endless gun-metal chains working in a shoot, and having upright pieces of wood fixed on them transversely at short intervals.

5. A direct connection between the hop-weighing room and the copper-side by means of a shaft, closing with a door on the copper stage and with a trap-door on the floor above. The hops, weighed up in bags, are thrown down this, and even if there are several different quantities they can be thrown down in the reverse order to that in which they will be required, so that the bag which will be wanted last lies at the bottom, and the one which will be wanted first at the top of the heap, and so on.

Minor, but far from unimportant points are:—

1. That the fermenting room should have its **windows facing north** if possible [windows of southerly and westerly aspect have to be shuttered up in summer time].

2. **The walls,** where the "thrust" of weight above is not excessive, **should be made hollow,** and this is especially the case in fermenting rooms, where the conditions favouring growth of mildew ought to be as restricted as possible. To this end **glazed bricks** as a lining for the walls are highly recommended.

3. Roofing should, generally speaking, and especially over coolers, be of tiles, which do not cause such rapid condensation of the vapour given off as slate roofs do.

[Pan tiles are better than plain tiles, a "square" of the former being hardly more than half the weight of a "square" of the latter, and moreover the studs or knobs, which catch upon the supporting battens, are less liable to perish than the pegs or pins used to retain plain tiles and slates in a similar position. The curves of the pan tiles form channels for the rain to run down to the gutters.]

4. The roofage area can be utilised for the collection of soft water for the boilers; but the tank in which such water is stored should neither be far from nor much below the level of the donkey-engine which pumps all water (except that which may be carried in by an injector) into the boiler.

Flooring of Cellars.—The large flagstones, at one time so much used for the flooring of racking cellars, have now got into disrepute owing to the fact that, unless of great size and exceptionally well set, they become loose, with the result that liquid and yeasty matter of a very offensive character accumulates beneath them. Amongst the best materials are either Claridge's Seyssel asphalte, which the writer has known to withstand the stress of ten years' hard wear without needing repair, or Stuart's granolithic paving material, which would probably not cost more than half as much as the asphalte. The granolithic is unquestionably a splendid material (excellent for malt-house floors too), and can be formed into large slabs capable of sustaining considerable weight.

Cheaper but nevertheless lasting flooring can be formed of Portland cement concrete, prepared as previously directed, the final face being of the same material, but rather finer in texture, and applied in the form of grout, *i.e.*, in a freely liquid state, and finished off quickly. Such a floor might, on an emergency, be fit for use in two days from completion.

The hard dark-coloured bricks, such as are used in stables, make a flooring cheaper almost than concrete. They can be laid " on bed " or " on edge," the latter where a smooth surface is desired. But to make a thorough job of the floor there should be an understratum of concrete, or failing this, the soil beneath the bricks should be well rammed and bottomed with stones.

The Well.—In the arrangement suggested for a 70-quarter brewery the well is planned within the four walls of the brewery, and if room can be spared there for withdrawing buckets, rods, etc., when necessary, the nearer it is to the engine the better, and a sheltered position renders the blocking of the rising-main by frost less probable than it might otherwise be. In the case of an Artesian well the pumps may be placed in the actual bore tube, the well being beneath the engine-room, and traps being made in the floor to get at the working parts.

I must, however, confess to a preference for an independent pumping arrangement in the shape of a **gas engine,** which is speedily got to work (in a minute or two at the outside), and the cost of which after the first installation is comparatively trifling.

Such an engine is also very useful as the motive power of the barley hoist or of the elevator carrying malt just thrown off kiln up to bins in the adjoining malthouse, seeing that these calls, coming at irregular intervals, sometimes cause inconvenience and interrupt the regular routine of brewing operations when they are made upon the ordinary steam motive power of the brewery.

Various methods of supporting the sides of wells are recommended, the old method of steining with brickwork being somewhat superseded, amongst which may be named (1) Steining with concrete, *i.e.*, a wooden drum being let down as the excavation proceeds the interspace between the side and drum is filled up with concrete. (2) The employment of ready-prepared concrete cylinders, which may be of large diameter, *e.g.*, 4 feet, and which, as excavation proceeds, carry themselves down by their own weight. (3) The employment in a similar way of cast or wrought-iron cylinders.

The driving of side headings, especially in the chalk formation, has already been recommended (Chap. III.), but where there is a reasonable chance of tapping a good spring, albeit at a considerable depth, it is usual to excavate the first part, say for 100 feet or so, and to bore the rest, the barrels of the three-throw pumps, prolonged by stand-pipes, which come well above the highest water level, being fixed at the bottom of the excavation, or as an alternative the pump-barrels may be fixed so as to be above the water level, but with a suction-pipe going downwards and fitting into the bore-pipe itself.

Pumps, as usually fitted in breweries, are either suction, or rather lift or force pumps (three-throw pumps giving a continuous stream), rotary, or centrifugal.

The **three-throw pump** is merely a triplet form of the common pump, the buckets, fitted on short rods known as plungers, working downwards in the barrels, and there being a valve or "clack" in the lower part of the plungers on which the buckets fit. There is also a clack in a distinct chamber at the lower part of each barrel, and this opens upwards in response to the suction caused as the plunger is drawn up, admitting liquid to fill the vacuum. As the plunger descends again *its* valve is forced open, the liquid rushing through it, but closes again directly the plunger begins to ascend. Thus at each downward and upward stroke the three plungers force upward as much liquid as can occupy the space between them and the bottom valves or "clacks." There are also three delivery valves in the box to which the upper parts of the barrels are bolted, relieving the plungers of the pressure of a high vertical column of liquid. An air chamber of copper, at the base of the rising main, minimises the pressure on the pipes.

The alternate or successive motion is got from a crank with two deeply **U**-shaped bends (and which is best made of wrought iron, though very large cranks are sometimes cast) forming three curves, on each of which one "throw" is fitted.

These are practically the only pumps of the three sorts named which can suck, and they are therefore used in wells; they are also used for pumping wort from hop-back to coolers, there being an impression that rotary pumps have, compared with them, but inferior lifting power.

However incorrect this view may be, rotary pumps certainly have but very inconsiderable power of suction, unless fitted with a "foot-valve," and must accordingly be placed below the level of the liquid they have to raise so that it may flow into them, but, when fitted with a foot-valve, it is said that they are capable of drawing water some twenty-five feet.

Rotary pumps may be made in the form of an elliptical case with two flattened sides, through the latter of which two spindles pass, closer to one another than to the rounded ends. On each of these spindles is a wheel with four cogs or less, gearing into each other in the centre, and working closely against both the rounded ends and the flattened sides of the case. The liquid, compressed by the outer cogs directly they begin to come together, is prevented from escaping, otherwise than up the outlet pipe, by the gearing of the cogs in the centre.

Sometimes they are made with a single spindle on which a disc of metal is keyed, this disc having four deeply U-shaped cavities in its circumference. In each of these a cylindrical roller, very nearly as long as the case is wide, is placed, and these, of course, rotate with the metal disc, at the same time revolving on their seating, so that wear and tear of parts is equalised as much as possible. The centrifugal force, driving these outward, forces them closely against the inner circumference of the pump-case, and thus they drive before them any liquid rising into the hollow case, and force it into the corresponding outlet pipe in its upper part. As many as 400 revolutions per minute may be advisable with these pumps, but they will do their work with much slower speed.

Centrifugal pumps act somewhat differently, and require a high rate of speed, at least 700 to 800 revolutions a minute, which speed is got by having the driving belt pass from a large pulley on a shaft, revolving at ordinary pace, to a very much smaller pulley on the spindle of the pump, whereby the speed of the first shaft's revolution is multiplied by the number of times that the diameter of the large pulley exceeds that of the smaller.

The construction of the pump is as follows. In the middle of the case into which the inlet pipe leads is a relatively small wheel, revolving with the spindle, and this wheel is fitted with a number of bent paddles. These, as soon as the fluid flows in, seize hold of it in their rapid revolution and dash it by centrifugal force against the inner circumference of the case, whence it flies off, at a tangent, up the outlet pipe.

[It will be remembered that a tangent is defined as a straight line touching a circle, but not cutting it, as is the case with one at right angles to the latter's diameter, and the pipe in question is placed at a tangent to the circumference of the pump-case.]

Before we touch upon the vessel in which the motive power is generated,—viz., the boiler,—let us devote a few pages to motion in general, and the way in which it is transmitted, for the benefit of the inexpert.

Motion may be transmitted (1) **By gearing,** or (2) **By belting,** and, as a matter of fact, a combination of the two is generally adopted.

With the former a breakage, though of comparatively rare occurrence, is a somewhat serious matter, involving stoppage of operations for a shorter or longer time; with the latter it is generally merely the lacing of a strap, or maybe the strap or belt itself, which can be promptly put to rights.

It is true that a pulley (see lower down) sometimes breaks, if habitually subjected to great strains, but even a risk like this may be cheerfully faced, if the precaution has been taken to have split-pulley duplicates for important points. [A split pulley being one that has been cast in halves, so that it can be slipped on and the two halves bolted together, without the necessity of moving the shaft on which it has to be "keyed."]

In either case **Shafting**—a main shaft and a number of other shafts—will be required, and these, though wrought iron is the better material, are very usually cast. For the convenience of fixing, twenty feet is generally the limit of length, and where longer lengths are required **Couplings** are resorted to. These may be either permanent or movable (where the shafts are to be frequently disconnected).

Of the first class are the solid coupling or **box-butt**, the **flange** and the **claw-coupling**—most suitable for small, medium and large shafts respectively.

When the box-butt is used, the ends of the shafting are swelled out, both to enable the key-ways to be cut without weakening the shaft, and also in order that the box, which of course has to be of the same diameter, or only a fraction of an inch larger, may slip over collars on the shaft. This makes them clumsy for large shafts.

In flange-jointing the flanges are also keyed on, and the bolt-holes must necessarily be exactly opposite each other. A drawback, both of this and of the former, is their rigidity, which becomes apparent if the shafts were originally badly adjusted, or have got out of truth by wearing down of **the bearings,** or, at least, which would become apparent with heavy shafting. Light shafts " give " a little.

Claw-coupling is effected by means of two solid castings, the one of which has two or more projecting, square-ended teeth corresponding to hollows in the other. Their centres are so pierced that they can be slipped on to the shaft-ends, they are then fitted closely into one another, and held in their places by stout sunk keys, forming, as has been said, the strongest coupling for large shafts.

Of movable couplings—*i.e.*, where the shafts have to be frequently connected and disconnected—**the clutch** is the most usual. It is, in effect, a claw-coupling, save that, instead of both of the claw-castings being fixed by keys, one of them slides upon its shaft and is held in its place, as long as the temporary connection is wanted, by some simple mechanical means.

Keys, of which mention has been made, are wedge-shaped pieces of metal, generally steel, used to secure wheels, riggers, etc., on to shafts, and they may be either hollow, flat, or sunk keys. The former are only adapted for light work, seeing that their under surface is rounded to the shape of the shaft, and that it consequently only acts by friction. Their chief recommendation is that the wheels, etc., fixed by them, can be easily shifted from one position on the shaft to another, which is not the case with either flat keys, which are flattened at the bottom, and fit closely on to a flat place filed on the shaft, or with sunk keys, which have a "key-bed" or "key-way" filed out for them in the shaft itself.

The latter, accordingly, is the best kind of key for fixing wheels subjected to heavy strains; the flat key is more used for securing pulleys (driven by belting) and wheels where the strain is light.

The key is also "sunk" into the boss surrounding the "eye" of the wheel or pulley, and it is in these, and not in the shaft, that the taper, corresponding to the taper of the key, should be made. The keys, of course, are driven home tight.

Sometimes a pulley, etc., may be required to slide along a shaft. A groove of the required length is then cut in the shaft, and the key slides with its pulley or wheel, being either dovetailed into the boss or having a head which fits into a round hole in the boss of the wheel.

Bearings * are the surfaces of contact between a shaft and its support, and they may be **bushes** (hollow cylinders of brass, steel, etc., in which the shaft revolves) or **journals,** consisting of movable pieces called **steps,** the better arrangement when the friction is considerable.

Plummer-blocks or Pedestals are a form of support for a shaft, consisting either of a standard bolted to the frame of a machine or connected with it by a bracket. The upper part of the pedestal is hollowed out to receive the bearings (steps), and above these a cover is placed and bolted down to keep the steps in position—*i.e.*, the

---

* The term is not limited, however, to surfaces of contact with rotating pieces. It is used in connection with to-and-fro movement—*e.g.*, slide-bars of engines, or with screw-movement. In the latter case the bearings are "nuts."

top step *in contact* with the shaft. Oil-cups, or better, self-acting Lubricators, are fitted on to the covers or caps, and oil-ways cut in the steps to carry the oil down to the shaft, where it comes in contact with them.

A familiar instance of plummer-blocks are the uprights supporting the bent crank of the three-throw pumps, attached to the hop-back, but the brackets which come from the walls in different parts of the brewery, and support the shafting, are virtually, though not nominally, plummer-blocks too.

Shafts are kept from moving lengthwise from their bearings by **collars** fixed on either side of the latter, and these may be either cylindrical pieces of larger diameter than the shaft and welded to it, or where such an arrangement would prevent the fixing of wheels or pulleys, **loose collars,** attached to the shaft by means of a screw, are used.

Bearings are fitted with lubricators to minimise friction, but **where pressure per square inch is excessive** it is found (*teste* Mr. T. Box in his rather technical book on mill-gearing) that the oil is squeezed out, so that the contact virtually becomes that of metal with metal. In such a case increasing the diameter and width of the bearing may have a good effect because, although the total pressure remains constant, it is distributed over a greater number of square inches. On the whole, however, increasing the diameter alone does not diminish the tendency to heating; for although the pressure will be spread over a greater number of square inches thereby, the *velocity* of the moving parts is also greatly increased.

The plan, therefore, where heating is feared, is to increase the *width* of the bearing, and with high speeds this should sometimes be to the diameter in the ratio $5 : 1$, whereas $3 : 2$, or an even lower ratio, is usual in ordinary cases. A wide bearing wears more evenly than a narrow one.

Where the driving is done by gearing, **wheels** of various kinds all provided with teeth are employed, but where the connection from shaft to shaft is by belting, the latter is slipped on to **pulleys or riggers.**

[It may be mentioned that the wheel or pulley, from which the motion is transmitted to another wheel or pulley, is termed the **Driver,** the second wheel or pulley being **the Follower.**]

Spur-wheels are those used to transmit motion from one parallel shaft to another (though, of course, if the shafts are very far apart, belting must be resorted to), and by giving suitable diameters to the respective wheels, the rate of revolution for the respective shafts can be made to vary at will.

Spur-wheels have either iron or wooden teeth (cogs), in the latter case being mortise wheels, and the distance from centre to centre of the adjoining teeth is known as the **pitch** of the wheel. A convenient ratio of pitch to length of teeth is 4 : 3 (inches), but rather closer than that with smaller teeth.

[There is a technical difference of opinion, whether this pitch is to be calculated as a straight line or chord from centre to centre, or as a curved line or arc. But the latter seems the better plan, as then the diameter of the wheels is in exact ratio to the number of teeth, which is otherwise not the case.*

Where shafts cannot be fixed parallel, but can be so placed with regard to one another that their ends come almost into contact, the shafts being also in the same plane, motion can be transmitted from one to the other by means of **Bevel wheels**. [Belting is, of course, an impossibility.]

---

* The diameter of a wheel is got by imagining the latter's "pitch-circle," *i.e.*, regarding it as a plain cylinder, driving its adjacent wheel (considered as another plain cylinder) by frictional contact. The pitch-circle is practically near the middle of the length of the teeth, rather above than below, and its diameter may be got by multiplying the number of teeth by their pitch and dividing by 3·1416 (ratio of circumference to diameter taken as 1). Thus the diameter of a wheel with 100 teeth and 2 inch pitch $= \dfrac{100 \times 2}{3 \cdot 1416} = 63 \cdot 66$ inches at pitch-line.

WHEEL-WORK. SHROUDING.

Bevel wheels, then, are wheels shaped upon a cone with the apex cut off (they are the *frusta* of cones), and have teeth running along the latter lengthwise and gearing into the teeth of the other apex-less cone. When the shafts are at right angles, so that the bevel-wheels are of equal size, and would, if a flat sketch of them, with the apex of the cone thrown in, were attempted, be represented each by an equilateral triangle, they are **Mitre-wheels.**

But for one purpose of the brewery, in which translation is generally from one shaft to another at right angles to it, viz., for driving the mashing machinery inside the mash-tun, deeply toothed wheels, one of the usual type the other a **Core-wheel** (*i.e.*, one with *cogs* at right angles to its diameter), will be found most convenient, as they can be readily thrown in and out of gear.

Mortise-wheels are the wooden-cogged wheels (hornbeam, with a transverse strength about three-tenths that of cast-iron, is the usual wood), which gear in with iron wheels. They are used for well-pumps, etc., to minimise noise. The teeth of the all-iron wheel are usually shorter than those where iron works against iron, because the cogs have to be made relatively thick for their length, and consequently the iron teeth, which gear in with them, must be proportionately slighter, which, were they of the usual length, would involve weakness.

The relative thickness usually is three-fifths the pitch for the cog and two-fifths the pitch for the iron tooth. The cogs are cut out square at the lower end, where they are driven into the mortises of the wheel, but where they gear in are slightly taper.

Wheels are sometimes **shrouded**—*i.e.*, the teeth are protected by a flange, coming up to part of the length of the teeth, say up to the pitch-line. If the flange comes up to the points of the teeth, the spaces between the latter become, in effect, mortises in the face of the wheel.

With wheels of equal strength shrouding is of no value,

because obviously only one of the pair can be shrouded, and their combined strength is determined by that of the weaker member. Moreover, for reasons too technical for insertion here, shrouding does not always impart strength. Its chief value is to reduce disproportion of strength, which occurs in certain cases, if the correct forms of teeth have been adhered to—*e.g.*, when a small pinion is working with a rack or large wheel. In such a case shrouding the teeth of the former may increase their strength 100%.

Other things being equal, the power exerted by a wheel increases with the number of teeth in gear at the same time.

Clearance is the portion of the pitch, which the tooth gearing-in does not completely fill, and which is allowed for slight errors of workmanship. With mortise-wheels little or no clearance is necessary, as the cogs can be trimmed to fit accurately.

Motion transmitted by Belting.—The method has certain advantages over wheelwork, where space is not particularly limited—viz., Economy; Power of putting shafts any distance apart within reasonable limits (nor does variation of distance alter rate of motion); Lessened risk of breakage (a sudden strain which might break wheelwork only causes a belt to slip on the pulley).

Pulleys or Riggers (as the wheel-like pieces on which belts turn are called) are generally curved on the surface of contact with the belt, so that the greatest diameter of the pulley is in the middle of its breadth. The curve is about half-inch per foot of rim.

This helps to keep the belt central on the pulley, the tendency of the moving belt being to rise to the pulley's highest part.

The rims of pulleys are turned after casting, which makes them balance better. It will be noticed, too, that the arms are sometimes curved, a form which gives best to the contraction of the rim, as it cools after casting, but otherwise straight arms, if properly proportioned and of oval section, appear to be the strongest.

Split pulleys have already been referred to.

A loose Pulley is one running free upon a shaft, and is useful for taking belts when not in use, to avoid friction of their edges. Such a pulley should have its boss made very deep, equal at least in width to its rim, and bushed with gun-metal.

It may be made to act as a fast and loose pulley alternately, in situations where it is inconvenient to slip a belt over a revolving fast pulley, a lever from some accessible place actuating it.

Belts, or bands, are fastened by lacing or riveting. Except where it is desirable to avoid any momentary friction beyond what is inevitable and necessary, the former is the better plan, enabling belts to be easily tightened when they stretch, as new belts, at all events, will.

When the shafts are wanted to travel in the *same* direction the **open belt** arrangement is adopted, but when the shafts have to turn in *contrary* directions **the belt is crossed.** The crossed belt brings a greater amount of its surface into contact with the pulleys than the open belt arrangement does, and this gives a firmer grip.

A belt will always slip first on that pulley the smaller arc of which is in contact with it; and with the open belt arrangement, except when there is a belt-guide, this will always be the smaller pulley.

The nice gradation of speed required in some factories, and got either by speed pulleys or cones, is not necessary in a brewery, but nevertheless there will be certain variations of speed, and everything will not be going on at a uniform rate. For example, the external mashing machine, say the form known as Steele's, requires to be driven rather fast—viz., at the rate of 120 to 180 revolutions a minute; consequently the pulley keyed on to the end of the shaft, which rotates inside the cylinder, that is *the follower*, should be only one-third the diameter of the *driving* pulley, seeing that for the crank-shaft of the engine 60 to 70 revolutions per minute should be the limit.

Internal rakes should revolve slowly, consequently the follower (in this case a cogged wheel) should bear to the driver the ratio of 3 : 2.

Wort-pumps again must not be rattled along fast, and here the following pulley may bear to the driver the ratio of 3 : 1.

Driving belts should be well greased every three months. After washing them with lukewarm water, leather grease is to be well rubbed in. The following recipe may be useful. Fish-oil 4 parts; lard or tallow 1 part; colophonium 1 part; wood-tar 1 part.

Saturation with castor-oil is also stated to have great effect in increasing durability of belts, in fact, to be the best preservative means known. Belts treated with it are less prone to slip, and it is said that this treatment sometimes increases their driving power by 50%.

Screws.—The two usual kinds (other than those familiar in carpentry work) are V or triangular threaded, and square-threaded [the thread is the ridge or projecting part; the distance between two consecutive threads is the pitch].

The former are used chiefly for studs, bolts, and set-screws; the latter for transmitting motion by means of slides, and in a brewery exclusively for moving a slide itself—*e.g.*, the slides at the bottom of a grist or grain-case, where the slide travels to and fro with the nut which is an integral part of it. The *pitch* of such a screw may be defined as the distance moved through by the nut in one revolution of the screw.

Screws moving from left to right, *i.e.*, as the hands of a watch, are right-handed screws; those moving in the opposite direction are left-handed.

The Boilers.—It will be impossible to treat boilers (and still less engines) exhaustively, but the writer will deal with a few of the main features, and touch on some points which experience has shown him to be of practical value. For the rest he must refer his readers to the usual manuals. There is, in particular, a capital little

STEAM BOILERS.

treatise, issued by the publishers of this volume, and priced at 6*d.*, called "The Safe Use of Steam."

The type used in breweries is usually the double-flued **Lancashire boiler,** a modification of the single-flued Cornish boiler, adopted because of the liability to collapse of very large flues, unless made of such a thickness of metal as to be unsuitable.

The flues, with the furnaces in their front part (upper half), pass first the whole length of the boiler (within the boiler, be it understood, thus largely diminishing its cubic content), then at the back of the boiler * the heated gases either divide and pass along two side flues, joining again when the front of the boiler is reached to pass along a flue beneath the boiler, which conducts them into the chimney-stalk or shaft. Or the progress is reversed, the gases first passing all together underneath the boiler to the front part, dividing there into the two side flues, from the ends of which they pass into the chimney.

In any case there are three outside flues, lined with firebrick, but having as much of the surface of the boiler exposed in them as is consistent with the proper support of the latter. As to whether it is better to take the gases into the side flues before the bottom one, or *vice versâ*, different opinions exist. With the former plan there is less risk of burning the boiler-plates, owing to sediment forming just where the fire would otherwise be hottest, and it is, maybe, more convenient for the back damper; but on the other hand, where the feed-water contains much carbonate of lime, etc., the fact that the hottest part is just where the water level is continually varying, greatly increases the formation of a hard "rock" there. [And this, be it remembered, in a position whence it is least easily removed, because in chipping men can only get a constrained sideways blow at it, instead of the downright blow at the bottom, whence,

* With the so-called **breeches-flued boiler,** the two internal flues, containing the furnaces, unite into one large cylindrical flue just behind the bridges.

moreover, " blowing off" will remove much before it gets hardened on.]

Moreover, the bottom is naturally the coldest part, and anything which relatively intensifies this increases the strain on the boiler. This was always a fault of Lancashire boilers, and Galloway tubes (slightly tapering tubes which pass through the internal flue diagonally) were invented to obviate this. These tubes are either welded into the flues or riveted, and certainly promote circulation of the water, increasing heating surface too and strengthening the flue itself.

The side flues must not be too narrow (say 9 inches, at least, in upper part for a 40 H.P. boiler), for heated gases will not go up into a narrow space if they can expand better elsewhere.

The **"setting-blocks,"** concave-topped blocks of fireclay, on which the boiler rests, should, with their brickwork beneath, be fairly deep (say thirteen courses of brickwork and the setting-block), which leaves a good space for ash and soot.

Furnace-bars are in 2 (or 3) lengths—very long bars are unmanageable—and have cross-bearer supports at their mid-length. In front they rest upon the **Deadplate,** at the back upon the **Bridge,** which is generally of firebrick. [Note that only firebricks *with smooth faces* should be used. Clinkers* stick on rough edges, and then in clinkering, portions of the brick, or perhaps the whole brick, may be torn away.] The depth of the grate is limited by the fireman's reach, and it will be usually 5 to 7 feet.

There are many **patent furnace bars,** but **Caddy & Co.'s Tubular** (applicable to coppers too) merit most attention. The bar itself is of cast iron, as other bars are, but unlike

---

* The injury to bars done by clinkers can be lessened by using chalk in the following manner. Two or three shovelfuls of dry chalk, in pieces about the size of a walnut, are to be placed on the bars first, and the fire laid and lighted over them. Half a shovelful should be thrown on three or four times a day when coaling up, and this will effectually prevent the clinkers from sticking to the bars.

BOILER FITTINGS.

others it is cast round a wrought-iron tube, which prevents it from warping, adds considerable strength, keeps the bar cool by allowing a current of cold air to enter, and conducts this air, suitably warmed, to the back of the furnace, where it helps the combustion of the unburnt matter given off from the fuel as smoke. The face of the bar is also chilled $\frac{3}{4}$ inch deep, so that clinkers do not adhere.

The combustion is also facilitated by stoking each furnace alternately, so that one is burning brightly while the other is giving off unburnt hydro-carbon matter, the heated gases from the former to some extent burning this matter from the "green fire."

The shell of the boiler is made of plates of wrought-iron or mild steel (containing about 0.1% of carbon), and from 3 to $4\frac{1}{2}$ feet in width, the lines of rivets connecting them running round the circumference of the boiler. Occasionally the **joints are welded,** and this, if properly done, prevents leakage and external corrosion; but that it is so is not easily ascertained for certain, so that riveting is the usual plan, the furnace-tube joints alone being welded. The boiler ends are fitted in and held, either by means of flanges or internal or external angle-irons, which are riveted on to the main shell.

Riveted joints have to be caulked—*i.e.*, the edges of the plates are burred down by means of a special tool, a kind of cold chisel.

The principal boiler fittings are:—

1. **Safety valve,** weighted to blow off at the maximum working pressure, say 50 lbs. for a brewery with non-condensing engine, and boiling, heating liquor, etc., by steam. [Precautions to be observed with this and other fittings will be given below under the Manchester Boiler Insurance and Steam Power Company's "Instructions to Firemen."]

2. **Gauge glasses,** connected at top and bottom with the boiler (but with shut-off cocks), to enable the fireman to ascertain that the water is at the proper level. There

is a blow-through cock at the bottom which helps to keep the tubes and their upper and lower inlets clear.

3. **Gauge cocks** (useful if the gauge-glasses break), one below the average water-level, the other well above it. In the absence of the gauge-glasses they must be tried frequently; as long as steam issues from the upper and water from the lower, the level is approximately right. Even when not in use they should be turned on periodically to keep them from furring up.

4. **Pressure gauge,** which purports to show the existing pressure in the boiler.

5. **Fusible plug,** a plug or disc of soft metal (lead), fixed in the hottest part of the boiler, the crown of the furnace-tube, so that if the water level gets below this and the plate becomes heated, the fusible plug will melt and the steam rush out to extinguish the fire.

6. **Steam whistle,** fixed in the upper part of the steam chest, if there is one, and with a spring to keep the steam inlet closed, until a certain pressure beyond that at which the safety valve blows off is reached, when the resistance of the spring is overcome, and the whistle by the continuous noise it makes calls attention to the fact. It is useful in the event of steam, through carelessness, getting up at night, or of the safety valve being overloaded.

7. **The float,** another water-level indicator.

8. **Man-holes,** one at the top, one (*alias* **the mudhole**) low down in front end of the boiler. These are taken out when the boiler is cleaned, and when they are replaced a close-fitting joint is made by means of a mixture of red and white lead well beaten up and stiffened with yarn. If these joints leak they must be remade at once. The manhole cover generally fits up from the inside of the boiler against a flange on a strengthening iron ring, and is held in its place by a bridge-bar, nut, and bolt.

9. **Blow-off cock** at the bottom of the front of the boiler and connected with a pipe running into the drain. This, besides being the cock used for emptying the boiler, is for periodically (every day, or every other day)

letting off an inch or so of the boiling water, preferably, so as not to risk shaking the boiler, when the pressure has got as low as 20 lb. This is especially useful when some effective agent, causing a sludgy precipitate, is used in the feed-water.

Obviously the blow-off cock must be accurately ground in to prevent leakage.

Adjuncts to a Boiler are:—

(i) **Donkey Engine and Pump.**—A compact combination, working independently of the main engine (and in this respect superior to the old form of feed-pump, which could only work when the engine was running). Its steam-piston and its pump-piston are at opposite ends of the same rod. Between each boiler and the donkey is a check valve, and the clicking of these as they rise and fall in their seats with every stroke is an indication that the pump is throwing, and not, in engineer's parlance, "taking the pet." There should be a small cock, the "pet-cock," on the boilerward side of the pump in the feed-pipe, and generally a stream of water issuing from this, on its being opened, is also a sign that the pump is working properly. Not always, however, for the pump will sometimes "take the pet" with very hot water, and, therefore, it is well to have provision for lowering the temperature of the water in the hot well.

The check valves are constructed so that they can be screwed down firmly on their seats, if it be wished to pump into one boiler out of two or more; otherwise the back pressure of steam, of course, keeps them tight when the pump is not working.

(ii) **The Injector.**—A subsidiary feed apparatus, which forces water into the boiler by the pressure of the latter's own steam (which, however, must be pure steam taken from the highest part of the boiler), and this, too, against the pressure of both steam and water in the boiler. No completely satisfactory explanation of its working is, as far as the writer knows, yet issued, but it undoubtedly depends on the admission of a jet of steam and the simultaneous admission of a larger quantity of water, in which the steam *instantly* condenses. Though much of the momentum is lost (say $\frac{12}{13}$ if the steam condenses in 12 times its weight of water) the united stream still rushes on at 130 feet per second at least, and this, combined with its concentration upon a given point (in which two funnel-shaped, *i.e.*, narrowing passages, doubtless play their part), will probably give the outline of the explanation. Or putting it otherwise, the combined steam and water jet still retains a velocity greater than that possessed by water alone issuing under the same pressure.

One thing is certain, that the injector will not act with water of a temperature above 120°—in some instances 90°—and this suggests that immediate condensation of the steam is an essential factor.

(iii) **Mechanical Stokers.**—Among the best known are those of Vickers of Earlestown, Lancashire, Sinclair of Leith, Cass of Bolton, and Andrews' Helix underfeeder, and of a somewhat different type, the sprinkling stokers (Bennis and Proctor).

The coals are fed either by hand or by a shoot into a hopper in front of the furnace, whence they fall, or are pushed, in a continuous thin stream on to the front of the fire, save in the case of the sprinkling stoker, which throws them (something like a person dealing cards) on to the top, and is thus better adapted for dealing with very fine coal which is practically in the form of dust.

In the former three stokers, the result is got by an alternating movement of solid firebars. The firebars move backward all together for a space of two or three inches, carrying the fuel with them, then they return into their original position one by one, but sliding under the fire. Then after an interval they all move back again together, and this continuous movement not only carries the fire regularly backwards, but breaks it up, and prevents the formation of clinkers. [Stokers of this type are superseding the old stoker of Jukes, in which firebars, linked together to form an endless chain, passed round two revolving drums, which kept them constantly and with them the fire moving slowly backward.]

The Helix-underfeeder consists of screws of wide thread, revolving in the direction of their length, which carry the coal from the hopper along channels under the grate, whence it is forced up beneath the fire, the latter being always fed from below.

It is said that the annual saving effected by using "slack" instead of larger coal (rendered possible by these mechanical stokers) may amount to as much as £100 per boiler. Further, they lessen the firemen's labour, and as the furnace doors have not to be opened, the usual inrush of cold air is avoided.

Boiler-heating (and copper-boiling) by Gas.—In this method, which has been adopted in one large brewery within the writer's knowledge, the coals are fed into a large retort and there converted into crude gas. No attempt is made at purification, but the gas is conducted direct into a flue connected with the boiler and kindled there, so that the whole flue is filled with blazing gas. Similarly, it is conducted underneath and round the coppers, which are, in effect, fire-coppers but without the necessity of stoking them direct, so that, instead of damping down the fires, it is only requisite to cut off the supply of gas.

Boiler Corrosion, External or Internal.—External corrosion will occur from several causes—*e.g.*, (a) careless setting in too much, and that impure, lime. (β) Setting on a damp foundation without proper means of drainage. (γ) Inattention to "weeps" (slight leakages) of the boiler plates at the rivets. (δ) Contact of ashes carelessly allowed to accumulate; alkaline salts contained therein in conjunction with damp attack the iron. (ϵ) Leakage round brass cocks, fittings, etc., attached to the shell of the boiler, inciting galvanic action between the dissimilar metals.

Internal corrosion is rapidly caused by the joint action of oxygen and carbonic acid, which all spring waters contain, in a moist state, though singly, or even combined, when dry, their action is inappreciable.

Grease (from lubricants) in condensed water used as feed is also most destructive, the *lime-soap* forming by its combination with lime salts decomposing again at high temperatures into a free acid, oleic acid, and a residue, which adheres to the surface, while the acid attacks the iron.

Sulphuric acid, developed under pressure from certain waters, notably those containing iron sulphate, may ultimately prove destructive, albeit produced in infinitesimal traces, seeing that, not being volatile, it accumulates.

Chlorides of sodium and magnesium are also destructive, especially in the presence of carbonic acid and air.

Incrustation (Boiler Scale).—This, the consequence of the feed-water containing carbonate of lime and silica (even more objectionable when organic matter is present too), is unwelcome, because it involves a loss of power from the fuel. [It is said that scale $\frac{1}{4}$ inch thick means a loss of 38%, while if $\frac{1}{2}$ inch thick it means a loss of 60%.]

On the other hand, it sometimes forms a protection against the corrosive agencies indicated above. For instance, at Glasgow, it was found that a range of new boilers, in which the freshly introduced supply from Loch Katrine was used instead of the former calcareous water, suffered rapid corrosion, while an old boiler, in which calcareous water had been used, but which had not been scaled before the introduction of the new supply, showed no signs of it, and it was actually found necessary to feed in *lime and water* until an artificial protecting scale was obtained. No condenser, possibly containing grease, being used, the corrosion could be traced with certainty to the limeless new supply.

Remedies are caustic soda, washing soda alone or mixed with lime, and patent remedies (*e.g.*, Anti-lithon). Caustic soda, which should contain not more than 2% of impurities (no common salt), is effective, but some of it is carried over by the steam into the cylinder of the engine, and is very destructive to all the packings with which it comes in contact.

Soda, besides preventing scale, corrects the acidity of water, and by absorbing carbonic acid, prevents its acting in the way of rusting.

"Anti-lithon," though somewhat costly, is very effective with certain calcareous waters, but in others its effects are less marked.

The **"Instructions to Firemen,"** given by the Boiler Insurance and Steam Power Company, Manchester, are so valuable that I shall append them here.

"Water gauges should be blown out frequently during the day and the glasses and passages kept open and clean. More accidents happen from want of attention to water gauges than from all other causes put together.

"Safety-valves should be tried at least once a day to make sure that they will act freely. Overloading or neglect leads to most disastrous results.

"Pressure gauges, where fitted with cocks, should be tried occasionally by shutting off the steam, and letting the pointer run back to zero. For this purpose the cock to the gauge should be arranged to open to the atmosphere when shut off from the boiler.

"Blow-off cocks should be taken apart, examined and greased every time the boiler is cleaned. Make certain that water is not escaping when the cock is supposed to be closed.

"Check-valves, or self-acting feed-valves, should be taken out and examined every time the boiler is cleaned. When the feed-pump is at work frequently satisfy yourself that the valve is acting.

"Fusible plugs should be examined every time the boiler is cleaned, and carefully scraped clean on both the water and fire sides. If this is not done the plug will be useless.

"To save coal, keep the boiler clean inside and outside. If there is a plentiful supply of steam keep a thick fire, but if short of steam work with a thin fire, but keeping the bars fully and evenly covered. Firing a furnace on each side alternately tends to prevent smoke.

"To preserve and keep the boiler in good repair, raise steam slowly. Never light fires till the water shows in the gauge glass. Never empty under pressure, but allow the boiler and brickwork to cool before running the water off.

"Clean the boiler inside regularly once a month, oftener if the water is bad. Clean all flues once a month, stop any leakages, and prevent any dampness in the seatings or covering. Carefully examine plates subject to direct action of fire, the underside of the boiler and any parts in contact with brickwork or with copper or brass, where water is present.

"If the boiler is not required for some time, and it cannot be conveniently emptied and thoroughly dried, fill it quite full with water, and put in a quantity of common soda.

"Should the water get too low, draw fires at once as a rule; or if the furnace-crown appears to be red-hot, it is best to smother the fire with wet ashes, wet slack, or any earth that may be at hand. The dampers may then be closed. If the engine is running or the feed-pump delivering into the boiler, do not stop them, but if not working do not start them, and do not attempt to blow off the steam until the fire is out, and the over-heated plates have cooled."

The Steam Engine.—This subject must be briefly dealt with, and mainly in connection with brewery work, text-books on it being numerous. Be it remarked, however, that, though the arrangement, in the Plan given for a 70-quarter Brewery, of having the malt-mills just over the engine-room is convenient for the shafting, and moreover allows of ready access from one to the other, the fine dust, which is bound to come down in quantity, is by no means conducive to that bright and smart appearance which every driver, who is good for anything, delights in.

Stationary engines are either **condensing or non-condensing**, the former being again either simple or compound (*i.e.*, expansion engines, in which high-pressure steam, introduced first into the smaller of two cylinders, passes, after doing its work there, into a second larger cylinder, and expanding, completes its work at low pressure*). These cylinders are generally placed either side by side, or one behind the other (Tandem arrangement), though occasionally with the larger cylinder horizontal, and the smaller inclined above it, with its connecting rod working upon the same crank pin.

The condenser (in condensing engines) will be in line with the cylinder, so that the tail-rod of the piston drives the plunger and piston-rod in the former. Condensers are either *jet* or *surface* condensers, the steam being condensed in the former by a jet of cold water, in the latter by contact with thin metallic surfaces, say brass tubes through which cold water is being forced. A pump (air-pump) connected with the bottom of the chamber draws off the water and any air.

Though expansion engines are seen in breweries, the usual type will be the horizontal non-condensing engine, the exhaust steam being passed through a heater (a large cylinder with a number of vertical tubes inside through which the "exhaust" passes, leaving any grease, due to lubricants, in a chamber at the bottom) in order to heat the water which the "Donkey" is pumping into the boiler.

It must be taken for granted that the reader knows how the steam acts on the piston (on alternate sides), and how the latter is made steam-tight in the cylinder, although working with a minimum of friction, and the section be concluded with an enumeration of working parts, with a word of explanation here and there.

The principal parts of an engine are :—Cylinder, Piston, Piston-rod, Crosshead (joining piston-rod on to connecting-rod, and working between guides on sliding surfaces), Crank-pin and Crank, or better than this a Crank-disc (a circular piece of bright cast iron, which translates the to and fro motion of the piston into circular motion), Fly-wheel (which by its momentum

---

* The steam may pass either direct from the small cylinder to the large, or there may be a receiver interposed, in which the steam can be uperheated by hotter steam from the boiler, passing through tubes.

carries the engine over the " dead-points," *i.e.*, the beginning and end of the piston's stroke), keyed on to the end of the crank shaft, which should be made of *steel*, the Fly-wheel itself being of bright cast iron. Steam-ports (openings for admission of steam into the cylinder, one on either side of the piston), closed and opened alternately by the Slide-valve (in the form of a hollow box, with accurately planed projecting ends). This valve is just proportioned so that, as it travels to and fro (driven by a rod worked from an eccentric keyed on to the crank-shaft), one port is *outside* its projecting end, and by this steam enters, while the other is *within* the hollow part, and is thus put into connection with the exhaust pipe. The valve of course works in a valve-casing, through which the steam-pipe passes, and which in larger engines is generally a separate casting bolted on to the cylinder.

To reduce friction, which, owing to the pressure of the incoming steam, is very considerable with valves of large surface, two valves, closing one port each, are adopted, and then they are, of course, worked by separate eccentrics and eccentric rods. The valve casing may also have, on the side remote from the crank-shaft, a screw-arrangement for reducing or enlarging the apertures of the ports, a very useful addition where the calls upon the engine are so varied as in a brewery.

The Governors are the two balls of metal suspended on either side of a vertical spindle, which, whenever the speed of the engine unduly increases, fly outwards by centrifugal force, and either by means of a lever and throttle-valve, or, in a more complicated manner, by reducing the *travel* of the slide-valve, cut off some of the steam from the cylinder, and so almost immediately correct the speed. They get their impulse from a belt running on one pulley, keyed on to the crank-shaft, and on another smaller pulley, the horizontal spindle of which has at its other end a pinion gearing into another pinion upon the vertical spindle whence the balls, above mentioned, depend.

STEAM-ENGINE. HOISTS.

The eccentrics are circular pieces of metal fastened on to a shaft *ex-centrically*, *i.e.*, at some point other than its centre, the distance between this point and the centre being known as their *eccentricity*. Round this circular plate a ring of metal, connected with the rod, moves freely; and it is obvious that, with each revolution of the shaft, the part of the ring connected with the rod will move *to* and *fro* for a distance equal to twice the eccentricity.

Thus the crank-shaft with its end farthest from the engine working in a plummer-block, will very probably have keyed on to it, first the fly-wheel, next a large pulley, round which a stout belt passes to a loose pulley overhead and from one-half to one-third the size, which, when made a "fast" pulley by means of a clutch, actuates the malt-rolls, then a toothed-wheel gearing in with another of such a size that the shaft on which the latter is keyed passes underneath the bed-plate of the engine and serves to drive the well-pumps, then the pulley for the governor belt, next the two eccentrics, and finally the crank-disc which of course must be nearly in line with the piston.

Lubricators are fitted to all points of friction; in most cases box-shaped receptacles for tow, saturated with oil; but for the slide-valves and piston the somewhat expensive lubricator, known as Brierley's Patent Climax Sight-feed, is found effective. One does for both purposes, the steam carrying the lubricant into the cylinder.

The above is, of course, a very incomplete account of the steam-engine, nevertheless the writer hopes it may help the pupil, who is not afraid of asking questions, to find out a good deal about it. It will, at any rate, supply him with some raw material for inquiries.

We will now deal with other parts of the plant in a cursory way.

Sack and other Hoists.—Use is generally made of friction gearing, where two wheels having a number (five or six) of square grooves in their peripheries, are so arranged that the grooves of one are opposite the thread-like projections of the other, and accordingly, when brought together, they interlock and form closely joined bearing surfaces. [The grooves, of course, run the length of the circumference, not as the indentations between the teeth of spur-wheels do.]

The usual arrangement is to have one such wheel, the smaller, keyed on to a revolving shaft, the larger wheel opposite to it, which is fixed on to the end of the spindle of a drum, being with the latter at rest, until both are

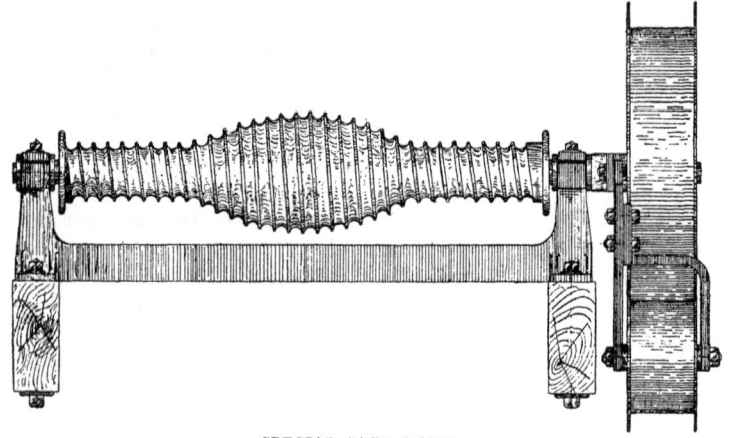

SPECIAL SACK HOIST.
SCALE ¾ IN. TO 1 FOOT.

raised by a lever. Directly the wheels interlock the drum revolves, and the sack, cask, or what not, suspended from it rises as desired. Descending motion is got by releasing the lever.

The best hoist that the writer is acquainted with is the patent of Messrs. Spencer & Co.,* Engineers, of Melksham, Wilts; a cut of it is annexed.

The enlarged barrel shown is for the purpose of in-

* They are also makers of a revolving dust-screen, capable of taking out about 75% of malt-dust during transit to store.

creasing the speed of chain *after* it has started and the smaller ends allow of a slower speed, both for starting the sack and landing it. The hoist is put in motion by a small pulley pressing on the driving belt and tightening it, and by this means any degree of tension can be put on it either for lifting or lowering sacks.

Barley and Malt Screens.—A simple but effective specimen of the former is one on the principle of an "overshot" waterwheel, made by Messrs. Boby. The barley coming out of a shoot on to a wooden wheel turns the latter round with considerable force. Below this wheel are two inclined wire slides, one over the other, the uppermost of which is moved to and fro by the revolutions of the wheel, and thus the needful check is given to the course of the barley, which comes into contact with the wires in such a way that almost every thin grain and much of that which is broken gets removed.

For malt I think the cylindrical form of screen, with mesh of three varying degrees of coarseness, preferable to the flat form, insomuch as it separates not only the dust, but thin corn and large stones too. The malt, in its passage through the somewhat inclined cylinder, first comes into contact with the finest mesh, by which the dust is removed; by the somewhat coarser mesh succeeding the small corns are removed, dropping into their special receptacle; through the next mesh, coarser still, the good malt falls; and finally, through the open end of the cylinder, peas, stones, and anything too large to pass the screens are discharged.

The Cold-liquor Back.—The size of this, the highest vessel in the brewery, must depend upon whether it is relied upon for attemperating or not. Some brewers use their well supply for brewing and cooling, but get their attemperating supply from the local waterworks, if there is reason to think the pressure from the latter will be more constant. But if attemperating is done with water from the brewery well, there should be a subsidiary attemperating-back kept always up *to the same level* by a ball-cock, so that the pressure may be uniform and the size of the main-liquor back should be *at least* on the scale of five barrels per quarter brewed. [Where, say, 1,000 barrels per week are brewed on the average, 160 barrels may easily be run out within twelve hours, and so the attemperating stop altogether, without speaking of the continuously diminishing pressure.]

Of course fresh liquor is the best for cooling, and the certainty of a copious well supply will render some reduction of size possible.

Liquor-backs are now generally made of cast-iron panels bolted together (joints made tight by planing the turned edges and painting them just before bolting tight), though Dantzic fir is still no unknown material. The width is about half the length, and they are made relatively shallow (3 to 4 feet), because the greater the area the more the weight will be distributed.

Hot-liquor Backs.—Their contents may be heated either by free steam from the boiler, by a coil, or by a tubular heater (Worssam's make). The former plan is objectionable for more reasons than one—viz., the risk of introducing impurities (perhaps not very great if the vessels are a good height above the boilers), the dilution of the water's saline properties, and the noise that free steam makes when so used. Coils must be placed so that the water from condensed steam readily drains away, towards the trap if one is used. In the latter case the pipes must be somewhat stronger than they would have to be if steam simply passed through the coil unobstructed, the pressure with a trap, which mainly lets the condensed liquid alone pass, being so much greater.

It is not easy to keep the joints of these pipes, of which several together, brazed to one flange, skirt the inside of the back, from leaking sometimes; further the contact of iron and copper, of which material the coil is usually made, in steam brings about a destructive galvanic action between the metals, which necessitates some form of insulation. Perhaps the worst defect is that, as the pipes

MALT-MILLS. 479

are necessarily some distance, relatively speaking, from the bottom of the back, the water below them does not get heated equally with the water above, so that, unless the mashing supply is drawn from well above the level of the coil, it is apt for some minutes to come down at a lower temperature than that required. [A bent-tube thermometer should always be inserted in the down pipe close to the "Steele" or other external masher.]

It is said that Worssam's high-pressure heater, by promoting circulation, obviates this drawback. The heater is, in effect, a large drum or cylinder of metal, through which a large number of tubes pass lengthwise. Steam (a pressure of at least 50 lb. recommended) is admitted into and passes through the drum, heating the water in the tubes, which immediately rushes out of their upper ends, and is replaced by cold or cooler water entering at the lower ends, and thus, till the desired temperature is reached, the entire contents of the vessel is kept in a state of more or less active movement.

The apparatus can be supplied with lining tubes of copper. These can be drawn out for cleaning, and are accordingly useful when the water is very calcareous.

[The same apparatus is fitted into wort coppers. It has been objected that the tubes would get choked with hops, but this is said not to be the case in practice. I am informed that it is used in one of the largest London breweries.]

Malt-mills consist of a pair (sometimes two pairs) of rolls, cast and turned to a true surface, and working together either by friction (one alone being driven), or gearing, which is the better arrangement for large mills. They are of course thoroughly cased in, but so that access can be got to the various parts. There will be a screen above, which may have a regular rocking motion imparted to it, and placed at a suitable angle for the unground malt to run down its length to the rolls, before reaching which it should have to pass an aperture, having a number of slight bars, close enough together to prevent any foreign bodies larger than the malt itself from passing through.

Malt-mills are sometimes furnished with an arrangement of magnets to withdraw any pieces of iron, and sometimes the rolls themselves are fitted with steel springs, to allow them to give a little if any chance foreign body too hard to be crushed should arrive. This safeguard is discounted by the fact that for rolls of any size the springs have to be so stiff as to be only a degree less unyielding than gearing itself.

When there are two mills—and it is better to have two than one very large one (maximum capacity of thirty quarters per hour)—there will probably be two large wheels (one a mortise wheel) between them, the driver wheel being keyed on to the shaft, on which the fast and loose pulley, mentioned in connection with the crank shaft, runs. The mortise wheel, with a plummer block on either side of it, transmits motion to a shaft, with which (when thrown in by a clutch) one of each pair of rolls rotates, the other roll of each pair getting their rotation by spur-wheels from it. A smaller spur wheel *cast in one piece* with one of these spur wheels, and gearing in with another spur wheel (of larger size) imparts a slower motion to the feed-roll, hereafter to be mentioned.

The levers opening or closing the slides, which regulate the feed, may be most conveniently acted upon by two short rods, connected into one by a piece, having a right-handed V-threaded screw at top and a left-handed similar screw at bottom, both working into nuts on the adjacent ends of the rods. Then a turn of the piece to the right shortens the connected rod and brings the lever down, while a turn to the left acts in a contrary way. A feed-roll, of smaller diameter than the crushing rolls, and deeply grooved in the direction of its length, working close over the back roll of the pair, is useful in distributing the feed.

The efficiency of the rolls depends on the size of their surface and the speed with which they are driven. A peripheral velocity of 180 to 200 feet per minute is a good limit, or say 60 revolutions for rolls of 1 foot diameter. Up to a certain point the yield of a pair of rolls of relatively small diameter can be increased by augmenting the speed of revolution, but if this be overdone they operate more by attrition than by pressure, and this tends to bring the grist into a too powdery condition.

When the mill has two pairs of rolls, one pair is set close (by means of set screws) to crush the thin malt, the other pair wider apart for the malt of average size. The malt, on its passage, has of course to be sorted out by a complicated system of different-sized meshes.

The Elevator (Jacob's Ladder).—An endless belt, on which tinned or galvanised iron cups are riveted, rotating, within an iron case, round a top and bottom pulley. It is advisable to have it driven from the top, as then, owing to the weight of the cups and belt giving more "bite," it is not necessary to keep the belt so tight, as would be necessary if the driving were from the bottom. There may be a screw arrangement connected with the lower pulley, enabling it to be raised or lowered so that the belt may be readily tightened as required.

There should be convenient doors, for inspecting the working of the cups, at some point or points in their upward career, and they should be allowed to run on for some minutes after the grinding is finished to ensure their being emptied. I also hold with giving the elevator case a few smart taps with a mallet, in order to detach as much of the adherent flour as possible. This should certainly be done after brown malt has been crushed. Black malt, I think, should be ground into sacks and be shot into the grist-case; the risk of colouring a following pale-beer brew is too great to admit of sending it up by the elevators.

Grist Cases, or Grist Hoppers.—Their position with regard to the mash-tun depends upon there being only an internal mashing arrangement (rakes), or on a combination of the latter with an external masher, of which that known as "Steele's" is the usual type. In the former case they will be directly over the mash-tuns, and will have four or more slides to allow the grist to be rapidly let into the mash-tun while the rakes are revolving.

In the latter, each "hopper" will only, generally speaking, have one outlet at bottom, with slide working with a square-threaded screw, and their position manifestly depends upon whether one Steele does duty for two tuns or not. In the former case the two hoppers will be, as it were, one structure, divided by a central partition.

Wrought iron, with as smooth an inner surface as possible, and painted inside and out, is now the usual material, but wood (well-seasoned deal), zinc-lined, has the advantage of not causing such rapid condensation of the steam, which inevitably finds its way into its interior.

The lower part of the grist-case should slope to the "Steele" at an angle of about 45°. A much less angle than that, meaning that the sloping sides are carried up unduly high (as I have seen them where exigencies of space have necessitated such an arrangement), causes the grist to come down by fits and starts, while a wider angle also interferes with the regular flow.

There should be an opening at the top, whence a man can push down every particle of grist within reach at the end of the mash, and *there should certainly be a movable piece, a shoot or box, between the bottom of the grist-case and the Steele.* Otherwise there is great difficulty in cleaning the parts round the slides properly, and pasty matter collects there which soon gets abominably sour.

The area allowed for a grist-case is about 12 cubic feet per quarter (for a hopper for whole-grain about 10).

External Mashers are either self-acting or require driving. The former type is generally used for small plants only, though it is possible, by having several (one connected with each outlet of the grist-case), to make them available for dealing with large quantities of grist. Ready detachability for cleaning is their recommendation in the latter case. Maitland's, Gregory's, or Riley's are,

I should say, the most usual forms, the first-named having revolving paddles actuated by the downward rush of the water, the last two having no mixing parts, but subjecting the ground malt, as it comes down through the inner part of the cylinder, to continuous fine jets of heated water proceeding from numerous holes pierced in the inner face of the cylinder's hollow jacket.

"Steele's," the most widely used form, requires driving. It consists of a shaft, with a number of short arms at right angles to it, rotating in a cylinder of iron or copper. The grist and liquor enter the cylinder at one end, at two separate openings, and when mixed by the revolving arms fall into the mash-tun at the other, the open end of the cylinder. This is the simplest form, but the machine may be fitted with a screw to feed the grist. There should be openings (closed during mashing) in both top and grist-case ends for cleaning out the cylinder.

Powerful "Steeles" are made which will mash sixty quarters in ten to fifteen minutes; but, personally, I think a lower power than that preferable.

The rate of speed may vary from 120 to 180 revolutions per minute, the lower rate being adapted to machines of larger diameter.

Mash-tuns and Mashing Tackle (Rakes).—Mash-tuns are either of wood (oak sides, bottom of Dantzic fir) or cast iron, the sides of the former tapering upwards slightly (to allow of the hoops being tightly driven), while in the iron tuns they are quite vertical. This, as Mr. Southey pointed out, causes "the goods" to rise better in iron tuns than in those of wood.

Iron mash-tuns, if properly managed, give no coloration to the wort, but in the leading pale-ale centres there is still a prejudice in favour of wood, and, where expense is no object, with gun-metal fittings.

Tuns of either material require to be thoroughly heated before use, but those of iron most of all, on account of the rapidity with which heat would otherwise be absorbed from the mash. A good plan is to turn in free steam, after having run in a sufficiency of *boiling* water to cover the false bottom.

The capacity of a mash-tun should be quite $3\frac{1}{2}$ barrels of liquor per quarter of malt, which allows a clear $2\frac{1}{2}$ barrels per quarter for mashing the malt with. The pro portion of depth to diameter recommended varies from equality (about 5 feet each) in 5-quarter mash-tuns to as 1 : 2 (7 feet and 14 feet) in full-sized 50-quarter tuns.

The largest mash-tuns which the writer knows of are 120 and 160 quarters respectively, but Mr. Southby thinks a capacity equal to 100 quarters should be the limit.

The internal mashing machine (or Porcupine)* consists of the following parts—viz., a vertical shaft, either driven by steam power from above, or from below (in which case it passes through a stuffing-box in the centre of the mash-tun bottom with a gland bolted on underneath). In the former case it works a foot-step (on gun-metal bearing, which is bolted to the bottom of the mash-tun inside) with a bevel wheel cast on, driving, as the vertical shaft rotates, a horizontal single or double rake-shaft, in line, by means of a bevel or bevel wheels gearing into it. The horizontal rake-shaft has a number (7 or 8) of *wrought* iron rakes bolted on, rotating with the shaft.

On the outer end of the rake-shaft is a toothed pinion, working on a circular rack, skirting the tun about halfway up. It is usual to have, one above and one below the rack, two rakes, which move with the shaft, but without rotating. These serve to push "the goods" from the edges.

In the largest mash-tuns it is necessary to have two tiers of rakes, one above the other, but driven from the same vertical shaft, although at different rates of speed.

Iron mash-tuns, of course, have to be lagged with felt or other non-conducting material, and boarded round.

Mash Tun Covers and False Bottoms.— The raised

* A name perhaps never heard now, though it survives in French as *Porc-épic Anglais*.

covers, with the sides closed in by shutters, sometimes seen, are not to be recommended.

The simplest arrangement is to have two nearly semi-circular covers (of well-seasoned wood, tongued), hinged on to a permanent narrow wooden bridge (just wide enough to allow of an opening being made in it for the bowl of the sparger to work). The two covers are properly counterpoised to allow of their being readily opened or closed, and fit down close on the upper edge of the mash tun.

The false-bottom plates, two semicircular, the rest roughly triangular, *stand, when down*, upon wooden feet, about $1\frac{1}{2}$ to 2 inches from the real bottom of the tun. They are either *drilled* with holes, from $\frac{1}{16}$ to $\frac{1}{8}$ inch in diameter (counter sunk and not over one inch apart), or have slots for drainage—long slits—radiating from the centre, the latter being now the more usual plan. Its drawback is that it tends to weakness of the cast-iron plate. Plates of copper or gun-metal (but not in an iron mash-tun, seeing that the galvanic action set up in the acid medium would gradually corrode the iron in contact) give the best drainage area for their surface, but are costly.

Spargers.—The simplest form consists of a bowl-like reservoir, revolving on a central pin, which is either a continuation of the vertical shaft, round which the rakes revolve, or, if there are no rakes, is fixed at right angles, to a bar which crosses the tun, and which can be raised or lowered according to the quantity of malt mashed. The arms, perforated with a row or double row of small holes, facing downwards when the arms are adjusted, and provided with screw-on caps, are screwed into sockets, communicating with the lower part of the reservoir.

It is important that the sparge-liquor should be delivered evenly over the whole surface of the goods. An appliance (Messrs. Wilson & Co.'s) for testing this is described on p. 312. Small spargers have two arms, larger more.

But if the mashing-tackle is driven from above the

tun, then the vertical shaft must pass through the bowl, the latter revolving on wheels running round a little circular platform on the former. As this arrangement involves more friction, greater pressure may be required to drive it. In either case the force causing the revolution comes from the water, rushing from the small holes in the arms, or impinging on transverse strengthening partitions within the bowl of the sparger itself.

Coppers; heated by Fire direct, or by Steam.

Fire coppers are either—

1. Closed dome, the form used in the large London breweries, especially for porter. The steam escapes through a pipe in the upper part of the dome, and sometimes there is a safety-valve too. Occasionally a shaft, driven from above, is fixed in the copper, and has arms at right angles, from which looped chains depend of just such a length as to sweep the bottom of the copper, as the shaft slowly revolves while the copper is boiling.

2. Open coppers, which are, of course, the easiest of *fire* coppers to clean (all fire coppers, however, want much more *scouring* than steam coppers do, and owing to this and the effect of the flame, wear out much more quickly than the latter), but require constant watching and *hard rousing* whenever they threaten to boil over. (See Fountains and Cones, below.)

3. Dome and Pan Copper. The dome is less rounded than in No. 1, forming, in fact, the bottom of the pan, which is generally of a capacity nearly half the *boiling* capacity of the copper. The sides of the pan are carried up in continuation of the sides of the copper, and there is an opening in the crown of the dome, from which a short, wide tube, firmly riveted on, is carried up level with the rim of the pan. There is also a hole, closed by a long-handled plug, in the lowest part of the pan.

When the copper is boiling strongly the plug is withdrawn, and the wort which boils out of the central aperture falls into the pan, and finds its way back at once through the plug-hole into the copper.

Towards the end of the boil, when the copper has steadied down, and it is desired to have some fresh wort ready "to save the copper" directly the first wort is turned out, the plug is replaced and fresh wort pumped or run into the pan.

I believe this to be by far the best arrangement for fire coppers, the only precaution necessary being to see that the plug fits well, and that no gritty matter gets round it or the plug-hole before the unboiled wort is pumped into the pan.

Size and Shape of Fire-coppers.—In Burton, as a rule, relatively small coppers (within 100 barrels) find favour, on the ground that less coloration ensues than would if the depth of wort were greater; in London, even for the largest plant, 350 barrels is considered a good working limit of size, it being preferable to have several coppers of comparatively medium size, than half the number of very large ones, as then one can much more easily be spared for repairs. [However, a size capable of boiling 500 to 600 barrels is not unknown.]

The bottoms of fire-coppers are dished upwards (in steam-coppers downwards), and the diameter always exceeds the depth. In some cases, where very free evaporation is desired, it may be as 2 : 1.

I look upon such proportions, however, as distorted and needless.

Furnace and Flues (Fire-coppers).—As with boilers, there is a bridge at the back of the furnace, and this extends upward to within a foot, more or less, of the copper-bottom. A flue, or flues, lined with firebrick, start from the combustion-chamber behind it, and go as high as the part—"the bench"—where the copper widens out.

On the flues, in relation to the furnace, and on the shape of the copper, the style of boil doubtless depends. As a rule, fire-coppers boil more from the centre, while steam-coppers boil from the sides (especially from that where the steam inlet is), but sometimes they boil from back to front. A well-known system of copper-setting depends on having a copper with very broad base, and with such coppers the boil will be central.

Coppers boiled by Steam.—These consist of a hemispherical copper pan made all in one piece (say of ½ inch metal for a 9 ft. pan), with a wrought or cast-iron jacket outside it, an average space of at least three inches, diminishing to one at top, being left between jacket and pan, and the steam space being, of course, made thoroughly tight at the junction. Wrought-iron plates for the jacket of a 9 ft. pan should be ⅜ inch thick, and it should be covered with some non-conducting composition (Leroy's or Pidduck's).

The sides of the copper—and in this case the *actual* depth may exceed the diameter somewhat*—are of less substance than the pan, but should be of a thickness averaging 7 lb. per square foot (No. 9, B. W. G.), and the edge at the top will be turned over 3 inch angle iron to keep the copper from buckling.

Wort is discharged through the centre of the bottom of the jacket, the delivery pipe passing through the steam space between it and the pan.

The fittings comprise a steam-inlet valve, actuated by a long handle carried up to the copper stage, so that steam can be immediately turned off by the man watching the copper, on its threatening to boil over; a safety-valve connected with the jacket to prevent undue pressure, and a cock in the upper part of the latter for escape of heated air, which, owing to the great expansive force of air when suddenly heated, is a necessary precaution.

There must be a condensed water outlet pipe and steam trap, so that condensed water only may pass to the condensed water tank. Steam-inlets, though often single, may be multiplied, and it is recommended to have three or even four for a large copper.

---

* The calculations in Chapter V. were made for steam-coppers having a depth greater than the diameter. With relatively shallower coppers evaporation would, of course, be more considerable.

A mercurial reducing valve, designed to reduce the strain while retaining the increased heat of high pressure in the boiler, may be added at a cost of £21, but a lock-up dead-weight safety valve of large area is thought to be as effective at a much less cost.

Fountains and Cones.—These are both appliances arranged to prevent coppers in strong ebullition from boiling over, and to promote circulation of the boiling wort, but as they are objectionable in more ways than one, they need not detain us long. Not only is there the danger, especially with fountains, if the upper pipe gets choked with hops, of their being forced bodily out of the copper by steam generated underneath, in which case a very serious accident might ensue, but there is the further drawback—still with fountains rather than cones—that the hops get so disintegrated as to be incapable of acting as an effective wort-filter in the hop-back.

A sketch of a fountain may be seen in any Brewing organ; cones, of the shape their name implies, except that there is a relatively large opening (18 inches to 2 feet) at the apex, are suspended, counterpoised so that they can easily be lowered or raised, within the boiling wort, which dashes through the opening at the top, and flows back through the space (some two inches) between the lower edge of the cone and the sides of the copper.

The Underback and Hop-back.—The size of the underback has been treated of in a previous chapter; it should certainly have a coil, but a single tube (as being more easily cleaned) is preferable here to the three or four smaller tubes brazed into one flange, albeit the heating power of the latter arrangement is greater for the same quantity of steam.

A circular form is most convenient for a hop-back (copper, with gun metal, slotted false-bottom plates), as it admits of sparging on the hops instead of pressing them. There should be an air-vent from under the false bottom; and this may be conveniently arranged in connection with the central support for the sparger.

Wort Pumps were referred to earlier in the chapter.

Coolers should be of iron or copper, the former of course being much the cheaper, and soon getting coated with an insoluble film of tannate of iron, which prevents any discoloration from the action of hop-tannin upon the metal. Unused iron coolers should be protected by a coating of whitewash.

Hanford-Stanford Atomising Plant.—This is a new departure, as to which no opinion can yet be formed. The wort is delivered on to the cooler (which may be fairly deep) in a more or less fine spray through a number of nozzles, a certain pressure being attained by appendages like ordinary safety-valves to each. These can be adjusted easily to any required pressure, and the fineness of the spray be increased therewith or diminished. Wires connected, one with each of the safety-valves, have their other ends brought on to a control board, easily accessible, where the adjustment is made.

It is stated that a saving is effected in refrigerating water by a sudden drop of 80° to 100° which occurs, and that this sudden fall of temperature causes a much freer precipitation.

[This system will, not improbably, be heard of in the future, but brewers, whose outputs are large, would wish to be assured of its causing no loss of time, which the lowering of temperature might not compensate for.]

Climax Aërator or Float Valve.—Consists of a hollow copper tube closed at the top, and passing through a circular, hollow copper float, flat at bottom and top. The tube is just big enough to pass easily over an upright tube fixed in the cooler outlet. If, now, this upright tube and the pipe down to the tap, between cooler and refrigerator, be filled with wort, and thereupon the tube with the float be placed over it in such a way that the flat under-surface of the float, sinking into the liquid, must prevent the access of any air to the upright pipe, it will be found, on opening the outlet tap to the refrigerator (whereby suction is begun), that the wort from the cooler, being higher than the refrigerator, will at once begin to syphon up the closed outside tube, and flow steadily down the inner upright tube and over the refrigerators.

The idea is that the supply of liquid running down is always taken from the top, and that consequently the brightest and coolest wort is run down. But to the writer it appears that the float and its connected covering tube are made much too heavy (*e.g.*, 8 lbs. for one of 16 inches diameter), in consequence of which the lower surface of the float is more than an inch below the top layer of the wort, which is accordingly the very portion that is *not* syphoned up.

If that were remedied, this ingenious and simple appliance would be of much greater value.

Refrigerators are of two classes, viz., (1) those in which the wort flows outside, exposed to view, and the water inside, and (2) those in which the wort flows inside the pipes and the water outside.

Class 1 is subdivided into vertical, horizontal, and circular.

Those where the wort flows outside are altogether preferable on the score of cleanliness, the vertical form being generally adopted where there is a sufficient fall. In this shape Lawrence's and the improved Baudelot are widely used, the former being made of corrugated metal (the water passages inside follow the corrugations), while in the Baudelot the tubes are of oval section and each provided with tiny projections like the teeth of a fine saw, which secure the even distribution of the wort.

In another make (S. Briggs & Co.) the tubes are of seamless copper, and have each a rib or feather which fits into a groove in the tube below, and the surface is thus everywhere accessible and the strength great. The chance which this construction gives of removing a damaged tube is one advantage over that of Lawrence's.

In no case should there be any brazed joints, for the alternate expansion and contraction occurring would be certain to ultimately set them leaking, and the waterways should be readily accessible (see hints on cleanliness, below). Lawrence's pattern is supported on trunnions, so that the whole refrigerator can be turned upside down, if found necessary, with comparative ease.

In all of these refrigerators the wort flows in one direction—viz., from top to bottom, while the water flows in the contrary direction, entering the refrigerator tubes at the bottom and making its exit at the top. [The water, after leaving the refrigerator, is sometimes carried into the hot-liquor backs for mashing next day. The plan—unless where water is scarce—is one of which the wisdom is doubtful.]

Of horizontal refrigerators the pattern put forth by Bridle of Bridport was the first resembling those now used, but nowadays Morton's, with great cooling surface, is the one most often seen. Inaccessibility for cleaning, as compared with the verticals, is the drawback of this and other horizontals.

Where space is limited, circular refrigerators are most effective. One (by Shears & Co.), standing beside a Morton, did, within the writer's knowledge, over two-thirds of the work, though occupying certainly less than one-third of the ground-space taken up by its horizontal competitor.

The quantity of cooling water required is a consideration. One of the authorities says that horizontals require at least twice as much as verticals. Verticals require two barrels, more or less (according to season), to cool down one barrel of wort.

Ice-making Machines.—In large breweries, especially where the water supply available for refrigerating is sometimes of too high a temperature for the purpose, ice-making machines are employed. They are rarely used (except on the Continent) to produce actual ice, English brewers preferring cold air, which is conveyed through the tepid liquor, or may be used in part for cooling the air of the fermenting room.

The machines before the public may be classified into—
  (1) **Air-expansion Machines.**
  (2) **Evaporation Machines** (divided into (a) Those with a compression pump, and (β) Those with absorption apparatus.

The construction of (1) depends on the fact that ordinary air compressed into one-fifth or one-sixth its bulk becomes enormously hot. If, then, this be done in a strong cylinder, and the heated air be afterwards cooled down, while under the same pressure, by allowing ordinary cold water to circulate amongst it through a system of pipes, obviously (such a vast number of heat units having been withdrawn) upon allowing the compressed air to expand to its original bulk, an enormous fall of temperature will occur. Windhausen, the leading pioneer of this principle, only uses a compression of *three* atmospheres, and gets a temperature of 58° Fahr. under zero!

Of course, in these machines the piston has great resistance to overcome, and very strong construction is requisite. For this reason, involving a higher first cost and more expenditure of coal, the principle has not found much favour with brewers, but seeing that *cooled air* is what the latter require, the writer cannot help thinking that it is the one best adapted to their requirements. And perhaps, as the extremely low temperature, named above, would not be required, some comparatively cheap and simple arrangement might be designed, to be worked by moderate power.*

The evaporation machines of both kinds depend upon the physical fact that many fluid bodies, on passing into the gaseous state, lock up heat—*i.e.*, render it latent. The main difference between them consists in the way in which the agent (ammonia or what not) is recovered after the cold has been produced.

* There is such an arrangement, worked by water power, delivering cooled air at a distance of nearly half a mile into the workings of a Devonshire copper mine.

In the compression system (Linde's), the gas as it leaves the refrigerator of the machine is pumped into a receptacle, and re-converted into a liquid by compression. In the absorption system it is brought into contact with some liquid, *e.g.*, water, which absorbs it, and whence it is afterwards recovered. This system is more elaborate, and machines on that principle have more parts; on the other hand, compression needs a good deal of power, and the piston is not easily made gas tight.

[In Linde's machines this is attempted by having a body of glycerine between two packings in a long stuffing-box, which also serves to lubricate the piston, but also unfortunately absorbs ammonia; and as it continuously drips away there is a certain loss to be reckoned with. I believe naphtha has been similarly employed with better results, as it does not absorb the ammonia.]

Ammonia—not the liquid known as such, which is only a solution of the gas, but the compressed and liquefied gas itself—is used largely, as implied above, for which its *low* boiling point and *high* latent heat well adapt it. As a matter of practice this gas, which should be anhydrous, *is* got by heating the ammoniacal liquor of commerce with steam, passing through a coil, which drives off the gas, and this gas, passing through sundry valves and traps (designed to remove watery vapour) into the condenser (this time into a coil, surrounded with cooling water), where it accumulates, is finally liquefied by its own pressure.

Hence into another vessel, the evaporator or cooler, where, the pressure being removed, it volatilises rapidly at ordinary atmospheric temperature, and in doing so renders latent an enormous amount of heat. This it abstracts either from water *passing through* a coil in the evaporator (as usual in breweries), or from a strong solution of calcic chloride, the so-called "brine," which rests in the coil till reduced to a very low temperature, and is then conveyed to the ice-making boxes. [The brine, of course, is used because it does not freeze at extremely low temperatures.]

The recovery of the agent has been indicated above as fully as our space will admit.

Agents other than ammonia can be employed. Ether, once much used, is now out of favour, but an apparatus constructed for carbonic anhydride is before the public.

A somewhat different machine—**the Vacuum Ice Machine** (on what was, I believe, M. Raoul Pictet's design, but has been improved by Windhausen)—must just be mentioned. It depends upon the fact that water, when the pressure upon it is reduced below a certain point, evaporates (and the nearer the reduction approaches an absolute vacuum, the more rapid is the evaporation) as to one-sixth of its bulk, so much heat being rendered latent in the process that the other five-sixths turn to ice. The only chemical used is pure sulphuric acid, and that is employed merely to absorb the watery vapour and cheapen production. It does not come in contact with the ice or volatilise at all.

It is said to produce ice more cheaply than any other machine; and though the ice, being opaque, may be less prepossessing than the clear blocks turned out of other machines, this does not matter in a brewery. That explosive agents are not required is, *per contra*, a recommendation.

Fermenting Vessels or Gyle-tuns.—The cleansing systems of fermentation have already been treated in some detail (Chapter I.), and therefore the remarks made here will be limited to the vessels adapted to the skimming system, the more so because " cleansed beers " have a preliminary stay of some forty-eight hours in such vessels.

Where a **Collecting or Gathering Vessel** (not shown on the plan of a 70-quarter brewery) is adopted, the wort *must* remain there for not less than twelve hours or till its gravity has been ascertained by an excise officer. The advantages of having one are (i) Uniformity of gravity when the contents are divided amongst smaller vessels. (ii) That, as samples are only taken whilst the fermenting wort is in them, the contents of fermenting vessels are not interfered with by the excise officer. (iii) The first dirty head (coagulated albuminous matter), and much sedimentary matter remain behind. (iv) Aëration—but not invariably a benefit.

Fermenting Vessels are generally of wood (slate has been tried, but is more sensitive to external temperature), viz., English or foreign oak, or Dantzic (yellow) fir. The timber should be well seasoned, *i.e.*, free from sap as well as from shakes and *knots*. [The latter, if they exist, must be bored out and the opening plugged with sound wood.]

The vessels are either round, oval, or square. The square shape is the more economical both of space and in other respects, as there need be no lost corners, and several can be constructed together with much saving of partition timber. The inside corners undoubtedly afford a harbour for dirt, and a patent (Ramsden's) for constructing them with rounded corners has been taken out.

In rounds and ovals the staves run upwards, say for twenty-four inches above the *highest* filling point, to form yeast boarding; this additional length being afterwards cut away from a few of the staves to form a manhole and dipping place. A frame is fitted into the manhole, and this is closed, if necessary, by movable boards.

I think the best way of seasoning *oak* vessels is to fill them with cold water in which salt, at the rate of a pound per barrel, has been dissolved, after one or two preliminary soakings, for a day or two each, with waste refrigerator liquor.

For seasoning fermenting vessels of fir, Mr Southby recommends the following course. First scald by filling with boiling water; on the following day run the water out, and whitewash with a mixture of $2\frac{1}{2}$ lb. of chloride of lime in one gallon of water. This having remained

YEAST RECEIVING BACKS.

on for 24 hours, a second wash, made of 1 part common hydrochloric acid (muriatic acid) to 4 parts water, is to be applied. Twelve or fourteen hours later the vessel is to be washed several times with water at 212°, and finally with bisulphite of lime solution, which destroys any smell of chlorine.

He also pointed out that quicklime injures oak, by forming a soluble compound with its astringent juices, whence it becomes soft and porous. On the other hand, it does not injure resinous woods, as it forms an insoluble compound with their resins.

The removal of the yeast by skimming is effected, generally, either through **a parachute** connected with a pipe penetrating the centre of the bottom of the tun, or through a **sluice** (Griffin & Pearce's), a smoothly planed slide of metal working against smooth inside edges of an iron frame, bolted on to the tun, the slide being raised or lowered by a rack and pinion on each side.

Sluices are, as a rule, arranged to work into a slate yeast back on the same floor, but where floor space is more of an object than height, there is no reason why the yeast should not be conveyed by a vertical shoot to the floor below. As *data* for the size of these yeast-receiving backs on the floor of the fermenting room (of course the bottom of the F. V. itself is really lower than this floor, the tun having been lowered through a hole cut therein, so as to rest on girders beneath), the following particulars may serve. When two fermenting tuns work into the same slate back ("yeast batch"), an allowance of two cubic feet, *liberal measure*, per barrel of the fermenting wort will probably always suffice, especially seeing that both tuns will not be working simultaneously.

But with stronger worts, and where the full content is fermented, that proportion will hardly suffice, unless precautions are taken to keep the yeast-back on drain. Thus a yeast-back 10 ft. × 9 ft. × 3 ft. 4 in. working out at 306 cubic feet, inside measure, is barely enough for a 150 barrel round, and the contents might occasionally—the yeast sluice having been open all night—be found in the morning to have worked over.

Fermenting vessels up to 150 barrels can generally be skimmed by hand, but above that size they require some form of **mechanical skimmer.** For rounds a skimming-board revolving round a central rod, and capable of being raised and lowered as well as rotated from the outside of the tun, pushes the yeast before it into a trough, which extends (instead of a parachute) from the centre to the edge of the tun, provided like the parachute with a down pipe, going through the bottom of the tun.

Squares may have a similar trough, extending along one of their sides, and into this a yeast-board, travelling on a wheeled framework, from end to end of the tun, pushes all the yeast.

Attemperators are made of tinned copper pipe, and are either fixed or movable, the latter not being adapted for tuns of large size, that of 80 barrels' capacity being about the limit. Beyond that they would have to be excessively cumbrous.

Fixed attemperators of tinned copper pipe, which should be *oval* in section, as this gives more cooling power than the round form, are made in lengths, bolted together in such a way that the whole forms a continuous coil circling the tun about three times. The water inlet is at the higher part of the coil, the outlet at the lower, and here the pipe carried to the outside of the tun, and which is continued by a rising pipe with a "swan-neck" end, should have a small draw-off cock for emptying the attemperator, in case of severe frost occurring when the fermenting vessel is not filled.

Movable attemperators are suspended with chains and balance-weights, and are connected with the mains by india-rubber hose. The whole weight is usually taken by a single wrought-iron chain, attached by a ring to which four short lengths of brass chain converge. The result is that if air gets into the pipes the attemperators sway about a good deal, and I cannot but think that suspension by four vertical chains (in connection with which a very simple arrangement for raising or lowering the attemperator might be made without counterpoise weights) would be preferable.

A Rotary Pump for rousing, raising, when the handle is turned one way, a continuous stream of wort, or when the action is reversed, pumping air into the fermenting wort, is a useful adjunct to the fermenting-room.

Casks are made of foreign (Memel) oak, as a rule. The timber should be free from worm-holes and sap. It comes to hand in lengths (*balk* or juggle) of rather over six feet, and of a thickness which admits of three stave lengths being got. Foreign oak, being straighter in the grain than English, admits of being split; English has to be sawn. Moreover, the latter warps when steamed.

Barrel staves are 31 inches in length; kilderkin staves 25 inches, and care should be taken to divide the timber lengths so as to avoid waste.

The pieces of which the heads are made are joined together by dowel pins (wooden pegs) and bevelled round, so as to fit into the croze grooves. The chamfered edges (afterwards painted) form the chime.

The hoops of hogsheads and barrels are known as the end, bulge, and quarter hoops respectively; kilderkins (generally*) and firkins only have end and bulge hoops.

Casks are classed as stout, intermediate, or slight, according to the thickness of the staves. The thickness of the heads and width of hoops also vary.

The thickness of the *staves* runs as follows.

	Stout.	Intermediate.	Slight.
	inches.	inches.	inch.
Hogsheads	$1\frac{1}{2}$	$1\frac{1}{4}$	1
Barrels	$1\frac{1}{2}$	$1\frac{1}{8}$	1
Kilderkins	$1\frac{1}{4}$	$1\frac{1}{8}$	1
Firkins	$1\frac{1}{4}$	$1\frac{1}{8}$	1

* Slight kilderkins, however, are hooped with six hoops, like barrels.

To Season New Casks.—Fill them with very hot liquor and salt. Most of the colouring matter and woody flavour will be extracted in thirty-six hours. Fill, however, for the first time, with black beer.

For pronounced "stinkers" there is supposed to be no cure, but the chloride of lime whitewash treatment succeeded by muriatic acid and bi-sulphite successively, each being driven in by steam, might certainly be tried.

For cases of moderate gravity, a treatment, which the writer lately derived from a foreign source, but, as yet, has had no means of testing, might prove useful. This is to treat the cask first with a strong solution of bi-carbonate of soda, and when this has well soaked into the pores, to drain the solution out and rinse with pure water, and then to treat again with water, acidulated with hydrochloric acid, whereupon an evolution of carbonic acid occurs, sufficient, it is supposed, to drive out putrescent matter. The use of permanganate of potash has also met with some success.

But, on the principle of *prevention being better than cure*, why should not brewers render their wooden plant, more especially their cask staves, impervious to putrescible matter by treating them with paraffin wax in the manner recommended by Dr. Graham eighteen years ago? His advice was to heat the wood slowly up to rather over 300° Fahr., and then to dip it into fluid paraffin wax at a temperature of 300° to 350° Fahr.

The staves are to be withdrawn as soon as all the air has been driven from their pores, and as the paraffin wax which now fills them is unacted upon by the strongest acids or alkalies, there is no fear of flavours being imparted to any fluid with which it may come in contact, because it does not dissolve at all. Owing, too, to the high temperature required for its solution, it is unaffected by boiling water, being in this respect superior to cask-enamel.

Cask-washing Machines.—The simplest form of effective arrangement for cask-washing (apart from taking out the heads of and hand-scrubbing each cask) is to have a series of nozzles, through which, by duplicate cocks, either steam or boiling water can be delivered. A modification is the Pontifex apparatus, where steam and water are admitted in a similar way, the water being boiled on its way, or within the cask.

Other machines have been designed to give a thorough revolving motion in all directions to the cask, which is charged with a few pebbles as well as half filled with boiling water. The most elaborate of these, which has not yet been surpassed, is the patent by Robinson of Bridgewater.

Messrs. Worssam also have a machine, which does not require any special fixing of the cask. Two parallel shafts are fixed in a wooden frame or trough, which may be below the ground level, and on these shafts eccentrics are keyed (four for each barrel, *i.e.*, two on each shaft), but so disposed that the longest distance, in each, from the key bed to the circumference, comes in a vertical line above the shaft *at varying times*, consequently the rotation of the shafts not only makes the barrel revolve, but the eccentrics tip up first this corner, as it were, and then that, so that the pebbles inside exert their friction, at all events, on most of the inside of the cask.

It is a question, however, whether the heads get such a scouring as is possible with the Robinson machine.

This chapter having already reached an inordinate length, I must pass over other pieces of plant, amongst which are yeast presses, yeast storage backs (less necessary if the slate yeast-backs described above are in a cool situation, and moderate fermenting heats the rule, but otherwise, with a cooling appliance connected with each, most useful), or Mr. Clinch's combined attemperator and rouser, which is understood not to have realised what was expected of it to the full extent, and conclude with a few hints on general cleanliness and general arrangement (taking the latter first) which have not yet come within our purview.

Supplementary Remarks on General Arrangement.—Waste pipes from any vessel used to contain wort or beer should never be directly connected with the drain, for two reasons. (1) The certainty of increased contamination by bacteria, and (2) the risk that, through a cock being left open inadvertently, loss of wort or beer might occur without being noticed.

Wort mains (of tinned copper pipe in moderate lengths connected by unions) should have a fall of at least one inch in ten feet.

Steam or water pipes may be of wrought or cast iron, but in either case the bends should be as easy as possible, avoiding *sharp elbows*.

[N.B.—It is well to specify that large cast-iron pipes should be cast in vertical moulds, as the thickness of the metal is more uniform, and it sets more compactly.]

Hollow cast-iron columns, on account of their liability to vary in thickness in different parts (note the hint in brackets above), are less used than formerly for supporting great weights, the preference being given to a smaller *solid* shaft with four ribs or feathers.

Steel girders are lighter and stronger than iron.

Supplementary Remarks on Cleanliness.—All mains and wort pumps should be periodically charged with a strong potash solution, even though hot liquor be pumped through before each brewing. Hot liquor should be pumped through, and the nearer boiling the better, at the close of each day's work. Steam is the best of all.

The screens of malt-mills are apt, with neglect, to get clogged to some extent, and become, so far, ineffective.

Liquor-backs should be emptied and cleaned every week, even when the liquor supply is pure.

In the mash-tun grains are sometimes left adhering to the cogs of the rack, etc. Wooden tuns sometimes have a rim, and beneath this is the neglected spot if any.

Wooden hop-backs and coolers should be treated with bisulphite, or frequently whitened with monosulphite made into a thin cream.

CLEANLINESS.

Refrigerators should neither be allowed to get coated with deposit outside, nor slime inside. For the latter, a periodical (monthly) charging with a solution of lime and washing soda mixed will suffice; for the former, except in the case of horizontals, which can be charged with potash solution, nothing but scrupulous brushing and plenty of water avails.

Racking hose and the sampling taps (if any) and racking cocks of fermenting vessels require attention, and finally, do not grudge time or labour spent in white-washing walls or keeping down the accumulation of cobwebs and fungoid growths in the less accessible parts of the brewery over coppers and coolers.

This may seem a vain saying to many, but we hardly know yet what condition of things is so trivial as to be incapable of bringing about a serious result.

APPENDIX A.

LIST OF THE HOP-GROWING PARISHES OF KENT.

Lettered to show in what division they lie, with nine Surrey parishes ranking as West Kent. E = East Kent; M = Mid Kent; W = West Kent; B = Bastard East Kent; H = The Hill; Wd. = Weald; S = Surrey (names of parishes in black letters).

Acol	E	Birling	M	Charing	E
Addington	M	Bishopsbourne	E	Chart-next-Sutton	M
Adisham	E	Blean	E	Chart, Great	E
Aldington	B	Bobbing	E	Chart, Little	E
Alkham	E	Bonnington	B	Chartham	E
Allington	M	Borden	E	Chatham	H
Appledore	B	Boughton Aluph	E	Chelsfield	H
Ash	E	Boughton-under-Blean	E	Chevening	W
Ash	H			Chiddingstone	Wd.
Ashford	E	Boughton Malherbe	E	Chilham	E
Ashurst	Wd.			Chislet	E
Aylesford	M	Boughton Monchelsea	M	Cliffe	H
				Cobham	H
Badlesmere	E	Boxley	M	Cooling	H
Barfreston	E	Brabourne	E	Cowden	W
Barham	E	Brasted	W	Cranbrook	Wd.
Barming	M	Bredgar	E	Crayford	H
Bapchild	E	Bredhurst	E	Cray, North	H
Bearsted	M	Brenchley	Wd.	Cray, St. Mary	H
Beckenham	H	Bridge	E	Cray, St. Paul's	H
Bekesbourne	E	Bromley	H	**Crowhurst**	**S**
Benenden	Wd.	Brook	E	Crundale	E
Bethersden	B	Broomfield	M	Cudham	H
Bicknor	E	Burham	M	Cuxton	H
Bidborough	Wd.				
Biddenden	Wd.	**Canterbury**	E	**Darenth**	H
Bilsington	B	Capel	Wd.	Davington	E
Birchington	E	Chalk	H	Debtling	M
Bircholt	E	Challock	E	Denton	E

HOP-GROWING PARISHES OF KENT.

Ditton	. M	Hardres (Upper)	. E	Loose	. M
Doddington	. E	Harrietsham	E & M	Luddenham	. E
Dunkirk	. E	Hartley	. H	Luddesdown	. H
		Hartlip	. E	Lullingstone	. H
EAST LANGDON	. E	Hastingleigh	. E	Luton	. M
Eastling	. E	Hawkhurst	. Wd.	Lydden	. E
Eastry	. E	Headcorn	. Wd.	Lydsing	. M
Eastwell	. E	Herne	. E	Lyminge	. E
Ebony	. B	Hernehill	. E	Lympne	. E
Edenbridge	. W	Hever	. Wd.	Lynsted	. E
Egerton	. E	High Halden	. Wd.		
Elham	. E	Higham	. H	MAIDSTONE	. M
Elmstead	. E	Hinxhill	. E	Malling (East and	
Elmstone	. E	Hoath	. E	West)	. M
Eltham	. H	Hollingbourne	. M	Marden	. Wd.
Eynsford	. H	Hothfield	. E	Meopham	. H
Eythorne	. E	Hoo	. H	Mereworth	. M
Ewell	. E	Horsmonden	. Wd.	Mersham	. E
		Horton Kirby	. H	Milton (by Can-	
FARLEIGH (East)	M	Hucking	. E	terbury)	. E
,, (West)	M	Hunton	. M	Milton (by Sit-	
Farnborough	. H			tingbourne)	. E
Farningham	. H	ICKHAM	. E	Milton Chapel	. E
Faversham	. E	Ifield	. H	Milstead	. E
Fawkham	. H	Ightham	. M	Minster	. E
Fordwich	. E	Ivychurch	. B	Moldash	. E
Frindsbury	. H	Iwade	. E	Mongeham	. E
Frinstead	. E			Monk's Horton	. E
Frittenden	. Wd.	KEMSING	. M	Monkton	. E
		Kenardington	. B	Marston	. E
GILLINGHAM	. H	Kennington	. E		
Godmersham	. E	Kingsdown	. H	NACKINGTON	. E
Godstone	. S	Kingsdown	. E	Nettlestead	. M
Goodnestone (by		Kingsnorth	. B	Newington	. E
Faversham)	. E	Kingstone	. E	Newenden	. Wd.
Goodnestone (by		Knockholt	. M	Newnham	. E
Wingham)	. E			Nonington	. E
Goudhurst	. Wd.	LAMBERHURST *	. Wd.	Northfleet	. H
Gravener	. E	Langley	. M	Northdown	. E
		Leaveland	. E	Norton	. E
HADLOW	. Wd.	Leeds	. M	Nursted	. H
Halling	. M	Leigh	. Wd.	**Nutfield**	. S
Halstead	. H	Lenham	. E		
Halstow (High)	. H	Leybourne	. M	OFFHAM	. M
,, (Lower)	E	**Limpsfield**	. S	Old Romney	. B
Ham	. E	**Lingfield**	. S	Orlestone	. B
Harbledown	. E	Linton	. M	Orpington	. H
Hardres (Great)	. E	Littlebourne	. E	Ospringe	. E
,, (Lower)	. E	Longfield	. H	Otford	. H

* Part in Sussex.

HANDY BOOK FOR BREWERS.

Otham	M
Otterden	E
Oxted	**S**
PADDOCK WOOD	Wd.
Patrixbourne	E
Peckham (East)	M
„ (West)	M
Pembury	Wd.
Penshurst	Wd.
Petham	E
Plaxtol	M
Pluckley	E
Postling	B
Preston-by-Faversham	E
Preston-by-Wingham	E
RAINHAM	E
Reculver	E
Ridley	H
Rochester	H
Rodmersham	E
Rolvenden	Wd.
Ruckinge	B
Ryarsh	M
SANDHURST	Wd.
Sarre	E
Seal	W
Seasalter	E
Selling	E
Sellinge	E
Sevenoaks	W
Sevington	E
Shadoxhurst	B
Sheldwich	E
Shepherdswell (Sibertswould)	E
Shipbourne	M
Sholden	E
Shoreham	H
Shorne	H
Sittingbourne	E
Smarden	B
Smeeth	E
Snodland	M
Southborough	Wd.
Southfleet	H
Speldhurst	Wd.
Stalisfield	E
Stanford	E
Stansted	H
Staple	E
Staplehurst	Wd.
St. Dunstan's	E
St. Lawrence	E
St. Margaret's	H
St. Margaret's (at Cliffe)	E
St. Mary's	B
St. Nicholas	E
St. Peter's	E
St. Stephen's	E
Stelling	E
Stockbury	E
Stodmarsh	E
Stoke	H
Stone	H
Stone-by-Appledore	B
Stone-by-Faversham	E
Strood	H
Stourmouth	E
Stouting	E
Sturry	E
Sundridge	W
Sutton (at Hone)	H
„ (by Dover)	E
„ (East)	M
„ (Town)	M
Sutton Valence	M
Swanscombe	H
Swingfield	E
Tandridge	**S**
Tatsfield	**S**
Tenterden	Wd.
Teston	M
Teynham	E
Thannington	E
Throwley	E
Thurnham	M
Tilmanstone	E
Titsey	**S**
Tong	E
Trosley	M
Trotterscliffe	M
Tudeley	Wd.
Tunbridge	Wd.
Tunstall	E
ULCOMBE	E & M
Underriver	M
Upchurch	E
WALDERSHARE	E
Waltham	E
Warden	E
Warehorne	B
Wateringbury	M
Westbere	E
Westerham	W
Westwell	E
Whitstable	E
Wickham	E
Willesborough	W
Wilmington	H
Wingham	E
Witchling	E
Wittersham	B
Womenswould	E
Woodchurch	B
Woodnesboro'	E
Wootton	E
Wormshill	E
Wouldham	M
Wrotham	M
Wye	E
YALDING	M

INDEX.

ABERRATION (spherical, chromatic), 347
Acarus sacchari (sugar mite), 149
Accessibility of shafts, etc., 445
Acetic acid finings, 44, 428, 431
Acidity determined in malt, 234; in beer, 250, 251
Acids, 193, 194; terminations and prefixes, 195; tartaric and sulphurous as cutting agents, 43; acetic as ditto, 44; lactic and butyric, 202; suggested connection of butyric acid fermentation with "stink," 208; succinic, 204
Achroo-dextrin, 212, 290
Acrospire, 8, 55; noting growth of in proportion per cent., 282, 283
Aërial spores, 369
Aerobic and anærobic ferments, 376, 377
Albuminoids, 204; soluble distinguished from peptones, 205; determined in malt, 237—239; soluble and total by soda-lime process, 240—243; coagulating temperatures for 286 (*note*); coagulable, 317; turbidity caused by, 414—417
Albumose, 415
Alcohol, effect of its specific lightness, 156, 196—199; iodoform test for, 215; source of heat in fermentation, 379; absolute and proof spirit, 381 (*note*)
Alcoholometer (for determining original gravity of beer), 248
Aldehyde, 197, 198—199
Aleurone cells, 55
Algæ, 337
Alternation of generation (*see* Polymorphism)

Amides, 4, 57, 80, 206
Amido-compounds, 207, 208
Ammonia process, 102, 103; determination of free and albuminoid ammonia by, 266—268
Ampère, 184
Amylan, 200
Amylin (= of Dextrin), 297
Amÿlo-cellulose, 385, 386
Amÿlo-dextrin, 288—290
Amÿlöin (*see also* Malto-dextrin), 2, 47; bearing of theory on analysis of malt, 232—234; turbidity due to, 420
Amylpn (= of maltose), 297
Analyses, typical (water), 98, 105; (inadequate, 106), 128, 129, 130; (barley), 209; volumetric and gravimetric, 226, 227; (*see sub* Water, Malt, etc.)
Antiseptics, 38, 426—428
Anthracite, 12
Apparatus required in laboratory, 220, 221; preparation of, 222
Anhydrides, 195
Aperture, angle of (microscope), 348
Archimedean screw, 446
Arrangement, 441—452; supplementary remarks on, 501, 502
Artesian well, 110
Ascomycetes, 341
Ascospores, 46, 335, 399
Ash in rootlets, 85; in yeast, 375
Asparagin, 83, 203, 207
Aspergillus, niger, 328, 342; *glaucus*, 341
Atomicity, 187
Atomising plant (the Hanford-Stanford), 490
Atoms, 184; saturation of, 190

Attemperators, 28 (*note*), 498, 499
Attenuation, 16; final, 156, 381; influence of cane-sugar on, 383
Auto-saturation (or auto-combination), 19
Avogadro, 184
Avoirdupois compared with Troy, 219 (*note*)

BACILLUS, 335; *subtilis, amylobacter, ulna,* and *panificans,* 338; *viscosus* I. and II. (ropiness), 422, 423, 424; *viscosus sacchari* and *vini,* 425
Back-spear, 8
Backs, cold liquor, 477, 478; hot liquor, 478, 479
Bacterial theory of diastase, 86—89
Bacterium, 335; peptonising power of certain forms, 337; *termo, lactis,* and *aceti,* 337; *zylinum,* 338
Baffle-plate, 73
Balance (chemical), 223
Barfoed's solution, 275, 291
Barley, six-rowed, 53; four-rowed, 54; two-rowed, 54; Chevalier and winter French, 54; anatomy of, 55; choice of for malting, 57, 59—61; soil best suited to, 58; seed-corn for, 58; effect of artificial manures on, 59; over-ripe, 59; skinned grains, 60; mowburnt, 60; tests for germinating power of, 62, 63; punctures in foreign, 91
Bases, 193, 194
Basicity, 194
Bearings, 455, 456; reducing excessive pressure on, 457
Beer, decoction (lager), 21—24, 41; determination of original gravity (distillation process), 245; ditto (evaporation process), 246; tables for, 247; Field's alcoholometer for testing, 246; original gravity of acid beer, 249—251; solid residue (dry extract) of, analysis of, 251—253; albuminous matter in, 252, 253; what constitutes good, 276, 277; running beer, maltose ratio in, 284
Beggiatoa, 339
Belting, 461; preservation of, 462
Bi-carbonates, 115
Bigg, 54

Bins, malt, 445; formula for calculating strength of beams to support, 446
Bi-sulphite of lime. In malt-house, 66, 67. 122, 427
"Bite," 28
Bitters, other than hop, 144
Blackman air propeller (fan), 73, 74; cost of using, 74
Bohemian method of malting, 65, 66
Boilers, 462—472; Lancashire, 463; breeches-flued, 463; furnace bars for, 464, 465; shell of, 465; fittings, 465—467; adjuncts (*e.g.*, donkey-engine, injector, mechanical stokers), 467—469; corrosion, 469—471; scale, 470
Boiling, 316—320; objects of, 316; researches by Dr. Morris on sterilising influence of, 316; mode of adding hops, 317, 318; steam *v.* fire, 319
"Boiling fermentation," 27, 388, 390
Boss (of wheel or pulley), 456
Bottling, 433; Bass & Co.'s instructions, 435, 436; forcing tray test in connection with, 437, 438; simpler test for fitness, 438
"Break" in copper, attributed to lime and magnesia salts in steep liquor, 68
Brewers' lbs., 155
Brewings, working out the, 160
British gum, 291
Brown, Mr. H. (and Dr. Morris), 80, 297, 298; originator of forcing tray, 437
Brownian movement, 355
Burette, 225 (*note*)
Burton-unions, 36
Burtonising, 116, 123, 124
Bushes, 456
By-products (of fermentation), 366

CALCULATIONS, 160; of materials, 163, 164; mixing worts, 170—173; extracts, 174, 175; contents of round or square vessels, 177, 178
Caramel, 310
Carbohydrates in barley, 85, 199; supply of assimilable limits secretion of diastase and cytase, 81
Carbon, organic, in water, 99, 100
Carbonates in water, 115, 116

Carlsberg brewery, 47
Casein, 205
Casks, 499 ; to season new, 500 ; washing machines for, 501 ; descending platform for lowering, 447 ; hoist for, 448 ; stacking apparatus, 448
Cask-conditioning, 45, 48, 409, 418
Cellarage in chalk, 441
Cellars, temperature of, 434 ; of bottling, 435, 436 ; flooring of, 450
Cellulose, 199, 200, 201
Cellulose-dissolving enzyme, 79 ; a starvation phenomenon, 81 ; corollary of this in regard to bacteria, 86
Cement (malt-house floors), 65
Chlorates, 195
Chlorides in water determined, 258
Chlorine in water, 99 (*see* Chlorides)
Chlorophyll, 56
Choice of site for brewery, 440, 441
Chromogenic, 336
Cilium (*see* Flagellum)
Circulators, 16 ; Crockford's, 17 ; Bucknall's, 18 ; advantage of using, 17, 281
Cistern, 6, 64
Cladothrix, 339
Clarke's process for softening water, 125
Cleanliness, supplementary remarks on, 501, 502
Cleansing system, 32 ; in carriage casks, 32 ; in loose pieces, 34 ; in unions, 36 ; in pontos, 40
Clostridium butyricum, 323, 339
Clutch, 455
Coccus, 337 ; a form assumed by spores of *C. kühniana*, 339
Cochineal a more delicate reagent than litmus, 263
Cold, production of, in breweries, 492—495
Coldewe's arrangement for testing germinative power, 63
Collars, 457
Combes, 13
Combustion process (water analysis), 96
Compound radicals, 191
Compounds, 183, 184
Concrete, for main walls, 442 ; for cellar floors, 450
Cones, 489
Conidium (*see* Gonidium)

Conron's rakes, 304
Constants, 272, 273
Contamination (previous sewage), 96, 97
Coolers, 20, 490 ; climax aërator for, 490, 491
Copper, boiling down to get required gravity, 173 ; steam and fire, open and closed, 319, 320 ; fire coppers, 486—488 ; steam ditto, 488 ; mercurial reducing valve for, 489 (*see* "Boiling")
Correlation of growth, 332
Corrosion (*see* Boiler)
Cost price of beer, 178—181
Couch (couch-frame), 6, 64
Couplings (box-butt, flange, and claw), 455
Cowls (malt-house), 73
Creeper (*see* Archimedean screw)
Crenothrix kühniana, 339
Curing malt by dry air, 13
Cyto-hydrolyst (*see* Cellulose dissolving enzyme)

DEAD mashes, 16, 311, 312
Decoction system, 21 ; limited decoction, 24, 303—305
Decoction and infusion beers compared, 23
Dematium pullulans, 343
Desiccator, 222, 223
Dextran, 200, 422 ; (?) isolated by precipitation with alcohol, 424
Dextrin, 1, 288 ; its conversion, 2 ; free and combined, 3 ; place in carbohydrate group, 200 ; to increase ratio in beer, 284, 285
Dextrose, 144, 199, 200
Diads, 187
Diastase, 1 ; power of, 4 ; cause of germination, and secreted in absorptive epithelium, 80 ; naked in endosperm, 83 ; not diffusible, 83 ; bacterial theory of, 86—89 ; to limit activity in well-grown malt, 281 ; what it is, 286, 287
Diastasic ferments, 322
Dickmaische, 22
Diffusibility, 329 ; property imparted to albumen by asparagen, 83
Dispersers and dissipators, 13, 78 (*note*)
Dorsal side (of barley), 55
Double decompositions, 122, 125

Drainage (drains outside structure), 444
Dressing, 387, 389
Dropping squares, 31
Dry-extract (*see* Beer)
Drying-oven, 222
Dulcite, 197
Dumas, facts on fermentation demonstrated by, 366, 409
Dunge, 73

ELEMENTS, 183, 186; in nascent state, 203
Elevator, 481
Embryo, its parasitic relationship to endosperm, 81; solution of starch in its vicinity only (J. O' Sullivan), 82
Endosperm, 55
Entry of materials (brewing paper), 161
Enzymes, 321
Epithelium, 55; absorptive, 79
Equations, 186; dealing with starch transformations, 293, 294, 298, 299; dealing with fermentation, 367
Erosion, 82, 84
Erythro-dextrin, 212, 290, 291
Escourgeon, 54
Ethers, aromatic, in old vaulted beer, 50
Eurotium aspergillus glaucus, 341; *E. oryzæ*, 344
Excise charges, 175—177
Expenses ("progressive" and "unprogressive"), 179—181
Extract per quarter, 174; solid or dry, 174; ditto per cent., 174, 175
Eye-pieces (microscope), 349, 350; inspection of for flaws, 357

FAN (Blackman), 73—77
Feed, bright, importance of, 36
Fehling's solution, 146 (*note*), 223, 224; testing correctness of, 225, 226; to decide when right quantity is run in, 229,
Fermentation, normal, 26; slow distinguished from sluggish, 27; fiery, 27, 388; predisposing causes of fiery, 390; under pressure, 33; bottom, 40; secondary or complementary, 45—48, 433; definition of, 324; germ *v.* spontaneous generation theories, 325; with commercial yeast, 357—390; theories on, Pasteur's, 358; Traube's, 359; Brefeld's, 360, 361, 363; A. Mayer's, 361, 362; Nägeli's, 365; Bourquelot's (selective), 366; heat generated during, 378, 379; with pure cultures, 403—409
Fermenting room, windows and walls of, 449
Fermenting vessels, 495—498; seasoning them, 496, 497
Ferments in general, 321—346; table of, 322, 323; inorganic (?), 324; are fungi, 326, 329, 330; two distinct modes of reproduction, 334; acetic and lactic, concurrent action of, 379, 380; degeneration of, 386
Fibrin, 206
"Field" (microsc.), 348
Film (pellicle), 402; table of formation at various temperatures, 400, 401
Fining-out, 34, 421, 432
Finings, 42—44, 428—432; best acid for making, 428; according as hard or soft water used in brewing, 431; strength of acid, 428, 429; high acidity unfavourable to action of, 430; effect of temperature on action of, 431; favourable or unfavourable conditions, 431; methods of using, 431—433
Fixed pipes, steaming of, 446, 447
Flagellum, 330
Flaked malt, 305
"Flooring" (malt), 6
Floors (malt), 7; progress of average, 9
Forchammer process (water analysis), 269
Forcing-tray, 437, 438
Formula, empiric and structural, 184, 185; glyptic, 191; calculating percentage composition from, 187; formula from percentage composition, 188; formula of acetic acid, 187—190
Fountains, 489
Foxy smell, 384
Free, Mr., on malting, 73—77
"Fret," pastorianus, 413; ellipsoideus, 414
Froschlaich, 149
Furnace (kiln), 73
Fusarium hordei, 60 (*note*), 343

INDEX.

"Fuzzy" heads, 122

GALACTOSE, 146
Gas, boiling by, 469
Gas-engine for pumping, etc., 451
Gathering square, 26, 495
Germination, 8; dominant note of, 84; loss of useful substances during, 85
Germinative power, tests for, 62, 63
Glucose (commercial), 153; analysis of, 154, 227, 228; compared with invert, 154; glucose group, 146
Glucosides, 142 (*note*), 143
Glucoside-splitting ferments, 322
Glycerine, 196, 197; a by-product of fermentation, 366—368
Gomme de sucrerie, 149
Gonidium, 335—341
Grain, raw, 304, 305; torrefied, 306
Grain trap, 449
Granolithic flooring, 64, 450
Granulose, 79, 285
Gravitating (tower) principle, 443, 444
Gravity, 155—160; loss of some prevented by hops, 382
Green malt, 11
Grist (stout and porter), 307
Grist-case, 481, 482
Grown corns, 61
Gyle-tun, 25 (*see* Fermenting vessels)
Gypsum (*see* Sulphate of lime)
Gypsum-tank, 123, 124

HABERLANDT, test for germinating power, 62
Hansen, 46, 47; test for purity of water, 108; his pure culture method, 396—398, 399, 403, 404; table for yeast analysis, based on his observations, 400, 401
Hardening tank, 124 (*cut*)
Hardness of water, 111; degrees of, 112; quantity of various salts required to produce one degree of, 129, 130 (*note*)
Hayduck on influence of hop-extract on lactic ferment, 316
Haylofts and oat stores, 445
Hassell, Dr., his objections to permanganate test, 104, 105
"Head," 384; rise and fall in fermentation, 384, 385

Heating in stack, 61
Heisch test, 107
Hoists, sack or other, 475—477
Hop-back, 20, 489
Hop-shoot to copper-side, 449
Hops, 131—144; in copper, 19, 317, 318; Mr. Whitehead on, 132, 133; yield per acre, 131; varieties of, 132, 133; finest land in England for, 133, 134; Farnhams, 134; Worcester and Hereford, 134, 135; Kent, hop-growing parishes of, *Appendix*; Enemies of, 135, 136; cost of producing, 136; a good sample of, 137, 138; "fliers," "mashy" hops, 138; Bohemian and Bavarian, etc., 138, 139; American, 139; Belgian, 140; French, 140; sulphured, 140; constituents of, 141, 142; storing, 143; dry hopping, 143; turbidity due to latter, 419, 420; "yearlings," "olds," and "old-olds," 144; apportioning, 167; working out proportion at lbs. per barrel, 168
Hop-flavour, 425
Hop-resin and turbidity due to it, 417, 418; cause detected, 419
Hordeum, 53
Huxley, Professor, on protoplasm, 331 (*note*); fermentation simile, 358
Hydracids, 193
Hydration (hydrolysis), 56, 147; of malto-dextrin by secondary yeast, 299, 330
Hydrates, 194
Hydraulic power, 448
Hydrocarbons, 196
Hydroxides, 194
Hypha, 330
Hyphomycetes, 336, 340—344

ICE-MAKING machines, 492—495
Idle corns, 68, 69
Increase, 92
Indigo test for nitrates and nitrites, 213
Infusion method of mashing, 14, 15; infusion and decoction beers compared, 23
Initial heat, 15, 281; formula to calculate from striking heat, 169
Invertase 145 (*and note*), 151, 322
Invertin (*see* Invertase)

Inverting sugar in brewery, 146, 152, 153; probable influence on bacteria, 150
Involution forms of schizomycetes, 340
Iodine reactions, 211
Iodoform test for alcohol, 215
Iron, tannate of, 122; removal of from water, 122; proto-salts and per-salts, 195 (*note*); test for, 214
Isinglass, 43
Isomerism (isomers), 192, 193

JOURNALS, 456

KAINIT, 120
Keys, 455; key bed or keyway, 456
Kick-up, 31
Kiln, 12, 69—78; double kilns, 12; Stopes' instructions for, 78; Stopes on construction of, 71, 72; Hedicke's twin kiln, 72; test of fitness for, 11; King's automatic regulator, 77
Kiln-drying, 69, 70
Kjeldhal's method (nitrogen determination), 210
Krith, 189 (*note*)

LABORATORY, arrangement of, 218
Lactate of lime, 67
Lactose, 146
Laevulose (levulose), 145, 199, 200
Lager beer (stability as compared with English), 23
"Last runs," gravity of, 165
Last's patent ventilators, 71
Lautermaische, 22
"Length," copper, 19; making up copper lengths, 161—167; examples, 170; causes for loss of, 162
Leptothrix, 335, 339
Leuconostoc mesenteroïdes, 149, 150; factor in ropiness, 422
Liebacks, 68, 69
Liebig on fermentation, 358
Limited decoction, 24, 303—305
Liquor (unsparged) in coppers, 163
Loose pieces, cleansing in, 34

MAGNESIA (in water) determined, 257, 258
Malt, heaping after curing, 79; data for judging, 89, 90; sampling, 90, 91; maltose and dextrin in determined, 229—232; acidity in determined, 234—237; albuminoids in determined, 237—239; albuminoids, soluble and total, by soda-lime, 240—243; diastasic activity of, 243—245; ill vegetated (mode of mashing), 282; mashing average, 283, 284; flaked, 305; brown or blown, 308; patent, 309, 310; substitute for patent, 310; slack malt and moisture percentage in sound, 446 (also synoptic table)
Malt extract, treating with, 49
Malt-house, situation in regard to brewery, 63, 64; cistern, couch, etc., 64; kilns (*see* Kilns), cowls, 73; baffle plate, 73, furnace, 73; Blackman air propeller, 73—77; Last's patent, 71
Malting process, 1, 6—13, 53—92; Mr. Free on, 73—77; faulty drying, 75; chemical results of, 79; pneumatic, 91; economics of, 92
Malt-mills, 446, 479—481
Malto-dextrin (= amylöin), 3, 47, 294—302; effects of various salts on type, 119; place in carbohydrate group, 200; compound bodies, 294; different types of, 295; evidence for theory of, 295; isolation of, 297; formula for, 297; influence on sluggish fermentation, 386
Maltose, 1, 146; reducing power of, 147, 200, 201; determination of in malt, 229—232; free or combined, 232—234
Mannite, 197, 422
Mashes, dead, 311, 312; second, 313
Mashing infusion, decoction system, 14; general principles serving as guide in, 279—281; applying them to practice, 281—285; limited decoction, 24, 303—305; hot grist, 306.
Mashing machinery, external, 482, 483; internal, 483, 484
Mash-tuns, 483; covers of, 485
Metric system (Weights and Measures), 219, 220
Micrococcus, 335—337
Micromillimetre, 287

INDEX.

Microscope, 346—356; good qualities of, 347—350; immersion, 350; monocular and binocular, 351; penetration, definition and resolving power, 348; magnifying power of certain combinations, 350; parts of, 352—354; light for, 353, 354; practical makers of, 355, 356
Million, parts per, 220
Millon's reagent, 213
Molecule, 184, 189 (*note*)
Monads, 187
Monatonic, 187
Monilia Candida, 343
Moritz, Dr., on factors determining type or quantity of malto-dextrin, 301. 302
Morris, Dr. G. H., researches on *Gramineæ* (with Mr. H. Brown), 80; acidity percentage in wort, 116; amyloïns, 297, 298; on sterilisation due to boiling in copper, 316
Motion, transmission of, 454—461, 462
Mould, prevention of in malt-house, 66 (*see* Hyphomycetes); favouring conditions, 380
Mucedin, 206, 415
Mucors, 342, 343
Mulder on diastase, 80; theory of "Protein," 292
Mycelium, 331; abortive, 333
Mycoderma aceti, 323; *vini*, 323, 346; spherical bodies in vacuole of latter, 372

NASCENT state, elements in, 203
Nesslerising albuminous matter in malt, 237—240; (water), 266—268; solution for, 273
Newark method of turning floors, 8
Nitrates, 195, 212; qualitative test for, 255
Nitrifying organisms, 101
Nitrites, 195, 212, 213; Laurent on effect on fermentation, 101, 387, 388; qualitative test for, 255
Nitrogen, 209—211; total inorganic (water), 97; as ammonia, 100; as nitrates or nitrites, 101; organic, 99, 100; total inorganic, 102
Nuclei (yeast cells), 372

OBERTEIG, 24
Objectives (microscope), 249, 250

"Odds," 176
Oïdeum lactis, 343; *albicans, vini, Tuckeri, ib.*
Optical activity, 215
Organic carbon (and nitrogen), 96, 99, 100; ratio to one another and its significance, 100
Organic matter, test for, 214
Osmosis, 329
O'Sullivan, James (experiments on germinating barley), 82, 83
Oxides, 193
Oxygen required to oxidise organic matter (water analysis), 104, 268—271

PALEA, 55
Pancreatic juice, 322
Parachutes, 29
Parasitic moulds, 344
Parti-gyle, 26
Pasteur, Etudes sur la Bière, 43; solution, 328; researches, 357, 358; on pure yeast culture, 393, 394; on bottling beers, 437
Pasteurisation, 23, 41
Pastorianus (*Sacch.*), 344
Pathogenic, 336
Pediococcus cerevisiæ, 422
Pellicles (films), 402
Penicillium glaucum, 341
Pepsin, 323
Peptase, 3, 84; lactic acid a stimulus, 202; 323
Peptones, 57, 80, 205; biuret reaction for, 214
Peptonising ferments, 323
Pericarp, 55
Phenol-sulphuric acid test (for nitrates), 213
Phosphates, influence of, on butyric fermentation, 108
"Piece" of malt, 7
"Piece-liquor," 15
Pitching, 25, 26
Pitching-yeast, 25
"Pitting" (erosion), 82, 84
Plant-life differentiated from animal, 326, 327
Pleomorphic craze, 336
Plummer-blocks, 456, 457, 475
Plumula, 8, 55; isolated and mixed with starch cause erosion, 89
Pneumatic malting, 91
Polarimeter, 215—217

Pollution, temporary, of water, remedy for, 128
Polymorphism, 335, 336
Pontos, 40
Priming, 48, 49
Proteids, 4; Millon's reagent for, 213
Protein, as a compound radical, 192
Protoplasm, 330, 331 (*note*)
Ptyalin, 322
Pulley, 458, 460, 461; split, 454
Pumps, 452—454
Purchase or hire of brewery, 442, 443
Putrefactive ferments, 323

QUALITATIVE tests, 211
Quantivalence, 187

RACKING, 41, 42
Racking fined beers, haze after, 48
Radicles (compound), 191
Rakes, Conron's, 304, 483, 484
Raulin's solution, 328, 329
Raw grain, 304, 305
Reagents required, 221
Refrigerators, 20, 491, 492
Reproduction, two distinct modes of, among ferments, 334
Return wort, 311
Riggers (*see* Pulleys)
Roofing of brewery, 449, 450
Rootlets, 8, 9
Ropiness, 201, 422—425; predisposing cause, 423
Rotation, right and left-handed (Rotatory power), 216, 217, 291
Rousing, pump for, 499

SACCHARANS, saccharens, saccharins, saccharons, 200
Saccharometers, 156, 157
Saccharomyces, 323, 344—346; *cerevisiæ*, 46; *pastorianus*, 47; *exiguus*, 47; *minor*, 392
Saccharose (or sucrose), 145
Salicylic acid, 426, 427
Salts, 193—195
Sarcina, 337; *pediococcus cerevisiæ*, a sort of, 422, 423
Scale (rock) in liquor pipes, removal of, 117

Schizomycetes, 333, 335, 336—340, 344—346
Screens (barley and malt), 477
Screws, 462
Scutellum, 55
Secondary (or complementary) fermentation, 45, 47, 48, 433
Sedimentary yeast, 40
Selective fermentation, 366
Semi-gravitation, 444
Septa (septation), 331; cause of branching, 332
Settling-backs, 37
Shafting, 454
Silica (in water), 117, 118
Skimming, 25, 28; last skim, 31; mechanical, 498
Sluices, 29, 30
Soap-test, 263—266
Soda-lime method, 240—243
Solid residue (*see* Beer)
Solids (sol. or insol.) in water, 259
Sparger, 17 (*note*), 485
Sparging, 161, 162, 165, 166, 312, 313
Specific gravity, definition of, 158; to convert into brewers' lbs. and converse, 159
Sphærotheca castanei, 135, 344
Spiles, porous, 434; ordinary, 435
Spirillum, 335; *S. amyliferum* supposed to be phase of *B. amylobacter*, 339
Spirochæta (*see* Spirillum)
Sporangium, 342
Spore, sexual, asexual, 335; aërial, 369
Sporocarp, 342
Sporophore, 330
Sprinkling, 10, 66
Spurging-out (*see* Fining-out)
Squire, Dr., on Nägeli's theory of fermentation, 365
Staining (bacteria), 338 (*note*)
Standard solutions, 273—275
Starch, molecule of, 147 (*note*); 285—288
Steam-engine, 472—475; parts of, 473; donkey, 467
"Steele," revolutions required for, 461
Steeliness (from premature application of heat), 70
Steep (duration of), 65
Steeping, hard water for, 67; temperature of liquor for, 6, 65
Sterigma, 335, 341

Stewing of wort, 315, 316
Stillion beer, 33
"Stink," 427; suggested connection with butyric ferment, 203
Stock-beers, 44, 45
Stone-squares (Yorkshire), 38—40
Storage, 433; temperature of cellar, 434; of bottling cellar, 435, 436
Store yeast, 30
Stout and porter, 307—311; Irish method, 308; grist for, 310
Streptococcus, 337
Striking heat, formula to calculate initial heat from, 169
"Struck," 20
Succinic acid, 366, 368 (as by-product of fermentation)
Sugar-cane, 145, 146, 147—152; refining value of, 148; invert, 145, 146; impurities of common, raw, 149; extract given by, 159; apparatus for dissolving, 164, 165; glucose and invert, analysis of (gravimetric method), 226, 227; (volumetric), 227, 228; analysis of cane, 228
Sulphates, 195; in water, 113, 114; proportions desirable, 115; determination of, 255—257, 260, 261
Sulphides, 195
Sulphites, 195
Sulphur in hops, 140; tests for, 271, 272
"Swan-necks," 35
Sweating, 65

TABLES (original gravity), 247—250
Tannates (iron), 122
Tap-heats, 18
Temperature, of fermenting wort, 28, 29; tendency of high, 29; of kilns, 69, 70; of cellars, 434—436
Testa, 55
Tetracoccus, 337
Theories (chemical, vitalistic, and catalytic) of fermentation, 365
Tied houses, their status, a gauge of value of brewery, 443
Tiles (for malthouse floors), 64
Tit-corks, 435
Topping-up, 33
Triad, 187
Turbidity, 410—421; due to yeasts, 410—414; to bacteria, 414; to albuminoids, 414—417; to hop-resin, 417; to dry-hopping, 419, 420; to amylöins, 420, 421; to mineral matter, 421
Tyndall's, Professor, deduction (germ theory), 325, 326

ULLAGE, 23
Underback, 314, 489
Underlet, 15
Unions (Burton), 36
Univalent, 187
Ustilago Carbo, 344

VACUOLE, 372
Valence, 187
Valerianic acid, 141
Vatted beers, 49—52; stout vatting, 51
Viennese system, 21
Vitreous barley, 61

WATER, pure, 93; carbonic acid in, 93 (*note*); how results are expressed, 95; impure generally hard, 97; chlorine in, 99; ammonia process, 102, 103; permanganate process, 103, 104; purity data, 106; phosphoric acid and sulphates as evidence of pollution, 106, 107; Heisch (sugar) test, 107; Hansen's test for purity, 108, 109; spring and well, 109, 110; natural purification of, 111; sulphates of potash or soda, 120; carbonates of soda or potash, 121; sulphates in, 113, 114; bicarbonates, 115; circumstantial evidence of purity, 116; silica, 117; chlorides, 118; common salt added, 119; iron in, 122; Clarke's process for softening, 125; Professor Wanklyn's suggestion for accelerating this, 126; easy qualitative test, 127; colour and smell, 127; organic matter in, 127, 128; remedy for temporary pollution, 128
Water analysis, operative steps, 254—271; nitrates and nitrites, qualitative test for, 255; sulphates, 255—257, 260, 261; magnesia, 257, 258; chlorine (chlorides), 258; soluble and insoluble solids (due

to constitution of water), 259; precipitate on boiling (temp. hardness), 259, 260; tabulating results in, 260—262; alkaline carbonates in, 262, 263; hardness of, 263; free and albuminoid ammonia, 266—268; oxygen required to neutralise organic matter, 268—271

Weevil, 91

Weights and Measures (Metric System), 219, 220

Well, 450; well-sinking, 110

Wheels, driver and follower, 458; spar, 458; pitch of, 458; bevel and mitre, core and mortise, 459; shrouding teeth of, 459, 460

Wild yeasts, 46, 395

Withering, 11

Working out the brewings, 160

Wort, raw or return, 311; stewing of, 315; limit of fermentable density, 378

YEAST, mechanical function of, 21; colour of, 26; huge excess of cells over bacteria, 320; microscopic examination of, 354, 355, 371—373; acting on its own tissues, 364; loss on washing, 364 (*note*); commercial never of one type, 368; high and low, 369; sub-varieties, 370, 371; old cells detected, 372, 373; cells should be of regular size, 373; severe ordeals, which it can survive, 374; limitations of, 374, 378; analysis of high yeast, 375; needs material and nitrogenous food, 375, 376; poverty of outcrop, 386; ratio of increase in fermenting wort (table), 390; bakers', 391, 392; culture from a single cell, 393—409; pure culture in France, 404—408; in Australia, 408, 409; turbidity due to, 410

Yeast-bite, 28, 31, 425, 426

Yorkshire stone-square system, 38—40

ZOOGLÆA, 337
Zygospore, 335
Zymases, 321
Zymogenic, 336

www.ingramcontent.com/pod-product-compliance
Lightning Source LLC
Chambersburg PA
CBHW071410160426
42813CB00085B/757